ENTERTAINMENT:

A Cross-Cultural Examination

A TAXONOMY OF
CONCEPTS IN COMMUNICATION
by Reed H. Blake and Edwin O. Haroldsen

COMMUNICATIONS AND MEDIA
Constructing a Cross Discipline
by George N. Gordon

ETHICS AND THE PRESS
Readings in Mass Media Morality
Edited by John C. Merrill and Ralph D. Barney

DRAMA IN LIFE
The Uses of Communication in Society
Edited by James E. Combs and Michael W. Mansfield

INTERNATIONAL AND INTERCULTURAL COMMUNICATION
Edited by Heinz-Dietrich Fischer and John C. Merrill

EXISTENTIAL JOURNALISM
by John C. Merrill

THE COMMUNICATIONS REVOLUTION
A History of Mass Media in the United States
by George N. Gordon

COMMUNICATION ARTS IN THE ANCIENT WORLD
Edited by Eric A. Havelock and Jackson P. Hershbell

EDITORIAL AND PERSUASIVE WRITING
by Harry W. Stonecipher

ENTERTAINMENT
A Cross-Cultural Examination
Edited by Heinz-Dietrich Fischer and Stefan R. Melnik

Humanistic Studies in | H | S | the Communication Arts
| C | A |

Entertainment:

A
CROSS-CULTURAL
EXAMINATION

☆☆☆☆

Edited, with an Introduction
and a Select Bibliography
by
HEINZ-DIETRICH FISCHER, Ph.D.
and
STEFAN REINHARD MELNIK, M.A.

COMMUNICATION ARTS BOOKS

HASTINGS HOUSE, PUBLISHERS
New York 10016

Library of Congress Cataloging in Publication Data

Main entry under title:

Entertainment, a cross-cultural examination.

  (Humanistic studies in the communication arts)
(Communication arts books)
  Bibliography: p.
  Includes index.
  1. Performing arts—Addresses, essays, lectures.
2. Mass media and the arts—Addresses, essays,
lectures. I. Fischer, Heinz-Dietrich, 1937–
II. Melnik, Stefan R.
PN1584.E57   790.2   79-66
ISBN 0-8038-1945-5
ISBN 0-8038-1946-3 pbk.

Published simultaneously in Canada by
Copp Clark Ltd., Toronto

Printed in the United States of America

CONTENTS

ACKNOWLEDGEMENTS

We wish to extend our thanks to everyone involved in the compilation of this book, in particular to the authors who submitted contributions, copyright holders, translators and the countless people who supplied us with information.

We are especially grateful to the following—who would otherwise remain unmentioned—for their invaluable help: Prof. Dr. Oskar Anweiler, Dr. Ilse-Renate Wompel, Mr. Friedrich Kuebart and Ms. Ingrid Dickhut.

The Editors

FOREWORD

THIRTEEN YEARS AGO, if I remember correctly, a not entirely undistinguished sociologist teaching in the American west wrote a book (on a grant from the National Association of Broadcasters), the pith of which was that the general thrust and function of mass communications in our time and place might well be almost entirely to provide pleasure and to entertain. Those of us who were then concerned about responsibilities of the cinema, press and broadcasting, he held, were largely elitists, a bunch of snobs riding in a plush-lined trolley on the wrong track.

The volume received considerable passing attention as I recall, largely because it so neatly echoed various establishment interests at the time, all in defense of the *status quo.* Hadn't a generation of students been taught that certain media were largely "entertainment" vehicles (as opposed to "orientation" and "information" conduits) and that mass communications, in spreading "culture for the millions" (another current phrase), was probably performing its natural function in a democracy by tickling the popular funnybone most of the time? You bet they had, along with warnings that various "elite" critics of contemporary media were hurling our nation back towards the Middle Ages of all places, against the grain of the common good and welfare of our culture.

I am referring here, of course, to a propaganda line, repeated in symposiums, articles, debates and on TV talk shows that should bring happy tears of nostalgia to the eyes of those of us who participated—even as adversaries—in what seemed to be a debate but was actually a public relations campaign bought and paid for mostly by the people who gave us all of those Western adventures on screen and television, now mercifully departed—at least from America—and their counterparts in the worlds of newspapers, magazines and paperback books.

Thirteen years seems to me today like thirty years! The worst of the Vietnam war and the peculiar relationship of the mass media to that abortive conflict, a national recession, *The Making of A President* (book), Watergate,

All The President's Men (book and film), and the so-called "porno-plague" all waited ahead of us as we argued, in effect, about whether some angels on the head of a pin should be dancing to rock n'roll or watching *Sunrise Semester* on CBS. If we had doubts about the benevolence of the mass communication establishment's plan for us, culture-clowns like Dr. McLuhan were only too willing to articulate visions of "global villages" and hot and cold running demiurges to, in the end, confound common sense with a doctrine of hope claiming that what we said to one another mattered much less than how we chose to say it.

In a way, it was indeed an age of innocence, as all past times are, during which galaxies of arguments and counter-arguments revolved in perfect circles around a pivotal concept of "mass culture," polarized into two and only two camps. Were we going to use our instruments of mass communication, broadly speaking, to *educate* the masses or to *entertain* them?

How naive, it seems now, that we thought that we had any choice! In our usual, parochial fashion, our eyes were mostly on our navels. Had we but looked to Cuba to the south, Canada to the north, China to the east and/or Britain to the west, the hollow fraud of the choice we thought we had would have rung loud in our ears. But no, our discussion was self-contained, self-justifying. The media, to borrow a neat but incorrect phrase from Jeremy Tunstall, were Amererican, weren't they? *All* TV was American TV! *All* newspapers were American newspapers! *All* movies were American movies! *All* media publics were American publics! *All* entertainment was what entertained Americans!

So much, I suppose, for the past, except to note that even thirteen years ago the subject started a brilliant musical comedy lyric running through my head. Entertainment is ". . . where a chap kills his father and causes a lot of bother," or ". . . some great Shakesperian scene, where a ghost and a prince meet and everyone ends in mincemeat." How clearly I remember this song that still amuses me because of its obvious irony which seems to evade so many academic analysts of television and radio programs, films and, even and especially, newspapers. Soberly they look but they do not see the true nature of what is on our daily buffet table of deadpan doom, stand-up comics, crossword puzzles, advice to the lovelorn in soap operas and soapy syndicated columns as well as video pancake pundits who view with alarm the present inflation, deflation, crisis, war, conference, crime wave, shortage, automotive defect and carcinogens in mother's milk. *All* of it, my friend, is *entertainment*—to somebody, usually a person with brains. And our cup runneth over!

Possibly I am dense, but after a lifetime's study of the drama, I cannot think of a playwright, serious or comic, in the history of the theatre who was not an entertainer. (The possible exception is Robert Browning, but nobody produced his plays.) What painting was painted if not to entertain in some fashion its viewers? What major novel—past or present—has not been an entertainment or, like *Moby Dick*, the stimulus for many types of entertainment?

What statue? What poem? What symphony or rock album? What autobiography? What movie review? What good military history, well told?

I suppose I might go on forever to make the simple point that universal entertainment has been and is one of civilization's prime and main aims since its beginnings. And, by and large, people have succeeded pretty well in amusing one another. Entertainment and sex (or a combination of the two) have been the main means of accomplishing this end in most periods of history, just as they are at present.

In retrospect, our non-argument a baker's dozen years ago centered upon who was going to entertain whom with what in the USA by means of what medium of public communication. What we could not understand at the time, I think, was that we had less choice in the matter than we thought we did. A nation obsessed with violence will entertain by exploiting violence one way or another in its various media, and neither marching mothers nor "violence profiles" will stop it as long as free speech even titularly exists. A people passionately in love with junk food and flashy gadgets will amuse themselves with entertainments that center on these edible and non-edible toys one way or another, especially if one remembers that *all* advertising is entertainment—of a sort. As I shall shortly show in a most indecorous book, a civilization that exalts the sexual orgasm to the apogee of mysticism will necessarily be entertained beyond measure by communications designed to deliver nothing but a genital tickle. And so on.

By no means am I referring solely to an American phenomenon, incidentally. In principle, all popular entertainment follows the same cultural pattern wherever it occurs, and, let me add, it occurs everywhere that folks have leisure and wealth enough to be entertained: not much of a requirement. What remains ambiguous is precisely what anyone ever means when he or she says, "That's entertainment!"

To continue my outrages a bit further, if any deep or fundamental dichotomy exists between "education" and "entertainment," I have yet to find it. And this present volume, a cross-cultural study of the latter has, thank heaven, only muddied the waters of this cute convenience still further for me. I hope it will for you too. I also hope that this survey of what seems to be entertaining whom these days on a global basis causes us all to pause and think about the neat set of categories into which our now aged or deceased sociological mentors asked us to put all mass communications decades ago.

What were they again? Ah, yes. "Surveillance," "correlation," "transmission" and, of course "entertainment." What useful tools! As practical as calling a newspaper like the *Daily Racing Form* a medium of "information" or a movie like *Night and Fog* "entertainment," or classifying Barbara Walters under the heading of "orientation." (Frankly I much prefer Farah Fawcett-Majors as an "orientation" medium.)

Entertainment, as any of us who have tried to manufacture it will tell you, is a terribly serious business both in its creative and receptive phases. Many of the greatest and most civilized cultural monuments of mankind were created to entertain, just as an unspeakably horrible living theatre of the absurd at Auschwitz entertained both the commandant and staff of that particular monument to barbarism. In my time, I have attempted to examine the relics of many of these particular amusements, as well as those that entertain both the few and the many today in different places and for different reasons right now. I remain humble in the light of the numerous paradoxes and ironies I think I have just begun to comprehend.

If this volume of articles, painstakingly collected from around the world, by Heinz-Dietrich Fischer in Germany and Stefan R. Melnik from England and at present in Germany (with abusive encouragement from me in the United States) does not cause you to reconsider your own prejudices, predispositions and postures concerning the nature and function of entertainment, the publisher assures me that you can try to get your money back. In truth, you do not deserve it. You have grown obsolete while the world around you is changing—and fast.

George N. Gordon
Institute of Communications
Muhlenberg College
Cedar Crest College

INTRODUCTION

THE BOOK we have compiled presents a selection of work that has been written on various aspects of what we loosely term "entertainment communication." We have chosen the term not so much for its clarity and precision but because we wish to focus attention on a whole area of communication, especially mass communication, that has been relatively neglected, neglected because of research emphasis on questions and issues that are considered to be more important and significant (e.g., information, education, influence, ethics of communication, public opinion). The area of communication the book covers can be summarized as follows: either a) the content of that which the communicator produces and supplies, with the prime intention—actual or apparent—of entertaining his audience, or b) the content (of anything from a variety show to a newspaper editorial) as it is used by the recipient for purposes of entertainment. The term "entertainment" includes the concepts of diversion, escape, companionship and play, to name only a few. All media have properties of entertainment, either through the content they supply or through the entertainment value they possess per se, although some media are more entertaining than others (e.g., television is more so than a newspaper), which is a result of both their history and the context within which they are used.

All the contributions to this book emphasize and explain the importance of entertainment as supplied by the media. It occupies a major portion of the leisure time that is at the disposal of most individuals in developed industrial societies. Such leisure activity is characterized by passive participation as opposed to active participation, the latter activity being termed recreation. The boundaries between the two are not rigid, however, as for example in novel reading, wherein the recipient must exercise his imagination. The functions of entertainment, as far as the individual is concerned, are manifold and, when taken together, are at least as important as those of, say, information. For example, human existence without regeneration, which entertainment helps to effect, is as inconceivable as human existence without education. Furthermore, it must be stressed, as many of the articles point out, that there is no such thing as "pure entertainment." All entertainment contains messages and values whether intended or not. Used deliberately, entertainment can be as effective in realizing political, social and economic aims as conventional tools of persuasion. Yet there has been little large-scale and coordinated research into the phenomena we have subsumed under entertainment communication.

We hope that this book will fulfill a number of needs, at least to a certain extent. It should be regarded as an attempt to point out where research and theoretical discussion is necessary, although comprehensiveness cannot be claimed. Perhaps the most glaring omission in this compilation is a discussion of some aspect of comic strip and magazine production or consumption. Moreover, the bias of the book is almost exclusively weighted in favor of entertainment as provided by the mass media rather than by theatre, the story teller, the home movie and other forms of group or individual media—which is mainly the result of limitations of space. We have purposely avoided subjects of research within an area that has already received considerable attention: the effects of the portrayal of violence, sex and such in entertainment.* Similarly, in making our choice of material for the book, we have avoided the inclusion of more articles written specifically and exclusively on the much discussed "uses and gratifications" approach, which is especially relevant to the area of entertainment communication.** Each article was thus chosen or commissioned with a view to its originality or to a particular research deficit.

The book is aimed at the college or university student and at people involved in the production of entertainment, as well as the general reader interested in the subject. If the compilation is successful in sensitizing the latter two groups toward certain questions and aspects of entertainment production and consumption, it will have fulfilled another function. As far as the student is concerned, it meets a number of requirements. The articles and select bibliographies constitute a source book bringing together research—often disjointed and uncoordinated—from a number of academic disciples. It provides an insight into patterns of entertainment with which the student is less familiar (i.e., those outside the United States, together with a survey of some non-American approaches***), research findings and issues with regard to the phenomenon of entertainment to which he has little or no access. Furthermore, if the collection helps in redressing the present balance at colleges and universities favoring study of the informational or educational aspects of communication, then it will have more than fulfilled its purpose.

---

* An extensive resumé of findings and knowledge—or lack of such—that this subject of research has supplied us with, together with an excellent and comprehensive bibliography, is to be found in Josef Hackforth's new publication (see Bibliography at the end of the book).

** In this context we would recommend the reader to refer to the discussion and bibliographies in the publications by Blumler and Katz, Lundberg and Hultén, and Katz and Gurevitch (see bibliography).

*** One exception has been made to this rule: Stephenson's exposition of a "ludenic theory of newsreading" has been included in the collection because of its seminal importance for non-American academic interest in entertainment communication.

The select bibliography at the end of this book contains some of the more important publications relevant to entertainment communication. It makes no claim to being comprehensive. We have included publications from a variety of disciplines, including psychology, sociology, history, literature and communications science. Each of them contains a useful or extensive bibliography for those interested in looking into some aspect of entertainment communication in greater depth. A number of works on the subject of leisure have been included for those interested in relating entertainment to other forms of leisure activity.

*   *   *   *

THE FIRST ARTICLE presented (1: pp. 2–19) is devoted to a description of the development of entertainment within the mass media and the status accorded to the accompanying research (when and if it was carried out). It also provides a summary of the various definitions given to entertainment followed by a synthesis of them. The synthesis establishes boundaries within which the various approaches to entertainment can be accommodated. Such definitions have determined our understanding of the term, whether or not it can be used reasonably for purposes of research. Although the article concentrates on the phenomenon and concomitant academic discussion in Germany, the vague nature of the term, the lack of research, the forms entertainment has assumed in mass media—all are part of a common experience, as many of the contributions to this book either implicitly or explicitly indicate.

Entertainment forms show remarkable continuity over the ages despite the fact that the original media through which they were presented have frequently been replaced by relatively new (mass) media. In the past, all entertainment was presented in front of a limited number of people who had gathered together at a particular place and time for the express purpose of being entertained— such forms of entertainment (e.g., theatre) and their modern variants (e.g., pop concerts) now exist alongside forms of mass entertainment (e.g., television), which are characterized by their lack of immediate feedback. Despite the fact that the majority of contemporary entertainment is presented through mass media, many if not most of its original elements have been preserved or adapted. For instance, audience participation or reaction is important for the entertainer performing on stage, in the market place and such, in front of a limited audience. In mass media production one attempts to introduce this element artificially in order to help both the performer (in live programs) and the audience at home through means of a studio audience, for instance. Paul Taylor (2: pp. 22–33), through his study of such a studio audience for television comedy, provides us with an insight into such artificial techniques, which ensure the success of a comedy production or series; he discusses why a studio audience and/or "canned laughter" are used and outlines the problems and limitations encountered in such television productions. Further studies are needed on the techniques used in the production of television comedy and other forms of entertainment together with their respective functions (e.g., the use of music in creating suspense, the use of symbols in drama or in the performance of pop music).

Popular literature as a form of entertainment communication has been neglected by researchers, perhaps because of its purportedly non-existent literary value or because of the sociologist's and mass communication specialist's predominant interest, when they look at mass entertainment, in its more modern and overt forms. This is surprising. Popular literature is, together with the entertainment to be found in newspapers, the first form of mass entertainment experienced by society. Popular literature has always been criticized, been accused of having negative effects on the recipient, as Peter H. Mann shows (3: pp. 34–42). Nonetheless, it fulfills quite definite functions for millions of people, functions that differ little from those of the last century. Reading of such literature has apparently been affected only slightly by the introduction of other mass media because of its different characteristics, and hence, its different functions (e.g., the medium requires the reader to become engrossed in what he is reading, requires him to form his own mental images) and still constitutes a major leisure-time activity.

Continuity of form is most overt in television productions of stage plays, transmissions of concerts, and such. The most ancient forms of entertainment are often either adapted or transplanted wholesale for the modern media. But this isn't without effect on a culture. Traditional centers of social communication, for instance, lose their significance; the traditional form of entertainment in its traditional setting faces extinction and only its successor presented by the mass media remains, as Kazem Motamed-Nejad points out in his survey of story-telling in Iran (4: pp. 43–62). Tetsuo Makita, in a brief account of historical drama on Japanese television (5: pp. 63–73), also stresses the continuity between the modern form of entertainment he deals with and its traditional antecedents with which the audience is familiar. This continuity is probably one of the reasons for the high popularity ratings of historical drama.

Parmar discusses the effect of this form of mass entertainment on popular culture. He stresses the need for continuity not only in form but also in the medium through which the content is presented for purposes of national development. All that is needed is modification of the messages transmitted. Presenting traditional forms in conjunction with the original media through which they were presented—singing, recitation of poetry, puppetry, and so on—constitutes a way of approaching the target audience more directly and effectively, especially if it is an audience which has little access to mass media, and if it does, takes little notice of the advice given unless its own experience, opinion leaders, and such, give it more substance. Moreover, the feedback, complicated in the case of mass media, is instantaneous—a factor allowing flexibility in adaptating to each respective audience, its moods and predispositions (6: pp. 74–82). Perhaps some of Parmar's observations also apply to modern industrialized society. Is theatre, for instance, more effective in communicating ideas than television "armchair theatre;" does more discussion take place before or after a performance in the latter than in the former?

Experience seems to show that some media are better suited to some tasks than other media: film and television for entertainment, whatever the term may mean; newspapers for information, and so on. The article by Jürgen Hüther (7: pp. 83–91) points out that this is not necessarily the case. Audiovisual media of all kinds, despite the fact that they concentrate on entertainment, are just as capable, if not more so, in presenting information and, more especially, in functioning in an instructive capacity, as both practical experience has shown and their capabilities in theoretical terms indicate. If such media favor programs of an "entertaining" nature, there is no reason why programs with educational content cannot incorporate elements to make them entertaining and thus capable of attracting a larger audience. Here we have a different facet of continuity and one that has to be given due attention when producing for a mass audience.

☆   ☆   ☆   ☆

Theories of entertainment *per se* are practically nonexistent. All attempts at theory embracing the concept of entertainment either implicitly or explicitly have related it to a wider context, as the articles we have chosen demonstrate:

Wilmont Haacke (8: pp. 94–98), one of the first specialists in public communication studies (*Publizistik*) to take a special interest in entertainment communication, discusses the phenomenon in relation to other forms of leisure activity it accompanies or has replaced (e.g., circuses) and outlines its necessary functions in terms of stimulating regeneration and maintaining social stability and in helping to create the necessary environment for acceptance of certain otherwise unpopular measures.

Henk Prakke (9: pp. 99–104) makes one of the first attempts to relate various forms and elements of entertainment with one another in a systematic manner. They are all subsumed under a so-called *socius function*—as distinct from the media's information and opinion-forming functions (although information and commentary is also capable of becoming entertainment). *Socius function* can be substituted by the word "companionship," something which has hitherto been largely overlooked in relation to the media and which is, according to Prakke, possibly their most important function.

To date, Stephenson's play theory of mass communication has probably had the greatest impact on traditional approaches to the phenomenon of entertainment. The theory constitutes an attempt to relate various mass media activities to each other in terms of play. The article we have chosen analyzes newspaper reading from this particular perspective (10: pp. 105–114). The author puts the reading of humorous articles, articles on foreign affairs and classified advertisements on a par with each other, and argues that newspaper reading is to be explained primarily by the pleasure it brings rather than by other factors.

In his view, many "objective" reasons given for reading a newspaper are mere rationalizations—underlying reasons are more convincing. Another article, written by David Victoroff (11: pp. 115–119), has been included on the role of play in mass communication. His approach is an orthodox Freudian one explaining the efficacy of verbal and visual advertising in terms of the pleasure derived from "psychic economy."

Sinclair Goodlad (12: pp. 120–128) argues for a need to relate mass entertainment with other forms of cultural experience. Entertainment, in his view, is comparable with religion, for instance, and in part replaces it as a form of human cultural activity in which ritual, morality and the reinforcement of individual identity are important elements. In attempting to show the relationship between television viewing, sport spectatorship, religious activity and such, he goes beyond first-order theorizing. Furthermore, he argues against a *uses and gratifications* approach, stating that it attempts to give a precise account of audience responses to specific media content, an impossible task in his view.

The article by David Chaney and Judith Chaney (13: pp. 129–143) takes a closer look at the audience for mass leisure (a concept that embraces our wide concept of mass entertainment) and criticizes the dominant traditions in studies of the audience for mass leisure. They emphasize the ways in which membership of such an audience does "not preclude creative enthusiasm or a discriminating self-consciousness about the aesthetics of leisure activities, or a desire to relate leisure enthusiasms to other aspects of life in such a way as to make a style of life consistent and comprehensible." Hitherto neglected in research are the processes by which individuals develop and express their taste in a mass context. It is the aim of their paper to present a way of analyzing this process.

The following article (14: pp. 144–152) argues a case for adopting a uses and gratifications approach in view of the dead-end that the concept, entertainment, leads to in heuristic terms and the relative lack of research in the field of "entertainment," which is not of the stock-taking kind. There is a need for groundwork in relating mass media (or media) activities with one another and with other activities (especially leisure activities) in personal and social terms. Such an approach is basically pre-theoretical, although consensus is required as to the concepts one should adopt. The *approach* can be useful for all attempts at theorizing (indeed, at a general level, various articles in this collection interpret uses in terms of particular theoretical frameworks). Entertainment as a term, however, cannot be forgotten and it serves one important function, that is, sensitization toward the fact that (mass) communication research has generally paid little attention to the wide field the term encompasses.

The article by Mansurov (15: pp. 153–178) is included in this collection not primarily because of an explicit theory relating to entertainment, but because of its exemplary character. In systematic research, a research program is required. In this respect, Soviet attempts are unequaled in their efforts to relate mass media use and use of cultural establishments with one another—if not in quantitative then certainly in terms of audience needs and preferences. The functions mass media and cultural establishments perform, eleven in all, are summarized at the end. Entertainment as a concept is rarely mentioned, although the area it encompasses has been given full, due attention. Such basic research provides a good basis from which to proceed and look into further relationships.

*   *   *   *

The myth that "pure entertainment" exists is one that is slowly but surely being dismantled. Entertainment fulfills a variety of social functions and hence cannot avoid being political in the widest sense of the term. The extent to which it is significant in political terms is open to debate, but probably less so now than used to be the case. There are conditions in which entertainment serves to help reinforce a particular political system or to dismantle it or, at a micro-level, reinforce or dismantle views that are fundamental to certain political issues.

Klaus Mäding (16: pp. 180–189) sets out to demonstrate that mass entertainment can help to maintain the *status quo*, even in a society such as one finds in Hongkong, where the social and political tensions below the surface are extremely high. A study of popular literature in the Colony shows that it attempts to deflect readers away from pursuing their "authentic interests," even when it touches upon issues of particular importance for the reader within the context of the society in which he lives—although the author is careful to point out that readers are not only manipulated but can manipulate what they are reading themselves. Luis Ramiro Beltrán also looks at the way in which mass media content contributes towards maintaining a particular *status quo* (17: pp. 190–195). He focuses his attention on mass entertainment in Latin America, a great proportion of which is imported from the United States or modeled on North American examples. The television programs shown are conducive toward maintaining the existing order through the particular set of ethics (which he lists) that they promote.

Husband discusses the way in which mass media entertainment contributes to sustaining a "dominant culture suffused with racist assumptions" and investigates the extent to which this is done (18: pp. 196–207). The example he has chosen: Great Britain. The author argues that mass entertainment (among other forms of mass communication) reinforces the black community's perception of its rejection while helping to legitimize the racial myths and antagonism of the white community. The same in all probability applies to sex discrimination or to prejudice against any group in society—both of which finds expression in entertainment and are possible subjects for further study.

In the article that follows (19: pp. 208–233) a look is taken at the interrelationships between the Olympic Games and mass media (concentrating on television), showing us the magnitude some forms of entertainment are capable of assuming. Apparently there are forms of entertainment with the ability to attract a world audience with all the consequences this entails (e.g., in terms of international politics, the pressures on persons presented or focused upon, further homogenization of culture). Why is such entertainment capable of attracting a world audience? An *Eigendynamik* (self-induced dynamic) seems to be at work here—a combination of prestige, tradition, audience expectation, "playing around" with technology, nationalism, the out-of-the-ordinary. The question of expense is suddenly lost sight of and organizational barriers and difficulties fade at national and international level.

Peter Kaupp (20: pp. 234–246) outlines the many attempts that have been made to distinguish among different kinds of fiction according to criteria of standard, production, readership qualities and such, showing that most attempts imply some form of value judgment, a factor that has helped to obstruct research of a more interdisciplinary nature. He suggests that research should look at "entertainment literature" more closely and as a whole (the term embraces all the various levels of literary entertainment) in terms of the various social functions it performs. He stresses its social significance but also maintains that there are definite limits to its influence in social and political terms. In this context, differences in quality assume secondary importance.

*   *   *   *

In looking at modern mass entertainment, its economics and production should not be lost sight of (i.e., the communicator-orientated approach). It is these that determine what the audience or readership obtains, although supply cannot function independently of demand. But apparently there is enough leeway for supply to ensure that certain developments can take place—standardization, homogenization of culture, lack of attention to the wants of minorities even if they are considerable in size (every recipient belongs to one minority or other; for example, he may wish Indian *ragas* to be shown on television—a minority demand—while still enjoying televised football—a majority demand). What happens as a result? To find out we should look at trends in the development of mass media as well as the institutions themselves more closely.

Werner Zeppenfeld (21: pp. 248–257), for instance, describes what is happening within the record and tape (or "recorded sound") market in West Germany, showing that although there are no discernible trends toward greater economic concentration at present, there have been considerable shifts in the relative business positions of the major competitors—to the advantage of United States companies. At the same time he shows that only large companies have any chance of entering the market in a big way. Such trends are accompanied by an internationalization of taste, which inevitably, means in accordance with Anglo-American standards. On another front, other mass media offer no counterbalance to trends towards homogenization because they themselves are dependent on the products of the recorded sound industry—for financial reasons. Vincent Porter (22: pp. 258–272) looks at the relationships among other mass media industries: the American film industry, the European film industry and European television establishments, and discusses the implications of certain trends for European film production. Television draws audiences away from the cinema, a trend increased by the fact that television also presents films—which can be purchased inexpensively from the United States, for instance. This puts the European film industry in jeopardy—especially if it attempts to maintain standards of quality—unless it resorts to strategies such as co-production and agreements controlling the presentation of films on television.

Halloran and Murdock (23: pp. 273–285), in a rare study of its kind, describe some of the organizational pressures and economic forces television producers—here specifically of television drama—profess to experience as well as their express cultural ideals and political aims (should they have any)—all of which came to light as a result of numerous informal interviews with members of a British television company. If we are to answer the question "why is entertainment what it is," such studies, looking into the process of creating television entertainment, are also necessary. Professional attitudes and aims represent only one aspect of this. The two authors demonstrate that it is necessary to get away from an oversimplified and cliché approach—creativity versus commerce—and show how complex decision-making is and what factors have to be taken into account. Many productions do not concur with optimum commercial requirements. Economic considerations need not be the only factor guiding entertainment production.

Gerhard Schmidtchen argues for balanced media production, maintaining that it is most effective in terms of audience satisfaction (24: pp. 286–298). The author points out that early media research was guided by pessimistic theories, especially with regard to entertainment. Using the example of radio, he attempts to point out where the weakness of such theories lies. Light music, for instance, is particularly favored by young people. It can play a role in the management of emotions and constitutes an important impetus for sub-cultures that bring social innovation about. A sufficient supply of entertainment is essential to ensure the audience's attention to political and cultural programs of a high standard. Frustration, particularly among young people, is translated into strong aversion against such a station. Listeners who are dissatisfied with a station only pay half as much attention to its political information programs as those who are contented. Here the interesting and significant hypothesis that entertainment is a precondition to receptivity toward information has been posed and subject to successful testing.

Finally, we present the views of two practicioners (25: 299–305; 26: pp. 306–314): what functions they believe entertainment fulfills and what social responsibilities they feel they have. Whereas Rohrbach takes on the critics and defends his division's record of production, Petur outlines the kinds of problems researchers face as well as the questions they have to answer if they wish to assist practice in any way.

Part One

☆☆☆☆

ENTERTAINMENT
IN CONTEXT

1   *Heinz-Dietrich Fischer*

ENTERTAINMENT: AN UNDERESTIMATED CENTRAL
FUNCTION OF COMMUNICATION

Heinz-Dietrich Fischer:

Entertainment—An Underestimated Central Function of Communication

☆ THE ABSTRACTION "entertainment function," applied to the communications media and so frequently used in an undifferentiated manner, is relatively vague, principally because the term "entertainment" can be made to mean so many different things. A deeper look reveals just how many strata the constituent components of entertainment effected by, or accompanying mass media occupy. However, neither the producer of entertainment—the communicator—nor its consumer—the recipient—seem able to describe what elements constitute entertainment and precisely how and with what effects an audience is entertained. Both the English concept of entertainment and its German equivalent, *Unterhaltung*, as they are generally understood, include only a part of the spectrum of potential forms, processes and effects that can be subsumed under them.[1] This applies equally to the term "entertainer," for which there is no German equivalent, and which at best is associated only with partial functions.

In introducing this subject, it must also be pointed out that the research deficit concerning the forms, patterns of reception and possible effects of entertainment content transmitted through mass media is considerable. Ever since the beginnings of journalism education and research establishments at a university level at the turn of the century—initially in the United States but soon followed by universities in Europe—entertainment communication as a subject has been largely overlooked or neglected because of its supposed comparative triviality.[2] Moreover, the preference schools or departments of journalism showed for the vast field of political communication is understandable when the circumstances of their establishment are considered. For instance, the First World War or the period immediately following the Second World War saw

▶ This is a rewritten and enlarged version of a previously published contribution written in German. Dr. Heinz-Dietrich Fischer is Professor of Journalism and Mass Communication at the Ruhr-University, Bochum, West Germany. The article was translated by Stefan R. Melnik, M.A.

the setting up of establishments primarily concerned with propaganda research, a subject with which they could also legitimatize their existence.[3]

Furthermore, early pioneers in communication research tended to be either trained historians or political economists and thus almost automatically orientated toward research in the field of *res publica* on which their respective traditional disciplines had been focused. Generally, a wealth of communications literature corresponding with this state of affairs was the outcome. Because the new subject had to fight for recognition amongst older, more established disciplines, its proponents usually avoided any area that might seem unusual or superficial. Within the field of political communication, the phenomena connected with the media's role in opinion formation and the way in which they handled news were given most attention. Accordingly, research concentrated for a long time on news and commentary as presented by the media and related theoretical questions. The discipline has been slow in expanding its horizons so as to include areas of communication that, in spite of their long tradition, were initially regarded as peripheral. Although some research was done in later years (e.g., on certain newspaper contents such as the arts, sports and local pages, which had originally been neglected), the amount has remained relatively small right up to the present day.[4]

As a result, research in such an area is no less desirable now than it has or should have been in the past. Whether a lack of awareness concerning the importance of the functions entertainment performs or a taboo on all subjects that are almost arbitrarily considered to be unworthy of study by the scientific community is more to blame for this state of affairs is a question of secondary importance and will not concern us here. It is possible to say, however, that for a long time universities were reluctant to consider work submitted on popular literature, indeed on popular culture in general, to be worthy of academic merit.

Yet that which is taken to be entertainment—initially without further reflection—in newspapers, for instance, perhaps has as long a history as the press itself.[5] As long ago as in 1690, in a dissertation entitled *De Relationibus Novellis*, submitted by Tobias Peucer at the University of Leipzig, the term was mentioned in connection with communication: "The purpose of the new (!) newspapers is to supply its readers with information about current affairs and events together with some useful advice and entertainment."[6] Precisely what he meant when using the term entertainment is not clear and it would be a purely speculative exercise to correlate it with any elements of present day newspaper content. Such an attempt would be all the more suspect when one bears in mind that even today no generally accepted definition of entertainment exists. Not only has the term been subject to semantic change, it is also interpreted to mean different things by our contemporaries.[7]

However, it must be pointed out that certain early literary genres undoubtedly correspond with at least part of the modern concept of entertainment. In this context, special mention should be made of the popular novel with its origins in the eighteenth century. In the words of one author, they were "the most widely read books of the day, showing great variety and satisfying qualitatively very different needs."[8] The genre was first typified in the early second half of the nineteenth century under the label of *chivalry, crime and suspense*, which adequately characterized its subject matter.[9] It was only in the 1920s that new academic interest was shown for this kind of literature under the influence of research originating in philological faculties. The Austrian, Marianne Thalmann, coined the term *Trivialroman* (non-serious fiction), under which all the various forms of popular literature were subsumed.[10] The term was substituted for all previous attempts at finding an adequate descriptive term for the genre but has progressively become associated with a number of negative connotations. Later such literature also came to be termed *Konfektionsliteratur* ("made-to-measure" literature). Recently, this genre has increasingly been termed *Trivialliteratur*.[11] According to Greiner, the consumption of such literature is looked down upon as a form of mental pastime even today.[12] This attitude is no different to that of past generations when, for instance, Schiller could call the novel-writer the poet's half-brother.[13] Nonetheless, it is now an established fact that novels written by authors such as Zschokke and Lafontaine ruled the literary market during the Goethe era, 150 years ago, and not the "classics" as one would like to believe.[14]

Similarly, the inclusion of entertaining elements in daily newspapers primarily concerned with political life was met with disapprobation. Meunier and Jessen stress that the newspaper as it had developed during the course of the seventeenth century was anti-feuilletonistic in its very conception and purpose.[15] The introduction of entertaining articles of various kinds is a relatively new innovation, as Wilmont Haacke points out, dating back only to the nineteenth century. The persistent practice of printing such entertaining news "below the line" was indicative of the value it was accorded by the communicator (in stark contrast to its popularity among readers!).[16] For this reason the switch-over to a medium that was far more flexible than the newspaper for the purpose of supplying entertainment, the magazine, occurred at a relatively early date.[17] The prototype for a successful entertaining family magazine, *Gartenlaube* ("arbour"), later to be looked upon with amused condescension, gained the highest circulation of any nineteenth century periodical, using a recipe that in its own words consisted of "entertaining and educating in an entertaining manner."[18] A number of journals even had titles that openly proclaimed their intention to entertain, for instance the *Blätter für litterarische Unterhaltung* (Paper for Literary Entertainment), first published in 1826 by Friedrich Arnold Brockhaus.[19]

Turning our attention back to the newspaper, the term *"feuilleton"* has its origins, as Dovifat points out, in the era of the French Revolution. Abbé Julien Louis de Geoffroy, a priest writing for *Journal de Débats* during this period, was the first journalist to publish feuilletonistic articles on a formal and regular basis, albeit in a supplement primarily intended for advertisements. The subject matter included "theatre, art, literature; experiences of town life and travel and all kinds of news coming from behind the scenes; the immediate environment and day-to-day life which were not always important but nonetheless worthwhile, for some readers even significant; all attractively written. Because in most cases its content differed considerably in style from the loud and pathetic manner in which political affairs were reported, and often purposely conveyed a personal note, light, lively, friendly, and human, the whole genre, which was more than just a stylistic form and incorporated a way of looking at things, was given the name *feuilleton* (light reading matter)."[20] All newspaper columns or pages which in any way seemed connected with culture, entertainment and enlightenment were eventually categorized under this term, although a feuilletonistic style is possible in all columns.[21] During the 1848 Revolution at the latest, the first definite tendencies toward politicizing feuilletonistic newspaper pages and articles are clearly discernible. A study of feuilletonistic journalism in Berlin's daily newspapers of the time bears this out: the desire on the part of the communicator to influence his readers politically through the use of light (as opposed to serious) political journalese, polemic and satire, as well as political poetry is unmistakable.[22] The use of entertainment for political ends is a topic to which we will return.

Habermas provides us with an insight into developments within the realm of culture during the course of the last two centuries and postulates an increasing polarization between the public and the private spheres of life. He maintains that the above mentioned *Gartenlaube* "already represents the idyllic mystic genre through which the flourishing cultural tradition maintained by the grand bourgeois family of past generations through their patronage of literature was passed on to the petit bourgeois town family but which the latter could only imitate. The arts almanacs and poets' journals, whose tradition in Germany dates back to 1770 . . . and which was maintained by Schiller, Chamisso and Schwab in the following century, were replaced around 1850 by a variety of family literary journals, such as . . . *Gartenlaube*, published by sound financial enterprises which were in a position to foster (large-scale) reading habits of almost ideological fervor. Such literature, however, still required the family as a literary sounding board."[23] According to Habermas, the phenomenon we find emerging in the mid-nineteenth century was given the (albeit dubious) nomenclature "mass culture," "precisely because culture attempts to broaden its base through adapting itself to the relaxation and entertainment needs of consumers with a relatively low level of education instead of trying to raise the intellectual outlook of a greatly enlarged reading public so that it could participate in a culture that was still fundamentally intact. . . . Involvement with culture requires practice, whereas the consumption of mass culture leaves no lasting imprint—the latter supplies the kind of experience that regresses rather than accumulates."[24] Here he subscribes to the views held by Adorno as set out in the well-known essay on the fetishist characteristics of music and the regression in music appreciation.[25]

Finally, Habermas outlines the significance of the role played by the popular mass press, for example, in increasing the chasm between the private and the public:

economic conditions that urged the masses to participate in public politics denied them the standard of education that would enable participation of the

kind and quality practiced by the bourgeois newspaper reader. The direct consequence was the penny press, which in the early 1830s reached a circulation
of between 100,000 and 200,000 copies, and, during the mid-nineteenth century, the rise of the even more widely circulated "weekend press," which offered the kind of "psychological relief" (that) has been a characteristic of the
commercial mass press ever since. Parallel developments are to be seen with
the beginnings of Emile Girardin's newspaper enterprise in Paris after the July
Revolution and the rise of Benjamin Day's *New York Sun* in the United
States. Half a century was to pass, however, before Pulitzer acquired the *New
York World*, a newspaper which, at about the same time as the London based
Lloyd's Weekly, reached circulation figures approaching the million mark, and
which, through use of the techniques of "yellow journalism," for the first time
really reaches the masses. . . . A decrease in the political dispositions of an
enlarged electorate was encouraged through compensation with the means of
"psychological relief," which became the objective of self-interested, commercially oriented consumer demand. The earlier penny press already showed
how circulation could be maximized: through depoliticizing the content—"by
eliminating political news and political editorials on such moral topics as in-
temperance and gambling."[26]

As a result of such experience, Socialists have attempted to conceptualize
and construct alternatives or even a counterculture, which to date seems to
imply no less than politicizing human leisure totally. The founders of Socialism were far more broad-minded in this respect than many of their more dog-
matic successors. For instance, the young Marx thought that man should be
free to use leisure as he pleases, perhaps fishing and hunting on occasion before
returning of his own free will to affairs of state.[27] And no less a person than
Engels meditated on the qualities required of a writer of humor: Such a man
requires the "gift for grasping and putting across the delicate sides to a day's
events."[28] In an early work, *Die Deutschen Volksbücher* (German Popular Literature), the following view can be found expressed: Popular literature has a
duty to "cheer up, animate and amuse" its reader, "but it also has to make him
aware as to his moral responsibilities, allow him to realize that he possesses
strength, rights and freedom, as well as awaken his courage and love of the fa-
therland."[29]

The negative or hesitant approach of the socialist press in general toward
feuilletonism is well documented.[30] The history of the Social Democratic Press
shows that it took a long time for the party to consent to the inclusion of any
kind of entertainment in the widest sense of the term. The great reformer of the
German Social Democratic Press, Bruno Schoenlank, was fighting a lost cause
when he proposed a modernization of newspaper contents to the party leadership at the turn of the present century. He remained alone in his advocacy of
certain changes, despite the fact that the innovations that he had introduced
into his own newspaper, the *Leipziger Volkszeitung*, including weekly satirical
gossip columns, readers' letters, political caricatures and arts pages matching
modern requirements, had led to a 75 percent increase in circulation. "Influ-
ential circles within the party as well as the party newspaper editors regarded

such innovations to be superfluous clever tricks" and feared that they "were basically suited only for diverting the worker from his emancipatory struggle."[31] Doctrinaire belief in the supposed persuasive power of articles purposively and ambitiously written with political education in mind as well as the constant monotonous repetition of the same old political theses failed to give socialist newspapers the qualities that were needed in order to attract a greater readership. Such newspapers continued to be no more than peripheral press products. It is an open question as to whether such a policy was purposely intended, perhaps emanating from a general desire to distinguish oneself in terms of content clearly and unmistakably from the bourgeois press.[32]

The First World War, which in certain respects created the preconditions for a rearrangement of communication structures,[33] also saw the first real breakthrough with regard to the inclusion of entertainment in mass communication. This was mainly due to the influence of film, a medium which had been in existence since the 1890s, but which had now reached such a level of technical perfection that it could rank alongside the older mass newspaper. Originally, film had been considered only to be an entertaining gag and circus attraction. With the increasing popularity of cinema, however, it wasn't long before the state realized that the new mass medium had enormous potential, which it accordingly put to systematic use. The first prototypes of the feature film were produced. Kracauer points to the psychological significance such early film entertainment had:

> Scores of patriotic dramas, melodramas, comedies and farces spread over the screen—rubbish filled to the brim with war brides, waving flags, officers, pirates, elevated sentiments and barracks humor. When, about the middle of 1915, it became obvious that the gay war of movement had changed into a stationary war of uncertain issues, the moviegoers apparently refused to swallow the patriotic sweets any longer. A marked shift in entertainment themes occurred. The many pictures exploiting patriotism were superceded by films which concentrated upon peacetime subjects. By resuming part of their normal interests, people adjusted themselves to the stabilized war. A multitude of comedies emerged, transferring to the screen popular Berlin stage comedians in proved theatrical plays.[34]

A similar entertainment function to that of film was initially accorded to radio in the early 1920s when it was first introduced. Because radio had often established itself as a commercial medium—this is the case both in Germany and in the United States—newspaper owners were quick to voice their protest. In Germany their official mouthpiece, *Zeitungs-Verlag*, demanded an early struggle against radio advertisements arguing that radio was "only comparable with concert performances and entertainment or with evening lectures."[35] Radio maintained its professed sole aim of providing entertainment, especially light music, at least until the end of the 1920s. Such programming policy proved later, after the Nazi seizure of power in 1933, to be a thorn in the sides of the new regime, as their reform of radio broadcasting clearly bears out. Radio was ideally suited for use as an instrument of propaganda. This even applied to music! The extent to which radio policy toward music was subject to radical political and racial restructuring can be gauged by the following decree issued by the Ministry of Propaganda:

> We require that all radio stations establish a permanent multi-purpose radio orchestra under the direction of a full-time artistically representative and gifted conductor. The orchestra must consist of at least fifty musicians so that light music can be performed whenever required, even when only a smaller number of musicians is available. We want to see foreign dance bands excluded as well as the elimination of Negro jazz as broadcast by the Berlin station. Melodious popular tunes sound infinitely better when performed by stringed instruments and the awful croaking of muted trumpets and saxophones together with the usual noise from the percussion is cut out. We demand that greater attention be paid to folk tradition when choosing the medium of expression or the pieces to be performed. It isn't enough simply to perform folk music in front of the microphone. Over and above this there must be continuity in emphasizing the mutuality of folk and art music to the exclusion of foreign stylistic elements as far as possible. In order to achieve racial awareness with regard to music therefore, the music of racially related peoples should be given priority over the compositions of alien races. [36]

Film, however, was undisputably the entertainment medium par excellence in the 1920s and 30s. Typifying Hollywood as a "dream factory," [37] which equally applies to its German counterpart in Babelsberg near Potsdam, aptly describes the concept of a modern entertainment industry. However, its products could easily and all too frequently be adopted for political ends. One of Goebbel's first tasks as Minister of Propaganda for the National Socialist Regime was a tactical one: to greatly improve the material well-being of producers of entertainment and thereby create ties, which could then be used for the purpose of integrating such talent into his universal concept of public communication. Top film personalities received incredible salaries end enjoyed great prestige. The relations between political functionaries and artists were marked by tacit assent and mutual respect: in this connection one need only think of the official meetings and congresses at which artists and politicians praised each other's achievements profusely, the many evening receptions given by Hitler and Goebbels to which film celebrities were often invited, as well as the many honors and titles that Goebbels awarded with such predilection. Actors and producers involved in the production of National Socialist films lived a life of ostentatious luxury even after developments during the Second World War had driven the rest of the population to the brink of starvation. During the mid 1930s the salaries of German film stars had already reached levels that would have seemed astronomical during the Weimar Era. Without doubt the point of such financial incentives had been, at least to a certain extent, to prevent the further emigration of well-known authors, producers, actors and such, and the further artistic sterility and emptiness that this would have entailed. [38]

The National Socialists needed such stars if they were to use film as effectively as was intended in propagating the so-called "new individual." Stars, producers and scriptwriters, in cooperating and thus allowing themselves to be used for the production of such films, which were political in everything but veneer, contributed to the entrenchment of National Socialist rule. This was the case precisely in those products that were characterized by their escape from reality and mendacious optimism. Most film talent could see no reason for resistance: providing that they were willing to accommodate the interests of those in power they had everything they wanted—a secure source of income and what they perceived as artistic "freedom." Their pecuniary benefits and rewards, including even a generous health scheme, however, were coupled with their submission to political control, exercised in the last instance by the Ministry of Propaganda. The very fact that this state of dependence could at any time be used as a means of repression helped to ensure the effectiveness of such indirect methods. *Filmschaffende* ("film-makers"), as they were called, either failed to recognize such dependency for what it was or suppressed their qualms on this matter. The history of National Socialist film shows that many prominent film personalities even went so far as to put their talent at the disposal of attempts to popularize the regime's anti-semitic, belligerent and inhumane ideology. Such people thus helped consciously and directly in the ideological stabilization of the National Socialist system.[39]

Again and again diversion—*Zerstreuung*—is named as a determining factor of entertainment communication. It enables the individual to "escape" from the monotony and pressures of everyday life. In this connection, American mass communications research speaks of the media's *"escape function"* and considers this in many situations to be the central function of mass communication.[40] A predisposition on the part of the recipient to seek escape has often been used as a basis for attracting his attention away from the many burdens and deprivations he has to endure and for subliminal political persuasion in times of crisis and war. Even Goebbels, who had initially given crude direct techniques of political propaganda absolute priority, eventually came to realize during the course of the war that the will to resist could be strengthened through the creation of an "internal" compensation for the many restrictions and hardships that had to be endured and, with this in mind, paid increasing attention to the release offered by escape, which was a component part of radio and film entertainment.[41] In order to stress the urgency of his new radio program policy, he issued the following instruction:[42] "German radio entertainment is of vital importance for the purpose of providing relaxation and relief both on the home and war fronts. For this reason, the category must be given special attention and care in the programming of German Radio." *We Transmit Cheerfulness, Donate Joy* was the title given to one of the variety programs produced in 1942 for members of the army and wounded fellow combatants.[43]

The above description of some of the countless forms and manifestations of mass media entertainment as well as the uses to which it can be put and the effects it can have raises a number of theoretical questions to which we will now briefly turn. There are a number of authors who maintain that mass media entertainment has done nothing more than to adapt an age-old recipe: namely that of *panem et circenses*.[44] The theory whereby a full stomach and entertainment are enough to keep the masses contented (or at least to prevent rebellion) has a large following and constantly reappears in academic literature. However, the "proof" has remained somewhat arbitrary. All that can be said with any certainty is that some definite correlation exists between the perusal of political aims and the satisfaction of the human demand for play as a precondition for these.[45] This applies equally whether one looks at the phenomenon of the Roman gladiatorial contest, a psychologically cleverly arranged state or party event or the spectacle surrounding the Olympic Games. The precise nature and extent of this correlation is a subject that deserves thorough investigation.

Play, whether in the form of games or subjective play (including humor), is considered to be an important part of human pleasure-seeking activity. This seems to apply to all forms of participation in play, whether active (e.g., playing tennis, telling a joke) or passive (e.g., the spectator or audience watching a football match, reading a crime story). The relationship between play and pleasure as well as its mechanisms and functions have been the subject of research in almost every branch of the human sciences. In Psychology, for instance, the first serious attempt to analyze the phenomenon of humor, albeit psychoanalytically, was made by Freud seventy years ago.[46] Important and perhaps the first impulses for the rediscovery of play as a constituent part of human *coexistence* stem from the Dutch historian, Johan Huizinga, in his now classic study, entitled *Homo Ludens*.[47] In Social Anthropology, as E. T. Hall for instance shows, play in its various forms is considered to be an integral component of culturally significant human activity. Further seminal work on the subject has been published by T. S. Szasz (*Pain and Pleasure*)[48] and R. Caillois (*Man, Play, and Games*),[49] to name perhaps the most important. In Mass Communications Research, however, it wasn't until a relatively recent date, when William Stephenson published his now well-known work entitled *The Play Theory of Mass Communication*, that interest was shown in the subject. He equates the play involved in, for instance, reading with communication pleasure, an all-embracing concept including even the pleasure derived from the reading of news on national and international affairs.[50]

But as has already become apparent in the first part of this paper, there is more to entertainment than just the provision of play. Indicative of a new approach toward the subject of entertainment communication, free from the many prejudices and taboos that used to surround it, is the work of two authors who almost simultaneously began to look into the relationship between mass media and entertainment supply. Gerhard Prager's essay, which appeared in a number of publications under the title *Unterhaltung—ein Unterhalt des Menschen* (Entertainment—A Support for Man), is regarded as a basis for further work on the subject.[51] Whereas he only concerned himself with outlining the positive aspects of an entertainment ideal, Wilmont Haacke wrote a number of articles looking into the question of opinion formation through entertainment, later frequently to be used as a starting point for research.[52] Haacke was one of the first to demonstrate convincingly that opinion formation and change had been effected through entertainment, although he doesn't attempt to test this empirically. His conclusions find support in a judgment by the German Constitutional Court shortly before his work appeared. The famous judgment against the plan for a German Television Corporation as conceived by Adenauer included the following passage: that the contribution that television makes toward the formation of public opinion "is not effected solely by newscasts, political commentary and programs about the political problems of past, present and future but also by radio plays, musical performances, cabaret and even the settings in which a program is recorded." Haacke sees this judgment as a recognition of mass media entertainment as an opinion-forming force and thus as a public rather than private responsibility.[53] That entertainment can be used as a means of achieving political ends and often is, with considerable effectiveness, is something that has only recently been fully realized. Haacke, for instance, took Hagemann's view that "for most of the present-day reading public the newspaper supplies . . . a means of general stimulation, relaxation and passing away the time"[54] as his starting point. He went on to formulate the following hypothesis, stating that as a rule the recipient uses communications content in inverse order of its objective importance (i.e., entertainment before information and commentary).[55]

In Holland at about the same time, Henk Prakke attempted to coin a special term—*socius function*—under which the entertaining elements of communication could be subsumed, thus constituting the third branch of the triad of mass communication's functions, the other two being information and commentary. He goes beyond the actual content of communication and its structure so as to include the media themselves when expounding the concept of a socius function (e.g., when he maintains that it is analogous to the function that a companion or a conversation partner during leisure might fulfil). The function consists of the following components: a stress on the so-called "human side of life"; initiation of contact between the recipient and an undiscovered and exciting outside world; promotion of his own prestige through keeping up with the news; compensation for his need for companionship; and enabling the repression of personal loneliness.[56] Later, Prakke was once to describe the socius function as "that part of public communication which supplies relief from the execution of work and from thinking about one's purpose in life."[57]

The communicator always has to bear in mind that it is the recipients' emotions at which entertainment is directed and that it gains its special effectiveness through this very fact. Hagemann sees entertainment as the "expression of a drive for play stemming from the need to free oneself from the purposive restriction of everyday life" precisely because entertainment doesn't necessarily have to have a particular, objectively perceptible purpose. "Entertainment is characterized through trivialization of important matters, exaggeration of petty trifles, comparison of non-comparables and confusion of the comparable (i.e., through its playful distortion of reality), and constitutes a form of mental pastime which easily catches on."[58] The socius function initially manifests itself on the part of the recipient as a reservoir into which information, commentary and entertainment flow. First of all he has to be soothed, amused and diverted. Only then, when he is fully relaxed, can his attention be focused on the opinions and convictions he is presented with.[59] In short: Hagemann maintains that the recipient's need for relaxation must first be satisfied before he can successfully be fed with difficult information and exacting commentary. Wilmont Haacke goes further and stresses the primacy of the entertainment function: "The first aim of public communication is entertainment" and points out that instruction and influence "are almost always contained in entertainment."[60]

The concept of an entertainment function encompassing so many factors and so vitally important for human existence is not completely new. Bernard Berelson's famous study into the effects of a newspaper strike on newspaper readers pointed to similar conclusions. The answers to the question as to what readers missed most without a newspaper can be categorized under headings such as: vicarious involvement with others (human interest), escape, and such.[61] The controversial Canadian prophet of a forthcoming communications revolution, Marshall McLuhan, maintains that the media *per se*, especially the electronic media, possess entertaining qualities and not only their content. Similarly, William Stephenson speaks of the communication pleasure media supply us with, where entertainment as a newspaper or program category is seen as only one of its many contributory means. If one looks into the McLuhanite postulate—already indicated in the attractive title to one of his publications: *The Medium is the Message*—more closely, he does no more than point out that each medium has its own immanent qualities and shortcomings, suiting it for particular tasks more than for others, with the implication that there are differences in the priority entertainment is given.[62] The American, Ralph L. Lowenstein, had made the same observation some time before, albeit from the perspective of the communicator, schematizing them as follows:[63]

1. Book
   a) commentary
   b) entertainment
   c) information
2. Magazine
   a) commentary
   b) entertainment
   c) information
3. Newspaper
   a) information
   b) commentary
   c) entertainment
4. Radio
   a) entertainment
   b) information
   c) commentary
5. Film
   a) entertainment
   b) commentary
   c) information
6. Television
   a) entertainment
   b) information
   c) commentary

According to this particular scheme, three media—radio television and film—are primarily entertainment oriented.

After all that has been said so far it should be clear that the traditional concept—that the form entertaining elements assume are primarily or even totally determined by the communicator and correspondingly consumed by the recipient—is misleading. The recipient has a far greater role than was realized: entertainment is far more a result of his mechanisms of selection and interpretation. Basically, a change in the intended function of information and commentary occurs when, according to Prakke, the recipient enriches the messages he receives with entertaining elements. Such a shift from the intended to the actual that the socius function often entails can occur in all areas of public communication, thus making more exact definition of what entertainment is or at least could be much more difficult. Entertaining elements, one could provisionally say, are always present in the communications process but they are given different entertainment value by each individual recipient. One must proceed on the assumption that each person has a subjective valency with regard to his perception of communications content.[64] The content that can be used to fulfill various recipient needs in line with the socius function outlined above also has, according to Prakke, conversational characteristics. Incidentally, Stephenson equates communication pleasure with the conversation effected through mass media. As one can thus see, entertainment, as far as form and content are concerned, means different things for both the communicator and the recipient.

Those involved in the production of mass communication content, for instance in broadcasting, often construe differences between various forms of entertainment on the basis of "quality." At the most basic level, one differentiates between light and intellectually more demanding forms of entertainment (in German between *leichte Unterhaltung* and *gehobene Unterhaltung*). The distinctions made between light and serious music provide a good illustration of this practice. Typical of the highly subjective distinctions made between light and "serious" entertainment is the one supplied by Fröhner: "light entertainment is meant to enable the audience to pass the time away pleasantly, allow it to "unwind" psychologically and provide relief," whereas a more "elevated" form of entertainment "doesn't only aim to distract and divert but concentrates on directing the audience's attention to matters of artistic and spiritual significance." According to Fröhner, this doesn't necessarily imply that light entertainment is superficial in character. All forms of entertainment, however, so he goes on to say, have a common denominator: namely, that entertainment doesn't aim to supply any objective facts or opinions.[65]

Many examples can be cited of attempts on the part of the communicator to confront the recipient with views or ideologies communicated in the guise of entertainment. This enables—so it is thought—the former to penetrate the conventional psychological barriers operating against their adoption. In fact, it is possible to go so far as to claim, as Friedrich Knilli does, that "entertaining the German viewing public has more in common with hard politics than with the intimacy of the home." Here Knilli is referring above all to the family series largely imported from the United States, which many commentators, in view of their popularity, regard as telegenic entertainment incarnate. He criticizes the fact that most of these series preach a world without problems or where problems are simply and easily solved and that that which is supposed to be "unpolitical entertainment creates its own political guidelines and strategies of action." The fact that many are the controversial "adventure" and "crime" series, whose popularity depends at least in part on the portrayal of violence, adds a further dimension to this problem.[66]

Thus we find an artificial and rigid codification of entertainment in the press, film, radio and television, dating back to the late nineteenth century, the early twentieth century, the 1920s and 40s respectively. The stereotyped layout of the arts pages or feuilleton are most probably the direct result of such stricture. Experimentation is discouraged. Similar observations can be made with regard to other media (e.g., the monotony and lack of originality of radio and television programs originating in departments preprogrammed to produce "entertainment" and nothing else—which results in the recourse to age-old and seemingly successful recipes).[67] At the same time, the uncertainty of communicators when asked to define or describe entertainment's characteristics is alarming. Symptomatic for this state of affairs is the fact that none of the three top show producers interviewed on German television a few years ago could say more about the nature and function of entertainment than that it contributes toward diversion.[68] Of course this also applies to the recipient, as audience research repeatedly shows.

With regard to the present discussion and controversy surrounding the topic of entertainment, Dieter Stolte, a leading figure in German television, has the following sobering comments to make (which put a lot of negative criticism into perspective):[69]

> 'Pure' entertainment was subject to ideological cross-fire. The medium (television) was accused of 'total manipulation.' The conformist and reactionary efficacy attributed to entertainment was attacked in general and undifferentiated terms. One polemicized against the authoritarian models presented above all in television serial output. . . . The ground for such aversion to entertainment had been well prepared, for there is little that German criticism in the field of culture has devaluated as much. Not only has television been criticized on grounds of supposed inferiority and lack of standards but so have all entertainment forms that mass and popular culture have produced since the eighteenth century. This contempt applies equally whether the entertainment form was the popular novel, the theatrical farce, the operetta, the pop song or the feature film. That the assault originated in two camps locked in earnest combat with each other—the pedagogically serious leftist German subculture and that of the elitist rightist senior schoolmaster-type—didn't make the criticism any more sound. Defamation was a matter of principle and argument was rarely found on concrete, demonstrable fact . . . their thoroughness was evidently based on an irrational core.

This devaluation of popular culture in general and modern mass entertainment in particular rests on foundations, according to Stolte, that fail to take the following two factors into account:[70] The first of these is

the—in cultural and historical terms—relatively new crystallization of a heterogenous reading, listening and viewing public with regard to level of education. . . . It is wrong for the cursory observer to conclude that standards of
taste have declined. He doesn't have the means with which to compare with
the mass taste of earlier times. In the past, namely, the educated person had
neither the opportunity nor reasons for attending to the interests and intelligence of the ordinary man on the street. The cultural environments of
both groups didn't meet at any point (apart from church and religion, in
which the priest acted as mediator). This mutual exclusion between the two
levels of culture still operates today. What the one group finds pleasure in—
grand ballet, Brecht, literary cabaret—is an unreasonable demand on the
other; and vice versa: what the latter enjoy most—an entertaining and amusing
show—is looked down upon by the former and regarded as insipid silliness.

The second factor, so he continues, is the subjective nature of the concept: standard of taste. One "tends to turn one's own standard of taste into an
absolute. The educated, the intellectuals see in their own entertainment
requirements the true needs of all other people. Wishes to the contrary are subject to the verdict that they are an expression of inferior "mass taste." The pedagogical expert, Horst Wetterling, described this phenomenon in the following
terms:

> If the others don't wish to conform to one's own image of man, then their
> desires are simply taken to be a mark of inferior capability. Yet these desires
> make sense . . . (especially) with respect to entertainment and diversion.
> . . . Who denies that they are not always made use of? Moreover, there is a
> simple reason as to why products, in which contemporaries seek entertainment
> and diversion, frequently show certain limitations: the non-cooperation of the
> elite. The elite is always ready to criticize standards but not to offer a helping
> hand. It is able to disparage the consumer of such products but not to support
> him. He is able to interpret play and its various manifestations but not to initi-
> ate play.

Against this background Stolte says:

> It is no wonder that the work of the television entertainment producers is ob-
> served and criticized so widely by anti-entertainment television critics. . . .
> The criteria for criticism are to be found in the aesthetic ideals of the high cul-
> ture to which they belong. From this position, entertainment, to put it simply,
> fulfills no other function than to stultify and lead the public astray. Criticism
> can only function as a stimulating regulative within the feedback system of
> producer, audience and critic if it plays its role taking the audience on the one
> hand and the producer on the other into account.[71]

Entertainment is less the result of the aims of the communicator than the
interpretation of communication within the process of reception. On the part
of the recipient, psychological predispositions, physical condition, level of education, group membership and situative factors (e.g., playing cards while
watching television) play the decisive role in determining what is to be perceived as entertainment. For this reason, all attempts at defining entertainment

a priori, using formal content categories, cannot be satisfactory. Erwin Scheuch aptly comments that entertainment is that which the recipient uses as entertainment.[72] And what he finds entertaining does not necessarily have to be content in its traditional operational definition within mass communications research (i.e., it may be a printing error, a slip of the tongue in radio or television, things that are often more entertaining and contribute more to conversation than prestructured content, whatever intention lies behind it.)[73] Another form of entertainment communication is to be found in the so-called "daydreaming effect," which Palmgreen described as "thinking about anything other than what is being communicated to the daydreamer at a particular moment."[74] People often perceive or use radio and television programs as a permanent switched-on source of background noise or flickering images without really paying attention to what is going on. Prakke's socius function embodying constant companionship can thus be intriguingly corroborated.

It should be clear from the above observations that the audience defines entertainment for itself. As Ulrich Saxer stresses, this sector of communication brings a great disparity between the intention behind the content and "real communication" to light. "As far as the communicator is concerned, his contribution to public entertainment . . . doesn't only consist of that which is marketed under the label by a long way."[75] And Scheuch supplements this observation by saying that "the viewer can turn almost anything into entertainment."[76] From that which has been said in this context, we can draw the following conclusion: Entertainment in the eyes of the communicator is the manifold attempt to free the recipient from the constraints of his work environment, using various forms of mass communication. On the other hand, the recipient can perceive almost anything as entertainment. As a rule, an incongruent relationship can thus be said to exist between the two partners in the communication process.

NOTES

[1] Cf. the rather detailed discussion on this aspect in Heinz-Dietrich Fischer's "Unterhaltung als Kommunikationsproblem," in *Das gedruckte Wort. Zweite Festschrift für Anton Betz,* ed. Karl Bringmann (Düsseldorf, 1973), pp. 107–30.

[2] Cf. Francis Earle Barcus, "Communications Content: Analysis of the Research, 1900–1958. A Content Analysis of Content Analysis" (Ph.D. diss., Urbana, Illinois, 1959), p. 83.

[3] Cf. Heinz-Dietrich Fischer, "Die traditionsreichste Publizistik-Fakultät der Welt. Sechs Dezennien School of Journalism der University of Missouri," *Publizistik* 14, no. 2 (Konstanz April–June 1969): 207–22.

[4] Cf. Heinrich Brandes, "Publizistik als Gegenstand der Wissenschaft. Ein Beitrag zur Entwicklung der deutschen Zeitungswissenschaft in den Jahren 1916 bis 1941" (Ph.D. diss., University of Leipzig, 1942).

[5] Cf. Otto Groth, *Die Geschichte der deutschen Zeitungswissenschaft* (München, 1948).

[6] Quoted from Karl Kurth, ed., *Die ältesten Schriften für und wider die Zeitung* (Brünn–München–Wien, 1944), p. 103.

[7] Cf. the relatively broad spectrum of meanings in Jakob Grimm and Wilhelm Grimm, *Deutsches Wörterbuch* 11, sec. 3 (Leipzig, 1936): col. 1606–11.

[8] Marianne Thalmann, *Die Romantik des Trivialen* (München, 1970), p. 10.

[9] Cf. among others Hansjörg Garte, "Kunstform Schauerroman. Eine morphologische Bergriffsbestimmung des Sensationsromans im 18. Jahrhundert" (Ph.D. diss., Leipzig, 1935).

[10] Cf. Marianne Thalmann, *Der Trivialroman des 18. Jahrhunderts und der romantische Roman* (Berlin, 1923).

[11] Cf. Heinz Otto Burger, ed., *Studien zur Trivialliteratur* (Frankfurt a.M., 1968); Jochen Schulte-Sasse, *Die Kritik an der Trivialliteratur seit der Aufklärung. Studien zur Geschichte des modernen Kitsch-Begriffs* (München, 1970).

[12] Martin Greiner, *Die Entstehung der modernen Unterhaltungsliteratur. Studien zum Trivialroman des 18. Jahrhunderts* (Reinbek bei Hamburg, 1964), p. 11.

[13] Cf. Friedrich von Schiller, "Über naive und sentimentalische Dichtung," in *Schillers Werke* VIII, ed. Ludwig Bellermann (Leipzig–Wien, 1895): pp. 310 ff.

[14] Kurt Ingo Flessau, *Der moralische Roman. Studien zur gesellschaftskritischen Trivialliteratur der Goethezeit* (Köln–Graz, 1968), p. 2.

[15] Ernst Meunier and Hans Jessen, *Das Deutsche Feuilleton. Ein Beitrag zur Zeitungskunde* (Berlin, 1931), p. 18.

[16] Cf. Wilmont Haacke, *Handbuch des Feuilletons* I (Emsdetten, 1951), pp. 173 ff.

[17] Cf. Margot Lindemann, *Deutsche Presse bis 1815* (Berlin, 1969), pp. 232 ff.

[18] Cf. the motto from the first edition of this periodical in *Facsimile-Querschnitt durch die "Gartenlaube,"* ed. Heinz Klüter (Bern–Stuttgart–Wien, 1963), p. 29.

[19] Cf. Gerhard Hense, "Friedrich Arnold Brockhaus (1772–1823)," in *Deutsche Presseverleger des 18. bis 20. Jahrhunderts*, ed. Heinz-Dietrich Fischer (München, 1975), pp. 82–90.

[20] Emil Dovifat, "Feuilleton," in *Handbuch der Zeitungswissenschaft*, ed. Walther Heide, I (Leipzig, 1940): col. 976 f.

[21] *Ibid.*: col. 977.

[22] Hans Becker, "Das Feuilleton der Berliner Tagespresse von 1848 bis 1852. Ein Beitrag zur Geschichte des deutschen Feuilletons" (Ph.D. diss., München, 1935; Würzburg, 1938), p. 127.

[23] Jürgen Habermas, *Strukturwandel der Öffentlichkeit. Untersuchungen zu einer Kategorie der bürgerlichen Gesellschaft* (Neuwied, 1962), p. 180.

[24] *Ibid., pp.* 182 ff.

[25] Cf. Theodor W. Adorno, "Über den Fetischcharakter in der Musik und die Regression des Hörens," in *Dissonanzen* (Göttingen: 1956), pp. 9 ff.

[26] Jürgen Habermas, *op. cit.*, p. 186 f.

[27] Cf. Karl Marx, "Deutsche Ideologie," in Karl Marx and Friedrich Engels' *Historisch-kritische Gesamtausgabe. Werke—Schriften—Briefe* V (Berlin, 1932).

[28] Friedrich Engels, "Die deutschen Volksbücher," in Kark Marx and Friedrich Engels' *Werke*, Suppl. Vol. II (Berlin, 1968).

[29] Quoted from Heinz Knobloch, *Vom Wesen des Feuilletons* (Halle [Saale], 1962), p. 153.

[30] Cf. Harald Feddersen, "Das Feuilleton der sozialdemokratischen Tagespresse Deutschlands von den Anfängen bis zum Jahre 1914. Mit einem Überblick über das sozialistische Feuilleton vom August 1914 bis Mai 1922" (Ph.D. diss., University of

Leipzig, 1922); Konrad Schmidt, ed., *Feuilleton der Roten Presse, 1918–1933* (East Berlin, 1960).

[31] Paul Mayer, *Bruno Schoenlank, 1859–1901. Reformer der sozialdemokratischen Tagespresse* (Hannover, 1972), p. 68.

[32] Cf. Kurt Koszyk, *Zwischen Kaiserreich und Diktatur. Die sozialdemokratische Presse von 1914 bis 1933* (Heidelberg, 1958).

[33] Cf. Heinz-Dietrich Fischer, ed., *Pressekonzentration und Zensurpraxis im Ersten Weltkrieg. Texte und Quellen* (Berlin, 1973).

[34] Siegfried Kracauer, *From Caligari to Hitler. A Psychological History of the German Film*, 4th ed. (Princeton, New Jersey, 1971), p. 23.

[35] Winfried B. Lerg, *Die Entstehung des Rundfunks in Deutschland. Herkunft und Entwicklung eines publizistischen Mittels* (Frankfurt a.M., 1965), p. 195.

[36] Quoted from Joseph Wulf, ed., *Presse und Funk im Dritten Reich. Eine Dokumentation* (Gütersloh, 1964), p. 325.

[37] Cf. Hortense Powdermaker, *Hollywood—The Dream Factory* (Boston, 1950).

[38] Wolfgang Becker, *Film und Herrschaft. Organisationsprinzipien und Organisationsstrukturen der nationalistischen Filmpropaganda* (Berlin, 1973), p. 63.

[39] *Ibid.*

[40] Cf. Paul F. Lazarsfeld and Robert K. Merton, "Mass Communication, Popular Taste, and Organized Social Action," in *The Communication of Ideas*, ed. Lyman Bryson (New York, 1948), pp. 95–118.

[41] Wolfgang Schütte, *Regionalität und Föderalismus im Rundfunk. Die geschichtliche Entwicklung in Deutschland 1923–1945* (Frankfurt a.M., 1971), p. 188.

[42] The complete document is reprinted, *ibid.*, pp. 189 *f.*

[43] Cf. Heinz Barkhausen, comp., *Filmbestände. Verleihkopien von Dokumentar- und Kulturfilmen sowie Wochenschauen 1900–1945* (Koblenz, 1971), no. 627, p. 51.

[44] Cf. Ludwig Friedlaender, ed., *D. Junii Juvenalis Saturarum Libri V*, vols. 1–2 (Darmstadt, 1967), p. 463 (= Liber quartus, Satura X, col. 81).

[45] Cf. as a special historical example for the realization of such an aim: Karlheinz Schmeer, *Die Regie des öffentlichen Lebens im Dritten Reich* (München, 1956), pp. 52 *ff.*

[46] Cf. Sigmund Freud, *Der Witz und seine Beziehung zum Unbewußten*, paperback ed. (Frankfurt a.M., 1958).

[47] Cf. Johan Huizinga, *Homo Ludens. A Study of the Play Element in Culture*, paperback ed. (Boston, 1950).

[48] Cf. Thomas S. Szasz, *Pain and Pleasure* (New York, 1957).

[49] Cf. Roger Caillois, *Man, Play, and Games* (New York, 1961).

[50] Cf. William Stephenson, *The Play Theory of Mass Communication* (Chicago and London, 1967), pp. 45 *ff.*

[51] Cf. Gerhard Prager, "Unterhaltung—ein Unterhalt des Menschen," in *Rundfunk und Fernsehen* 7, no. 3–4 (Hamburg, 1959): 233 *ff.*

[52] Cf. Wilmont Haacke, "Meinungsbildung durch Unterhaltung," in *Publizistik* 6, no. 5–6 (Bremen, September–December, 1961): 338–54.

[53] *Ibid.*, 340.

[54] Walter Hagemann, *Die Zeitung als Organismus* (Heidelberg, 1950), pp. 42 *f.*

[55] Cf. Wilmont Haacke, *Handbuch des Feuilletons* I (Emsdetten, 1951), pp. 168 *ff.*

[56] Hendricus Johannes Prakke, "Die Soziusfunktion der Presse," in *Publizistik* 5, no. 6 (Bremen, November–December, 1960): 558. See Chapter 9 of this book.

[57] Henk Prakke et al., Kommunikation der Gesellschaft. Einführung in die funktionale Publizistik. (Münster i.W., 1968), pp. 160 f.

[58] Walter Hagemann, Vom Mythos der Masse. Ein Beitrag zur Psychologie der Öffentlichkeit. (Heidelberg, 1951), p. 33.

[59] Cf. Max Weber, Gesammelte Aufsätze zur Soziologie und Sozialpolitik. (Tübingen, 1924), p. 441.

[60] Wilmont Haacke, Handbuch des Feuilletons II (Emsdetten, 1952), p. 308.

[61] Cf. Bernard Berelson, "What 'Missing the Newspapers' Means," in Communication Research 1948–1949, ed. Paul F. Lazersfeld and Frank N. Stanton (New York, 1949), pp. 111–29.

[62] Cf. Marshall McLuhan, The Medium Is the Message (New York, 1967).

[63] Ralph Lynn Lowenstein, "The Elements of Mass Communication" (Unpublished paper, Columbia, Mo., 1969).

[64] Cf. Henk Prakke et al., Kommunikation der Gesellschaft, p. 75.

[65] Rolf Fröhner, Kritik der Aussage. Sprache, Mitteilung, Ausdruck und ihre publizistische Problematik (Heidelberg, 1954), pp. 77 f. (The author not only entangles himself in contradictions—if entertainment is not superficial, it must in some way be significant; opinions are often matters of artistic or spiritual significance; and matters of artistic or spiritual merit are always to a certain extent based on fact, etc.—but fails to recognize that a documentary or an expression of opinion can function as entertainment.)

[66] Friedrich Knilli, Die Unterhaltung der deutschen Fernsehfamilie. Ideologiekritische Kurzanalysen von Serien (München, 1971), p. 7.

[67] For example, both of the West German Television networks have so-called "Unterhaltungs-Abteilungen" (program departments for entertainment); cf. ARD-Jahrbuch 1977 (Hamburg, 1977), pp. 138, 142, 146, 149, 151, 154, 158, 162, 167; cf. also ZDF-Jahrbuch 1976 (Mainz, 1977), p. 40.

[68] Statement made during a live program, "Wünsch Dir was" (moderated by Vivi Bach and Dietmar Schönherr), co-production of the television networks of Austria (ORF), Switzerland (SRG), and West Germany (ZDF), March 25, 1972, 8:15–10:10 p.m., Middle European Standard Time (according to the author's stenographed notes).

[69] Dieter Stolte, "Die Unterhaltung im Fernsehen—Auftrag, Angebot und Nutzung," in Unterhaltung im Fernsehen: Klimbim am laufenden Band?, ed. Adolf-Grimme-Institut (Marl, 1977), pp. 12 f.

[70] Ibid., p. 13.

[71] Ibid., pp. 13 f.

[72] Cf. Erwin K. Scheuch, "Unterhaltung als Pausenfüller—Von der Vielfalt der Unterhaltungsfunktion in der modernen Gesellschaft," in Unterhaltung und Unterhaltendes im Fernsehen, ed. Gerhard Prager (Mainz, 1971), p. 42.

[73] Cf. Heinz-Dietrich Fischer, "Unterhaltung als Kommunikations problem," p. 128.

[74] Philip Palmgreen, A Daydream Model of Communication (Lexington, Kentucky, 1971), p. 12.

[75] Ulrich Saxer, "Publizistik und Unterhaltung. Die Probleme der Legitimation und der Definition," in Neue Zürcher Zeitung, Vol. 1993 (International ed.), no. 21 (Zurich, January 22, 1972), p. 51, col. 3.

[76] Erwin K. Scheuch, "Unterhaltung als Pausenfüller," p. 43.

Part Two

☆☆☆☆

CONTINUITY IN ENTERTAINMENT

Paul Taylor:

The Studio Audience for Television Situation Comedies

☆ IT IS DOUBTFUL, as one commentator has noted, that the end result of comedy should be to produce laughter.[1] Most expositions on comedy, in fact, tend to ignore the audience, and therefore laughter, and rather concentrate on defining and delineating the attributes of comedy in an attempt to map out what sort of a view of life is generally posited therein. The works of many playwrights and authors, from Aristophanes through Shakespeare to Wilde and from Rabelais through Sterne to Thurber, have been subjected to critical analysis. Here, of course, one is really talking about comedy with a capital "C," "respectable" drama and literature with supposed artistic merits. As such, these works have been seen as existing in perpetuity, as part of a store of material in the fabric of the public domain. A lack of performance, in the case of drama, does not impinge on their existence.

Of course, performance continually revitalizes and allows for the possibility of reinterpretation, and further provides for a dramatic dialectic through the process of feedback.[2] Styan has argued that it is misleading to maintain a linear Aristotelian perspective for drama, a perspective which disentangles plot, character, thought, diction, music and spectacle. Rather, we should try and understand drama as the *total* theatrical experience, where the nature of the occasion is paramount. He suggests a Gestalt theory of drama whereby the total experience of the theatre is greater than the sum of its parts. One's concern in an approach to drama should be for ". . . reaction and 'feedback,' all the alchemical changes that occur during the reception of theatrical signals."[3] The audience completes the circuit.

Obviously, the audience is an integral part of this process and the point I wish to develop is the general nature of the "theatrical" audience for television situation comedies with specific reference to their role as generators of feedback. One point should, however, be noted at this juncture: While the end

▶ This is an article written especially for this book. Paul Taylor is engaged in research at the Centre for Mass Communication Research at the University of Leicester, England.

result of comedy may not be to produce laughter, if laughter is not produced then Heads of Comedy will eventually roll.

Laughter

While there have been many theories of laughter and comedy (Greig gives 363 works bearing partly or wholly on the subject),[4] very few actually deal with laughter as communication. Hayworth is a notable exception, although his hypothesis that laughter functioned as a signal to the members of the primeval group that they could relax in safety is not directly relevant here. Duncan argues persuasively that comedy allows communication through laughter by stressing that "laughter breaks down the distance subjective concern creates between individuals"[5] and further that ". . . even though our group laughs at us, it does not shut us off from joining once again. Laughter offers us an open and simple way of re-establishing communication. Once we join in laughter, the burden of ridicule is lifted."[6]

Television Situation Comedies [7]

Almost every situation comedy that is transmitted on British television is recorded in a studio in the presence of an audience that ranges in size from about 250 to 350 people. The reason is twofold—the presence of a (hopefully) laughing audience enables the cast of the program to build up the script and to time their lines and, secondly, audience laughter is supposed to give cues to the television viewers watching in their homes.

Timing

It is now conventional wisdom that to play comedy successfully one needs "timing," though this apparently magical "you've got it or you ain't" quality tends to escape precise definition. Fry and Allen come as near as anybody in their description of a Jack Benny joke:

> A robber accosts Benny with "your money or your life." Paaauuuusssseeeeee. Finally the robber demands, "Well?!" To which Benny replies, "I'm thinking! I'm thinking!"[8]

Fry and Allen then proceed to analyze the performance:

> The timing, or rhythm in that exchange is especially crucial. Even before the spoken punchline, "I'm thinking! I'm thinking!" is delivered, an initial punchline is presented in the lengthening pause. As the pause extends longer and longer, underlining the miser's conflict of priorities, more and more people begin laughing. Timing, itself, becomes the joke.[9]

Performers certainly stress timing as a key element in good comedy playing and this is as true of the stand-up, joke-telling comedian as it is of the actor or actress playing a role in a situation comedy.[10] Obviously, timing is dependent on some sort of reaction to any given joke or line. During rehearsals for situation comedies, attempts are often made by both media professionals (the producer and/or director, assistant floor manager, and such) and onlookers (members of the cast, friends, an academic researcher here and there) to give some sort of response and indication of how everything is going to the performing actors. However, until a program is actually performed in front of a large, expectant audience, no one can accurately predict where all the laughs are going to come. The presence of an audience raises performances to concert pitch and allows the creation of a relationship built on feedback.

One scriptwriter I interviewed said of situation comedies recorded without an audience:

> They've put a laughter track on afterwards and it just isn't the same. It's absolutely essential if you're doing comedy for the actors to have something to time against. Timing's all essential and you've got to have an audience, hopefully laughing, for the actors to work with.

Similarly, a producer of a number of situation comedies said:

> I think it's nice for the actors to have (laughter) because it does enable them to time it—the timing is the essence. It encourages them, so long as they are reacting of course, and that gives them an extra lift because they know that they're entertaining immediately.

For the cast, certainly, a favorable and definitely audible reaction improves performance by supplying a response against which both pace and intensity can be measured and timed. Laughs can also be milked; anecdotes are legion of how the better actors and actresses can immediately respond to an unexpected laugh (or more importantly, to an unexpected silence) in such a way as to capitalize on the situation. To play comedy well, some reaction is needed and as the response of the millions of home viewers cannot be tapped, a surrogate is used instead. This reaction has been aptly, if not effervescently, described by a successful husband and wife comedy acting team:

> You embrace them into your moves and move with them . . . you dance with them . . . (a good audience will) move like a sea, they weave around like corn, and you do dance with them.[11]

Both partners agreed that, for them, it is very nearly impossible to act comedy without a studio audience and if there isn't one, the wife will rely on the reactions of cameramen, prop boys or anyone else who happens to be about.

Cues and Contagion

A number of writers[12] have suggested that "cues," in classifying that which follows the cue as humorous, have a great deal of importance in any study of humor and laughter. While these cues may take many forms, from the usually lighthearted or frivolous opening music to the general publicity surrounding the program, the most specific and the most easily recognizable cue is that of hearing laughter on the soundtrack—one automatically knows that something is supposed to be funny. One exception to this is the American program, M*A*S*H, which has no laughter soundtrack at all; it can only be assumed that the presence of a sufficient number of other cues, coupled with the fact that this writer happens to find it funny and believes that many others do too, obviates the need for such a definite cue as audience laughter. It is certainly possible to turn on any British situation comedy midway through the program and immediately know that one is watching a show that ought to be comic.

Apart from providing cues for the home audience, the recorded studio audience response is reckoned, at least by many scriptwriters and producers of such programs, to have a contagious effect. There is some academic proof[13] that such contagion exists, although the circumstances surrounding some of these experiments cannot be directly paralleled to the process of the mass media in that the ambience has normally consisted of an interpersonal face-to-face reaction. In a reference to an earlier experiment (1973) one psychologist has noted:

> The findings of the experiment vindicated the utilization of dubbed laughter, showing that when adults are solitary recipients of humor, they laugh more if there is laughter accompanying the presentation.[14]

The experiment referred to involved university students and the material presented was in joke cartoon format. It is, however, possible to extrapolate, with some supportive evidence gleaned from those works mentioned *supra*, that the sound of laughter will tend to determine any particular program as supposedly funny—whether the larger, home audience then tend to rate such a program as funnier has been a matter of some debate. Whether the home audience enjoys a show more or less does not directly concern us here; what does matter is that the people responsible for writing and producing comedy programs tend, in the main, to be convinced that laughter is contagious and that, therefore, the presence of a studio audience is a necessary evil. As one scriptwriter told me:

> It's on the assumption that laughter is infectious and that if you're watching a comedy program at home, all by yourself or just you and the wife, and you hear people laughing, that tells you it's a funny show. Now I'm not saying that that's good reasoning; I think that's the reasoning.

It certainly would appear to be the reasoning prevalent in the minds of many decision makers in the mass media. While most practitioners vehemently deny that canned laughter is ever used, this denial is often by way of a *mea culpa*.

The use of canned laughter generally falls into the nebulous area of technical continuity, wherein such use is justifiable when, for example, a laugh has been cut off in mid-vocalization because of a retake or when there has been some mechanical or artistic failure that results in a retake at which the audience does not feel predisposed to laugh again. The defensive attitude of those working in television is somewhat understandable—canned laughter is certainly used in the sort of situation where an absence of laughter would create an un-called for atmosphere of high drama. When it is patently obvious that a line is intended to raise a laugh, it is quite unnerving to hear such a line received in a hushed silence. It would appear, though, that the use of canned laughter in Britain is quite restricted, mainly because there is a realization that its use does involve a degree of artistic cheating. The position in America would appear to be much more developed, for, as one American scriptwriter expressed it:

> Another terrible thing that goes on today, which means that there is really no point in fighting in a story conference over whether something is funny or not, is that they can easily state it's *going* to be funny—because they are going to push the laugh machine.

> We're breeding a whole set of people holding the reins, who never worked with an audience in their lives. They simply don't know what it *means* to work with an audience. The guy comes in with the machine and he plays it like a piano. As he does it, the producer says, "No, wait a minute; I want a smaller laugh," or "I want a bigger laugh." [15]

A Closer Look at the Studio Audience [16]

Once it is accepted that the presence of a studio audience is desirable as a method of generating laughter, for both the cast in a situation comedy and for the home audience, the problem that confronts the television companies is how to best fill the seats. Fortunately, for them, the problem is immediately dissipated because of the large number of applicants for tickets. The BBC, in fact, states in a leaflet giving general information that "owing to the enormous demand, we are unable to send tickets more than once for any series."

Although there is a slight difference in the case of the commercial com-panies, the tendency is to do what the BBC does—allocate tickets on a first come, first served basis. The amount of tickets for any given program will vary a great deal depending mainly on the size of the studio and on how many tickets are requested as complimentaries by the producer, his staff and others connected with the show (these may make up to 50% of the audience). The remainder of the tickets will be distributed between parties (to ensure a reason-able attendance) and individuals. Preference is given to people living away from the place of recording, as it is assumed that they will be coming to London for a day out and that it may be their only chance to see a program. After that, applications are dealt with on a purely rotational basis. Both the BBC and the commercial companies operate "waiting lists," and applicants are offered tickets when their name reaches the top. Official policy suggests that applicants are refused only on two grounds—that of minimum age (varying between fourteen and sixteen years for situation comedies) and that of physical handicap. [17]

Attempts are made, sometimes at the request of the producer, to try and "match" an audience with a particular show. It is then up to the ticket units and offices to try and distribute the tickets available to gain the most "suitable" audience. A reasonably close working relationship with the producer is obviously desirable in this respect and a general awareness of the nature of particular programs is a necessity.

I have argued elsewhere [18] that there seems to be a bias both toward middle age and toward women as members of the studio audience, though it should be emphasized here that this view is based on limited experience (by attendance) and not on any sort of analysis of the participants. It does, however, seem certain that the studio audience is not representative of the general public at large, and I have heard estimates from producers and scriptwriters alike that the number of women in the audience will be anywhere between 70 and 90%. The bulk of the parties come from what may be loosely termed "social clubs," with a (presumably unintended) bias toward Women's Institutes and Mother's Unions.

Having assembled this audience, the next stage in the proceedings falls in the lap of the "warm-up" man. Already feeling under some obligation to react "properly," since the tickets are free, the audience is then jollied along into a state of ready participation. The function of the warm-up man is to both get the audience into a relaxed and receptive frame of mind and also to stress their forthcoming importance. It is continually emphasized that we, the audience, should laugh loud, long and often and that without such participation, the show cannot really be a success. By joking about the strange surroundings of wires and lights and cameras, the warm-up man attempts to defuse the situation of any of the technical processes. The whole affair is coated with a friendly, chatty gloss which tends to detract from the actual proceedings—which are that a situation comedy is being recorded for future transmission.

It is almost possible to detect a slight hint of embarrassment in the warm-up man's voice when, in his role as choirmaster and conductor, he asks the audience to laugh again at a retake—a request, stripped of its environment, as far-fetched and incredible as asking somebody to laugh again when you tell the same jokes within the space of a matter of minutes. However, the audience tends to laugh again, possibly because of sense of familiarity with the material as well as their general, prompted obligation. In fact, one producer told me that ". . . some producers automatically do the first scene twice. Unless it goes exceedingly well, they pretend that technically they want to do it again because very often you get more and better laughs the second time."

The technicians are usually made the scapegoats when there is any holdup in the process. There is a continual stressing that the cast are there to entertain and, conversely, that the audience are there to be entertained and to react accordingly and that if it was not for the producer, the floor manager and the cameramen, all would go smoothly. Although the necessity of getting as best a recording as possible may be mentioned, the emphasis is clearly laid upon the immediacy of the process as if one were approaching a normal theatrical show. When actors fluff their lines, necessitating a retake, audience sympathy is directed—by the warm-up man—toward the cast and their antipathy is drawn against the people who demand the retake. One approaches an almost ludicrous situation in which an actor who is clearly failing to do his job, and would be reminded of such failure in the theatre by unfavorable audience reaction, is exonerated and his mistake transferred. When things are going smoothly, the importance of the technical processes is minimized. When retakes are necessitated, they become all important and the technicians must act as scapegoats.

There are, of course, several reasons for retakes, and it would be unfair to put too much of the blame onto the cast. Technical hitches certainly do occur, though in my limited experience mistakes are likelier to come from people in the gallery than from the floorstaff and cameramen. It would be wrong, however, to imply that retakes are only made from technical or practical necessity. For a number of reasons, a scene or a line may not be working out as well as it has done in rehearsal and the producer may deem it advisable to try and recapture the lost "magic." Also, as was noted before, a supposed laugh line that is greeted by silence creates an almost threatening atmosphere; in this case, the producer has the option of turning to canned laughter (or euphemistically "turning the volume up a bit") or of doing the piece again after alerting the audience that it is supposed to be funny.

In brief summary, it can be posited that the presence of a studio audience is seen as necessary by the media professionals for the interrelated reasons of providing laughter for the cast and for the home audience. While no special importance should be attached to the following quote because of its length, the argument given therein is, I believe, both persuasive and correct. Further, it gives a clear indication of how much the media professional (in this case a scriptwriter with some production experience) is aware of the nature of the process. In reply to a question about the necessity or otherwise of a studio audience, the person replied:

> One hundred percent necessary. Lots of people have tried to do comedy without an audience; now this is the whole point to me . . . an actor who plays comedy has to time his laughs. He has to time his reaction. He cannot do this in any other way but with people there. In the studio audience at (television company) we have about four hundred people in the audience. A lot of people say "I can't stand that canned laughter." At (television company) we never put any laughs on a show . . . (the studio audience are) sitting there and they see it acted in front of them. The actor must do two things—he must be with the audience but not play to the audience. A television camera, you can look right into it and the camera comes in close and they see your eyes . . . you are in the camera but you are in reality playing to that audience. The actor, when he's playing situation comedy, must have an ear on the studio audience—he never plays to the studio audience, he's got to remember the camera, he's playing to the camera, but he's timing his laughs through the studio audience. Now the actor . . . is making a rapport with the studio audience so there's a sort of umbilical cord between the actor and the studio audience. Now if the audience like him, those four hundred people will laugh . . . now this is recorded onto tape, and when it goes out there's usually three

or four people. This is your audience. Now when you are watching that tape on the box, the contact that the actors have made in the studio with the audience is then transferred to you. Now this is my theory and it works.

Inherent Drawbacks

There are several immediate and practical limitations that the presence of a studio audience automatically imposes upon the creation and the production of a situation comedy. Firstly, the amount of filmed as opposed to "live" material is restricted (though, of course, this is subject to the strictures of a budget anyway). Unless there is a large percentage of actual performance in the studio, one cannot expect to get a suitable audience response. While the monitors receive as much, if not more, attention than the "stage," the audience is still there because of the very theatrical nature of the process—the primacy of the occasion is paramount. One of the great differences between a television situation comedy and a stage play is that in the latter it is most rare for an actor to exchange unscripted remarks with the audience or to appear out of character in any way whatsoever, curtain calls excepted. The illusion of the theatre is notably absent from the television studio, but a balance, favoring performance, must be kept, otherwise the whole affair gets perilously close to just presenting an audience with a half hour film and expecting them to laugh out loud. Once one accepts the desirability, if not necessity, of a studio audience and the emphasis on performance that that entails, then it becomes apparent that the "action" of situation comedies is severely limited.

Bound to a studio and to the concomitant circumstances of restriction in the number, shape and size of sets available, the writer is constrained to adopt certain practices and approaches that have slightly less flexibility than those of his counterpart in the theatre and a great deal less than those of the film writer. Perhaps more important in this respect is the question of time. The fact that most situation comedies are of approximately a half hour in length seems to derive from early radio shows, which themselves owed something to the "American Invasion" of radio during the war. Advertisers thought that half an hour was about the right time span to keep someone amused. In the studio, the recording of a half-hour program can take anything from an hour to two hours to do. To enable the audience to be gathered, the process cannot start too early and either 7:30 p.m. or 8 p.m. are the usual times. Because of union agreements, the studio must be cleared by, usually, 9:30 p.m. or 10 p.m. and, as there is a premium on studio space, it is absolutely imperative that a show be recorded in its allotted time span to avoid all sorts of complications of revised schedules. Given the essential time needed for set changes, costume changes and the almost inevitable retakes, it simply would not be practical for a situation comedy to run much longer than it does at the present time. If one is to record a show with a live audience, one is faced with a potential limitation on creativity, as it must be assumed that half an hour is the optimum length for a program.[19]

A further limitation arises when the plot calls for some outdoor filming, as is often the case. Without any significant feedback, the cast must time their lines with the intention and hope that the laughs will come where they are supposed to. The film will be shown, in sequence, during the recording of the live segments of the show and the audience laughter will be mixed with it. Obviously, as no one can predict with absolute accuracy where the laughs will come and of what duration they will be, pregnant pauses on film may remain vacant instead of being filled with laughter or unexpected laughter may drown out subsequent lines.

On a more general level, several perspectives can be identified which tend to militate against the creators of situation comedies. There is, for example, the chance that the home audience will react against and not with the sound of laughter—although the weight of evidence tends to suggest that hearing laughter boosts mirth reactions and perceived funniness.[20] It is likely that this is so only because cues are being given that point to the material in question as being humorous. If some of the home audience either do not need or reject these cues or refuse to participate in the "choral" aspects of group laughter, then it would appear that annoyance, rather than encouragement, may be the end result.

Also, although the studio audience may be intended to act as a surrogate for the home viewers, there could well be a clash of tastes between the two that drastically undermines the concept of contagion. On this point, *inter alia*, a scriptwriter had this to say:

> For me, the studio audience is the key to the whole problem of situation comedy and what I dislike about it most. If you're doing something that is relatively sophisticated and you're doing that in the theatre, that will find its own audience . . . the audience that comes is the audience that is ready to appreciate and understand. Now, generally speaking, the audience that comes to situation comedies in the TV studios is the equivalent of the coach party audience. It's usually, in my experience, seventy percent women, it's usually elderly, outings from Darby and Joan clubs. Certainly, in very general terms, they're not a very sophisticated audience. In order to make them respond, you have to do a not very sophisticated show. The trouble is that studio audiences are not selected with care. Whereas an immense amount of time and effort goes into writing the script, rehearsing, designing the sets, choosing the film locations, every damn thing, how do they choose the audience? They just send out at random the three hundred and fifty tickets to the first coach parties that write in regardless of the nature of the show.

If, as is implied in this quote, there is a difference of character between the two audiences, then it seems reasonable to assume that in this respect, with the best intentions and the cheeriest laughter in the world, one man's meat is still another man's poison—if one only finds something mildly funny, the sound of guffaws are likely to be offputting rather than enhancing. A further quote can be used to expand this:

The worst thing about television situation comedy in my opinion is the studio audience: because what's funny to the audience is frequently not funny to the viewer. I know that programs that go best in the studio sometimes seem the least funny at home. I think it's . . . because of viewer resistance to audience laughter which they think is canned, which in fact isn't, and also because what makes a live audience laugh is different. It's like the difference between stage acting and film acting and the difference is enormous . . . in the theatre you have to do it bigger. A studio audience forces a compromise on you which very few people have learned to cope with. Most people find it a problem . . . acting big for the studio audience to make them react because it's obviously humiliating if you do the program . . . and they only laugh once every five minutes.

The presence of a studio audience, then, is partially responsible for this hybrid form of television, which mixes conventions from both the theatre and film. Situation comedies are not entirely unique in that variety shows and quiz programs, for example, also have their audiences to provide a reaction, usually loud and sustained clapping. Comedy, however, is unique: there is a constant pressure for laughter, not just thoughtful smiling or acceptance. Audibility of reaction is the key element. Everything in the studio process is geared to gathering and relaxing a theatre-sized audience and making them laugh. While it may be doubtful that the end result of comedy should be laughter, it seems wiser, in this instance, to agree with Woody Allen that "when it comes down to survival, it's laughs that a comedy has to have. There's no way out of it."[21]

NOTES

[1] Potts, p. 10.

[2] I am both following and adapting the models of communication suggested by Shannon and Weaver, de Fleur and Riley.

[3] Styan, p. 26.

[4] A very extensive bibliography can be found in Goldstein and McGhee, and these editors are constantly expanding and updating it.

[5] Duncan, *Communication and Social Order*, p. 331.

[6] Duncan, *Language and Literature in Society*, p. 55.

[7] Some people would prefer to call them domestic comedies or character comedies, but the designation chosen here seems to be the most common.

[8] Fry and Allen, p. 136.

[9] *Ibid.*

[10] See, for example, Nathan, Wilde and Fisher for an abundance of quotes from performers on this topic.

[11] John Alderton and Pauline Collins in the *Radio Times* 19.4.75, p. 7.

[12] Including Berleyne, McGhee, Chapman, Emerson, Fuller and Sheehy-Skeffington, Fuller. Adorno, writing of American situation comedies, says, "These types (of programs) have developed into formulas which, to a certain degree, have pre-established the attitudinal pattern of the spectator before he is confronted with any specific con-

tent and which largely determine the way in which any specific content is being perceived" (p. 482).

[13] Chapman ("Social Aspects of Humorous Laughter") and Fuller both review the literature.

[14] Chapman, *ibid.*, p. 156.

[15] Fry and Allen, pp. 93–94.

[16] I am indebted to the BBC Ticket Unit and to the Thames Television Ticket Office for much of the information in this section.

[17] Because of the vast amount of technical equipment in a television studio, the seats for the audience are steeply banked to afford a comprehensive view. For practical reasons of wheelchair maneuverability and conditions of insurance, it is deemed unwise to admit physically handicapped people. The age limit for children is presumably related to a potential lack of understanding (and therefore laughter) of what is often "adult" material.

[18] "Laughter and Joking—the Structural Axis."

[19] A half-hour situation comedy lasts about 24 minutes and between 28 and 29 minutes on the commercial companies and the BBC respectively. Probably the most common complaint I heard from writers concerns the brevity of this period, one writer adding: "Those five minutes are the difference between a story with a plot and an anecdote without one."

[20] Fuller.

[21] Lax, p. 75.

REFERENCES

Adorno, T. W. "Television and the Patterns of Mass Culture." In *Mass Culture*. By Rosenberg and White. New York: Free Press of Glencoe, 1964.

Berleyne, D. E. "Humor and Its Kin." In *The Psychology of Humor*. Ed. by Goldstein and McGhee. New York: Academic Press, 1972.

Birenbaum, A., and Sagarin, E., eds. *People in Places*. London: Nelson, 1973.

Chapman, A. J. "Funniness of Jokes, Canned Laughter and Recall Performance." *Sociometry* 36 (1973): 569–78.

Chapman, A. J. "Social Aspects of Humorous Laughter." In *Humor and Laughter*. Ed. by Chapman and Foot. London: Wiley, 1976.

Chapman, A. J., and Foot, H. C., eds. *Humor and Laughter: Theory, Research and Applications*. London: Wiley, 1976.

Chapman, A. J., and Foot, H. C., eds. *It's a Funny Thing, Humor—International Conference on Humor and Laughter*. Oxford: Pergamon, 1977.

De Fleur, M. *Theories of Mass Communication*. New York: David McKay, 1966.

Duncan, H. D. *Communication and Social Order*. New York: O.U.P., 1968.

Duncan, H. D. *Language and Literature in Society*. New York: Bedminster Press, 1961.

Emerson, J. P. "Negotiating the Serious Import of Humor." In *People in Places*. Ed. by A. Birenbaum and E. Sagarin. London: Nelson, 1973.

Fisher, J. *Funny Way to Be a Hero*. Frogmore: Paladin, 1976.

Fry, W. F., and Allen, M. *Make 'Em Laugh—Life Studies of Comedy Writers*. Palo Alto: Science & Behavior Books, 1975.

Fuller, R. G. C. "Uses and Abuses of Canned Laughter." Paper presented at the International Conference on Humor and Laughter, Welsh Branch, British Psychological Society, Cardiff, 1976.

Fuller, R. G. C., and Sheehy-Skeffington, A. "Effects of Group Laughter on Responses to Humorous Material, a Replication and Extension." *Psychological Reports* 35 (1974): 531–34.

Goldstein, J. H., and McGhee, P. E., eds. *The Psychology of Humor.* New York: Academic Press, 1972.

Greig, J. Y. T. *The Psychology of Laughter and Comedy.* London: George Allen & Unwin, 1923.

Hayworth, D. "The Social Origins and Functions of Laughter." *Psychological Review* 35 (1928): 367–84.

Lax, E. *On Being Funny—Woody Allen and Comedy.* New York: Charterhouse, 1975.

McGhee, P. E. "On the Cognitive Origins of Incongruity Humor: Fantasy Assimilation Versus Reality Assimilation." In *The Psychology of Humor.* Ed. by Goldstein and McGhee. New York: Academic Press, 1972.

Nathan, D. *The Laughtermakers.* London: Peter Owen, 1971.

Potts, L. J. *Comedy.* London: Hutchinsons University Library, 1949.

Riley, J., and Riley, M. "Mass Communication and the Social System." In *Sociology Today.* Ed. by Merton, Broom and Cottrell. New York: Basic Books, 1959.

Rosenberg, B., and White, D. M. *Mass Culture—the Popular Arts in America.* New York: Free Press of Glencoe, 1964.

Shannon, C. E., and Weaver, W. *The Mathematical Theory of Communication.* Urbana: University of Illinois Press, 1963.

Styan, J. L. *Drama, Stage and Audience.* London: C.U.P., 1975.

Taylor, P. A. "Laughter and Joking—the Structural Axis." In *It's a Funny Thing, Humor.* Ed. by Chapman and Foot. Oxford: Pergamon, 1977.

Wilde, L. *The Great Comedians.* New Jersey: Citadel Press, 1973.

Peter H. Mann:

Romantic Fiction and Its Readers

☆ ALTHOUGH 36 percent of the men and 26 percent of the women[1] in Britain claim not to read books at all, 16 percent of all people say that reading is their main leisure pursuit[2] and 28 percent of the men and 38 percent of the women claim to read at least a book a week.[3] Most of the reading done by women is of fiction (74 percent), which is a far higher proportion than that done by men (31 percent).[4] This essay deals with the most popular form of fiction read by women—romantic fiction—which accounts for a quarter of all women's reading.

Light romantic fiction is rarely discussed in the review pages of daily or weekly newspapers or weekly and monthly magazines, yet it is the most popular of all reading with women. Little of this genre has pretensions to great literary merit and it is not seriously intended by its publishers to have any long term literary value. Romantic fiction is, for the most part, ephemeral literature that gives great pleasure to its many readers but has few functions outside of this. To scholars of "literature" it is therefore rarely of any interest, though to sociologists and students of the mass media of communication it is of great interest.

Romantic fiction is read mainly for personal pleasure rather than for intellectual stimulus. Its function is to provide its reader with relaxation and distraction in her leisure hours. (The word "her" is used because there is no evidence that men provide any recognizable proportion of the readers). Much of romantic fiction is written to a limited number of formulae so far as plots are concerned. Although there are a number of variations, the basic plot is usually that girl meets boy, for some reason girl does not initially like boy, but in the end girl recognizes that she does like boy and there is then a "happy ending" with marriage envisaged. There are special types of romantic fiction in which other factors may be used to pad out the basic romantic theme. What are known as "gothic" romances, which are very popular in the United States, may center

▶ This is an original article written especially for this book. Dr. Peter H. Mann is Reader in Sociology at the Department of Sociological Studies, University of Sheffield, England.

the action on an old house wherein the heroine is threatened by strange forces. "Mystery" romances may incorporate a crime into the plot, so that the heroine and hero find themselves embroiled in the detection of the criminal. "Historical" romances may use all sorts of periods of history from medieval times to the Edwardian period in Britain, though the Regency period is greatly favored by some authors because of its elegance in dress and manners.

What might be called the "contemporary" romance is set in the present day though exotic backgrounds in the West Indies, Africa, Australia and the Pacific may be used to add glamour to the story. Romantic fiction is always changing gradually to reflect the views of its readers, but it rarely attempts to go beyond the more conservative mores of its period. For the most part it is reflective of current moral codes rather than challenging to them, and it is fair to say that the predictability of the romance is an important element in offering its readers a story that will neither surprise nor shock them. Immoral behavior, especially pre-marital or extra-marital sexual liaisons, either do not happen or, if they do occur, are clearly labelled as wrong and likely to result in unhappiness. Marriage is not questioned as being the goal of all heroines and the dominance of the male in the relationship is accepted with hardly any questioning. It is not surprising therefore that romantic fiction is not liked by militant feminists.[5] It is interesting to note, however, that romantic fiction has a very long history and not only has survived the many social changes in the past century and more, but has even increased in its popularity over the past ten years.[6]

The Historical Setting

Richard Altick, in his scholarly work *The English Common Reader*,[7] which studies popular reading from 1800 to 1900, points out that in the first half of the nineteenth century politicians worried about the effects that increasing literacy might have on the general population and fears of rebellion inspired by demagogues were often in their minds. However, when fears of rebellion decreased at the end of the 1850s, people then began to worry about the possibilities of reading leading to moral corruption. Altick claims that "the Society for Pure Literature was as characteristic of the sixties as the Society for Useful Knowledge had been in the thirties."[8] Clearly the middle years of the century were years of uncertainty for many people who thought seriously about the effects of spreading literacy.

In the world of books, the novel from the "circulating library" so enjoyed by women had been an object of suspicion among men for many years. Even in 1775, Richard Brinsley Sheridan in his comedy *The Rivals* had Sir Anthony Absolute warn Mrs. Malaprop of the danger to women: "Madam, a circulating library in a town is an evergreen tree of diabolical knowledge! It blossoms through the year!—and depend on it, Mrs. Malaprop, that they who are so fond of handling the leaves will long for the fruit at last."[9]

The puritanism of the mid-nineteenth century is well exemplified by comments made about Mechanics Institutions by a Dr. J. W. Hudson, who said, "Those Institutions which had adhered to their original scheme, rejecting novels from the library and newspapers from the reading room have, for the most part, become extinct . . . while their officers declaim at the apathy of the working classes. Others have been led into unhealthy excitement by weekly lectures, frequent concerts, ventriloquism and Shakesperian readings."[10] The dangers of too much reading by women is indicated in a letter to the London *Evening Standard* in 1891, noted by Altick: "Many are the crimes brought about by the disordered imagination of a reader of sensational, and often immoral, rubbish, whilst many a home is neglected and uncared for owing to the all-absorbed novel-reading wife."[11] Of course, no empirical evidence was ever brought forward to substantiate such sweeping statements as these, but undoubtedly many people must have believed that too much novel reading was dangerous to women. The very fact that critics, such as the letter-writer to the London newspaper, should single out novel-reading for attack can be taken to indicate the popularity of light fiction.

In the 1930s, the famous author George Orwell ran a bookshop in Hampstead, which included a circulating library in the services it offered. Orwell himself recognized the great popularity of romantic fiction and also made one of the first comments based on observation about its readers. He noted that his library customers ranged from "baronets to bus conductors" and that the most popular author was the romantic novelist, Ethel M. Dell, with Warwick Deeping second and Jeffrey Farnol third. About Ethel M. Dell he wrote: "Dell's novels are, of course, read solely by women, but by women of all kinds and ages, and not as one might expect merely by wistful spinsters and the fat wives of tobacconists."[12]

The Situation Today

After the 1939–1945 war, the growth of book publishing was at first hampered by shortages of all kinds, but as these were overcome, the popularity of paperbacks (which had been launched on the mass market by Allen Lane, the founder of Penguin Books, in the late 1930s) increased enormously and gradually the commercial lending libraries closed down as people became accustomed to buying their own copies of popular fiction in cheap paperback editions.

Today, popular paperback books can sell literally in millions and, though British publishers are reluctant to give many details about their print runs, it is said that popular authors such as Wilbur Smith and Arthur Hailey have initial paperback print runs in this country of half a million copies.[13] Sales of over a million copies for popular thrillers are by no means uncommon and authors such as Alistair Maclean, Hammond Innes, Len Deighton and Frederick Forsythe are household names. In women's romantic fiction, the fame is more restricted, but authors such as Jean Plaidy, Denise Robins, Georgette Heyer and Barbara Cartland are extremely well known to the general public. In a recent national survey, Plaidy, Heyer and Cartland were among the six most popular writers named by women.[14] In another national survey of both men and women, romance accounted for 20 percent of all light reading done by respondents over a four month period[15]—and as the data did not separate men from women it is clear that the readership of romance by women alone must have been much higher than 20 percent. Another survey, in this case of the borrowers from public libraries in a midlands area of England, showed that two-thirds of the people using the lending library were just looking for "any novel of interest."[16] Clearly light fiction is a very important element in people's reading habits in Britain and romantic fiction has an important position in the interests of women.

The Functions of Light Fiction [17]

As has been indicated, light fiction is a somewhat heterogeneous collection of different sorts of books written for different sorts of readers. Judged by the criteria for criticism used in analysing "English literature," much of light fiction may seem shallow in plot and trivial in content. To judge light literature by the criteria developed for the assessment of "heavy" literature is akin to using the same criteria for evaluating, say, Wagner's *Ring Cycle* and *Oklahoma* or Shakespeare and a typical West-end farce. Because of the use of the same criteria for the two sorts of books, few useful comments on light fiction have been made by serious literary critics.[18] Richard Hoggart wrote: "Some critics have also, in the last thirty years, been unwilling to try to analyse the social and moral significance not just of "high" literature, but of "low" literature or mass literature. . . . Here one thinks again of *Scrutiny*, of Mrs. Leavis' *Fiction and the Reading Public* and of a few brilliant essays by George Orwell."[19] The Leavises are certainly extremely "literary" people and it is debatable as to whether their perspectives on popular, mass literature are appropriate to that genre. Queenie Leavis' book begins by claiming to be objective but rapidly becomes a polemic against "popular" literature, and even such authors as Rudyard Kipling, Arnold Bennett and Gilbert Frankau come in for strong criticism.[20] This is very interesting today, when Kipling is recognized as an important writer, Bennett is being rediscovered and discussed seriously[21] and only Frankau seems to have been forgotten.

The most important functions of light fiction are social ones rather than literary ones. Light fiction is essentially leisure reading and its aim is to provide simple relaxation for the reader. Light fiction can compensate the person who has a dull and uninteresting job. The spy thriller or the war adventure story can offer a vicarious experience to the man who has a humdrum job and a dull leisure life too.[22]

Light fiction is in competition with other forms of leisure entertainment such as television, the radio, the cinema and newspapers and magazines—all of which are mass media of communication. Television is by far the most time-consuming leisure activity in Britain today, with an estimated seventeen hours per week of viewing for adults.[23] But to compare television viewing with reading of fiction is misleading. Television viewing, which often takes place in the general living room of the house with other people is essentially a passive form of behavior. The viewers merely watch the images presented to them. Reading, by contrast, is an active form of leisure, which requires a certain standard of literacy and which requires the reader to form his (or her) own mental images. It is not uncommon to refer to people being "lost" in a book, when they are so engrossed in their reading that they are mentally quite removed from their physical setting. The reader constructs a mental world of his own; the television viewer merely receives a world created for him and several million other viewers. The book reader therefore creates his own characters and scenes in his mind and the act of reading is therefore a very personal and *private* form of activity.

The creation of privacy in the act of reading is one explanation for the popularity of the reading of light fiction by women. A great deal of leisure reading is done in the evening or during the weekend when people want to relax. For women who have onerous work during the day, looking after children and homes and husbands, cleaning, cooking, and perhaps doing a job outside the home as well, leisure time reading of fiction enables them to "get away" from the domestic environment for a while and to live vicariously as a young and attractive heroine in a romantic situation. To be successful, therefore, a successful writer of romantic fiction must be able to tell a story clearly and simply, to engage her reader's interest in the opening pages and to provide a heroine with whom the reader can identify (even if the story is told in the third person) and a hero to whom she can react strongly. Such writing skills are by no means as common as some people might think and to become a successful author of romantic novels is not easy. For women who are successful, the financial rewards can be high, as this type of fiction has a mass paperback market.

A Survey of Readers

The author of this essay has been engaged in research into books and readers since 1967[24] and has been fortunate in gaining the cooperation of the most successful publishers of romantic fiction in Britain. Mills & Boon of London now publish fourteen romantic novels in hardback each month. From these, ten titles are selected for publication in paperback each month, and a further four titles that were published five or more years earlier are re-published each month in a series called "classics." All fourteen paperbacks published each month are "contemporary" romances, though Mills & Boon have just launched (May 1977) a new series of historical romances. The print run for the ten new romances each month exceeds a million copies, which are sold in Britain and around the world except for Canada and the United States. In North America a sister firm called Harlequin Books publishes twelve paperbacks each month and their print run is even higher than that of the British company. The books, which all originate from the editorial department in London, are translated into thirteen foreign languages; the company has also fully or partly-owned subsidiaries publishing their books in Germany, Holland and France. These details indicate the widespread popularity of the romances.

With complete cooperation and considerable help from Mills & Boon I was able, in 1968, to carry out a survey of their readers; in 1973, five years later, at my request, I made a follow-up study.[25] In both instances the survey was done by sending a postal questionnaire to women on the Mills & Boon mailing list who receive the company's catalogue three times a year. The questionnaires asked the readers for details about themselves, such as age, marital status, education, occupation, and about their leisure interests and attitudes to romantic fiction. From the large responses, over two thousand replies were taken at random on each occasion and punch-card analysis was made from these. It must be noted that the sample frame—the published mailing list—is made up of women who are interested enough to fill in a form at the end of a Mills & Boon book asking to be put on the mailing list. They are therefore genuinely interested readers, not just casual ones.

Before beginning the first survey, I shared in some of the popular stereotyped ideas about the readers of romantic fiction—that women who read romantic fiction are either young girls or aged spinsters. Both of these stereotypes are quite wrong. As Table 1 shows, the ages of the romance readers are widely distributed, with a slight peak in the age-range 35 to 44. Romance readers are younger on the whole than the general female population, and with the increasing popularity of the books between 1968 and 1973, the average age of readers has declined:

Table 1 Age of Readers

Age Groups	Percent 1968	Percent 1973	National 1973 Women Aged 15 and Over
Under 15	1	1	—
15–18	6	6	8
19–24	10	13	10
25–34	21	23	15
35–44	21	25	15
45–54	17	16	16
55–64	12	9	16
65–74	8	4	12
75 and over	4	2	8

Readers of romances are not predominantly spinsters, although the younger average age of readers does naturally give more unmarried women than the national distribution. However, as Table 2 shows, only a third of romance readers are unmarried and two-thirds either are or have been married.

Table 2 MARITAL STATUS

Marital Status	Percent 1968	1973	National 1973 Women Aged 15 and Over
Single	34	33	23
Married	55	60	63
Widowed	10	6	14⎫
Divorced	1	2	⎭

Nearly half the readers have children of varying ages living at home, 11 percent having children under the age of five and 20 percent having children under the age of eleven. A third of the readers are full-time housewives and 30 percent are housewives with either a full-time or part-time job. Only 22 percent are unmarried and working. Of those with jobs, 10 percent have professional or technical posts and 51 percent have clerical occupations. A further 30 percent have either shop or factory jobs.[26]

Romance readers are a good cross section of the population so far as education is concerned. Bearing in mind that for many years the minimum school-leaving age in Britain was fourteen, it is interesting to see that only 20 percent left school at aged fourteen or below, and 47 percent left at the age of sixteen or more. Twelve percent were at school or college until they were eighteen. Comments on questionnaires have indicated that women with responsible jobs in computing, offices and retail distribution management often enjoy reading romances after a hard day's work for pure relaxation.

Three-quarters of romance readers borrow books from public libraries (which is much higher than the national average of under 40 percent)[27] and their reading is by no means restricted to Mills & Boon romances. When asked in the 1973 survey to name other authors or publishers whose books they read, over 60 percent did so. The 1968 survey also showed that the women who read romantic fiction read, on the average, slightly better quality newspapers than the general population and tend to enjoy films and television programs where there is a good story.

It is clear from the two surveys that the Mills & Boon readers are above the general cultural level of women in Britain in their education, occupations and general leisure interests. This is not to suggest in any way that they are "bookish" intellectuals. On the contrary, they are likely to be lower-middle or working class women who lead active lives and who simply enjoy reading as their leisure activity. The fact that book reading gives privacy and enables them to "escape" temporarily from their worldly cares is extremely important. In the 1968 survey, one woman added to her questionnaire a message for the publishers. She wrote: "Between the covers of your books I can ignore the television, transistors, politicians and the weather. I thank you most sincerely for the happiness your books have given me." After a statement like that, there is no more a mere sociologist need say.

NOTES

[1] The Euromonitor Book Readership Survey, Euromonitor, London, 1976. Table 12, p. 28, and Table 11, p. 27.

[2] *Ibid.*, p. 12.

[3] *Ibid.*, Tables 11 and 12, pp. 27 and 28.

[4] *Ibid.*, Table 19, p. 34.

[5] See Germaine Greer, *The Female Eunuch* (London: MacGibbon & Kee, 1970), p. 171.

[6] For a popular discussion of romantic fiction with historical examples, see Rachel Anderson, *The Purple Heart Throbs* (London: Hodder & Stoughton, 1974). Unfortunately the author does not give detailed citations of the references she uses.

[7] Richard D. Altick, *The English Common Reader. A Social History of the Mass Reading Public, 1800–1900* (University of Chicago Press, 1957). This is an excellent survey of popular reading in the nineteenth century.

[8] *Ibid.*, p. 368.

[9] Richard Brinsley Sheridan, *The Rivals*, I:ii.

[10] Altick, *English Common Reader*, p. 202.

[11] *Ibid.*, p. 232.

[12] Sonia B. Orwell and Ian Angus, eds., *The Collected Essays, Journalism and Letters of George Orwell*, I (London: Secker & Warburg, 1968), p. 244.

[13] Private communication from a publisher.

[14] The Euromonitor Book Readership Survey, Table 24, p. 44.

[15] Book Promotion Feasibility Study, Research Summary, prepared by Masius, Wynne-Williams & D'Arcy-MacManus for the Booksellers' Association of Great Britain & Ireland (London, 1974), p. 16.

[16] J. N. Taylor and I. M. Johnson, *Public Libraries and their Use*. Department of Education and Science Library Information Series No. 4. (London: H.M.S.O., 1973), p. 21.

[17] For a fuller discussion of the functions of reading see Peter H. Mann and Jacqueline L. Burgoyne, *Books and Reading* (London: André Deutsch, 1969), especially chapt. 3.

[18] This point is also discussed in Peter H. Mann, *Books: Buyers and Borrowers* (London: André Deutsch, 1971), chapt. 5.

[19] Richard Hoggart, "Contemporary Cultural Studies" (Occasional Papers No. 6, March 1969, Centre for Contemporary Cultural Studies, Birmingham University), p. 4.

[20] Queenie Leavis, *Fiction and the Reading Public* (London: Chatto & Windus, 1932).

[21] See Margaret Drabble, *Arnold Bennet: A Biography* (London: Weidenfeld & Nicholson, 1974).

[22] For an interesting discussion of the compensatory function of leisure, see Stanley Parker, *The Future of Work and Leisure* (London: MacGibbon & Kee, 1971); Joffre Dumazedier, *Towards a Society of Leisure* (New York: The Free Press, 1967) is also interesting and refers to books in chapt. 9.

[23] Book Promotion Feasibility Study, p. 13.

[24] See *Books and Reading* and *Books: Buyers and Borrowers* (already cited) and *Students and Books* (London: Routledge & Kegan Paul, 1974).

[25] See Peter H. Mann, *The Romantic Novel, a Survey of Reading Habits* (London: Mills & Boon, 1969) and *The Facts about Romantic Fiction*, (London: Mills & Boon, 1974). The 1969 survey is now out of print, but photocopies of this and of the 1974 survey are obtainable from Mills & Boon, 17–19 Foley Street, London, W1A 1DR.

[26] These details are taken from the 1973 survey (published in 1974).

[27] See W. A. J. Masterson, "Users of Libraries: a Comparative Study," *Journal of Librarianship* 6, no. 2 (April 1974).

Kazem Motamed-Nejad:

The Story-Teller and Mass Media in Iran

THE ROLE OF STORY-TELLING IN SOCIAL COMMUNICATIONS

☆ STORY-TELLING as a rhetorical art is one of the most ancient and effective tools of communication among human societies. For centuries this impressive instrument of thought and expression has served both as a means of getting together as well as a source of amusement among human groups. At the same time it has played a significant role in promoting spiritual harmony and social consensus within groups. In common with other traditional means of cultural expression, story-telling too is losing its hold on popular attention, confronted as it is with the sophisticated means developed by modern technology in the field of mass communication. And unless concerted measures are taken for its preservation, this precious heritage of the past is doomed to gradual extinction. However, it is still within the pale of possibility to save this traditional institution from decadence by adapting it to the needs and aspirations of the present generation through special programs developed for radio, screen and television answering to the tastes and the propensities of the present-day audiences of the electronic "mass media."

The special importance that story-telling bears on the course of development of human communication and the role it plays in the social life of a community necessitates a comprehensive insight both into the operation of this process of communication and the cultural heritage of the community concerned.

▶ This extract from a research paper, prepared for the *Comparative Popular Culture Seminar on Traditional Media* (East-West Communication Institute, Honolulu, Hawaii, 7th July–1st August, 1975), is reprinted here with the kind permission of the author. Dr. Kazem Motamed-Nejad is Professor and Vice President of the College of Mass Communications, Tehran, Iran.

Story-Telling in Its Historical Perspective

Generally speaking, story-telling embraces reciting of stories, relating of tales and recounting of legends epical, religious and entertaining, the method of narration and performance varying from one situation to another. However, the stereotype we have in mind here is the kind of story told before an audience through highly stylized forms of narration to the accompaniment of animating and amusing gesticulations. The following definitions should help toward a precise understanding of this particular form of story-telling:

Story-telling is a narrative, true or fictitious, in prose or verse, about some event or incident presented before an audience, with appropriate animating gestures. It carries an appeal more to the heart than to the head, projected as it is to the emotions of the audience. It is also at variance with rhetoric, since the subject matter of the story is entirely unrealistic and its presentation through hyperbolic exaggeration deifies the hero and elevates him to the supernatural.

The purpose of the story is as much to entertain as to excite the feelings and emotions of the audience. Through absorbing stories, delicacy of oration, significant gestures and skillful histrionics, the story-teller brings the audience under his spell to such an extent that it visualizes him as the actual hero and, in fact, as one who could singly play the role of each of the characters.[1]

Described in different words, story-telling is an art in which the performer recites a poetic composition or a narrative of events before the audience using all his oratorical talents and body movements to the best advantage, in as much as he not only entertains them but makes them dumbfounded with amazement and, while doing so, pours forth on them his homilies and gems of advice. In order to achieve this he must necessarily have a complete control over his voice and be able to fluctuate his tone in keeping with the subject matter and the occasion, making it loud or soft as may be necessary to answer the needs of his performance. Contemporaneously, through changes in facial expression, he puts on, intermittently, a mien of anger, love, tyranny or oppression. With such artful maneuvering of tone and expression, he gives vent to his urges and inner desires. Putting his words in the mouth of the hero, he laughs with him, weeps with him, draws forth cries of joy and then drowns into grief with him.

The origin of story-telling is shrouded in mystery. Presumably it took its birth in primordial societies. "It may be speculated that recital of stories and events came into being after man developed the faculty of speech. As a rule, toward sunset, when the members of a clan or a tribe gathered together around the fire, lit to provide warmth or to frighten away the wild animals, they used to listen to the strongman or the headman or the magician of the tribe narrate accounts of the wars he had witnessed, of his encounters with wild animals while hunting and, in particular, of the strange phenomena of nature."[2]

In this manner the narratives about heroes, of their feats of valor and the tales of individuals and their superhuman deeds were conveyed to the listeners in those societies. Some of them, in turn, narrated the stories to others in the community and, in order to gain personal distinction and to preserve it, added gestures to the words and even exaggerated the events. In the course of time, many of them made additions to these stories of adventure in the light of their own individual tastes and abilities. This will explain how the great epics of Iran and of the rest of the world are an outgrowth of those primordial beginnings.

It is worthy of note that, before the invention of script, the rudiments of the literature and mythology of countries sprang up through mouth-to-mouth circulation of the stories. It was only after the development of script that they were reduced to writing and put together in book form. Notwithstanding their compilation, the verbal recital of stories still continued, since everyone could not read and learning was the privilege of a few. At the same time people preferred to watch and listen to the story-teller in the actual act of performance, with all its zeal and motion, rather than merely read the stories in cold print. The story-teller, therefore, still abides.[3]

Before the advent of Islam, story-telling in Iran was accompanied with music. Since music was taboo according to the Muhammadan religion, the recital of stories alone, shorn of their musical content, survived in this period and burgeoned out into different divisions. During the first three centuries of Islam, the performances were confined to the past national and epical stories of Iran. Since the beginning of the fifth century Hejri, however, the story-tellers became their own composers and these compositions found their way into script in exactly the same form and style in which they were delivered orally.

During the Mogul period, story-telling leaned toward tales that were quasi-epical and quasi-religious. The Safavi period saw story-telling at the zenith of its popularity. The Quajar reign too was one of considerable prosperity for the profession. Thereafter, with the inauguration of "Quahve Khanez" (teahouses) in Iran, these places became the centers of the story-tellers' activities.[4]

Story-Telling in Iran

The earliest documentary source of information about story-telling in ancient Iran are the memoirs of Ibn Nadeem in his treatise *Alfehrist*. According to Ibn Nadeem, nocturnal story-telling was introduced by Alexander the Great to keep his soldiers up and awake at night, as a strategy against being ambushed by the enemy. A group of performers told them stories that kept them roaring with laughter. Thereafter, the later kings made use of *Thousand Stories*, a collection of a thousand tales. The same treatise gives particulars about the origin of the compilation, later known as *Thousand and One Nights* and, even more popularly, as *The Arabian Nights*, and also the circumstances underlying the recital of the stories to one of the kings by Shahrzad, the legendary story-teller.[5]

There is good ground for conjecture that the narration of events in pre-Islamic Iran was a versified recital to the accompaniment of a musical instrument, presumably the "Chang" (lyre). This mode of performance rested on a technique known as "Quavvali," in which the musician switched intermittently from song to dialogue and dialogue to song in subtle shifts. Evidence of such versified performance exists both in the music and the story-telling of that period. With the ushering in of the Islamic era, the "Quavvali," now stripped of its musical content, was no more than a mere narration of events. To make up for it, the performers resorted to other strategies, including reliance on dramatization. It was thus that the art of story-telling preserved itself for posterity during its first impact with Islam.[6]

Story-Telling During the Struggle for Independence in the Post Islamic Period

In the early centuries of Islam, story-stelling took the shape of national epics. The story-tellers of the period emphasized the glorious past of Iran in their themes. These played on the national pride of the Iranians and so vehemently held their attention that no efforts on the part of the central Islamic government could stem the overwhelming tide of public impetuosity.

In this age of struggle for Iranian independence from Arab influence, the freedom fighters gave currency to patriotic stories in glorification of their ancestors in order to antagonize the people against the rulers of a foreign race. It was not before long that, in order to keep themselves in power, these rulers were compelled to fabricate faked family trees designed to trace their geneologies to famous Iranian Kings and heroes of the past. It is significant to note that the story-tellers, by serving as a medium for communication of these stories to the public, made a worthy contribution in this campaign.

Public interest in the art of story-telling also prompted many of the poets to enlist the support of the story-tellers to broadcast and popularize their own compositions.[7]

According to historians of the time, there still existed descendants of blueblooded Iranian families who preserved the old traditions and the ancient tales of Iran through recitals or mouth-to-mouth relay. This clan of people called "dehquans," who in all probability held ground till the Mogul period, served to arouse anti-Arab feelings as one of their noblest duties.[8]

Story-Telling During the Turk and Mogul Rules

Starting the middle of the fifth century Hejri, the gradual disappearance of epics and epical narrations with their emphasis on chauvinistic racial glories as an instrument of propaganda against the Arabs, the end of political movements, the old religious prejudice, the domination of Turkish rule and intermarriages with Turks and Arabs, helped the gradual drift of religious epics and their recital toward the quasi-religious and the quasi-historical.

It should be worthwhile to mention that toward the end of the fifth century Hejri, the defeat of the movements, which promoted the revival of the ancient glories of Iran, engendered a feeling of frustration among sections of the society, and this gradually reflected in the works that still endured. The shift among others, who pinned their hopes on mysticism and gnosticism or on promotion of Shiism, which was equally a result of the same setback, was not without its effects on the institution of story-telling.

The middle of the sixth century saw, on the one hand, a common disposition among the story-tellers toward mysticism and, on the other, its use as religious propaganda.[9]

One of the agencies employed by the Shiites to propagate their religion after achieving power were the "munaquabkhans" or "eulogists." They went about reciting odes in praise of Ali and the other Imams in streets and market-places; at the same time they assailed with profanities some of the Caliphs who they reckoned as usurpers.

The "Sunnites" (the orthodox Muslims as they were so called) were not sitting idle against the Shiite campaign. They too had their trained panegyrists, known as "fazilkhans," who extolled the virtues of Abubakar and Umar through laudatory verses in public places.[10]

The most interesting feature of what has been stated above was that these stories (in this case religious) were recited at determined locations, and the people knew in advance where the praises of Ali or those of the Caliphs were to be sung. It is probable that the "munaquabkhan" or the "fazilkhan," as the case may be, ensconced himself at a vantage point on a raised dais so as to have a good command over his audience.

Panegyrizing stayed even after its original need ceased to exist. It then continued on the sideline as a marginal activity with the professional jugglers who devoted a considerable time of their performance to reciting praises of Ali and Abulfazil.

With the invasion of Iran by the Moguls in the seventh century Hejri, story-telling entered on a new phase. Although little direct historical evidence exists over three centuries of their reign, a study of the happenings of that age shows that few inhibitions were placed on the performance of this art. Further, the expanding popularity of historiography and the abundance of quasi-historical and -religious epics of the day points to the fact that story-telling must have made further strides in keeping with the literary and cultural trends of the time.

The Progress and Extension of Story-Telling in the Safavi and Quajar Reigns

The Safavi rule, which was marked by a period of political stabilization, centralization and also of extensive urban development, saw the art of story-telling at its highest point of popularity and also its burgeoning into new branches.

After the end of Safavi rule, the narration of religious stories continued side by side with the recital of the Shahnameh and other legendary tales. Sir John Malcolm, whose well known book *The History of Iran* was published during the reign of Fateh Ali Shah Quajar, gives the best commentary on the art of story-telling in Iran. In this book Sir Malcolm refers to the King's story-teller as an essential feature of the royal court. He describes him as one who is highly competent, who is well versed in the history of the country and who possesses deep knowledge of events. He must be an expert in classical poetry, witty and refined. Iranians, he says, have many diversions, but miming in its western form is not one of them. Their story-teller combines a variety of skills in one person, who with the power of his oration, change of motions, undulations of voice, tricks of facial expressions and other similar artifices could alternately portray anger and forbearance, happiness and sorrow, king and beggar, lover and beloved, affluence and indigence, command and submission. Story-telling, he says, is a very respectable and a paying profession and the incumbent of this office at the royal court enjoys the supreme privilege of the King's audience at all times.

According to Elwell Sutton, another English traveler, Edward Scott Worthing had visited Shiraz in the year 1217 Hejri (lunar year) and had said this about the recital of the Shahnameh:

> Another kind of amusement is to listen to the recital of the Shahnameh. The reciter is a person who repeats before others, parts from this national epic of Iran in a loud sweet voice. This entertainment is of impressive sublimity and is a source of immense delight to the foreigner.

He goes on to add: "Although I did not know many of the Persian words used in the recital of the battle between Rustam and Sohrab, I could nevertheless comprehend each and every word from the tone of his recital and his gesticulations."

TYPES OF STORY-TELLING

During the course of historical evolution, story-telling has developed into numerous categories that can be classified under three major titles: epic, religious and entertaining.

"Quisse Khani" (narration of stories) and "Shahnameh Khani" (recital of Shahnameh) are the most popular forms of epic and heroic story-telling and they are still prevalent in many parts of Iran. Varieties of religious story-telling such as "Hamleh Khani," "Rauze Khani," "Pardeh Dari" and "Sokhanvari" have been in full swing since the Safavi age, but except for "Rauze Khani" (preaching and chanting) they have all disappeared. Among the entertaining narrators, mention must be made of minstrels and jugglers.

Heroic and Epic Story-Telling

"Quisse Khani" and "Shahnameh Khani" are the two types of epic story-telling whose popularity has been preserved. "Quisse Khani" consists of narrating adventurous tales and heroic legends handed down from mouth to mouth.

These stories are declaimed before an audience, using a deep resounding voice and a captivating address. The most popular of such romances, dating back to the pre-Safavi period, are "Eskandar Nameh" (adventures of Alexander), "Darab Nameh" (The book of Darius), "Hossein Kurd," "Sammak Ayyar"[11] and "Amir Arsalan." "Shahnameh Khani," as the name denotes, is a recital of stories from the Shahnameh, the greatest national epic of Persia. It is a colossal work of about sixty thousand rhyming couplets, ranging thematically over the whole factual and imagined life cycle of ancient Iran, from the creation to the coming of the Islamic Arabs. The language is simple and hard, deliberately archaic and designedly low in Arabic content. The chief hero of the epic, Rustam, has been identified as Iran itself, maintaining its identity age after age against the barbarian powers surrounding it. The heroes constantly fight against dragons and demons (symbolizing evils) or are engaged in the age-old struggle between Iran and Turan.

Shahnameh Khani was usually performed in coffeehouses and traditional palestras called "ZoorKhaneh." In his book of travels to Iran during the Safavi rule, Cavalier Chardin has referred in several instances to this type of story-telling. It is worthwhile to quote some of his comments about this traditional art:

> Tabriz square is the biggest plaza that I have ever come across in the world.
> . . . At any time of the day and night the place is swarmed by thousands of
> citizens who converge to be entertained by a variety of performances put on by
> magicians, acrobats, clowns, jugglers, musicians, singers and reciters of heroic
> stories of ancient national heroes.

At the present time, in certain coffeehouses in Tehran and other major cities of Iran, recital of Shahnameh is still in vogue. Radio and television have also displayed great interest in this native art and contributed to its revival after long decadence.

Religious Story-Telling

Religious narrations such as Hamleh Khani, Rauze Khani, Pardeh Dari, Ta'zieh Khani and Sokhanvari flourished during the Safavi rule, but some of them went into eclipse in subsequent periods.

Hamleh Khani: This type of narration consisted of recitals from a book by the name of Hamleh Heidari. The main plot of the book pivoted around the life of the prophet of Islam and the first holy Imam, Ali, and related the war they waged against the infidels and pagans.

Rauze Khani:[12] Rauze Khani is a particular form of religious story-telling mainly centering around the tragedy of Karbala.[13] This sort of narration started in the Safavi age and can by performed at any time of the year on various occasions, reaching to a peak within the first decade of Moharram. Such preoccupations, still prevalent in Iran, are normally organized by merchants and statesmen, who gather together professional Rauze Khans to get on with the act.

The Rauze Khan often ascends a pulpit to gain better command over his audience. The chief aim of this performance was to arouse people to tears by reciting and chanting the calamitous episodes of the martyrs of Karbala. At the end of such ceremonies a great feast is given by the organizer. Rauze Khans are, as a rule, divided into preachers and chanters. The preachers are responsible for guiding people to the right path of salvation, whereas the chanters recite in wailing tones the tragic incidents that befell the holy Imams. The chanters were expected to possess a pleasant voice and a certain knowledge of the principles of music. They should also have a good command of the relevant subjects and a better grasp of the mentality and disposition of their audience.

Ta'zieh Khani—The Passion Play of Iran: The origin of this type of theatre is shrouded in obscurity, but it is believed to reach back to antiquity. Among ancient national celebrations, there seems to have been in particular a performance of the agonies of Siavash, the epic Iranian hero. Like the Greek and Roman tragedies, the final outline of Ta'zieh shows reliance on religious origins.

Strangely enough, in spite of being situated between the two greatest theatre cultures of the world—Greece and India—and sharing a long history of cultural and artistic exchange with both, Iran has never proved to be a fertile ground for drama. Why this should be so has puzzled many scholars. Goethe, one of the great admirers of Persian literature, regrets that there is no Persian drama to match the Persian epics and lyrics. Had he known that an indigenous Persian drama had come into being at the time of his birth, he might have taken an interest in it. What is fairly evident is that with the rise of Shiism, a type of religious drama evolved whose subject matter had to do with the martyrdom of Ali, Hossein and some of the other Imams. During the Safavi rule, the dominance of Shiism gave a great vogue to Ta'zieh. Later, the Quajars actively support the presentation of religious plays. Thus Ta'zieh, as it is performed in modern Iran, owes much of its substance and many of its conventions to the Safavi and Quajar periods. But unfortunately, while the western nations are experiencing a renaissance of religious drama, this once powerful and still beautiful tradition of dramatic art is fading out of existence in Iran, and serious efforts must be expanded to prevent its extinction.

If the sources of the stage conventions of Ta'zieh are not fully known yet, the origin of the stories that make up the subject matter of most Ta'ziehs is to be looked for in the Shiite hagiography. Ali, the first Iman of the Shiites, was martyred at the hand of an assassin. Almost twenty years later, his son, Hossein, accompanied by a small band of brave followers, was surrounded by the army of Yazid in the desert of Karbala. Being denied water, the trapped warriors fought desperately and died to the last man. The story of the death of these men of faith, especially of Imam Hossein and his half brother, the heroic Abbas, forms the central theme, not only of Shiite martyrology and mourning rituals but also of the largest body of religious plays.

Ta'ziehs were, as a rule, performed by non-professional actors belonging to various crafts. Though scenery was kept at a minimum, ample use was made of costumes, usually green and black for the saints and red for the antagonists. The plays were generally written in verse, but the actors often disregarded this and took initiative according to their talents and preferences as well as the mood of the audience.

Ta'zieh Khaneh—Playhouses: The plays were presented on a raised platform surrounded on all sides by a zealous audience whose prior knowledge of the plot and faith in its veracity greatly enhanced the emotional impact of the play. These places which were equally used for other religious ceremonies, both joyous and mournful, were called Tekieh, and were sometimes large enough to seat thousands of spectators. But the most popular were those of average size, accommodating a few hundred people, which were built through the contributions of wealthy merchants and the people of the district as a religious and public service. During the Quajar rule, there was a competition for the most splendid Tekieh and even the British and Russian Embassies were drawn in to arrange temporary Tekiehs for each Moharram.

The most famous Ta'zieh playhouse in this period was the Tekieh Doulat, the royal theater, which played a leading role in the development of this drama. According to many western travelers and diplomats, performances at the Tekieh Doulat—with its huge stage and arena, with its royal boxes and those for diplomats and ministers and with its hundreds of actors and singers costumed fantastically in brilliant colors—overshadowed many operas and theaters in European capitals. Hundreds of camels and horses were brought into the arena under the light of thousands of candles and crystal lamps when the Ta'zieh was performed by night. An account by a nineteenth-century Iranian historian of the performance of a Biblical story, *Joseph and His Brethren*, staged on a Tekieh Doulat reads:

> It was a fantastic performance, something unforgettable. Some twenty thousand candles were burning and in front of royal and government boxes, beautiful crystal lamps were glittering. The Egyptian caravan that arrived at the well into which Joseph had been thrown consisted of some two hundred camels loaded with boxes and materials and on each camel sat a Negro dressed in (a) white Arab shirt and a red hat.

According to a British diplomat of this period, Sir Lewis Pelley, Ta'zieh was the greatest drama in the world if the success of a drama is to be measured by the effect it produces upon the audience for whom it is composed.[14]

With the social and political changes at the beginning of the twentieth century, Ta'zieh slowly lost its splendor and gradually retreated to the provinces and rural areas, where it seemed to be fading out.

Fortunately, however, a few years ago some people became aware of the artistic and social value of Ta'zieh Khani, and as a result, articles on Ta'zieh began to appear in periodicals, new collections of manuscripts were published, musicians hailed Ta'zieh as the preserver of Iranian music, producers started to use Ta'zieh techniques in contemporary theatre and finally, five years ago, for the first time, Ta'zieh was shown on television during Moharram and at the Shiraz Art Festival.

Sokhanvari—Elocution: The tradition goes that two brothers by the names of Khalil and Jalil laid the foundation of the Sokhanvari in the Safavi period. The principal goal was to glorify the House of Ali and to promote the cause of Shiism. After a short time, Sokhanvari took its final form, that is to say two Dervishes in a coffeehouse or Tekieh recited poems in eulogy of the Shiite saints and refuted the Sunnites' practice.[15] The two Dervishes emulated in excelling one another in the laudations and eulogies. Such performances were presented at night, particularly during Ramazan, the fasting month, and sometimes lasted until dawn.

Recreational Story-Telling

Story-Telling by Wandering Story-Tellers: This type of narration was normally undertaken by wandering story-tellers and actors. In the province of Azarbeijan, there existed bards and minstrels called Ashegh (lovers), who both recounted stories and chanted sweet songs to the accompaniment of music. In certain characteristics they can be compared with the Greek rhapsodists of antiquity.

Story-Telling by Jugglers: Jugglers, magicians and clowns sometimes also narrated stories in addition to performing their particular feats and wonders. These story-tellers, numerous in number, attracted large crowds of people. Humor and witticism coupled with enthralling gestures and melodious songs, making animals dance and setting them fighting with one another and, finally, magic and acrobatic feats all combined to draw a large audience seeking entertainment.

Story-tellers were generally of two major categories, the Shamayel[16] Gardan and the Naghal. Shamayel Gardan was an itinerant story-teller equipped with a very large canvas which he unrolled wherever he could gather an audience. Upon this canvas a dense crowd of characters were painted; these were the focus of his stories to which he referred during the course of narration. His stories, usually religious in nature, were well-known to his listener. He recited with an expert sense of pacing the tension, accompanied by appropriate gestures, body movements and changes of voice, pitch and volume. Depending on the size of the town and whether or not it was a market day, the story-teller would often quickly exhaust his potential audience and be forced to move on.

More popular than the itinerant Shamayel Garden, were the resident Naghals. These men were usually professionals and usually worked in the same coffee houses for many years. This attachment to a particular coffeehouse had two advantages. First, the narrator could build up a loyal audience, a certain core of which would be present to hear him every day. Second, it allowed him to tell longer stories. Some of these narrators told stories from the legendary adventures of the Shahnameh[17] and other epic stories written after its fashion. Others narrated mysterious stories of the Ayyars and their escapades. Some were skilled at creating supernatural worlds of fairy tales and enchanted lands;

others dramatized religious tragic episodes moralizing on every act of devotion by the holy Imams.

COFFEEHOUSES, THE LAST HAVEN FOR STORY-TELLERS AGAINST THE INROAD OF MODERNISM

Structure, Function and Historical Background

Before the craze of modernism and the advent of sophisticated means of transmission in Iran, people had a variety of places to go for such entertainment, which provided more genuine pleasure than their counterparts in modern life, i.e., movies, restaurants, cafeterias. Mosques, Tekiehs (religious playhouses), public squares, market places and coffeehouses were the popular centers of public attraction. People could, almost at any time and always free of charge, enter these places to entertain themselves by the amusing and instructing performances of story-tellers, reciters, chanters and preachers. In lieu of modern cafeterias, there existed large teahouses in every corner of Tehran and all provincial towns. Some of these coffeehouses were so huge as to cover an area of several thousand square meters, where hundreds of people could gather to converse, to exchange information and to enjoy a variety of diversions.

The advent and development of coffeehouses, the definite date of whose introduction to Iran is not known, probably began before the reign of Shah Abbes the Great. Early in his reign there existed large coffeehouses in Isfahan, so it is very likely that the drinking of coffee in this country had become a habitual practice sometime before Shah Abbas. During his rule, numerous coffeehouses were to be found in larger cities, particularly Qazvin and Isfahan. Early in the evening, people of all classes and crafts, merchants, writers, poets and painters held their friendly night circle. The inside of the coffeehouses was normally adorned with paintings of religious leaders, Kings and princes, national heroes and wrestlers. Some of these paintings depicted well-known episodes in the Shahnameh and reflected a spirit of heroism and epic. The main factor that gave rise to the creation of these pictures was the same as that which caused the composition of national epics.

During the Safavi period, coffeehouses were normally spacious places with clean whitewashed walls and entrances on all sides. The interesting feature was that these houses were often constructed in the same size and shape and adjacent to one another, with no walls to separate them. The inside was covered with rugs and carpets and the audience would sit on the floor. Many lights and lanterns were suspended from the ceiling and were lighted at night. In the center was a very small pool that overflowed with crystalline water. The reflection of the overhanging lights on the clear water of the pool resembled the sky with glittering stars. In these coffeehouses, in addition to watching various performances, people could drink tea, smoke pipes and water pipes, play chess and backgammon and other local games.

Social Reasons Behind Coffeehouse Popularity

The flourishing of coffeehouses in Iranian cities was closely linked with urban development in this country. At the outset these coffeehouses were used as meeting-places for the affluent and the intelligentsia. Before the Safavi period, the well-to-do gentry used to frequent taverns and the religious class crowded mosques, where political and social issues were handled and settled.

The prevalence of coffeehouses in the Safavi period can be attributed to the following factors:

1. Development of urbanization, construction of roads, population growth, city dwelling by diverse classes of society, including workmen, small merchants and the intelligentsia, which accentuated the need for the establishment of new social centers.
2. Social regimentation resulting from unified attitudes and ideologies. (The firm establishment of Shiism as the official religion of the country.)
3. Introduction of coffee and tea to Iran, which were non-existent prior to this period.
4. Weakening of the family life and patriarchal authority, at least among the lower classes of society, necessitating the formation of centers other than family circles.

New Social Role of Coffeehouses

Toward the end of the Quajar period, with the boom of business and the rise of merchants, coffeehouses gradually assumed a new role and function. Coffeehouses were no longer quiet centers for amusement of particular groups, but they were serving the merchants and small traders. In this period, the coffeehouses often sprang up at city gates, road intersections and trade routes, where commercial affairs were discussed and handled. In the course of time, the thrilling stories of Alexander in pursuit of the elixir of life and of Rustam proceeding with his seven labors were replaced by business and mundane affairs and later on by political discussions of immediate concern.

STORY-TELLING VERSUS THE NEW MEDIA OF MASS COMMUNICATIONS

Story-telling as an ancient dramatic art and a traditional method of communication has experienced gradual decline since the rise of modern technology and the advent of new means of mass entertainment. Coffeehouses have been replaced by modern centers of attraction and even in the few remaining coffeehouses and teashops, television has superseded the story-teller. People spend their leisure time either at home watching television or they go out to movie houses, cafeterias, cabarets and so forth. The alluring fascination of modern distractions, which are for the most part shallow and deceptive, has overshadowed the more genuine art of story-telling and stripped it of the great appeal and popularity it once enjoyed. Fortunately, however, in Iran, like many other ancient countries of the East, certain types of traditional means of communication such as story-telling and other dramatic performances are being actively patronized and supported in order to protect and preserve the valuable manifestations of traditional culture against the onset of technology and modernism.

To further acquaint ourselves with the present position of story-telling in relation to modern mass communication media, we present hereunder a brief study of its contact with radio, television and cinema and commercial publicity. We have also reviewed and evaluated the current efforts that are being made for the revival and promotion of this traditional art vis-a-vis the modern conditions brought about by modern technology.

Story-Telling and Cinema

The advent of moving pictures, the so-called "seventh art," has undoubtedly inflicted the hardest blow on story-telling and other traditional diversions. However, it has indirectly and to a small extent directly, contributed to its revival and preservation. The long cherished stories once declaimed and dramatized in coffeehouses appeared in wonderful new presentations on the cinema screens. Western film producing companies have so far created numerous films based on the fascinating stories of Alladin and the Magic Lamp, Alibaba and the Forty Thieves, The Robber of Baghdad and the Seven Voyages of Sinbad and numerous other tales and legends adopted from the repertoire of the old story-tellers, and have amused millions of people through the medium of cinema.

One of the earliest films produced in Iran in 1933 carried the name of *Firdusi* and was focused on the life and adventures of this great poet, whose treasury of ancient stories, Shahnameh, has ever been the inexhaustible source of story-tellers and Shahnameh reciters. Four years later Layli and Majnoon, an old Arabian romance and perhaps the most remarkable cognate of Shakespeare's Romeo and Juliet, appeared on the screen and immediately won public acclamation.

During the post-war period, after several years of recession, local film producers displayed a fresh interest in the old Iranian legends and restarted making films on such stories. The first film produced in this period was named *Zendani Amir* (the prisoner of the prince) adopted from old Islamic sources. During the ensuing years, numerous other films were screened on the basis of the popular romances and national epics. In addition to numerous cinematic representations of the folk tales and popular romances, in many films there were also scenes of story-telling and Shahnameh reciting performed in the traditional manner.

Story-Telling and Radio

Radio as an oral and aural means of communication has, like story-telling, a firm and far-reaching control over word and sound. As such, it has done incalculable harm to this traditional mode of entertainment. Paradoxical though it may appear, it has, for the same reason, also helped to preserve and maintain the original characteristics of the art.

As mentioned earlier, the establishment and expansion of radio in Iran resulted in a serious setback to this ancient technique of communication and entertainment, inasmuch as it even went out of favor in teahouses, which, for a time, were its last refuge. In fairness to the radio, however, we must say that, by exploiting its close similarity with story-telling in its communicative behavior, it has also strived to preserve this popular age-old entertainment through interesting and imaginative programs developed for this purpose. In pursuance of this objective, with the inauguration of the first radio transmitter in 1939, various story-telling programs were offered along with the normal programs.

At present, story-telling programs consist of the following:

Story-Telling Under Morning Physical Exercises Program: This program, which was broadcast between the hours of 5 and 6 in the morning, was ordinarily comprised of three parts, each occupying a total of 15 minutes on the average. It covered:

1. Recital of verses of wit and wisdom from classical poets and the Shahnameh.
2. Miscellaneous recitals from the Shahnameh in authentic times.
3. Singing of lyrics to the accompaniment of bells and drums, on the pattern of "ZoorKhanes" (palestras), in which three musicians participated.

Story-Telling for Workmen: This program, which is particularly directed to workmen, was on the air on Thursdays for three to seven minutes between 12 noon and 1 p.m. In this program, the famous contemporary story-teller, Murshad Ghulsmali Haghighat (who has been conducting it since 1966), after briefly summarizing the story of the previous week, recited different stories from the Shahnameh, at the same time giving necessary explanations about their background and relevant incidents.

Story-Telling Under "Iran Zamin" Program: This program was scheduled between 4:30 p.m. and 5:30 p.m. every day of the week, except Thursdays and Fridays. It included two kinds of story-telling:

1. Recitals by the singer Ghulsmali Haghighat from the Shahnameh, similar to those for the workmen, from 4:30 p.m. to 5 p.m. on Sundays. There were, however, actually seven broadcasts from October 1974, the data of its inception, till the middle of March 1975. It has now been regularly on the air since mid-April of this year.
2. Stories of the Chivalrous, a program which is a combination of dia-

logue and drama, themes of which are based on the Shahnameh and other Iranian epics. Scheduled for every Wednesday between the hours of 4:30 p.m. and 5 p.m., this program too had seven runs between October 1974 and the middle of March 1975; since mid-April it has been regularly on the air every Sunday.

Tales for Children and Teenagers: This program, broadcast daily from 7:15 a.m. to 7:30 a.m. and 10 a.m. to 10:30 a.m. from Radio Iran, features entertaining and educative fables, tales and stories for children and adolescents.

Story-Telling at Night: Over the years, Radio Iran has produced and broadcast this special program of night stories, which is on the air every night between 10 p.m. and 10:30 p.m. As mentioned in the earlier part of this paper, these stories, bearing continuous theme and plot, are presented in installments, serially, on successive nights on weekdays. A complete and self-contained story is featured only one night a week. In earlier years, the stories either were derived from *The Arabian Nights* and narrated in the mouth of the legendary Shahrzad, or they were selected from the works of other ancient story-tellers. A new trend has developed lately, favoring foreign stories as well. Taking note of this drift, Radio Iran has made necessary modifications to suit the listeners' tastes. In consequence, the program has changed its content and technique of narration and has, in a way, assumed the form of a radio play.

Story-Telling and Television

Like the radio, television has done considerable harm to the traditional profession of story-telling and has taken away much of its original splendor. At the same time, this communication phenomenon of the century, through its unlimited potency for attracting and holding the attention of its viewers, has and is doing a tremendous job through recitation of traditional stories in the form of serials and other special broadcasts portraying story-telling, as far as circumstances permit, in its original authentic setting.

During the last few years, in the course of its movie programs, National Television has on occasions exhibited cinema films based on ancient stories. It has also, of late, presented to Iranian viewers serials of its own film productions dramatizing old Iranian stories, and made use of animated cartoons for relating stories of special interest to children. Television has also now brought under its purview most of the story-telling programs originally developed by radio. It may be said without fear of contradiction that on account of the unlimited potency television possesses as a medium of communication, through its use of printed and spoken words, pictures in motion, color, music, liveliness, vivacity and sound effects—all rolled into one message—it has far excelled radio in its sense appeal. In the discourse that follows, we will briefly relate the part television has and is playing under its various programs in the field of story-telling and in the preservation of this ancient art.

Story-Telling Through Films: In the course of the last few years, N.I.T.V.

has developed and produced special programs of Iranium stories in serials. Some of the stories have a social and historical significance, while others carry a timeless appeal, having been told over the ages or recited by professionals. For instance, National TV has lately produced a series of films based on the famous tales of *The Arabian Nights*. In this series the noble legendary events are so delicately blended with contemporary social events that they carry the viewer alternately from the world of fancy to the world of reality and back to the regions of fancy again.

*TV Tales for Children:*N.I.T.V. presents a special program for children daily between the hours of 5:30 p.m. and 6 p.m. Also, on Fridays, a program under the title *Bache Ha, Bache Ha (Children! Children!)* is exhibited from 6:30 p.m. to 7:15 p.m. Parts of this program are specially devoted to narration of tales for children. In the portion entitled "Yeki bood, Yeki nabood" ("Once Upon a Time"), a female narrator tells ancient Iranian tales with the help of stationary paintings, kept steadily fixed on the TV screen for the while. This program also makes use of animated cartoons for telling amusing stories to children.

Narration of Stories on Television: The special programs produced and broadcast by Radio Iran for several years failed to attract sufficient attention of Iranian TV. After September, 1974, however, a production mainly consisting of recitals from the Shahnameh was included in TV programs. Since the initiation of this program, viewers were treated to between two to seven such story-telling recitals of ten to twenty minutes duration every week till March 12, 1975. Since the month of April, 1975, however, the story-telling programs on TV have taken a more definite shape and have been presented with remarkable regularity every day of the week (except Thursday and Friday) between 6:30 p.m. and 6:45 p.m.

Story-Telling and Commercial Publicity

Story-telling with all its historical antecedents and social acceptance has made its way not only to radio and TV programs and the movies, but into the field of commercial publicity. The bulk of cinema, TV and radio advertisements are now presented in the form of traditional tales and versified stories.

In the TV commercials projected nightly, at appointed hours, immediately before programs with larger audiences and in advertisements displayed in cinema houses prior to the start of the main feature, goods like refrigerators, washing machines and dishwashing machines are introduced with verses and ancient stories.

Help is also occasionally taken of a hero in the story by associating him with the use of goods offered for sale. A make of razor blades is demonstrated shaving the tough bushy beard of Rustam, the hero of *Firdusi's* Shahnameh, with perfect speed. Similarly, the advertisement for a brand of shoes, makes Amir Arsalan, the hero of a story of adventures, wear a pair of the shoes on a long and arduous journey in his tough struggle to conquer the enemy—and all this without a scratch or a mark of wear on the shoes.

In the final analysis, it may be claimed that despite their powerful influence, the electronic mass media have been unable to dispense with the narration of tales and stories as a necessary attraction for their programs. In fact, they have to draw increasingly on this ancient communicative technique, deeply rooted as it is in the culture of Iran. At the same time, we must not be oblivious to the fact that the rapid strides made by modern means of communication in their march for progress are essentially responsible for the general indifference toward the traditional art of story-telling. This emphasizes the need for effective action to save it from total oblivion.

If the measures taken in support of story-telling and other domains of ancient Iranian culture and art prove effective against the onrush of Industrial Culture, their gradual annihilation could possibly be arrested. Excellent examples of these expedients are the Shiraz Arts Festival, Art and Culture Festival and Toos Festival.

CONCLUSION

On the whole it must be conceded that story-telling, in sharp contrast with bygone days, has ceased to play an essential role in social life, and faced as it is with the alluring manifestations of an industrial world, no efforts can bring it back to its pristine glory.

In the present state of our society, even the teahouses, which were considered to be the last refuge of this dying art, have lost most of their appeal. Whatever programs are still offered in those places (also called coffeehouses) are no better than a superficial imitation of the traditional and fail to evoke public response.

As has been previously indicated, modern media have dealt a serious blow to the art of story-telling. Most of the programs under this and other titles do not afford any real support to the art. In fact, as matters stand at present, the media stand to gain more from its traditional appeal than they contribute toward its promotion.

Even the steps taken within the framework of programs designed to preserve and maintain ancient art and culture have not, by themselves, proved adequate. Unless they are accompanied by precise and imaginative programs, with inbuilt incentives for creating the right mood for public participation, no desirable or effective results could be expected.

It may be said without fear of contradiction that story-telling as an oral medium has been one of the most fascinating ways of group communication. Aided by the present audio-visual means it can, more than ever, help promote social harmony and mutual understanding. In those developing countries where oral communication has thrived and flourished for centuries, story-telling programs, based on pressing social themes, can be extremely helpful in creating common awareness for promotion of literacy and raising standards of life.

In the special circumstances of the developing countries, the moral aspect of the stories is of significant importance. Stories of this type, based as they are on praise of honesty, cordiality, bravery, manliness, tolerance, fellow-feeling, support of the deprived, encounter with the oppressor and such other moral virtues, could go a long way to neutralize the undesirable influences of the Industrial Civilization. They would at the same time create repugnance and a capacity for resistance against selfishness, exploitation, unconcern for others, violence, promiscuity and similar other evils of the machine age. Such stories should, however, be drawn largely from Iranian and oriental cultures, which are rich in moral content. The stories selected for presentation, however, should be those that have something in common with present-day life.

It is suggested that for a better acquaintance with the transitional role story-telling has played in oriental societies and its overall impact on the metamorphosis of their communicative behavior an extensive research would be timely. A closer study would more precisely identify the course that the art of writing and printing took to develop in those countries. It would also shed more light on the question of whether or not these societies could, before resolving the problem of illiteracy and without the advantage of widely circulated newspapers or of the modern audio-visual means like TV and radio, take a leap forward toward a richer life, depending only on improved oral communication. It is through such research that we could obtain a deeper knowledge of the revolutionary changes that have occurred, in communicative behavior, over the course of time. Based on such information, we could make appropriate decisions regarding the nature and content of messages for the mass media, relevant to the educational needs of our society.

NOTES

[1] Behram Beizai, *Dramatic Art in Iran* (Tehran, 1965), p. 60.

[2] Sadegh Homayouni, *Ta'zieh Khani* (Tehran, 1975), p. 24.

[3] Behram Beizai, "Story-Telling—Dramatic Art in Tehran," *Journal of Music* III, no. 65 (Month of Khordad, 1341): 9–10.

[4] Dr. Ahmad Mohammadi, "A Glance at the History of Dramatic Art in Iran," *Art and People*, nos. 129 and 130 (Months of Tir and Mordad, 1362): 19–25.

[5] Behram Beizai, "Story-Telling," 10–11.

[6] Behram Beizai, *Dramatic Art in Iran*, pp. 60–61.

[7] *Ibid.*, p. 62.

[8] *Ibid.*, p. 63.

[9] *Ibid.*, p. 65.

[10] Dr. Zabih-ul-Safa, *History of Iranian Literature* II (Tehran-Ibnsina-1336): 192–94.

[11] In the context of popular romances, the Ayyars were mainly male urban dwellers of the small merchant and craftsman class who united in voluntary, semi-secret, frater-

nal organizations devoted to the cultivation of certain group and individual values, such as honesty, generosity, hospitality, bravery and personal honor and to the maintenance of civil order and organization when the central political power broke down.

[12] "Rauze" is a word of Arabic root signifying a garden. However, as an expression used here, it means recital from a book called Rowzat-Al-Shohada or The Garden of the Martyrs.

[13] The tragedies of Hossein, the Third Imam.

[14] It is noteworthy to stress that Ta'zieh is not, as conceived by many scholars, only a religious passion play but also a clear manifestation of patriotic sentiments and national integrity. Patriotic elements so evident in the Iranian national epic (Shahnameh) are also noticed in Ta'zrieh.

[15] The Sunnite sect is regarded as the Orthodox Islam, whereas Shiism is considered a revolutionary protestanism.

[16] "Shamayel" is an Arabic word meaning pictures, particularly of the saints and holy Imams.

[17] The stories of the Shahnameh are normally divided into three categories: legendary, semi-historical and historical.

REFERENCES

Arlan Pour, Manuchehr. *History of Persian Literature*. Teheran, 1973.

Bricteux, A. *Contes Persans*. Paris, 1910.

Brockett, Eleanor. *Persian Fairy Tales*. London: Frederick Muller Limited, 1970.

Browne, Edward. *A History of Persian Literature in Modern Time* (1500–1924). Cambridge, 1924.

Cejpek, Kiri. "Iranian Folk-Literature." In *History of Iranian Literature*. By Jan Rypka. Dordrecht, Holland: D. Reidel Publishing Company, 1968.

Chardin. *Voyage du Chevalier Chardin en Perse*. Paris, 1723. 4 vol. Nouv. ed. par Lanles. Paris, 1811, XVCL.

Chelkowski, Peter. "Dramatic and Literary Aspects of Tazieh Khani-Iranian Passion Play." *Review of National Literature* II, no. 1 (Spring 1971). Iran.

Christensen, Arthur. *Contes Persans en Langue Populaire*. Copenhague, 1918.

Clouston, W. A. *A Group of Eastern Romances and Stories from the Persian, Tamil and Urdu*, with Introduction, Notes and Appendix. Glasglow: Privately Printed, 1889.

Gerhardt, Mia I. *The Art of Story-Telling. A Literary Study of "The Thousand and One Nights."* Leiden, Netherlands: E. J. Brill, 1963.

Hanaway, William L., Jr. "Formal Elements in the Persian Popular Romances." *Review of National Literature* II, no. 1 (Spring 1971). Iran.

Kazemeini, K., and Babayan, S. S. *Zoorkhaneh, Iranian Ancient Athletic Exercises*. Teheran, 1964.

Kurti, Alfred, tr. *Persian Folktales*. Originally published as *Persische Volksmarchen*. Tr. into German by Arthur Christensen. Dusseldorf: Eugen Diederichs Verlag, 1958. Tr. from the German by Alfred Kurti. London: G. Bell and Sons, 1971.

Lacroix, Petis de, tr. *Les Mille et un Jous. Contes Persans*. Nouv. ed. par A. Loiseleur. Paris: Deslongchamps, 1939.

Lormier, D. L. R., and Lormier, E. O., trs. *Persian Tales*. Written down for the first time in the original Kermani and Bakhtiari and translated. London: Macmillan, 1919.

Mehdevi, Anne Sinclair. *Persian Folk and Fairy Tales.* London: Chatto and Windus, 1965.

Masse, Henri. "Croyances et Coutumes Persanes, Suivies de Contes Et." In *Chansons Populaires,* 2 vols. Paris: Maisonneuve, 1938.

Nackchabi, Ziay-ed-din, D'Afres la Red de Mohammed Qaderi. *Touti-Nameh, ou les Contes du Perroquet.* Tr. de l'origin Persan par E. Muller. Paris, 1934.

Phillot, D. C. *Some Current Persian Tales. Memoirs of the Asiatic Society of Benga* I, no. 18. Calcutta, 1906.

Renan, Ernest. *Les Teazies de la Perse* (Nouv. etudes d'Histoire Religieus), pp. 185–215. Paris, 1884.

Rezvani, Medjid. *Le Theatre et la Danse en Iran.* Paris: G. P. Maisonneuve et Larose, 1962.

Sykes, Ella C. *The Story-Book of the Shah, or Legends of Old Persia.* John MacQueen, 1901.

Tavernier, J. B. *Les Six Voyages de Jean-Baptiste Tavernier,* Qu'il a Fait en Turquie, en Perse et aux Indes Pendant Lespace de 40 Ans. 3 vols. Paris, 1679–1681.

Virolleaud, Ch. *Theatre Persan.* Paris, 1950.

Tetsuo Makita:

Television Drama and Japanese Culture with Special Emphasis on Historical Drama

☆ TELEVISION-VIEWING is an overwhelmingly preponderant activity in the lives of the Japanese. The national average for time spent watching television is surpassed only by that for duration of sleep and for time at work, respectively. If we take the following facts into account—that a third of the population is not economically active and that less than 1 percent are not exposed to television at all—we can also say that television viewing is the most common activity in Japan (with the exception of sleeping, of course) despite its relatively recent origin.

What has made the Japanese become so preoccupied with television? The main reasons are perhaps to be found in the medium's handiness and its domesticity. Furthermore, as Hidetoshi Kato points out, a specific cultural tradition has also contributed to the present state of affairs outlined above. "The Japanese had had such animated arts as shadow picture and lantern picture shows before motion pictures were introduced. On the basis of these traditional arts Japan has built its motion picture culture and television culture." [1]

The influence of traditional culture is most conspicuous in the various dramas shown on television. Of these the NHK's historical drama series are the largest in scale and have been tremendously successful in terms of audience popularity. This paper primarily seeks to analyse these series. Yet it may also serve as an introduction to the study of Japanese culture.

The Audience and Television Drama

Before looking at our subject matter in greater detail, some background information will be presented; it should help the reader to relate historical drama with other forms of drama on television as far as the recipient is concerned.

▶ This is a revised version of an article first published in *Studies of Broadcasting* (International Edition), no. 10 (Tokyo: Nippon Hoso Kyokai (NHK), 1974), pp. 57–76. Mr. Tetsuo Makita is a member of the NHK Public Opinion Research Institute.

Table 1 MOTIVES FOR WATCHING TELEVISION DRAMA

Viewers Watch TV Drama in Order:	Total Percentage	Age Groups Giving the Most Affirmative Replies
Simply to enjoy without any particular reason	40	Females: 13 to 19 years of age, in their 20s, in their 30s
To take a rest or feel relaxed	35	Males: in their 40s
To think about the way in which various people live	32	Males: in their 60s Females: in their 40s
To gain help in leading their own lives	31	Females: in their 20s to 60s
To satisfy their interest in the customs and manners, eras and places shown on TV	29	Males: in their 30s and 60s Females: in their 30s and 40s
To see their favorite actors and/or actresses	20	Females: in their teens and 30s
To enjoy the film version of a book they had liked	19	Females: in their 40s
To enjoy the acting	15	
To enjoy events that don't take place in real life	13	Males: in their teens Females: 13 to 19 years of age
To forget worries	13	Males: in their 50s Females: in their 60s
To enjoy exciting things	10	Males: in their teens Females: in their teens
Other replies	—	
TV dramas are seldom watched	3	Males: in their 40s

Sample: 2,712 persons from the ages of 10 to 69
Source: NHK Survey, 1971

Motives for Watching Television Drama: The Japanese see television primarily as a means of entertainment. Television drama is one of its most favorite forms. As Table 1 indicates, the audience watches television drama mainly for the pleasure and diversion it provides. Frequently, no particular reason is given for the enjoyment of drama. Furthermore, many viewers hope to acquire enlightenment of some form or other, that is, something instructive or helpful in a cultural or practical sense.

Audience Preferences in the Field of Television Drama: Drama is classified in a recent survey as follows: 1) domestic drama, 2) sword drama, 3) mystery, detective and action drama, 4) youth and school drama, 5) historical drama, 6) semi-biographical drama, 7) love stories, 8) serious drama, 9) stories of foremost sportsmen and 10) westerns.

Brief explanations may be necessary for categories that are thought to be peculiar to Japan:

Domestic drama depicts various events that take place in ordinary family life. It deals with relationships between husband and wife, mother and daughter-in-law, parents and children, neighbors, and such.

Historical drama often takes its subject matter from the Japanese feudal age (latter part of the twelfth century to the mid-nineteenth century). The heroes are selected from the ruling class of society, i.e., the *shogun* or *samurai*, who actually lived and exerted great influence upon their times.

The feudal age also provides the setting for sword drama. Both the heroes and events, however, are completely fictional. The heroes are either *samurai* (warriors) or *yakuza* (armed vagabonds), skilled in sword-fighting. In many cases they are lonely and nihilistic in character, but by no means tolerant toward evil-doing in society. Assigning reward to the good and punishment to the wicked thus constitutes the essence of such drama.

Semi-biographical drama depicts the course of a real or fictitious person's life with its many ups and downs, concentrating on his vitality and ability to survive in the face of the many difficulties with which he is confronted.

Males prefer historical and sword drama while women prefer domestic drama, semi-biographical drama and love stories. While young people prefer

Table 2 AUDIENCE PREFERENCES IN THE FIELD OF TELEVISION DRAMA

Subject	Total Percentage	Age Groups Favoring Each Respective Category
Domestic drama	47	Females: 13 to 19 years of age, in their 20s to 50s
Historical drama	43	Males: in their 30s, 50s and 60s
Mystery, detective and action drama	40	Males: in their teens Females: in their teens
Comedies	37	Males: 13 to 19 years of age, in their 20s
Sword drama	35	Males: in their 40s to 60s
Serious drama	32	Males: in their 60s Females: in their 30s to 50s
Semi-biographical drama	32	Females: in their 20s and 30s
Love stories	19	Females: 13 to 19 years of age, in their 20s to 40s
No desire to see television drama	3	Males: in their 20s and 30s

Sample: 2,712 persons from the ages of 10 to 69
Source: NHK Survey, 1971

Table 3 CORRELATION BETWEEN MOTIVES AND PREFERENCES

	Domestic Drama	Historical Drama	Mystery, Detective and Action	Sword Drama
Simply to enjoy without any particular reason	(1) 43%	(3) 38%	(1) 41%	(3) 34%
To take a rest or feel relaxed	(3) 40%	(5) 36%	(2) 39%	(1) 43%
To think about the way in which various people live	(4) 38%	(1) 43%	(3) 35%	(3) 34%
To obtain help in leading their own lives	(2) 41%	(3) 38%	(5) 30%	(5) 31%
To satisfy interest in the customs and manners, eras and places shown on TV	(5) 32%	(1) 43%	(4) 32%	(2) 35%
N =	1,264	1,172	1,090	949

Source: NHK Survey, 1971

mystery, detective and action drama, middle-aged and elderly viewers prefer serious drama (cf. Table 2).

Correlation Between Audience Motives and Audience Preferences: Table 3 is self-explanatory. Worthy of mention is the fact that a fairly large number of people hope to learn something from drama. In other words, even the most entertaining drama or, for instance, a sword drama has an educational function in the broadest sense of the term. In the case of historical drama, instruction and help take precedence over diversion and relaxation as far as audience motivation is concerned. The fact that the NHK's historical drama series have enjoyed great popularity suggests that they play an important and specific role in Japanese cultural life.

The NHK's Historical Drama Series

Duration and Frequency of Broadcasts: NHK Television initiated its historical drama series in 1963 and has continued to broadcast such series regularly every Sunday between 8 and 8.45 p.m. up to the present day. They are thus transmitted during peak viewing hours (when the greatest number of poeple are at home [Sundays: 83%] and when they are concerned primarily with diversion and relaxation). All 39 hours per year are allocated to one series (52 weeks @ 45 minutes = 39 hours).

Although programs are usually changed or modified in April and November, such series begin in January and end in December—thus corresponding with the traditional rhythm of Japanese life, which puts greatest emphasis on New Year's Day and New Year's Eve.

Historical Background: Most of the subject matter for historical drama is drawn from the feudal age (1180–1867) during which *samurai* regimes controlled Japan. A brief description of the history of the feudal age will help the reader to form a conceptual framework within which historical drama can be understood.

There were four distinct periods of *samurai* rule. Political power was exercised by the *Shogun* (the title was officially bestowed by the *Tenno* [Emperor] of Japan).

The earliest *samurai* regime was the *Kamakura*-Regime (1183–1333) established by *Yoritomo Minamoto*. This was followed by the *Muromachi*-Regime (1336–1573). The three years in between saw the return to the old system of *Tenno*-court government, a significant historical event in that impetus was given to the traditional *Tenno* system. The last stage of the *Muromachi*-Regime is characterized by disintegration and turmoil, brought about by the diminishing power of the *Muromachi-Shoguns*, and is thus called the "turbulent age." The third, the *Oda-Toyotomi*-Regime (1568–1598), was transitional in nature but of great historical importance. It is characterized by the cultural creativity which emerged after years of disturbance. This period is often called the "Japanese Renaissance." The fourth, the *Tokugawa*-Regime (1568–1867) was the last and the longest. During this period the feudal system attained its greatest maturity. Almost all prototypes of Japanese life and customs date back to the peaceful years under this regime.

The critical years between the four periods outlined above constitute the richest source of Japanese tales and still stimulate the imagination of writers and novelists.

During the feudal age the *Shogun* wielded supreme political power. The status of *Tenno* was a hereditary one, higher than that of *Shogun*, but it conferred very little political power upon its holder. Especially after the *Muromachi*-Regime, the *Tenno* was virtually excluded from the struggle for supremacy, although as a spiritual symbol he still exerted considerable influence over the whole of Japan.

Characteristic Motifs: As mentioned above, historical drama depicts the life of a hero drawn from Japanese history as well as the important events brought about by his conduct. The themes of the various series are outlined below (Table 4):

1. *Tragic factor:* Almost all the historical dramas shown on television show some inclination toward tragedy, which includes elements such as the hero's death and unrequited love.

a) *Death:* According to Carl G. Jung, the hero's life in mythology has a pattern common throughout the world consisting of the following component elements:[2]

Table 4 OUTLINES OF THE NHK's HISTORICAL DRAMA SERIES
AND THE PERIODS IN WHICH THEY WERE SET

Title	Year of Broadcast	Historical Period	Outline
Hanano Shogai (Flowery Life) 27.7% (average of viewers watching series)	1963	1840–1860 Transitional period between the feudal and modern age	Agony of Ii Naosuke, chief minister during the last days of the Tokugawa shogunate, who was assassinated on account of his initiative in lifting Japan's self-imposed ban on economic and political contact with foreign countries.
47 Royal Samurai of Ako 31.5%	1964	1701–1702 Feudal age—The stable period of the latter samurai regime	Story of the 47 samurai who by their united efforts avenged their master, the Lord of Ako.
Taikoki Story of Taiko 43.3%	1965	1540–1598 Turbulent age—The latter part of the second samurai regime and the ensuing samurai regime	Success story of Taiko Hideyoshi, who ultimately came to reign over the whole country despite his humble origins as the son of a footman (lowest class of samurai).
Minamoto no Yoshitsune 34.0%	1966	1173–1189 Transitional period between aristocratic rule and the first samurai regime	Life of Minamoto no Yoshitsune, a tragic hero, who, after destroying the enemy force of the rival Heike family thanks to his military genius, was killed by his brother.
Three Sisters 27.8%	1967	1864–1868 Transitional period between the feudal and modern age	Fate of three sisters of a samurai family who lived through the disturbances during the last days of the Tokugawa shogunate.
Whither Ryoma 21.4%	1968	1853–1867 Transitional period between the feudal and modern age	Life of Sakamoto Ryoma, who was assassinated on the eve of the Imperial Restoration, the realization of his plan for modernizing the ancient feudal system.

Title	Year of Broadcast	Historical Period	Outline
The Heaven and the Earth 35.0%	1969	1530–1578 Turbulent age	The lifelong struggle between *Uesugi Kenshin*, a war poet, and his worthy opponent, *Takeda Shingen*.
The Fir Tree Remained 29.9%	1970	1642–1671 Mature period of the last *samurai* regime	The latter half of the life of *Harada Kai*, chief retainer to the *Sendai* clan, who succeeded in bringing peace to his master's family through sacrificing his own life.
Haruno Sakomichi (Life is a Continuous Climb) 22.1%	1971	1594–1646 Initial stage of the last *samurai* regime	Life of *Yagyu Munenori*, chief superintendent of the *Tokugawa* shogunate, which adopted the spirit of the art of *Yagyu*'s fencing for use in political life.
New Tale of *Heike* 20.9%	1972	1118–1185 Transitional period between aristocratic rule and the first *samurai* regime	Struggle for political power between the nobility and the *samurai* is described, centering around *Tairo no Kiyomori*, head of the *Heike* family.
Story of the Conquerors 22.5%	1973	1517–1582 Turbulent age	Ambition of *Saito Dosan*, formerly an oil man, who died during the course of conquering the whole realm.
Katsu Kaishu 22.0%	1974	1839–1868 Transitional period between the feudal and modern age	Life of *Katsu Kaishu*, a founder of the Japanese navy, who surrendered the castle of *Edo* without bloodshed.
Genroku Taiheiki 20.7%	1975	1686–1702 Feudal age—The stable period of the last *samurai* regime	The fatal confrontation between *Yanagisawa Yoshiyasu*, a person close to the Shogun, and *Oishi Kuranosuke*, the leader of the 47 royal *samurai* of Ako.
Wind, Cloud and Rainbow 23.8%	1976	?–940 Aristocratic age	Story of simultaneous rebellions, led in the east by *Taira no Masakado* and in the west by *Fujiwara no Sumitomo*.

1. The hero is born miraculously, unrecognized by contemporaries, and displays superhuman powers during the early part of his life.
2. He distinguishes himself and rises to power rapidly, victorious in combat against evil powers.
3. He is apt to fall victim to the sin of arrogance—which causes his downfall, go to ruin or to die as a result of treachery or "heroic" self-sacrifice.

The lives of almost all the heroes who appear in these television series correspond with Jung's schematic characterization. Moreover, the heroes in these series are well known to the Japanese and it is generally known that most of them will meet with a tragic death. The audience, even halfway through the series when the hero is in the prime of his life, is always aware that his life will end in tragic circumstances. The fact that many viewers write to the NHK asking that the hero's life be "spared" is a reflection of such awareness. Thus every episode of such a series is colored by a feeling of impending tragedy as far as the recipient is concerned.

Of the fourteen dramas listed in Table 4, eleven end with the death of their respective heroes. The deaths may be categorized as follows:

i) The hero is killed unreasonably before he has completed what he had set out to do (five dramas).
ii) Although the hero gains prosperity himself, he dies with an uneasy conscience because he has been unable to appoint a successor (three dramas). (In one of these dramas the hero's family is ruined after his death. The Japanese are fond of stories in which those who have become prosperous rapidly go to ruin. This is a reflection of a belief in the mutability of life originating in Buddhism.)
iii) Death through self-sacrifice (one drama).
iv) Death after feeling satisfied that he has accomplished all his aims (two dramas).

b) *Unrequited love:* Many women make an appearance in the company of the various series' heroes. In most cases love affairs end unsuccessfully, hindered by factors typical of the feudal age. During the feudal age, for instance, the daughters of *samurai* were treated as political tools. So-called marriages of convenience were the outcome. Furthermore, there were four distinct classes during the feudal age, i.e., the first: *samurai*; the second: farmers; the third: artisans; and the fourth: tradesmen. A *samurai* was not allowed to marry outside his class.

The tragedy depicted in these series, composed of such elements as the hero's death together with the uncertainty it brings and unrequited love as a consequence of feudal customs, strongly attracts the emotions of a Japanese audience.

2. *Modernity:* One of the characteristics of these historical dramas is the fact that they portray the past in such a way that their relevance for present-day

life is apparent to all who watch. The results of the questionnaire survey outlined above show that a majority of those who liked historical drama primarily wished to learn about (and learn from) the way in which other people led their lives. Viewers are interested in the hero's ideas and actions and seek to apply what they have seen to contemporary conditions.

a) *Practical ethics:* During the feudal age Japan was composed of numerous small feudal states, each of which was ruled by a *daimyo* (lord) who was subject to the *Shogun*. When the power exercised by the *Shogun* was weak—as in the case of the "turbulent age"—a stronger state would attempt to establish its primacy over other states. When the shogunate exercised supreme power over the whole nation, small states found themselves in an awkward position, facing either removal to other territory or abolition at the hands of the *Shogun*.

The drama series can be classified in terms of the political processes they depict as follows:

i) Process in which a small state attempts to reestablish a centralized political system and place other states under its control (six dramas, of which two portray the success and four the failure of such an attempt).

ii) Process in which a ruler tries to maintain supremacy (four dramas, of which two portray success and two failure in doing so).

iii) Process in which a small state under another state's control struggles against the latter's attempts to destroy it (two dramas, of which one portrays success and the other failure of the struggle).

iv) Process in which a new political force emerges, destroying the state hitherto exercising power (two dramas).

Principles that can be applied to various contemporary situations and conditions are promoted by such drama. For the viewer, for instance, a series might suggest ways of improving the organization of companies, groups, and the like, criteria whereby appointments to vacant positions should be made, ways of dealing with complex human relationships or how relationships with other companies and such can best be regulated. It might also encourage the viewer to adopt an innovative frame of mind with regard to new ideas and techniques.

b) *Modern production techniques:* Producers in charge of historical drama production constantly try to find new ways and means of presenting drama in an attractive and appealing manner in order to ensure high popularity ratings. In a few cases, for instance, they experimented with the insertion of film sequences drawing attention to contemporary aspects of the situation being depicted. When a modern city or the like suddenly appears in the midst of a historical drama, the effect is to startle the viewer.

Why is this done? Producers give the following explanation: the dramatic element in television drama mostly lies in the interaction between the experiences the viewers themselves have gone through and those which are being represented on the screen. If the television drama itself recreates such interaction, it will strengthen and enhance the way in which the viewers react to what is being shown.

Background of Interest:

1. *Tradition of mass entertainment:* The historical story was one of the principal genres in the various entertainment media that preceded television. Almost all the stories these series have drawn upon have repeatedly been told from time immemorial by *biwa* (lute)- playing minstrels, by *kabuki* (professional story tellers), in popular literature and on the cinema screen—and are historical stories with which the Japanese are familiar. Accordingly, the tragic elements embodied in "death," "uncertainty" and "unrequited love," for instance, are a part of the cultural tradition that influences the thoughts and attitudes of the Japanese.

2. *Present social conditions:* Professor Yozo Horikome gives us an explanation as to why people in modern society are so interested in history:[3]

> The type of person required by a modern society characterized by increasing mechanization and organization is the "average" person, not the one displaying individuality. Those who aspire to individuality, a quality originally required by human nature, come to have an interest—for various reasons both positive and negative—in the role played by individuals appearing in history.

The extraordinary growth of the Japanese economy after the war has caused chronic inflation and an environmental crisis constituting a threat of the contemporary life-style of the Japanese. Against the background of such prevailing conditions, people's interests are moving away from the "material" and toward the "mind." And it may be said that people have begun to resort to history as a means of seeing their identity.

Social Influence of Historical Drama:

1. *Decline of cinema: Hanano Shogai* (Flowery Life), the first historical drama series presented by the NHK, is to be remembered for the fact that its cast included the first film stars to appear in a television program. This constituted a turning point. Since then many film stars have made appearances in television programs. Historical, sword and home dramas featuring stars who had made a name for themselves elsewhere have come to attract more people to the television screen.

With the improvements made in the quantity and quality of television entertainment programs and with the appearance of other forms of leisure activity, the cinema audience has rapidly decreased in size. The contemporary cinema audience is mainly composed of people in their teens and twenties.

Japanese films have also changed gradually as a result of this development. The luxurious feature film using many stars at one time has disappeared. And subject matter has changed in such a way that it doesn't overlap with that presented on television,[4] i.e., *yakuza*'s (armed vagabond's) destructive action, grief of those who have lost their homeland, eroticism, and the self-tormenting behavior of young men.

2. *Theatre success:* New stars in the theatrical world have become famous through their performances in these series. Furthermore, the story that was selected for each respective series is performed at some theatre during that particular year.

3. *A boom for publications on history:* 1965 and 1972 experienced booms in the sale of books on history. The series shown on television are thought to be an important factor in explaining the phenomenon. The majority of the historical series shown on television have been based on books. Since 1968, such books have occupied higher rankings on the best-seller lists thanks to the boost provided by these series.

4. *Creation of new sightseeing resorts:* In many of these series, events take place centering around present-day Tokyo and Kyoto. We also notice that all areas of Japan except Hokkaido have served as locations at one time or another for the various historical drama series presented to date. Hidetoshi Kato demands that the popular novel and the feature film should not only guide people in their way of life but also guide them to various places.[5] These series may provide one way of doing this. In 1969, for instance, when the series entitled *Heaven and Earth* was being televised, the location used for filming various scenes turned into a sightseeing resort. The number of visitors to the location, *Kawanakajima*, an ancient battlefield, was about 120,000 a year before the series was televised. During the year after the beginning of the series, 1,100,000 visited the place. Since then an annual average of 600,000 have visited the site.

NOTES

[1] Hidetoshi Kato, *From Side Show to Television* (1965), in Japanese.
[2] Carl G. Jung, *Man and His Symbols* (1965).
[3] Yozo Horikome, *History and Man* (1965), in Japanese.
[4] Cf. Tadao Sato, *Literary Yearbook* (1972), in Japanese.
[5] Hidetoshi Kato, *Ibid.*

Shyam Parmar:

Traditional Folk Forms in India
and Their Use in National Development

☆ TRADITIONAL FOLK MEDIA are tools of a special nature. Their special nature is derived from the fact that they have no grammar or literature. They are nurtured through oral and functional sources. In perspective, traditional folk media provide channels for the expression of the socio-ritual, moral and emotional needs of the society or societies in which they are to be found.

Social anthropologists believe that the dominant characteristics of traditional folk media persist and never die. But in the process of transmission over time, most of the contents of these media become blurred, and sometimes even the rubrics of the media forms themselves cannot be sustained. So long as the contents satisfy psychological and social needs, they are carried forward by the people themselves. If the media forms are found to be vital enough to survive against the onslaughts of the modern age, people of their own accord make provision to put fresh contents into them. All such modes of communication have to establish their worthiness as expressive agents in accord with the commonly accepted behavioral patterns of their respective cultures. The more folk forms prove their susceptibility as expressive channels, the more they are regarded worthy of use by society. The contents, however, may change or get distorted regardless of their structural characteristics. For example, the *alha*, one of the popular ballad forms of Uttar Pradesh and Madhya Pradesh, has survived over the ages both in content and structure. The Government of India has, during various Five Year Plan periods, exploited this form extensively in order to establish rapport with the people. Fully aware of the extent to which the masses appreciated the style, several folk poets conveniently inserted new words so as to meet the communications requirement in rural parts of the country. Even political parties and sales promotion agencies use *alha* reciters to get their messages across. Its utilization has widened its impact, even in cul-

▶ Reprinted from *Traditional Folk Media in India* (New Delhi: Geka Books, 1975) with the kind permission of the author. Dr. Shyam Parmar was Head of the Department of Traditional Media at the Indian Institute of Mass Communication in New Delhi until his recent death.

tural regions where it is traditionally at home. More examples from other areas can be cited in order to support this point.[1]

Reaching the Grass-Roots

The bare fact that, despite the availability of modern means of communication, traditional folk media continue to exist, entitles them to the increased attention of mass media experts. Their use is possible in those countries where the literacy rate is poor, mass media reach appears to be limited, or the mass media seem less trustworthy to a large number of rural people on account of their alien nature and *modus operandi.*

Studies have indicated that messages intended for downward transmission to rural communities by urban-orientated experts were ineffective at their destination points. They have also shown that between traditional and modern societies communication flow is not an easy and smooth process.[2] Generally, when dissemination is carried out in a society with many different cultures, messages are not received at the receiving ends with their intended meaning.[3] However, with increasing communication among the people of India, it is becoming apparent that "cultural isolation" is never total.

A Communications Model

A communications model relating to the use of traditional folk media in India is depicted in the diagram below. The model is confined to the field assigned to the Directorate of Field Publicity, which is the biggest user of traditional folk media in the country. The Song and Drama Division, its sister organization under the Ministry of Information and Broadcasting, complements its activities by broadcasting live programs via modern media of communication, most of which are arranged in the rural areas by mobile units of the Directorate of Field Publicity.

In the following model, the "Coordinating Agency" and "Impact Study Groups," shown in dotted lines, have been proposed by the author. Both units seem to be necessary in order to insure desired impact at the grass-roots and effective feedback at the source.

The messages the policy maker at the source (A) intends to disseminate are passed on to the regional offices (B). At B, the messages are integrated into the regional programs and then handed on to the field units (C). In the process of "implementing the orders," the messages are handed over by C to the channels (D). In the form of live performances, D has the major role to play. Personal media—Block Development Officers (BDO), Village Level Workers (VLW), Agricultural Extension Officers (AEO), and such—contribute to the further dissemination of the messages. Impersonal media (e.g., film and print material) make the operation into a multi-media one. Traditional folk artists usually find it very hard to integrate the messages C asks them to incorporate, folk forms proving to be quite rigid. More often than not, they also fail to conceive the

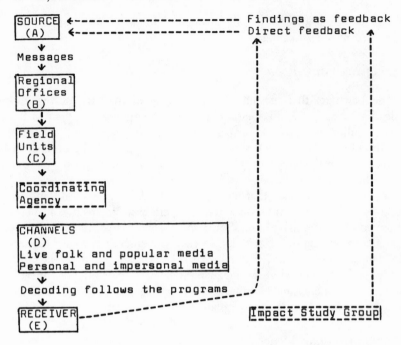

messages along the lines intended, illiteracy being the main reason for this. The Song and Drama Division claims:

> Scripts of folk media programs are traditionally prepared by the artists them-selves and mostly such programs are extemporized as per changing require-ments of circumstances and audience. In such cases, the direction and treat-ment are approved beforehand by local officers on the spot.[4]

In such cases, C usually acts simply as an official unit carrying out in-structions in whatever possible way. In certain cases, C also proves to be igno-rant of the modes of communication locally available. This state of affairs increases the problems at headquarters (A): how to make fullest use of these special tools for the diffusion of information in what circumstances, by whom and where?

Two decades of experience have proved that there is great scope for more imaginative use of traditional folk forms. What needs to be looked at, however, is the gap that exists between A and E. The author visualizes that this gap can be bridged by a coordinating agency that can work at a regional level in collab-oration with the field units, helping local artists to incorporate the messages in-tended for dissemination into existing folk forms so as to leave their vital char-acteristics intact. Such an agency should be composed of artists and script writers possessing sufficient knowledge about their target audiences and compe-tent in dealing with the message passed on from A. Collaboration with such persons who understand the folkways, dialects, mores and taboos of our rural and tribal communities as well as the aims of the policy maker is bound to produce the desired results. To quote Dr. Everett Kleinjans:

> One possible choice is to frame the message differently for the people with different cultural backgrounds. The categories of one language or one culture are not adequate for those of another. Or to put it in another way, no two cultures have the same set of meanings nor do they use similar symbols to represent similar meanings. In cross-cultural communication, the message must be given the proper form and style so that the receiver gets the message which the sender intends.[5]

Together with the addition of research-based feedback, this approach may perhaps remove the deficiencies of the present communications model.

In India this model-based arrangement may be feasible because most cultural values are inherent both at A and E. In the communications process, when traditional values interact with contemporary values, the former have to undergo certain changes. Yet they don't lose their basic characteristics because of the strength of their motifs and symbols.

The Folk-Urban Continuum

Indian society—with its complex family system, castes, ethnic groups and clans—has not lost its deep associations with folk culture. In remote villages and in tribal communities, indigenous strands of basic Indian culture have survived to the present day because continued use has been made of oral and functional folklore. This fact emphasises the strong links Indian society has with the past. Despite the acceptance of modern innovations, cultural perpetuity is discernible in our attitudes and taboos.

Cities in India have grown with pockets of rural population within their boundaries. The percentage of urban dwellers in 1971 was 19.87 as against 17.89 in 1961. Of the total urban population, 52.48 percent is literate as against 23.60 percent of the rural population. With nearly 80 percent of the rural members of society illiterate and also beyond the reach of the electronic media, it is the use of traditional media that brings about a sense of cultural unity. Although cutlural diversity exists in one form or another, it is the common values accepted by all kinds of societies, both rural and urban, that need to be traced so that existing folk forms can be coordinated with the new media.

Traditional Tools of Communication

Traditional folk media should not be confused with the technology-based mass media. Technology-based mass media disseminate messages to heterogeneous audiences, whereas the traditional folk media cater for ethno-rural communities through the functional role of folklore. Folklore, by employing the vocal, verbal-musical and visual folk art forms transmitted to a society or group of societies from one generation to another, represents a form of communication itself. The various forms are indigenous and have served society as tools of communication for ages. They were integrated during the course of time into the complex body of socio-cultural behavior, determined by the anthropomorphic existence of the people to which they belong. The components of traditional media therefore co-exist with rituals and ceremonial activities as well.

The audiences catered for by the traditional media are not diverse in cultural fabric like the audiences of the technology-based mass media. They consist of local, regional and ethno-linguistic communities. At the same time, however, in the wider dissemination process effected through mass media, the audiences associated with traditional folk media are not cut off from the vast heterogenous audiences. On the contrary, traditional media assist in the further dissemination of the messages transmitted through mass media.

Illiteracy and the Inadequate Spread of Mass Media

The two important factors that obstruct communication in the country are a high rate of illiteracy and an inadequate spread of mass media. Literates constitute under 30 percent of the total population and the reach of the electronic media is of the same order. This means that over 70 percent of the population are virtually cut off from information about social and political affairs and from developments in the field of science. Illiteracy[6] barricades our growth in many other fields. Even if radio acts as the first source of agricultural information for one in ten farmers, interpersonal communication in the form of *chaupal charcha* or *baithaks* are still needed for an effective dissemination of information.

A crucial role is played by opinion leaders of rural elites who adapt and channel messages so as to conform with the traditional norms of rural communities. Local proverbs and sayings facilitate speech communication and help to break down traditional resistance to new ideas. The adoption of folkloric elements in face-to-face communication allows communication in terms of the recipient's decoding capacity.[7] A survey of communication sources used in the process of adopting high-yielding varieties of crops in thirty-three villages, conducted in 1968 by the Indian Institute of Mass Communication, reveals the importance of the *gramsevak* (village level workers): He continues to funtion as a link with farmers with regard to most agricultural matters.[8] UNESCO's report on literacy for 1969–1971 indicates that mass media are increasingly being used in order to eradicate illiteracy. At the same time it also points out that organized radio-listening or television-viewing followed by group discussion are considered to be more effective. Of course, radio is a vital instrument, but for purposes of persuasive communication it plays a secondary role.[9] That is why in most developing countries oral communication is used to help in interpreting the content presented by the electronic media.

Any communications network with which the masses are unfamiliar, which does not function in accordance with their cultural predispositions and institutional values, will have little impact and significance. Studies have stressed that no mass·media can exist in a cultural vacuum.[10] The aims of communication can only be fully realized when the contents and channels used are in accordance with the people's attitudes and behavioral patterns. This is the reason why communication in India is largely communication through non-mass media, an observation that has frequently been made. It occurs within a framework that includes the following traditional folk forms of entertainment, usages and institutions:

1. Traditional folk theatre or rural dramatic forms, including tribal mimes and dance-dramas
2. Puppetry
3. Oral literature-cum-musical forms (folk musical styles, ballads, *harikatha, kabigan,* story-telling and so on
4. Fairs and festivals including social, ritual and ceremonial gatherings
5. Traditional youth clubs like the *ghotul* of the tribal Murias of Bastar or the *dhumkuria* of the Oraons of Bihar
6. Folk dances
7. Ritual symbols, traditional designs and miscellaneous motifs
8. Sound signals and speech surrogates

This is only a broad categorization. There are many more regional variations.

Marriage of Traditional and Mass Media

In order to bridge the gap between the new technologies available and their use by farmers or to eliminate the deficiencies in the dissemination of socio-political and cultural information effectively, a coalition between technology-based mass media and traditional modes of communication is essential. Within the total communications network, the avoidance of folk media may keep the major part of the population ignorant of many useful things.

Although a wide range of development projects are under way, most of the activities and achievements in various parts of the country go unnoticed and messages of importance are not diffused properly for want of means. Despite the spread of mass media, many ethno-linguistic groups in India did not know for a long time that Mahatma Gandhi was dead. We find several instances of a communications gap which are obviously the result of a low level of literacy.

Informal Communication Behavior

Within the various ethno-linguistic groups and peasant societies, communication behavior is not always of a formal nature. In their social activities and festivities, messages are disseminated through means of poetry, legends, ballads, mimicry, puppetry and other forms of drama. In many tribal and agricultural communities, dancing as a means of informal communication supplements other forms of communication. Singing inspires such communities in their day-to-day work and very often promotes coordination in manual work.

Traditional folk singing, akin to speech, serves as a mode of specialized communication. It is to be found in all activities from cradle to grave. Thus, in illiterate communities, communication is channeled through the different genres of folklore. It is claimed that "folk culture has its own wide network of communication" and it "does not depend solely on . . . tradition for the transmission of its elements."[11]

The Concept of Field Publicity

Owing to the limited reach of the electronic media, the concept of field publicity was introduced by the government in order to give a new dimension to the process of communication. Field publicity techniques involve direct confrontation with the masses, using various forms of media. Contact with the masses is maintained not only through film shows, exhibitions, posters, folders, pamphlets, seminars and discussions, but also through the respective traditional folk media of entertainment popular in different parts of the country, which are employed to achieve effective reach.

Studies have shown that the hold of traditional media on the rural and semi-urban masses is still strong. The *Vidyalankar* Study Team[12] observed that the media of song and drama, because of their great appeal with the masses and their quality of being able to touch the deepest emotions of the illiterate millions, are matchless as means of mirroring popular responses to national challenges. Realizing the potential of these verbal-musical and visual folk media, some State Directorates of Public Relations and non-official organizations make imaginative use of traditional live entertainment forms. The Song and Drama Division has made several experiments, employing many of these forms for the dissemination of ideas and innovations. In 1973 a total of 11,673 performances were given by the 361 private folk troupes on its roster. The following breakdown of these performances gives a general idea as to the range and variety of traditional media made use of by the division as well as the relative frequency with which each medium is used:[13]

1. Drama (including folk plays)   1,253
2. Poetic symposia (*kavi sammelan, mushaira, kavi darbar,* etc.)   95
3. Composite programs (concerts, folk dances, etc.)   2,404
4. Folk and mythological epics (including *burra katha, katha-prasangam,* etc.)   910
5. Folk recitals (*qawwalis, palla, villupatu, ras, kabigan,* etc.)   1,708
6. Puppet shows (including *bomalattam*)   1,309
7. Ballads (*alha, powadas,* etc.)   1,706
8. Religious discourses (*harikatha, bhagwatkatha, daskathia,* etc.)   1,861
9. Programs on a no-cost basis   427

The coalition between modern mass media and existing traditional media creates a process of interaction. The electronic media seldom replace the traditional media. Each new mode of communication superimposes itself on the existing mode. In this process, the former takes over certain functions of the latter. However, the basic functions are retained by the existing mode because of its local characteristics and association with social functions. As modern technology has not disrupted the structures of our society and community life, traditional media provide tremendous opportunities for bridging the communications gap if used in an organized and integrated manner.

The strategy quoted below—taken from the working document prepared for the expert group meeting on the integrated use of folk media and mass media in London in 1972—seems to be a logical approach:

> A wise strategy would try to bring about a mutual reinforcement of the advantages of both traditional and modern media. It would also see to it that the effectiveness of the traditional forms did not vanish because of their inability to face up to the competition of the mass media, and that these media did not lose their impact as soon as the novelty of their use wore out. A practical approach to this multiple problem lies in the marrying of the two types of media. After all, both are simply two different points on the same continuum. As the puppet, the "vintage" folk form of today was yesterday's innovation, so the film, today's innovation, is likely to be tomorrow's vintage medium.[14]

The Advantages of Folk Media

The advantages of the traditional folk media over radio and television are many, particularly in the rural and tribal areas of the country. They may be summarized as follows:

1. Traditional folk media are the most intimate of media as far as the masses in all parts of the country are concerned. Their primary appeal is to the emotions rather than to the intellect.
2. They command an immense variety of forms and themes to suit the communications requirements of the masses.
3. They are local and live and able to establish direct rapport with the audiences as they antecede the mass media.
4. They are easily available.
5. Their flexibility allows accommodation of new themes.
6. They are enjoyed and approved by all age groups.
7. When compared with the sophisticated mass media, folk media are low cost means of communication.

NOTES

[1] Cf. Shyam Parmar, *Traditional Folk Media in India* (New Delhi: Geka Books, 1975), pp. 16–119.

[2] Everett M. Rogers and F. Floyd Shoemaker, *Communication of Innovation: A Cross-Cultural Approach* (New York: Free Press, 1971), p. 84.

[3] Edward T. Hall and F. W. William, "Intercultural Communication: A Guide to Men of Action," in *Human Organisation* 19 (1960), pp. 5–12.

[4] Report of the Ministry of Information and Broadcasting, 1973–74, p. 98.

[5] Everett Kleinjans, *Crossroads in Communication* (Singapore: Asian Mass Communication Research and Information Centre, 1972), p. 13. The publication contains the text of the address delivered at the opening session of the First Assembly of AMIC held in Singapore on 2nd December, 1971.

[6] According to the recent census, 386 million people in India do not know how to read and write. Though the literacy rate has gone up, the number of illiterates shows an increase of 88 million in two decades. This can be attributed to the population explosion.

[7] Vinod and Urmil Bhandarai, "Baithak as a Channel of Communication in Rural Areas," in *Journal of Family Welfare* 14, no. 2 (December 1972): 52–62. The study shows that the institution of *baithak* could be geared to involving people in interpersonal communication.

[8] A. V. Shanmugam, *Agro-Information Flow at the Village Level* (New Delhi: Indian Institute of Mass Communication, 1968).

[9] P. C. Chatterji, "Broadcasting and Social Change," in *Sunday World* (New Delhi, 29th April, 1973).

[10] James W. Markham, *Voices of the Red Giants.* (Iowa: University Press, 1967), p. x.

[11] Indra Deva, "Folklore Studies," in *A Survey of Research in Sociology and Social Anthropology* III (New Delhi: Indian Council of Social Science Research, 1972), p. 205.

[12] Reference may be made to the *Report of the Study Team on Five Year Plan Publicity.* The study team was appointed under a resolution of the Government of India in the Ministry of Information and broadcasting, dated 3rd April, 1963. An assessment was to be made of the impact of the publicity programs on the people as well as a report on measures to widen their impact and improve their efficiency. The report was submitted to the Government in 1964.

[13] Annual Report of the Ministry of Information and Broadcasting, 1973–74, p. 98.

[14] The Expert Group Meeting was sponsored by UNESCO and convened by the International Planned Parenthood Federation (IPPF), London, 20th–24th November, 1972.

Jürgen Hüther:

Comments on the Functional Change of Television Viewing as a Leisure Pursuit

☆ IF WE ARE TO BELIEVE the prognoses of futurologists with regard to the year 2000—and there is no reason why we should not in so far as these prognoses are based on empirical data—modern civilization as represented by the industrialized nations is in the process of transformation from a work-oriented into a leisure-orientated society. Because the amount of leisure is by and large directly related to the length of the working week, it has proved easy to document this trend clearly through the indices relating to the latter: in Germany, for instance, during the last half-century, the working week has been reduced in length by more than half.[1] Both contemporary societies and those of the future differ from those of the past, the difference being characterized above all by the following two criteria, partly interconnected, mutually conditioned and independent of the various different political systems and social structures in existence:

1. Industrial technology, characterized by mass production and automation as well as by a steadily increasing amount of leisure.
2. The existence and continuous expansion of mass communications media in their different forms, and their increasing utilization.[2]

Holzer points out that mass communication can be looked upon as a functional requirement especially in the case of democratically constituted industrial nations "because it is fundamentally they—through the supply of basic social knowledge and current news—that turn the individual into a *homo politicus* and enable self-determination as well as individual responsibility."[3]

Contemporary industrial nations, often apostrophized rather precipitately as leisure societies, having experienced a continual reduction in the length of the working week, are witnessing a decline in the importance of the time spent working at least in quantitive terms because the life of the population today is

▶ This is an original article written especially for this book. Dr. Jürgen Hüther is Professor of Media Didactics and Pedagogical Field Research at the Department of Pedagogy, Hochschule der Bundeswehr (College of the West German Armed Forces), München.

no longer determined by the daily working process alone. Nowadays leisure does not so much represent a privilege of certain social strata, having undergone a process of democratization in many spheres. Moreover, the increasing amount of leisure is accompanied by rising income through which consumer demand for new products is stimulated and new consumption opportunities are offered. However, this doesn't mean that equal distribution of opportunity transcending the social structure exists with regard to the possibilities of access to individual kinds of leisure activity. Differences specific to various social strata continue to exist, mostly in terms of the "quality" and "cultural standard" of leisure activities as seen by the middle classes. One can agree with Opaschowski when he ascribes these differences to those of opportunities in society regarding development of individual capabilities and communication between groups and not primarily to the material disadvantages of certain social strata.[4]

A lot of evidence exists indicating that a functional relationship exists between the amount of leisure and the time spent in using the media. Statistical data for West Germany show that during the past one and a half decades, parallel with the increasing amount of leisure, media consumption was also subject to continual growth. The following all showed considerable increase:

- Sale of daily newspapers between 1964 and 1976 from 19.8 million to 22.5 million copies
- Illustrated magazines during the same period from 43.3 million to 74.9 million copies
- The number of radio licenses between 1961 and 1977 from 15.9 million to 21.8 million
- The number of television licenses during the same period from 4.6 million to approximately 20 million
- Average weekday media consumption between 1964 and 1975 from 3.1 hours to 4.5 hours[5]

The fundamental significance of the increasing amount of leisure and use of mass media has given rise to earnest academic endeavors trying to keep pace with this rapid development. The question as to the influence of high media consumption on the leisure activity and the entire socialization process of the recipient is one of the main concerns of pedagogical and communications research analyses. Although results that cannot be underestimated, especially for pedagogical practice, have been the outcome, one cannot hide the fact that systematic and comprehensive studies on the mass media's influence and their total significance in the socio-cultural environment do not exist. This is surprising when one considers the twofold relevance of mass media within the socio-cultural system. They inform about, transmit and popularize political, cultural, social and further activities and measures on the one hand; on the other, they are also responsible for launching initiatives in these areas themselves.

A conspicuous shortcoming is to be found in literature on the subject of leisure: the fact that the mass media are not considered in their own right within the spectrum of life's contributory determinants. The use of mass media is subsumed generically under the term "leisure activity" and put on a par with a category of activities (e.g., model-building, playing a musical instrument), which fulfill the functions of a pure hobby. The results of mass communications research, however, have shown that such a comparison must at least be treated with considerable doubt. The use of mass media has become so much a part of everyday life that to say that it is experienced as a hobby or fad is hardly possible. It doesn't possess the characteristics of a consciously experienced leisure activity—or at least it doesn't do so any more—but has by and large become an established part of a normal daily routine that is taken for granted, guaranteeing information, entertainment and education on a regular basis. If one takes a formal definition of leisure as a starting point, however (i.e., the time the individual has at his disposal after subtraction of work or professional occupation and directly related activities, sleep, and time spent on personal hygiene and fulfillment of basic physical needs), and sees it as the time spent on activities, non-essential in material terms, which can be chosen according to personal ambitions and inclinations and which are not the result of his functional role, it stands to reason that media consumption should be included in this category. Nevertheless, there are indications that television—through its constant availability, the diversity of program choice, conveniency as well as high entertainment and information value—has enticed the recipient into a state of dependency from which he cannot easily escape.

The German television organization, *Zweites Deutsche Fernsehen* (ZDF), together with the Institute for Mass Communications at the Free University of Berlin carried out a joint experiment designed to assess the extent and implications of such dependency. Two families in Berlin were confronted with the following questions: "Imagine that removal men would come and take away your television set and you couldn't watch television for four weeks as a result. What do you expect, hope or fear during the course of the next month? Do you already feel so dependent on television and thus expect to be bored without a TV-set? Or does the prospect of rather lengthy abstinence promise a welcome opportunity to develop more activities of your own, something which you haven't been able to do because the "box" entices you to do nothing but switch on?"[6] These two families were given an opportunity to answer these questions themselves on the basis of experience. With their consent they were deprived of a television set for four weeks. The experiment was presented as part of a ZDF-serial, *betrifft Fernsehen*, which took a critical look at the medium of television, in February, 1976. The findings of this experiment: boredom, non-fulfillment, helplessness in doing anything with the time on one's hands, even tears. In both cases, the return of the television set was longingly looked forward to.

A further example, similar to the experiment outlined above, of the West German citizen's dependence on television: the "Gesellschaft für rationelle Psychologie" was able to persuade 184 men and women, constituting a representative cross section of the population, to agree to abstinency from television for one year in return for a measure of compensation of a financial kind. None were able to persevere. "The most resolute family put an end to their state of distress without television after only five months." Unexpected side effects of the experiment: "Peaceable husbands didn't only beat their children but also their wives and sought pleasure away from home."[7]

Such dramatic consequences of television abstinency are perhaps atypical. Nonetheless, they indicate, albeit overpointedly, the extent to which people today are increasingly becoming dependent on television, something which would be apparent to everyone if television were not habitual. An apt characterization of such a commonplace experience is to be found in a leading story published in *Der Spiegel*:

> In the meantime, the Sunday ride in the car doesn't last as long, the walk in the woods with the family has become more infrequent. If grandmother doesn't have a TV-set, the grandchildren are reluctant to pay her a visit—and if they do, then only briefly. For at home with the people from the Shiloh ranch things are at their nicest.[8]

Here one sees signs of a general and for the time being still undifferentiated change in leisure activities conditioned by television that can be characterized as follows:

1. The West German citizen increasingly spends leisure time on habitualized activity.
2. The use of mass media takes first place among various forms of habitualized leisure activity.
3. In comparison with other mass media, television is the most attractive medium and its use reduces the time spent on a range of other activities.

With regard to television, statistical evidence helps to underline this state of affairs. A time-budget study in 1970/71, commissioned by the ARD and ZDF, with a sample consisting of 16,277 West Germans, arrived at the following conclusion concerning the relationship between leisure and media use as well as media use and watching television.

RELATIONSHIP BETWEEN LEISURE AND MEDIA USE, MEDIA USE
AND TELEVISION CONSUMPTION[9]

Day of the Week	A Leisure hrs. mins.	B Media use hrs. mins.	B as a % of A	C Television hrs. mins.	C as a % of B
Weekdays	6 : 12	3 : 06	50.0	1 : 36	51.6
Saturdays	8 : 35	4 : 03	47.2	2 : 26	60.1
Sundays	9 : 17	4 : 07	44.3	2 : 43	66.0
Average per day	6 : 58	3 : 22	48.3	1 : 53	55.9

The above table shows that the West German youth and adult population (the respondents were aged fourteen and above) spend approximately half of their leisure time on media use. The differences between the percentages for weekdays and weekends constitute no more than slight fluctuations from the mean. Furthermore, television, with an average of 55.9 percent accounts for a large share of total media consumption. What is more, on Sundays a maximum 66 percent share was registered. The most recent studies available show that the average time spent every day on watching television has risen to 2 hours and 11 minutes (1972).[10] Watching television is herewith third in the list of activities governing everyday life (i.e., after sleep and work).

The research findings of the mid-1960s indicating that the level of television consumption was reciprocally related to social and educational status do not apply any more, nor indeed did they for the late sixties. Indeed the stereotyped common view, that television is an easy way of passing the time away especially as far as the lower social strata are concerned, will prove difficult to verify today in such a categorical form. During the course of its development it has proved possible for television to dissipate the initial scepticism of higher social groups and intellectuals with which it was confronted. The proportion of time spent watching television in relation to other media activities is by and large the same for all social and educational strata within society.[11] In this context, however, it is interesting to note that a study into the significance of television in the lives of adults showed that precisely those recipients who were more highly educated regarded the medium with ambivalent feelings: "On the one hand, viewing was a pleasant experience, on the other, one had the feeling that it was a waste of time, that one was lazy, that the time so used was lost. Television is thus a source of conflict between doing as one likes and doing what one thinks should actually be done."[12] In connection with this finding dating back to 1968, it remains to be ascertained if and to what extent a functional change has taken place or is still taking place in television as a leisure activity as far as both the recipient and program structure are concerned.

The press, radio and television hardly differ from one another in their fundamental public communication aims. Their content matter is equally determined by three factors: information, commentary and entertainment. Of course, there are considerable deviations with regard to the respective accents set that express themselves in the different weighting given to such aims. This is demonstrated by the fact that television in particular is playing a continually more and more important role in the process of education and further education. Generally it can be said that the daily press and within certain limits serious journals and magazines are committed mainly to information, whereas average radio and television programming is primarily committed to entertainment—even though broadcasting organizations might not say so explicitly or readily admit that this is the case. This observation is not connected with any kind of value judgment but only points to differing emphases, which are visible and necessary, reflecting the expectations recipients have with respect to each individual medium. There is adequate support for the view that such differing emphases are related to the recipient's consumer habits and desires. Two studies carried out during the mid-1960s both conclude that youths (72 percent) as well as adults (80 percent) see television primarily as a means of entertainment.[13] This almost certainly still applies today. Naturally television is still used mainly as a form of entertaining diversion and unproblematical passing away the time. At the same time, however, certain data—which must be interpreted with caution—seem to indicate the beginnings of a change in the way the audience approaches television: the medium seems to be gaining relative importance as a source of information while at the same time losing importance as a source of relaxation and distraction. Thus, for instance, an ARD-media analysis established that between 1964 and 1970 the percentage of those who saw television primarily as a source of relaxation and distraction fell from 76 percent to 71 percent and the percentage of those who wished to forget their everyday worries and cares through means of television from 65 percent to 52 percent.[14] On the other hand, it must be noted that the proportion of those who do not see television as a source of information rose by 1974 to 55 percent.[15]

As a whole, television in the Federal Republic of Germany must today be considered, in addition to its outstanding significance as far as entertainment is concerned, in its capacity as the most important means of information within the media spectrum, both with regard to the range and currency of information supply and the credibility of content. In this context, however, it must be understood that the recipient uses press, radio and television in such a way that they complement rather than compete with each other in the supply of information. The final or total amount of information he possesses on a particular topic is thus a mosaic of the bits of information supplied by a number of media. In the process of gathering information about a particular topic, the first source as a rule is television (in 1964 for 36 percent and in 1974 for 63 percent of the audience).[16] The credibility attributed to television, however, suggests a largely uncritical and unreflectingly trusting approach or attitude toward the medium. The viewer believes that he has a check on the reliability of what is being said through means of the synchronously transmitted pictures. This is because pictures *a priori* possess greater documentary value and a large degree of authenticity that cannot be manipulated, an erroneous assumption.

The fact that television is increasingly being put to systematic use for educational purposes is responsible above all for the gradual improvement in the medium's image outlined above; it is a medium that one is beginning to see as a means of transferring knowledge and not only of providing entertainment. Especially the Third Program, produced by the ARD, but also the ZDF (the two television organizations in West Germany) present a wide variety of educational programs designed for children below school-age, for schools, occupational training and further training, adult education and, in all probability as far as the future is concerned, even university level education within the framework of the non-residential university at Hagen.

Education should really be subsumed under information, rather than be separated from one another as the ZDF's program objectives with which it was commissioned—stipulating that programs should supply comprehensive information, stimulating entertainment, and education—would seem to suggest, for the simple reason that the transmission of educational content constitutes a form of information supply. This is stressed by Schardt, who emphasizes that television can only begin to impart education when information and education have points of departure in common.

> Our present notions of education which are orientated toward the self-fulfillment and development of man, notions which thus attach great importance to his immediate social and intellectual environment, can be combined with television's primary objective—the supply of information—without difficulty. The objectives of information and education prescribe the same subject matter and occurrences insofar as both are designed to enable one to observe and understand the environment and to impart facts, their interrelationships and ideas.[17]

The increased attention paid to a systematic supply of educational programs by West German broadcasting organizations is understandable against the background of the problems facing education during the mid-1960s, when the country seemed to be threatened by an educational catastrophe both in terms of an acute shortage of teachers and a lack of high school graduates. And, as is so frequently the case when deficits in the educational system become apparent, the technical media were called upon to help out, something which had hitherto been difficult to effect. Television was prepared to meet this challenge and its contributions were readily accepted by politicians and experts in the field of education. Educational programs, which became more varied and specialized in time both in form and content, can be categorized with respect to their didactic intentions as follows:

1. *Enrichment programs,* which tackle a single topic either isolatedly or together with other topics within the context of a series on some general theme (e.g., the German program *Rappelkiste,* for children below school age).
2. *Contextual programs,* mostly in serial form, designed for use within official curricula but which can be slotted into larger courses of instruction (mainly conceived for school broadcasts).
3. *Program series constituting independent courses,* using supplementary media, whose individual sequels are related to one another (e.g., a computer-programming course).
4. *Complete systems of instruction* with a complex, systematically designed syllabus, also using supplementary media, some leading to an officially recognized degree or qualification (e.g., the West German *Telekolleg,* a complete course leading to a technical school-leaving certificate or a technical college degree).

West German television's supply of instructional programs has become so manifold and complex during the past few years that it was recently decided to publish a separate program journal in addition to the long-established general program magazines, with the intention of supplying an orderly preview and survey of the educational programs to be shown on television.[18]

However, and in conclusion, the following must be said: Television's numerous activities in the field of education should not be overestimated as far as its efficiency as an instructional medium is concerned. There is no reason at all for euphoria, especially when one measures television's performance against its claim—which can be heard again and again—that it can guarantee a greater measure of equal opportunity within the educational system. As a rule, television hasn't succeeded in helping educationally underpriviledged viewers overcome their language and educational barriers or in persuading precisely those people for whom further education is primarily intended to follow the courses it transmits. Thus, a functional change in television from a pure entertainment medium to one that incorporates both entertainment and education to an equal degree can be observed when one looks at the program structure and the way in which it is reflected in audience research findings. However, we still have a long way to go before educational programs are used on a wide basis during leisure hours.

NOTES

[1] Cf. H. Lüdtke, *Freizeit in der Industriegesellschaft* (Opladen [West Germany], 1972), p. 13.

[2] Cf. L. A. Dexter, "The Basis of Mass Communications in Society," in *People, Society and Mass Communications*, eds. L. A. Dexter and D. M. White (London and New York, 1964), pp. 3–5.

[3] H. Holzer, *Gescheiterte Aufklärung* (München [West Germany], 1972), pp. 36 f.

[4] Cf. H. W. Opaschowski, *Pädagogik der Freizeit* (Bad Heilbrunn [West Germany], 1976), pp. 80 f.

[5] Source of data: "Freizeit und Massenmedien," in *Media Perspektiven*, no. 4 (1971): 81; *Media Perspektiven: Daten zur Mediensituation in der Bundesrepublik* (special number) (Frankfurt, 1977): 1, 10, 17.

[6] *ZDF Presse*, 9. Woche: 23. bis 29. Februar 1976, p. 22.

[7] J. Rzitka, *Manipulieren uns die Massenmedien?* (München, n. d.), p. 17.

[8] "Vorm Schlafengehen kommt der Kommissar," in *Der Spiegel*, no. 4 (1972): 52.

[9] The data are taken from Tables 15–18, in D. Stolte, ed., *Das Fernsehen und sein Publikum* (Mainz [West Germany], 1973), pp. 110–19. This time-budget study was primarily concerned with investigating television viewers' daily routine. The use of media as part of this routine was consequently not looked at in detail—e.g., as in more specialized studies using memory aids—with the result that lower values were recorded for media use than would otherwise have been the case.

[10] *Media Perspektiven: Daten zur Mediensituation*, pp. 1, 10, 17.

[11] D. Stolte, ed., *Das Fernsehen*, pp. 116, 123.

[12] Hans-Bredow-Institut, ed., *Fernsehen im Leben der Erwachsenen* (Hamburg, 1968), p. 203.

[13] Cf. J. Hüther, "Jugend—Fernsehen—Politik," in *Hearing 4* (Bonn, 1970), *Fernsehen im Leben der Erwachsenen*, p. 202.

[14] Cf. H. W. Opaschowski, *Padagogik der Freizeit*, p. 61.

[15] *Media Perspektiven: Daten zur Mediensituation in der Bundesrepublik.* (Frankfurt, 1975), p. 18.

[16] *Ibid.*

[17] A. Schardt, "Bildung durchs Fernsehen," in *Fernsehen. Ein Medium sieht sich selbst*, eds. W. Brüssau *et al* (Mainz, 1976), p. 293.

[18] *Sehen, Hören, Lesen*, Vorschau auf Bildungsprogramme im Fernsehen. The first number of this new quarterly was published in autumn, 1977.

Part Three

⭐⭐⭐⭐

ENTERTAINMENT
AND THEORY

Wilmont Haacke:

Mass Media—the Playground for Grown-Ups

☆ JOHANN WOLFGANG VON GOETHE, strolling in front of the city walls on Easter Sunday, philosophized on man's dependence on play and entertainment (*Faust I*). Adalbert Stifter too embroiders on this theme in his *Wien und die Wiener in Bildern aus dem Leben* (*Vienna and the Viennese; Scenes from Daily Life*) (Pesth, 1844). Both come essentially to the conclusion that relaxing and amusing forms of entertainment must be provided for the working people so that they may remain human. A socially engaged man himself, Stifter writes: ". . . and I am convinced that the majority of people have no choice but to spend the greater part of their lives in crowded urban factories doing a dull job and that they should be entitled to—and even be encouraged to—look about and amuse themselves once in a while."

Even the severest critics cannot change the fact that the daily ration of light entertainment dispensed by newspaper, magazine, movie, radio and television contributes to people's happiness and even broadens their horizon. Several socio-psychological studies have disclosed that audiences of mass media tend to retain the positive impressions rather than the negative ones, both during the performance and afterwards. Negative influences, on the other hand, can only be traced afterwards.[1]

Observing the bustling Sunday crowds in Vienna's *Prater* and rejoicing with them, Stifter remarks: "This, then, is healthy and real popular entertainment which the people provide for themselves; it does them a lot of good . . ." Modern people, however, are rarely able to really enjoy their ever increasing leisure time either in the evening or daring the weekend. The mass media *must* therefore make a combined effort—though each in its own way—to produce almost continuous light entertainment for the masses, without dulling their

▶ This article originally was published under the heading "Some sociological reflections on mass media" in *Gazette—International Journal of Mass Communication Studies* XVII, No. 1/2 (Deventer [The Netherlands], 1971): 45–50; reprinted here with kind permission of the author, Dr. Wilmont Haacke, professor emeritus of the University of Göttingen (Germany).

minds. Stifter notes that "since it must carry them through the whole of next week these people tend to prefer the wine of their amusement rather strong and sour."

Recent sociological findings have taught us that the mass media with their light programs greatly help people reduce their frustrations. Why not grant them their therapeutic value? In his amusing treatise, Stifter mentions that "a happy people is a good people and we, on the banks of the Danube, are well aware of the fact; so we are full of joy that we find ourselves in this happy situation where work and fun are so intermingled that one will never know which is the main interest of the Viennese." [2]

For all these reasons, the classic rulers provided circuses for their soldiers and civilians, the medieval nobles took part in tournaments for the *hoi polloi*, and the churches, cities and princes built theatres for the people. These enterprises were culturally and politically rewarding and Professor Lamprecht, the historiographer, sounds downright silly when he condescendingly writes that "any self-respecting prince used to employ as many 'court intellectuals' as 'court servants.' They used to 'keep' academies, learned societies and colleges just as they kept studs, dancers and harems." [3] Professor Lamprecht seems to be referring to the fact that it was not unusual that the dean of a college or some other university official was appointed court jester and that this post became his chief source of income. Disguised, these men were often able to speak up. It was, after all, their job to make scathing remarks. Thus they could occasionally bring about the correction of some social abuse. Later, in the nineteenth and twentieth centuries, cabaret artists carried on the court jesters' tradition. Of course, providing entertainment is by no means their main object, but they make it their business to ridicule officious and boastful politicians, whether they drive a carriage-and-six or a Daimler Saloon. Whether the audience is small or large, they are there to criticize injustice without restrain.

Keeping their example in mind, we have come to interpret well-devised entertainment as more than mere diversifying amusement and want it to contain some food for thought. The audience is meant to take part in the process of thought, not, to be sure, on a higher but on a more advanced, a more humane level. Indeed, in his day, the great clown Grock—*alias* Adrian Wettach Ph.D.—struggling in the arena with the impeding objects, was better known than his colleague Heidegger and his difficult linguistics. Maybe one day somebody will publish a thesis on the publicity value and influence of clowns.

Court jesters, cabaret artists, clowns and other entertainers are publicity men. Have they always been considered intellectuals as well, as René König kindly suggests when he writes that "the development of our modern industrial society has caused the economic integration of the professions: journalists, authors, literary men and even artists in political cabarets have become part of it."? [4] Especially the cabaret artists, closely resembling leader writers, authors, publishers and the like, freely express an opinion about world affairs that may be their own or somebody elses. The top people in these professions are the men and women who manage to give their seemingly esoteric but actually practical views on everyday occurrences with charm and without malice. All do their mental acrobatics in front of their audience and only the most sophisticated among them scorn the safety net: they all use some sort of camouflage. Ideologists are rarely flatterers; they therefore never meet with approval or build up a following. Great wits, however, especially the clerical humorists (i.e., Ulrich Megerle, *alias* Abraham a Santa Clara), have always managed to convert the great masses. Originality not being their trade, government officials had better keep off the stage.

For a publication to carry weight it must contain an element of entertainment, as Justus Möser argued in his columns in the *Wöchentliche Osnabrücker Anzeigen* (1766–11782). In these articles he suggests that dictated rules and censorship should be replaced by information that the people are likely to appreciate, understand, and sympathize with.[5]

Republished in book form, Möser's articles have been preserved for later generations under the name of *Patriotische Phantasien* (*Patriotic Phantasies*), (1774–1786). Even a man like Goethe found the four volumes fascinating.[6] A government official of the grand duchy of Weimar himself, Goethe had made a lifelong study of the problems of putting a government decision before the people to its best advantage. He actually practiced what we now call public relations, often inserting some entertaining remark in his texts. He was absolutely convinced that only pleasant prose would help people make the right decisions. Möser's passionate publications made him comment:

> A real professional, addressing the people in weekly publications, telling them what any well-meaning and considerate government puts into practice or at least tries to put into practice; explaining everything to all, not didactically but pleasantly.

In the heyday of German absolutism, Justus Möser realized that the best way to execute an unpopular measure is to make it sound pleasant. Any official would be well advised to read Goethe's portrait of Möser:

> Always superior to his subject, he manages to point out the bright side of serious problems. Sometimes he wears a mask and other times he doesn't. Cheerfully, often slightly ironical, he puts his arguments before his readers. An efficient man, he can be blunt and passionate, honest and well-meaning; with all these qualities well balanced, we cannot but admire his spirited skill and good taste. The choice of his subjects and his understanding and humorous treatment of them are so thorough that I know of no author to compare him with but Franklin.[7]

Nor has Goethe been his only admirer. The other media have long since developed their own ways to attract a public by providing light entertainment. Walter Hagemann, a political journalist of long standing, evidently never felt the charm of the feature pages when he argues in his otherwise excellent book *Grundzügen der Publizistik* (*Basic concepts of Journalism*) that "not all the items in the printed press are there by rights." According to *Herr* Hagemann, all incidental stories, sketches and other items that happen to drift into the *symbiosis* of a newspaper should be relegated to the feature pages.[8] I could not disagree more.

All able newspaper men—Caspar von Stieler calls them *Zeitunger* ("newspaperists")—mix the daily ration of colorful, fancy writing with the drabber items about humdrum events in order to break the monotony and banality of day-by-day journalism.

Paul Fechter, who, among other things, played a major role in the creation of the feature pages of the *Berliner Tageblatt,* the *Deutsche Allgemeine Zeitung,* the *Deutsche Rundschau* and lately the *Neue Linie,* has often declared that the only readable part of a newspaper was the feature pages.[9] With this remark he apostrophized the standardized press of Nazi Germany after 1933. Even before the Olympic Games of 1936, the voice of publicity in Germany on the subjects of government, industry and sports sounded like a loud brass band; still, some clever feature editors managed to produce the more subdued tones of chamber music in the areas of culture, and even sometimes to make some delicate political joke.

Apart from the publication of an abundance of news items, somewhat less comment, and some very cautiously dosed attempts at opinion forming, newspapers have always given pride of place to sensational journalism. Only after these functions had been completed did publishers turn to the more edifying subjects. Professional moralists have remarked that in this respect the two older media are increasingly following the example of the new ones and do so to their advantage.

Among the different kinds of motion pictures, the light and entertaining ones have for some time now been making the greatest progress, their producers being well aware of the advantages of this sort of entertainment.[10] As for radio programs, light music takes up far more time than all the other programs together and always has. Television developed new and interesting ways to hold the attention of its audience. Imitating the classic authors, it reaches its effect by involving the audience in the action on the screen. Modern people rediscover the magic of this old gimmick. How is it possible that people who willingly left their comfortable homes to be mere spectators will now happily take part in the action? Schiller provides the answer to this question in section XV of his *Briefe über die ästhetische Erziehung des Menschen (Letters on the Esthetic Education of Man)*: ". . . and it happens to be so that man is only willing to play when he is human in the fullest meaning of the word, and only when he is playing is he really human." Man dies but *homo ludens* is immortal.[11]

Only the publicity media make the individual feel regularly that he is appreciated as an actor even if he indulges in vulgar encounters like football matches. Every evening again the mass media tell him that he is not just a fool.

In this sense we have come to regard the contemporary mass media as a unique yet almost everlasting playground for grown-ups. Unlike other public gardens, it does not close at sundown; it rather tends to come into its own at that time of the day. Psychotherapists generally agree that the light entertainment offered by the mass media act as a remedy for frustration. It is remarkable that they operate at the same level as the magazines.[12] But they also appeal to people's higher feelings as Walter Hagemann reports in his *Publizistik im Dritten Reich* (*Publicity During the Third Reich*) (Hamburg, 1948).

Give the people circuses; afterwards it will be so much easier to arouse their passions, which can and have been used to make them war-minded. Who would have thought of it as the playground for grown-ups?

NOTES

[1] Alphons Silbermann, *Bildschirm und Wirklichkeit. Über Presse und Fernsehen in Gegenwart und Zukunft* (Berlin–Frankfurt–Vienna, 1966); cf. also Alphons Silbermann, *Vorteile und Nachteile des kommerziellen Fernsehens. Eine soziologische Studie* (Düsseldorf–Vienna, 1968).

[2] Adalbert Stifter, *Wien und die Wiener in Bildern aus dem Leben* (Pesth–Budapest, 1844), *passim.*; Wilmont Haacke, *Handbuch des Feuilletons I–III* (Emsdetten, 1951–53).

[3] Karl Lamprecht, *Deutsche Geschichte der neueren Zeit* III (Berlin, 1910).

[4] René König, *Soziologische Orientierungen. Vorträge und Aufsätze* (Cologne–Berlin, 1965), p. 242.

[5] Paul Göttsching, *Justus Mösers Entwicklung zum Publizisten. Mösers Schrifttum 1757–1766.* Ph.D. diss. (Frankfurt, a. M., 1935; Frankfurt, 1935); Otto Hatzig, *Justus Möser als Staatsmann und Publizist* (Hannover–Leipzig, 1909); Wolfgang Hollmann, *Justus Mösers Zeitungsidee und ihre Verwirklichung.* Ph.D. diss. (Heidelberg, 1937; München, 1937); Rudolf Lenzing, *Von Möser bis Stüve. Ein Jahrhundert Osnabrücker Pressegeschichte als Spiegel des Bürgertums.* Ph.D. diss. (Münster, 1925; Osnabrück, 1925).; Wilmont Haacke, *Die politische Zeitschrift 1665–1965* (Stuttgart, 1968); *Ibid., Publizistik und Gesellschaft* (Stuttgart, 1970).

[6] Cf. *Allgemeine Deutsche Biographie* XXII (Leipzig, 1885), pp. 385 *ff.*

[7] Johann Wolfgang von Goethe, *Dichtung und Wahrheit,* here quoted from his *Complete Works* XXVI (Stuttgart–Tübingen, 1829), pp. 239 *f.*; Wilmont Haacke, "Das Feuilleton des 20. Jahrhunderts", in *Publizistik* 23, No. 3 (Konstanz, 1978): 285–312.

[8] Walter Hagemann, *Grundzüge der Publizistik,* 2nd ed., ed. Henk Prakke (Münster i. W., 1966), pp. 49 *ff.*

[9] Paul Fechter, "Dichtung und Journalismus," in *Die Weltliteratur der Gegenwart,* II (Leipzig, 1924), pp. 209 *ff.*

[10] Alphons Silbermann, "Der arme deutsche Film," in *Ketzereien eines Soziologen. Kritische Äusserungen zu Fragen unserer Zeit* (Vienna–Düsseldorf, 1967), pp. 57 *f.*

[11] Johan Huizinga, *Homo Ludens* (Amsterdam, 1939).

[12] Cf. " 'Der Moloch muss gefüttert werden.' Gespräche mit Günter Gaus," in *Der Spiegel* (Hamburg) XXII, no. 29 (July 15, 1968): 86 *ff.*

Hendricus Johannes Prakke:

The "Socius" Function of the Press

☆ THE EXTENSION OF the discipline *press studies* ("Zeitungswissenschaft") to that of *publicistics* (i.e., public communication) puts old problems into a new perspective. This is the case, for instance, when we ask ourselves which functions in the publicistic process the communicator has in relation to the recipient.

The study of the press always focused its attention on the supply of news. The communicator supplies news to the recipient: in this capacity he acts as informer. To news, the former adds explanations and commentary: here he acts as commentator. However, he also acts in a further and third capacity when he offers entertainment. This I labeled the "socius function," a term I introduced in my Groningen lectures.[1] With film and broadcasting (that likewise inform and comment through newsreel, news broadcasts and radio and television commentary), this third function has come to the fore most clearly. Although it also manifests itself in the press, press studies have only considered this function in passing.

In his doctoral dissertation,[2] the Dutch professor Maarten Rooij (former chief editor of the N.R.C.—*Nieuwe Rotterdamse Courant*—the Dutch equivalent to *The Times*) also discussed the general "exigencies of the saleability" of a newspaper and concluded that the newsreading public in civilized society demands above all satisfaction of the individual's "need to know about the current circumstances in which he finds himself."[3] For Rooij, the inclusion of a certain amount of entertaining reading matter constitutes one of the exigencies of saleability. "The need for relaxation," he writes, "manifests itself throughout the entire readership spectrum." Curiously, however, when he states that "with good reason one wants to relieve tension, aroused by so many frequently disagreeable news items, by continuing to read one and the same paper,"[4] he seems to subsume the need for entertainment under the need for news.

▶ This article was first published in *Publizistik* 5, no. 6 (Bremen [West Germany], 1960): 556–60. It is reprinted here with the kind permission of the author. Dr. Hendricus J. Prakke was Professor of Publicistics at the University of Münster (West Germany) until his retirement in 1969.

Here the element of entertainment has been adapted much too much so as to conform to the "civilized" approach (i.e., looking at the press as informer-commentator). Although consistently neglected by the historiography of the press, the element of entertainment already had a role to play in the Dutch newspapers of the eighteenth century. Later, especially with the democratization of our society as a consequence of which the public at large took to newspaper reading, its affective significance became correspondingly more important. *This element of conviviality taken by itself is also a function of the press and as such we must venture to look into the significance of this third function, the socius function, more closely.* Where is the dividing line between "being informed" and "being thrilled"?

The Dutch author, Jef Last, tells us that in present-day Bali the "little man" (he is described as a "viewer of moments") prefers an American "Western" when he doesn't have the opportunity to see an Indonesian or Malaysian film.[5] The more fighting and killing, the better. "From such films the Indonesian forms his image of the American: a guy who drinks, kisses, shoots and thereby pockets the whole world. No American propaganda, however many millions are invested, can ever counterbalance the Indonesian contempt for the white man that the American film induces." And, as Last further comments, "they believe that everything they see must correspond with the facts because it was photographed. Historical films, fictional films, documentary films—all have the same reality value, especially for the villager."

Just as in this case the occurrences on the screen become part of the viewers' "knowledge of current circumstances," so Jef Last relates how on the other hand that which is intended by the press to be a contribution to the knowledge of current circumstances is enjoyed by the same Balinese as a fascinating story.

> In the evening, the teacher is still to be seen at the crossroads reading old weeklies out loud which were sent to him by the Ministry of Information. The teacher ("Dalan") then talks about big politics, about American imperialism, and the Chinese People's Republic, as well as about the sins of the Dutch. His pupils still have little or no idea as to where America or China are to be found on the map, but their imagination transforms wicked America and good-natured Russia into characters who resemble the legendary heroes from the "Wajang Kulit," the popular Javanese puppet theatre. The heroes' shadows appear on the screen and disappear again, they fight using miraculous weapons, and the atom bomb is no more astonishing for the audience than the mountains *Ardjuna* flings into the air. It's a wonderful tale that lasts as long as the *Dalan* reads.

For the recipient in this case, *topical information and commentary become fiction, elements of entertainment, whereas the before-mentioned film fantasy becomes topical information.* The Belgian professor DeVolder states with good reason that topicality is not an attribute of an occurrence as such, but originates in the relationship between the occurrence and man.[6] It should by no means be thought that this interplay is a Balinese peculiarity! When the principal character in the television dramatization of Galsworthy's *Forsyte Saga* died, it was as if a world-famous "flesh-and-blood" person had passed away. A London newspaper brought the news with a headline, wording the day's tragic event: "Death of Soames Forsyte."

During the 1955 London newspaper strike, the *Manchester Guardian* (then still published in Manchester) suddenly found itself in great demand. How unfamiliar this newspaper—"the best English newspaper but one"—must have been in terms of supply and content for both the hardened *Times* reader and for the readers of the boulevard papers. Someone asked a reader of the *Manchester Guardian* if he could briefly have a look at the comic strip and received the reply in a somewhat detached manner: "The Manchester Guardian has no comics." Whereupon the former commented: "Blimey, you miss real newspapers, don't yer?" Without a comic strip no real newspaper!?

There are people whose thirst for news is directed in the first instance toward finding out about the latest adventures of their comic strip heroes. And there are readers who like to be informed about the achievements of their football heroes first thing on Monday morning, and who don't regard the Dutch newspaper *Trouw* as a newspaper because, as a matter of principle it doesn't report on Sunday's football events.

In trying to gauge what is really happening, the scholar must, when studying the recipient, start by differentiating between various groups, each of which has its own news requirements, even if he has to replace the pure journalistic concept of "news" in favor of another more general concept in the process: essentially a diluted concept of "news," unless he accepts that the newspaper includes an element of entertainment, a separate third function. It would be most convenient if experimental technique could supply us with a comprehensive picture as to all the functions of the press in modern human society. However, one cannot very well arrange the necessary preconditions: "Let us do without a newspaper in our locality for a while."

Berelson used the opportunity offered by a two-week strike by news delivery men (July, 1945) to research into the question: "What 'missing the paper' means."[7] Although the first more or less spontaneous reply of those subjects interviewed stressed the importance of the newspaper as a source of news, a closer look indicated that only about a third of the readers missed newspapers primarily for this reason. It was found that the modern newspaper fulfilled a number of different tasks. The study in question delineated the five most significant of these:

1. *Information about and the interpretation of public affairs* (also as a touchstone for personal opinion).
2. A *tool for daily living* (radio programs and film schedules, commercial reports, advertisements for women shoppers, embarkation timetables, family announcements, recipes, fashion reports, weather forecasts and so on).
3. *Respite* (without doubt many people find relief from the worries and

routine of everyday life in reading the news and "human interest" stories with which they can readily identify. It is the same form of "escapism" that is to be found underlying frequent cinema going and radio and television program consumption).

4. *Social prestige* (the newspaper has conversational value. Being informed, being able to take part in conversation increases the reader's prestige among social contacts).

5. *Social contact* (to the reader, the personal note of certain columns suggests personal contact with their authors. Some respondents indicated that they missed the newspaper because, so to speak, some of their friends resided in its pages). [8]

If the above categories are analyzed functionally, they can be assigned partly to the press's function as informer, partly to its function as commentator. Moreover, the press also manifests itself very clearly here in the above-mentioned third function, for which I proposed the term "socius function." The newspaper as a companion, as a conversationalist in one's leisure time who breaks the boring and tiresome monotony of everyday routine by injecting a taste or flavor of the other world, where something always happens, something shocking, something great, something different! Every day, at the same time, one can count on its coming, its cheerful prattle, its romanticized news features and its headline sensations. The newspaper knows what life, true life really is!

Or so it is able to suggest—through its pictures and features in editorial columns as well as in advertisements: about the use of nylon stockings and lipstick, for instance; the increasing familiarity with divorce and similar issues (contemporary matters of interest or relevance as far as many people are concerned). Its influence grows in those areas where customs and mores lose their hold—especially on the young generation. Influence—for better or for worse—depending on how one looks at things! "All of a sudden you see such neat little hats everywhere," I once heard someone say. "They must have been in *Libelle* (a widely read Dutch women's journal)." Newspapers have the same effect!

The newspaper gains the confidence of the masses for the very reason that it plays the role of a socius (companion) rather than that of a commentator. In the first instance, people buy their favorite newspaper, which cannot be exchanged satisfactorily for any other newspaper whatsoever: it is *the* paper that has been brought in from the outside world and assimilated with one's personal environment, one's own familiar little universe.

Essentially, this tripartition of press functions runs parallel with the distinctions the German professor Walter Hagemann drew between his three categories: 1) news, 2) opinion, 3) novelties (news) in the sense of entertainment (sensation). [9] Wilbur Schramm's summary of the three aims of communication also invites comparison: the sharing 1) of information, 2) of an idea or 3) of an attitude. [10] Isn't "sharing an attitude" implicit in the socius function?

Here above all, a parallel—which invites comparative study—can be drawn between the press and other media of communications; also, surely, to the advantage of the press, which has accepted the third function in practice but which hasn't adequately recognized its significance theoretically. When dealing with this particular aspect, one shouldn't only consider those groups that satisfy their need to "know about current circumstances" differently than intellectuals. The intellectual also has his favorite newspaper and doesn't always look for news in the journalistic sense straight away. Usually, he too has his special friends who reside in its pages: columnists and cartoon heroes. So it is in the case of the above-mentioned Dutch quality newspaper, the N.R.C., which publishes an animal cartoon series, one of whose characters is a certain *Ollie B. Bommel*, a "gentleman of standing." Some of his characteristic sayings have occasionally been quoted even in our parliament. Thus the intellectual also experiences his daily puppet show, his "Wajang Kulit," despite the excuses he might try to make (e.g., that Mr. *Bommel's* adventures with robots of different kinds are disguised representations of current issues and as such have reality value).

A striking example of the peculiar relationship that may develop between the newspaper and reader—the total assimilation into the immediate personal environment—is given by the American author Hemingway in his novel *The Old Man and the Sea*.[11] Through following newspaper accounts of baseball matches, a lonesome old fisherman has developed a tremendous admiration for the crack, Di Maggio, whose father was also reported to be a fisherman. During his last great struggle—with a swordfish—it was this very character, whose almost physical presence he feels during the fight, that renders inspiration and support. Baseball heroes, as a critic suggested, became heroes of *Olympus* in the old man's eyes.

Isn't the press, supported by other mass media, the modern authority that canonizes boxers and statesmen alike after presenting them as glamor boys and transforming them into VIPs? Doesn't it create new sagas and legends in the same way that it may passionately treat a Napoleon or a Rembrandt, a Luther or a "Hauptmann von Köpenick,"[12] when some event or issue awakens new interest in these characters?

Indeed, it is in its socius function that the newspaper has much in common with film and broadcasting. Here, at a deeper level, it might perhaps be possible to gain much more insight into the loneliness and God-foresaken nature of modern man, which is at the root of our present-day crisis of culture. What is certain is that a journalist in this very function has the opportunity to pass on and stereotype, practically unnoticed, day after day, part of his own outlook on life. Being conscious of this power, he must beware of distorting reality and attempt to meet public taste with more valuable material and moral support than the world-known recipe of *war, sex and crime*. He will feel the need to look for a codex regulating the selection and relay of material based on a higher estimation of his public's requirements and inspired by the ambition to turn more aspiring topics into fascinating reading matter for a greater number of people; in short, he will feel the need for communications' ethics.

If we succeed in improving our understanding of the effects of the various media of communications in terms of their socius function, the resulting contrast and comparisons between the press and other media will prove fruitful for the discipline press studies; and above all, for the press itself, which, if it intends to maintain and confirm its publicistic primacy, has to remain conscious of its cultural responsibility in "society's dialogue."

To draw our conclusion: the extension of the discipline press studies to that of publicistics puts old problems into a new perspective. In particular, the functional theory of the press can thus be clarified to a great extent if we treat the socius function as an independent third factor governing the relationship between communicator and recipient.

NOTES

[1] H. J. Prakke, "Van Perswetenschap tot Publicistiek." Public lecture at the University of Groningen, Netherlands, 18th October, 1956 (Assen, (Netherlands, 1956), p. 35.

[2] M. Rooij, *Het economisch-sociale beeld van het dagbladbedrijf in Nederland* Ph.D., University of Rotterdam (Leiden, Netherlands, 1956), p. 63.

[3] *Ibid.*, p. 70.

[4] *Ibid.*, p. 63.

[5] Jef Last, *Bali in de Kentering* (Amsterdam, 1955), pp. 167–68.

[6] N. Devolder, *De Ethiek van de Pers* (Leuven, 1952), p. 16.

[7] Bernard Berelson, *What "Missing the Newspaper" Means. Communications Research 1948–1949* (New York, 1949), p. 111. Reprinted in Wilbur Schramm, *The Process and Effects of Mass Communications* (Urbana, 1955), p. 36.

[8] *Ibid.* pp. 40–42.

[9] Walter Hagemann, *Grundzüge der Publizistik* (Münster, 1947), p. 20. Re-edition (Hagemann-Prakke, 1966), p. 37.

[10] Wilbur Schramm, *The Process and Effects of Mass Communications.* (Urbana, 1955), p. 3.

[11] Ernest Hemingway, *The Old Man and the Sea* (London, 1952).

[12] "Der Hauptmann von Köpenick," revived in a German film in 1956. Text: Carl Zuckmayer and Helmut Käutner; direction: Helmut Käutner; leading part: Heinz Rühmann. Premiere in Cologne on the 16th August, 1956.

William Stephenson:

The Ludenic Theory of Newsreading

☆ IN THE PAST, newspaper reading has been studied from the standpoint of broad functions it may serve and not, usually, from a theoretical standpoint. Berelson,[1] for example, concludes that modern newspapers serve several roles for their readers. They provide information about, and interpretation of, public affairs; they are a direct aid in everyday life—for radio and TV programs, movies, business news, advertisements, obituary notices, and so on. They also may serve an *escape function*, transporting the reader, through comics and human interest stories, outside his "own world." They give information about social affairs, and have a vicarious function in matters of sensationalism, scandals and gossip generally. Kingsbury and Hart,[2] likewise, distinguish between "socialized" and "sensational" news: the former concerns serious matters of the world—foreign affairs, citizenship and such—while sensational journalism deals with sex, money sensations, salacious martial affairs and the like.

More recently, attention has been given to reasons of a more theoretical, if not speculative, kind for newspaper reading. Berelson, for example, considered that reading itself can be "a strongly and pleasurably motivated act"; mention was made of its possible *oral* character (an adult pacifier). He mentions, also, the relation of newspaper reading to feelings of insecurity: the individual feels lost without a newspaper because "he doesn't know what is going on." Motivation research[3] has suggested that people feel they have lost touch with things during the night, and that a newspaper re-establishes their world for them in the morning. The average person, according to this view, thinks of the world as a fearful place, he awakens in the morning in a state of tension, and, concerned about the unknown, needs a newspaper to make him "feel better." Berelson and others have also drawn attention to the *ritualistic*, near-compulsive character of some newspaper reading. More significant is the observation

▶ The article originally appeared in *Journalism Quarterly* 41, no. 3 (Iowa City, 1964): 367–74 and is reprinted here with the kind permission of the publishers. Dr. Stephenson was Distinguished Research Professor at the School of Journalism, University of Missouri until his recent retirement.

by Janowitz[4] that a community newspaper not only supplies content for parents grappling with children, but that it tends to be supportive of their way of life.

Berelson, Kingsbury and Hart, Janowitz and others in this field of endeavor all discover facts, all true in their way; and in some cases plausible enough explanations are offered for their truths. But the facts are not necessarily of greatest theoretical interest.

Nor do theories of learning do justice to the facts of newsreading. Kay,[5] for example, proposes that the conscious, (and sometimes the unconscious) motive for all newsreading is to obtain new information, either to apply toward the solution of a problem, or "because it evokes images that are different in some degree from images already stored in the reader's memory." He adds that if a reader knew beforehand what a paper contains, there would seem to be no reason for reading it. On the contrary, so it seems to the present author, people are apt to want to read about something they already know about: they see a football match and then are doubly pleased to see it again on a television rerun; they read about it again the next day in the newspaper and are delighted to read further commentaries about it the day after that.

Schramm[6] has dealt with newsreading in relation to pleasure-pain, in his well-known immediate versus delayed reward theory. One suffers the pain of today's bad news, Schramm proposes, in favor of a future pleasure, when one will be the better prepared to face reality.

The theory stems from Freud's pleasure-reality principle, which Szasz[7] has shown to be in need of considerable elaboration if it is to be an adequate theoretical formulation. In particular, Freud's theory was concerned with unconscious, "economic," *non*-ego-involving processes, whereas the enjoyment of newsreading seems, instead, to be highly ego-involving.

A New Theory of Newsreading

The present author came to feel, three years ago or more, that what had been long overlooked about newspaper reading was its *play*-like character.

What has to be explained about newsreading, fundamentally is the *enjoyment* it engenders. Even bad news is enjoyed, in the sense at least that *afterwards*, upon reflection, we can say that it was absorbing, interesting and enjoyed. So, also, *play* is enjoyed, though during the game we may be so intent upon winning that we are unaware of any feelings of pleasure. We are to propose that newsreading, in developed forms, is subjective play, and that communication-pleasure (a technical term used by Szasz) explains the enjoyment: newsreading is therefore attended, normally, by a certain inflation of the self. Newsreading, so regarded, is a complex subjective skill, the importance of which is little understood.

It is important not to confuse this theory with decision-making and games theory such as Kaplan[8] describes, following von Neumann and Morgenstern[9] and others. The theory of play is much more general than that of decision-making in games theory. Play has long been the subject of psychological and cultural anthropological study. Piaget's[10] research on the playing of children is of outstanding importance; and more recently Szasz,[11] following Mead, applies the theory of play to the myth of mental illness. Without knowledge of Szasz's work, we found it necessary to apply play theory to newsreading, the latter being a *modus operandi* for keeping in touch with one's world.

Theories of play abound. For some, it is abreactive, an outlet for harmful impulses; for others, it involves *wish-fulfillment*, as psychoanalytic doctrine teaches; for others it is fiction, to maintain one's feelings of personal values, as Janowitz suggested. All of these are fair-enough explanations of some aspects of newspaper reading. Reading about sex and money-marital scandals no doubt offers vicarious thrills to the starved and money-hungry. The hard-worked mother of a modern urban community, the cliche-ridden lower-middle classes of Warner and Henry's classic,[12] no doubt require some bolstering of the spirit. Freud's own view[13] on the nature of fantasy, however, was that only the neurotic have it, as children have the measles, and that in a sanely therapeutic world there would be no need of it.

Yet playing is "fun," as Huizinga[14] reminded us, and nothing in abreaction, or fantasy (which is as apt to be terrifying as not) or the maintenance of one's values explains, the fun of it.

The "pure play attitude," which Mead[15] described, is the stuff of myths, of religious pageantry and of the sport and fun of primitive peoples; but the child also plays, at being a mother, teacher, policeman, and the like. These persons are all around the child, affecting him; he depends upon his mother and teacher. Yet they are vague and uncertain figures for him. There is no *organization* in play of this pure kind: the child is one thing at one time and another at another without relation to the former—what he is at one moment does not determine what he is at another. The child is always *itself* in such play: he plays at being teacher, mother or policeman, but *he himself* is the mother, teacher or policeman.

Games have a different form. They are organized, with set rules, as in a game of baseball. What the player does in a game is in relation to a whole game, as anyone watching a Mickey Mantle can observe. More specifically, the player in a game has to put himself in the role of *others* in the game: he anticipates the catcher, pitcher or outfielder, and in doing so takes on the roles of these others, so that he is more than himself—these figures become part of his own *self-consciousness*, as Mead observed, so that one plays, in a game, with the attitudes of others.

Newsreading is to be thought of, therefore, as subjective play. In its most primitive form, one would have the "feebly socialized" newsreader, passing from one enticing bit of scandal to another entertaining murder; in a developed form, one has the skillful reader of the New York *Times*, pursuing his orderly way through a complex subjective minuet, in which there is order, elements of ritual and much else of a highly playful nature. The outcome is a feeling of enjoyment, as one says, *after* one has been so absorbed in the reading.

Application to Newsreading

Newspaper reading, subjectively regarded, has all the earmarks of play. At the "pure play" level, one reads one thing at one moment, and another at another, and what one reads at one moment has no relation to what is read at another. But with more developed reading, one is self-conscious for everything, as in a game.

Reading a newspaper is voluntary, not a task or duty: the reader can leave the paper alone if he wants to do so. Reading the paper is not part of the reader's ordinary, real life—rather, it is an interlude, an act of "pretending," a temporary event, satisfying itself and ending there. Thus commuter trains, at the New York terminus say, are full of newspapers, dropped and done with when the journey is over: but during the journey the men sit, two by two, each absorbed in his own newspaper—so silent, indeed, that one can readily discern the stranger on the commuter train (he will be talking to his fellow traveler). What indeed could be more mysterious than this sight, any morning, of hundreds of men, two by two, all behind newspapers, all deadly silent? There are rules in this game of newsreading.

Basically, one is disinterested, detached in some sense, when reading a newspaper. If one participates in a competition, or reads the classified ads for a specific purpose, or the departmental store pages for a particular need, these are additional to the newsreading *per se*. For the habitual newsreader, a newspaper stands outside the immediate satisfactions or needs of the day—it *interrupts* one's daytime activities rather than otherwise. Yet one reads a paper regularly, recurrently: it becomes part of one's way or style of life. As Cooley noticed, newspaper reading is *secluded*: one becomes absorbed in it—it has its place in the day somehow, whether it is at breakfast, or at a coffee break, in a commuter train, or in a chair with slippers in the evening. Thus it is hedged off from everyday surroundings, especially marked off, as a child marks out its space and time for a game of house.

Yet it creates a certain *order* in itself as in a game, a temporary grasp of the reader's own world, as the motivation researcher noticed. It casts a light spell upon one—not of rapture or capitivation, but of deep absorption, very like, again, the child's absorption in its game of house. It involves the reader in direct identifications, as he projects himself into the reading—the self is the "Hero," as in any T.A.T. test situation. One surrounds one's newspaper with an air of mystery, "secrecy" or "disguise": who hasn't claimed that his paper is better than the bare truth could attest? In reading a newspaper, who has not caught himself being self-important, or being effective (where others in the world outside are blundering along, making mistakes *we* wouldn't make)? Who hasn't caught glimpses of his own imcomparable good sense, his keener discernment and more accurate appraisal of affairs? The self is everywhere in the reading, as it is in the child playing. Down to the smallest detail, therefore, newspaper reading in its subjectivity seems to be play, mainly "pure play attitude," but with the attributes of a game in the rules and self-consciousness it deploys. We propose to call the theory *ludenic,* [16] meaning *playing* as inclusive of pure play and playing a game.

Practical Implications

These can be briefly dealt with immediately. A newspaper, from the ludenic standpoint, should lend itself freely to the attributes of play.

Characteristic of a game is its rules, its repetitions, its demand for fair play, the player has to be transported into a special place psychologically, if not physically as well, for the play. In newspapers this has its counterpart in certain fixed attributes of the format of a newspaper. Consider, for example, the old London *Times*. The familiar outside front page contained classified advertisements; one could find births, deaths, personals, each in its place, and always in the same place each day. The two center pages were next most distinctive, with the main news on the left page, and editorials and letters on the right. Even the editorials kept their orderliness: the fourth editorial was meant to be witty and to raise a smile. One knew exactly what to expect on each page, almost in every column on each page. All of this comports with high-order ludenic newsreading.

But how different are many newspapers today, where novelty replaces regularity! The Chicago *Daily News*, handsome in typography and chockful of feature articles, is a wilderness in comparison with the well-ordered gardening of the New York *Times*. Such is the way of the play of young children—one can never rely upon it being the same for very long. The most highly developed newspapers today, on our theoretical continuum, are the *Wall Street Journal*, the New York *Times* and (among news magazines) *Time*. Everything about *Time* is familiar. From play theory one would argue that if a paper fails to make it easy for a reader to play easily (i.e., according to rules implied by regular format), to that extent it is a spoil-sport. To that degree it is spoiling the "fun" of newsreading, the enjoyment of absorption in a newspaper.

Nothing may be more distracting, and destructive of a developed ludenic mood, than to have to chase a leading article or commentary into the remote pages of a newspaper. Nothing could be more hectic than the attempt, in many newspapers, to become magazines, with novelties and sensations on every other page, interspersed with advertising matter, which adds to the confusion—again, if one is a highly developed ludenic newsreader. On the other hand, the hectic appearance could be in tune with the lowly development of those newsreaders who are still at the primitive stage of "pure play." If research can indicate that such haphazardness, though appropriate for mere playful entertainment, is destructive of developed ludenic enjoyment, one might begin to see why the staid pages of the *Wall Street Journal*, or the New York *Times* or *Time* are so widely successful—not merely in circulation but in the enjoyment as such attending their reading, not merely in the wealth of their content but in the skillful development of the ludenic play they engender.

It is not merely a matter of familiarity. Nor does it suggest a return to old-fashioned or staid appearances. A newspaper or magazine, to fit a theory of developed newsreadership, should induce and encourage self-absorption. The editor thinks this means making it interesting, and no doubt there is something of the kind at issue. But interests, as in a primitive play or in a parade, may induce a scattering of the mind. Avid newsreading is contemplative rather than scatterbrained. What is essential is to induce absorption even if, as happens for the London *Mirror,* it is for ten minutes only of a reader's time.[17] Everything in developed newsreading has to be in proper place, and in proper sequence, so that one can move from foreign news to editorials, to letters, to comics and commentaries, in the orderly manner of a game. Photographs have to be in their orderly places, too, as well as advertisements. This is not to suggest regimentation of a newspaper's form, but merely that regard has to be paid to the newsreader's "play," and to the encouragement of developed newsreading habits.

Interview Material

Interviews with newsreaders bring to light a wide range of magical, ritualized and compulsive behaviors attending newspaper reading, as Berelson[18] has indicated. At least one woman in ten seems to read a newspaper backwards, from the back page forward, to judge by our data; some regularly read the commentaries from their end paragraphs forward. Not all such oddities, of course, are indicative of ludenic conditions—some people are compulsive readers, being satisfied, apparently, with reading nothing less than every word in the paper. There is a wealth of interview material, however, attesting directly to high-order ludenic newsreading: the following are typical statements made by men and women spontaneously about newsreading that are in line with the ludenic theory:

> I don't try to read the paper until I have time to get by myself.
> I wouldn't call newsreading *entertaining*: I feel the newspaper is a need and I feel satisfied once I've read it. My day isn't complete without it.
> My wife gets mad when I bury myself in a paper, and I don't want to be a cartoon husband, always hidden behind a newspaper. So I read at night when my wife is in bed. That's the time when I can be alone. . . . I get very involved. It's a habit.

Where, however, the reference is to purposes other than enjoyment, the remarks do not seem to indicate ludenic reading. The following, for example, are not of the unalloyed ludenic character:

> I just want a newspaper to give me the facts—in a way I can draw my own conclusions.
> I read papers because it is enjoyment of learning.
> I read to know what is going to happen: I'm curious.
> I want to see my predictions fulfilled.

These are not necessarily contra-indicative of ludenic reading, however, because the individuals may be giving *reasons* for newsreading, as rationalizations or the like, supraordinate to ludenic reading that goes on without their being aware of it.

The play in ludenic reading is serious, as a child's is. What is at issue is not the reading of a paper merely to "pass the time," to idle with, but reading as a serious interlude, about which one says that it is a habit, an enjoyable habit—but by enjoyment one means it is so as one looks back upon it. One may indeed smile, laugh or express alarm during the reading, all in attitude of concentration and absorption: it is afterwards, when one is reflective, that one speaks endearingly of the newsreading habit as something enjoyed. If one looks at interview material with play-theory in mind, one can usually readily discern the true play from mere entertainment (as "passing the time" or the like). However, there is no proof in such observations, however perspicacious the interviews.

Experimental Testing

A beginning has been made in experimental directions in various studies. In one case a Q sample (QS) of thirty-eight statements was collected from the writings of Berelson, Kingsbury and Hart, Schramm, Janowitz, Kay and others, each statement being a key concept about newspapers and newsreading. It was apparent that none of these concepts concerned newsreading in its subjective respects: all were *objective* (e.g., that "the news is different each day," that newspapers "serve educational purposes," "give a correct picture of the world," are "copious rather than discerning," "critically reflective," "biased," "report the interesting rather than the important," "have social consciousness," "perform an indispensable service for the government" and so on). These are objective in the sense of being attributes of the newspapers, not of the reader.

The present author added to QS statements that are subjective to the reader: that is, that newspapers are *enjoyable* to read, associated with *relaxation* and *leisure*, are *absorbing*, and that newsreading is a *habit* (you miss reading the paper if it doesn't come) and an *interlude* in one's everyday activities. All of these are in line with ludenic theory, and are clearly "human," involving one's feelings and understandings. The Q-sample thus included thirty objective and eight subjective statements. No one draws attention to this difference, however, when called upon to describe as a Q-sort his own *understanding* of newsreading. The subjective statements are taken along with the others and put into place in a Q-sort without anyone observing that most of the statements refer to newspapers as such, and only a few to newsreading as such.

Studies with this and similar Q-samples indicate that skillful, mature newsreaders give high saliency to the ludenic statements. We have learned to distinguish, with such Q-samples, between three main types of newsreaders, called M, P and N, respectively. The first are mature (M) well-rounded people, whose interests extend into national and international news and who couldn't get along without a metropolitan newspaper. Another (P) is a pleasure-reading type, interested in "livened up" gossip, sports and such, who take their news from television and *Life* or *Look*. The other type (N) are basically non-readers, rigid, poorly educated, fundamentalist people of rural areas, many of whom still regard newspapers as sinful. M are invariably ludenic newsreaders; P are often so; none among N find pleasure in newsreading, and none can say that they can become absorbed in it.

Discussion and Conclusion

Enough has been said to introduce the viewpoint that newsreading, in an habituated, ego-involving, but non-compulsive, form, has the marks of play-theory upon it. It is repeated day after day with absorption, sometimes intensely so; preferably one likes to be alone, with one's head buried in the paper; and the enjoyment is serious, and not that associated merely with entertaining features (comics or the like).

The enjoyment is current, whatever the nature of the news. But it is distinguishable from the immediate overt pleasure of the reader of type P, who laughs at the comics without really being ego-involved in the paper in any sense that it matters much to the person. Such is perhaps explicable as *immediate* reward in Schramm's well-known theory. But his theory of *delayed* reward does not touch upon the enjoyment of ludenic newsreading, which is also of an immediate kind, whatever else it may involve vicariously or by remote inference, and which occurs for the educated (M) or the uneducated (N) readers alike. For this a different theory is required. Szasz[19] has indicated that Freud's pleasure-reality principle, upon which Schramm based his theory of newsreading, is far short of satisfactory for ego-involving conditions. He proposes a new concept, communication-pleasure, to account for some forms of immediate ego-involving enjoyment. When two people meet and converse, they may say afterwards how much they enjoyed it. They have been interacting in a complex manner, now serious, now in fun, now at cross-purposes, now with gusto. The talking serves no apparent purpose as far as one can see—the one person isn't necessarily trying to convince the other, or to subdue the other, or to gain something. Neither is trying to please the other. Such is communication-pleasure. Quite different from this is communication which is *demanding*—such as occurs in a command for action, or a plea for help. Such may be called communication-pain.

According to this theory, communication-pleasure (with its self-satisfaction) is contrasted with communication-pain (which alone is apt to bring about change in a *status quo*). Communication-pleasure calls for no action; communication-pain is a command for action. There is a difference in the subjectivity at issue: in the latter there is apt to be a *loss* of self; in communication-pleasure there is a *gain* in self. We reach the conclusion, therefore, that ludenic newsreading is communication-pleasure. It calls for no action, but is enjoyable. It is deeply absorbing, but is about *status quo* conditions. The news is the same every day, in infinite diversity, with infinite subdivisions of the same stories every day, with infinite shadings and differentiations, but all the same story, told as to a child, over and over. The correspondence of this with content analysis of mass media in general, as in studies by Green,[20] Arnold,[21] and many others is apparent. It is in full agreement with the judgment of Wright[22] that, in general, people do not look for new experiences in the mass media but for a repetition and elaboration of their old experiences. Only in such a context, indeed, can they readily project themselves.

The theory that newsreading at its best is play, simple at the one extreme and highly developed ludenic at the other, is put forward for wider consideration. The practical implications should not be overlooked, that one can now begin to find reasons for concern about the format of a newspaper to suit the play of its readers. The theoretical matters are no less important, and can now be looked at more fully in play-theory terms.

Importance of Ludenic Newsreading

Though what we have now to say will be regarded as much more speculative than the above, it is of interest at this point to take note of another aspect of the present theory. Play, in Huizinga's theory, explains *cultures*, and of course there are remnants of play in many of the practices in which we call our "real" world—the legal profession, for example, still plays at winning cases rather than at necessarily eliciting the truth. There can be few professions, likewise, which give so many prizes, medals and citations to themselves as does journalism. This, surely, is playful. It is editorial policy, likewise, to print the "truth" in news: but news about Cuba in a British newspaper scarcely looks like that in ours. One does not suggest that newspapers in such cases are deliberately distorting the "truth." On the contrary, truth is difficult to find, and newspapers are merely buried in their own cultural milieus, communicating what they can within the limits each culture sets.

It is in this context, we suggest, that ludenic newsreading has its primary importance. Out of it comes freedom for the person, at times, to see through the cultural conditioning of news. It is not just that he becomes more penetrating in thought, but merely that he can at times *exist*, as a child does when he freely plays, and thus, every now and then, be free to push to one side the trappings of what everyone else swears is the truth. It is, according to this view, not incidental that the great newspaper editors, who are the most self-conscious of newsreaders and the most developed in ludenic respects, have been among the first to "see through" the current "news."

NOTES

[1] B. Berelson, "What Missing the Newspaper Means," in *Process and Effects of Mass Communication*, ed. W. Schramm (Urbana: University of Illinois Press, 1954).

[2] S. M. Kingsbury, H. Hart *et al.*, *Newspapers and the News* (New York: Putnam, 1937).

[3] D. Hyshka, "Motivation Research Looks at Detroit Newspapers," *Detroit Free Press*, 1955.

[4] M. Janowitz, *The Community Press in an Urban Setting* (Glencoe, Ill.: The Free Press, 1952).

[5] H. Kay, "Toward an Understanding of Newsreading Behavior," *Journalism Quarterly* 31 (1954): 15–32.

[6] W. Schramm, "The Nature of News," *Journalism Quarterly* 26 (1949): 259–69.

[7] T. S. Szasz, *Pain and Pleasure* (New York: Basic Books, Inc., 1957).

[8] M. A. Kaplan, *System and Process in International Politics* (New York: Wiley and Sons, 1957), Chap. 9.

[9] J. von Neumann and O. Morgenstern, *The Theory of Games and Economic Behavior* (Princeton: University Press, 1944).

[10] J. Piaget, *Play, Dreams and Imitation in Childhood* (London: William Heinemann, 1951).

[11] T. S. Szasz, *The Myth of Mental Illness* (New York: Harper Bros., 1962).

[12] W. L. Warner and H. E. Henry, "The Radio Day Time Serial," *Genetic Psych. Mono.* 37 (1948).

[13] S. Freud, "Relation of the Poet to Daydreaming," *Collected Papers* IV (London: Hogarth, 1929).

[14] J. Huizinga, *Homo Ludens: A Study of the Play Element in Culture* (Boston: Beacon Press, 1950).

[15] G. H. Mead, *Mind, Self and Society from the Standpoint of a Social Behaviorist* (Chicago: University of Chicago Press, 1934).

[16] The correct Latin, no doubt, is *ludic,* but there are times when euphony should take precedence over grammar; the pleasing sound of *ludenic* is much to be preferred over the harshness of *ludic.*

[17] T. S. Matthews, *The Sugar Pill: An Essay on Newspapers* (New York: Simon & Schuster, 1959).

[18] Berelson, *op. cit.*

[19] S. Szasz, *Pain and Pleasure.*

[20] T. S. Green, "Mr. Cameron and the Ford Hour," *Public Opinion Quarterly* 3 (1939): 669.

[21] T. Arnold, *The Folklore of Capitalism* (New Haven: Yale University Press, 1937).

[22] C. R. Wright, *Mass Communication: A Sociological Perspective* (New York: Random House, 1959).

David Victoroff:

The Ludenic Function of Advertising

☆ THE CONTEMPORARY social psychologist regards advertising primarily as a specific method of communication, a method corresponding with a particular social practice. This method, which one can term the language of advertising, makes use of many means of expression: spoken or written language, moving or fixed images, numbers, sound effects.

The efficacy of advertising language as far as the public is concerned is beyond doubt, a fact recognized even by the most resolute critics of advertising. And although nobody, so it seems, is fooled as to the objectivity of commercial advertising, a large proportion of the consumer public freely lend an ear to advertising language, more often than to other more impartial and serious sources of information.[1] What are the reasons for the public's partiality for advertising language? To this we wish to supply an answer.

In principle the hypothesis we wish to put forward is a straightforward one: the evident success of advertising language is explained by the fact that it provides us with a certain amount of pleasure.

In order to support this hypothesis, we will make use of an old notion, but one that still holds, although it is practically unknown to those directly concerned with advertising: the notion of psychic economy. This notion was developed by Freud and plays an important role in the psychoanalytic interpretation of mental processes. Freud alluded to it in most of his works, but without doubt the most systematic exposition is to be found in his book, *The Joke and Its Relation to the Unconscious.*[2] It is also on the basis of this exposition that we will briefly present the Freudian approach to the concept of psychic economy.

Freud postulates that all economy of effort, whether mental or physical, is a source of pleasure. The pleasure, however intense, that results from a witticism is the result of an economy of mental effort. Such economy occurs at two distinct levels: that of essence and that of form.

▶ This article was originally published in the XVè *Journées d'Etudes* I.R.E.P. (Institut de Recherches et d'Etudes publicitaires, Paris) and is reprinted here with the kind permission of the author. Dr. David Victoroff is Professor of Social Psychology at the Université de Caen, France.

At the level of essence, psychic economy corresponds with an alleviation of the control that censorship exercises over our conscious activities. Here the underlying source of humor is to be found. However, in order to define the phenomenon more exactly, Freud at this stage introduces the distinction between innocuous humor and tendentious humor. In the former case, pleasure results from an economy of mental effort dependent on the alleviation of the censorship that reason exercises over our cognitive activities: the adult truly becomes a child again and amuses himself in total freedom with words and ideas, paying no attention to the constraints of logic. In the latter case, pleasure corresponds with an economy of mental effort resulting from an alleviation of the censorship that morality exercises over our instincts: humor in this context constitutes an outlet for the satisfaction of prohibited impulses.

However, a further source of pleasure that is related to the language of humor also exists; it is located at the level of form. Its existence, accessory in nature but nonetheless significant, is evident in the techniques employed by the language of humor. Freud presents us with a very detailed list of these based on numerous examples of humor: condensation (with or without modification), the use of the same verbal material, double meanings, errors in reasoning, representation through opposites, unification, allusion, omission, and so on. The only and ultimate common factor among all these procedures is a tendency toward economy, "a tendency to compress, or rather, to economize characterizes all these techniques. Everything, as Hamlet says, seems to be a matter of economy ('Thrift, Horatio, thrift!')." [3]

Humor through its very form thus provides us with pleasure also: we always enjoy making small economies of mental effort even if this only means trying to express a multitude of ideas with a *minimum* of words. "In the complexity of our mental processes, economies of detail remain a source of pleasure for us as the experience of everyday life shows." [4] It is precisely this accessory pleasure related to form that allows the vigilance of censorship to slacken, thus enabling the deep source of pleasure that humor represents to burst open. In effect, this additional pleasure serves as a "*seductive bonus;* with the aid of a small amount of pleasure a considerable amount of pleasure is released which would otherwise be highly inaccessible." [5]

Using the "model" Freud constructed, we have incidentally shown how psychic processes put to play through means of a slogan or catch-phrase can brighten up a day again. In effect, it seems as if the slogan manufacturers are essentially trying to provide pleasure, namely by using a multitude of techniques in order to effect psychic economy at various levels. [6]

But the slogan isn't at present one of the most favored forms of public communication. To an increasing extent its place is being taken by the picture (*image*). Indeed, the history of public communication from its origins to the present day is characterized by the constant increase in space (or time) devoted to picture. We are convinced that the efficacy of the picture, such as used by advertising, can also be explained in the same way (i.e., pleasure deriving from an economy of mental effort).

Certainly such an approach may at first come as a surprise. Doesn't the advertising picture on the contrary have a vast array of means at its disposal? Indeed it is the profusion of form, the abundance and luxury of color, the multiplicity of graphic illustration that strikes us most about advertisements. At a general level, the use of a wealth of expression to express the same, an invariant characteristic of visual advertising, seems to contradict the principle of economy as expounded by Freud.

Is this to say that the interpretation of the advertising message in terms of economy is valid at the level of the slogan but not of the picture? We don't think so. On the contrary, we believe that precisely such an interpretation corresponds well with the basic reality of psychic processes when visual advertising initiates play.

In fact, it is the rhetorical approach that to our present knowledge seems to offer the most satisfactory description of visual advertising, one which far from excludes interpretation in terms of psychic economy. Indeed, one has to resort to this interpretation because it is the only way in which we can present a coherent insight into the mechanisms triggered off by looking at forms and shapes. Furthermore, by adapting the Freudian model, we will try to show that the techniques employed by visual rhetoric impart a certain pleasure resulting from psychic economies achieved at both the level of essence and the level of form.

The Level of Essence

As Jaques Durand has adequately shown,[7] all the techniques of classical rhetoric are to be found in advertisements. Conversely, the better advertising illustrations can all be interpreted in terms of rhetoric. By definition, a stylistic technique implies the transgression of a norm.[8] In the case of the picture, the norms most frequently concerned are those of physical reality. Here, representations are striking because of their elements of unreality, fantasy and absurdity: *inversion* takes the form of a person standing upside down; the *ellipsis* finds expression in the picture of a table without legs; the *hyperbole* is being utilized when a pea takes on the dimensions of a football; *rupture* or *discontinuity* in construction is being employed when the doors of a cupboard are opened, exposing a holiday landscape beyond.

Consequently, everything happens in such a manner that, at the sight of a world thus transfigured, the adult finds himself plunged into a magical universe, the universe of fairy tales appreciated so much by the child. Seen at a very general level, the absurdity of the rhetorical picture, taken at its face value, gives access to the kind of pleasure we enjoyed during childhood, which is now inaccessible as a rule; we freely enjoy words and things without caring about the constraints of reason.

Nevertheless, an absurdity or an ineptitude offends us, causes embarrassment, gives us a feeling of uneasiness. Such defensive reactions threaten to bar the path to the pleasure coupled with nonsense. Yet, after a few moments of hesitation, we discern a hidden meaning materializing at the heart of the absurdity itself. We realize that we find ourselves in the presence of nonsense containing a certain sense. It is this compromise between the demands of rational criticism and our desire to shake off the yoke that allows us to enjoy the pleasure to be gained from nonsense without any feelings of guilt.[9]

The Level of Form

Let us presume that the very fact that allows one to interpret the advertising picture in terms of rhetoric implies the existence of processes of persuasion analogous to those used in oration at a different level. Thus, an advertisement presenting a particular manufacturer's washing machine as the solution to a problem[10] constitutes a kind of visual argument, easy to understand even in the absence of any written message. In this respect, the resemblances as well as non-resemblances in appearance provide illustrations that are most convincing. The former are the equivalent of the line of argument that, relying upon the satisfaction of its users, aims at persuading the public not to call upon the services of any other make. The latter corresponds with the reasoning aimed at eliminating the competing makes as alternatives.

Briefly, the motifs at the visual level are the equivalents of those at a verbal level involving discursive techniques that tend to be longer and more complex. In this context, one may postulate that the great law that governs the visual advertisement is the law of condensation: the motifs of pictorial rhetoric seem to be like the condensed formulae used in written reasoning or in verbal expression. Presented in the form of data coexisting in space, they are understood as quickly and as easily as discursive operations that unfold themselves in time. The economy thus achieved constitutes precisely that *seductive bonus* that allows the liberation of the greatest pleasure: it can aptly be called ludenic pleasure.

All these considerations allow one to suppose that alongside its manifest function, which is essentially economic, and ultimately relatively limited role, advertising language serves in a latent capacity and its scope at the level of collective mentality is very far-reaching: in the midst of our technological civilization, so "rational" and yet so frustrating, it permits the rediscovery of the joy of play.

NOTES

[1] Cf. P. Kende, "La publicité et l'information du consommateur," *Communications* 17 (1971): 43–54.

[2] S. Freud, *Der Witz und seine Beziehung zum Unbewussten* (Leipzig and Wien: Franz Deuticke, 1905). Here, the French translation by Marie Bonaparte & Dr. M. Nathan (Paris: Gallimard, 1930) will be quoted.

[3] *Le mot d'esprit et ses rapports avec l'inconscient*, p. 48.

⁴*Ibid.*, p. 180.

⁵*Ibid.*, p. 157.

⁶D. Victoroff, *Psychosociologie de la publicité* (Paris: P.U.F., 1970), pp. 72 *ff*.

⁷J. Durand, "Rhétorique et image publicitaire," *Communications* 15 (1970): 70–95.

⁸If all techniques are transgressions, it is entirely evident that transgressions are not all techniques. Of course this observation does not invalidate the studies made on the subject of transgression.

⁹Cf. Freud, *op. cit.*, pp. 150–51: "The psychogenesis of the joke has taught us that its pleasure derives from the play with words or from the unfettering of nonsense, and the sense to be found in the joke only serves to protect this pleasure against criticism."

¹⁰J. Durand, *op. cit.*, p. 84.

Sinclair Goodlad:

Mass Entertainment in Perspective:
The Need for a Theory of the Middle Range

☆ THE PURPOSE OF this paper is to argue the case for a theory of the middle range that can relate mass entertainment, in particular spectator sports and television drama, to other elements of culture, notably religion and education. Empiricist sociology tends to dissolve the unity of cultural experience into a congeries of specialist areas of study (the sociology of religion, the sociology of education, the sociology of art and literature and so on) at the expense of meaningful connections. By contrast, grand unifying theory often does not lend itself to empirical testing and lacks the precision that would enable one to predict a given social structure from patterns of symbolic behavior or vice versa. The theory of society embodied in the study *Natural Symbols* by anthropologist Mary Douglas, it will be argued, not only offers a crucial link between aspects of culture that need to be considered simultaneously but also is a theory of the middle range, placing detailed observation into a comprehensive cross-cultural perspective.

This is not the place for an exhaustive review of the reasons for considering mass entertainment, sport, religion and education together. A few selected examples must suffice to suggest the interconnections that a theory must explain:

First, although common cultural origins do not necessarily imply common contemporary content, they should alert us to the possibility that certain cultural forms are in some ways interconnected. For example, both in ancient Greece and in medieval Europe, Western drama emerged from religious ritual.[1] Spence has shown how many sports also emerged from religious rituals. These observations by themselves would not be significant but for the evidence from later social history that mass entertainments seem to offer similar satisfactions to religion; as mass entertainments spread, so institutional religion appeared to decline. Bryan Wilson has argued that this correlation is causal.

▶ This is an original article written especially for this book. Dr. Sinclair Goodlad is lecturer in Associated Studies (Communication) at the Imperial College of Science and Technology, University of London.

. . . the entertainment industry . . . was from the outset a challenge to religion, offering diversion, other reinterpretations of daily life, and competing for the time, attention and money of the public. In its actual content, it may be seen as more than an alternative way of spending time, but also as an alternative set of norms and values. It replaced religion's attempt to awaken *public* sentiments by offering titillation of *private* emotions.[2]

Pickering has taken this argument further by demonstrating, with survey material, that religion may itself be perceived as a leisure-time activity, offering satisfactions in many ways comparable to those of mass entertainment.

Second, both religion and mass entertainment in the form of television drama are preoccupied with morality. A *Sociology of Popular Drama* demonstrates that drama with mass appeal (one possible definition of "popular") is overwhelmingly moral in the sense of being obsessed with, and affirming, conventional codes of morality. Peak television viewing hours are filled with sagas showing incorruptible agents of law enforcement—backed by vast bureaucracies, computers and "bionic" or invisible assistants—tracking down the workers of iniquity. The Western hero who delivers the small town or army fort from the clutches of "the evil one" may have given pride of place to the government agent who delivers the whole of civilization from some maniac, or to the militaristic star trekkers who impose the Protestant Ethic and the Spirit of Capitalism on whole galaxies, but the same obsession with codes of conduct is present.

Third, religion and spectator sports both collectively reinforce the individual's sense of identity. The Herberg thesis suggests a link between religion and national identity; Goodlad[3] suggests that field sports may be a form of ritualized territoriality. Others have been even bolder and argued that football, for example, may be a surrogate religion reinforcing the individual's identity as supporter of a given town or city. Edgell and Jary, observing that football is the most popular spectator sport in contemporary Britain, examine the capacity of football to generate for the individual spectator a wider, more universal sense of shared humanity and "the ultimate." Coles has represented football as a Durkheimian ritual, in which a sense of the sacred is generated and amplified through a social process. The feelings of supporters about the game are, he argues, similar to religious feelings. Group allegiances are displayed in symbolic ways through scarves, rosettes and car stickers; chanting execrates the opponents and celebrates the home team. Discussions in bars—and specialist publications—all affirm the individual's identity as supporter of a common cause, transcending his isolation and integrating him with a group.

Fourth, mass entertainments form the core of a leisure-culture that has singular implications for formal education. Murdock and Phelps have demonstrated great differences between the teachers and those taught in Britain in terms of the symbolic universes they inhabit. Teachers, for example, watch less television than their pupils, read different newspapers, and favor different kinds of music. The values the school represents are concerned with the intellect, with work, with production, with planning for the future; by contrast, the val-uses of the world of "pop" culture that is inhabited and enjoyed by the pupils are concerned with the body, with pleasure, with consumption and with enjoyment of the here and now. Many schools witness, in fact, a clash of symbolic universes, a running conflict between two (or more) systems of belief.

If we are to understand the interconnections between elements that make up an individual's culture, we must articulate a theory that illuminates the relationships between mass entertainment (such as television drama and spectator sports) and religion and formal education. More importantly, that theory must fit into a comprehensive account of social behavior.

There is an abundance of first-order theories in each of the sub-areas mentioned above, proposing hypotheses amenable to empirical investigation. For example, the proposition that "mass media fictions offer vicarious social interaction for the lonely" suggests the question: "Do socially maladjusted people (so defined by themselves or on any one of a series of indicators) consume more mass-media fictions than those who are not socially maladjusted?" Answer: Yes. (Goodlad[4] reviews some of the studies that support this hypothesis.) The conclusion is interesting and important, but it is of little theoretical interest until built into a more general theory of human behavior. Similar first-order theories concerning religion and personal adjustment can readily be proposed and tested against empirical findings.[5]

First-order theories help to sharpen up definitions, but they tend to generate almost too much data. For example, functional analysis requires a precise definition of the items to which functions are imputed. Are sports and drama the same thing? According to the thesis propounded by Huizinga in *Homo Ludens*, both are sub-categories of play. But, as I have argued at length elsewhere,[6] this categorization disguises important differences. Roger Caillois' discussion of the classification of games locates sports in one sub-category (*agon*) and drama principally in another (*mimicry*). But his classification still leaves drama poised uneasily between these two categories of *agon* and *mimicry*. Further work at definition is illuminating. Elizabeth Burns,[7] for example, emphasizes the element of mimicry in theatre, exploring the continuities and differences between the authenticating conventions by which the provinces of real life and theatre are defined. By contrast, J. W. Loy highlights elements of institutionalization and organization in sports, which go a long way in differentiating sports from drama. Separate areas of research are, through this disciplined process, marked out.

But this very process can be the undoing of functional analysis. For example, uses and gratifications research, an important sub-variant of functional analysis, requires precise definition and description of the item that is deemed to gratify a given member of the audience for a mass communication production. In an essay on the social significance of television comedy,[8] I have shown how one apparently straightforward system of content analysis can generate a grid of 420 possible types of observation to be applied to every unit of television comedy! And a unit can be a complete show, an individual joke, a sketch or a single line in a sketch! Add to this the fact that economy is the artistic virtue by which comedy is judged (so that several possible meanings may be telescoped into a single idea, sight or other comic element), and one soon perceives the impossibility of ever giving a precise account of the responses of audiences to specific television content.

Second-order theories try to go beyond the detail of first-order theories and explore the unity of experience. For example, one might see television drama, or television comedy, as a celebration of socially constructed reality. The phenomenological theories of Berger and Luckmann are hypnotizing in their scope. They seem to draw all elements of knowledge and social experience together. However, as Hamilton, among others, has pointed out, their theory is clearly non-empirical. It does, of course, have "mythic" value—which may account for its attraction to ideologues. Like the Freudian "myth," it is internally consistent and locates many elements of experience in a satisfying way.

A theory of society, to be fully articulated, needs *both* first-order theories and second-order theories; above all, it needs a way of linking them. A theory of the middle range might be expected to earth the grand unifying theories by specifying first-order theories (with their associated possibilities of empirical verification) by which they can be tested. Perhaps a necessary precursor to a theory or theories is an *agenda*.

An agenda can form the focus of attention of an academic discipline. It draws together ideas in some systematic way, but does not presuppose a direction of causality. Diagram 1 from *Conflict and Consensus in Higher Education* [9] suggests possible inter-relationships between twelve major areas of culture ranging from systems of technology to individual beliefs. The arrangement does not, be it noted, specify a direction of causality. Marxist theory would most likely propose causality from Technology, with individual beliefs part of a superstructure of culture. An alternative theory might give supremacy to the autonomous beliefs of individuals and demonstrate our freedom to alter all other elements of culture to express our wishes.

The elements of culture with which the present paper is concerned appear under Item 6. It is a moot point whether sports, religious ritual and mass-communicated drama reflect or determine our beliefs. Probably they do both.

As far as the effect of them (through Item 8) on education is concerned, it does not very much matter; either way, a marked difference of culture as represented by Items 6 and 8 will severely inhibit communication, the sharing of cultural values, through education.

A theory of the middle range takes one item from this agenda, without necessarily presupposing a theory of society, and explores its relationship with social structure. Such a theory is offered by Mary Douglas in *Natural Symbols*. She is concerned with a hypothesis to interpret the clustering of symbols. In reaction to the idea of compensation that, she argues, has loosely dominated the sociology of religion, she explores a replication hypothesis that allows for the power of symbols generated in a particular social setup to control it. That is to

DIAGRAM 1

PUBLIC ↑DIMENSION	*Instrumental*	*Expressive*
TECHNOLOGY	1. Systems or devices to achieve specific social objectives. ⟷	2. Social values incorporated in technology.
	↕	↕
ORGANIZA-TIONS	3. To affect the physical or social environment (e.g., businesses, factories). ⟷	4. Embodying beliefs about the physical and social environment (e.g., churches, political parties).
	↕	↕
RITUAL PROCESSES	5. Standardized organizational procedures, often showing no intrinsic link between ends and means (e.g., office parties). ⟷	6. Activities with no recognizable economic benefit to the participants (e.g., sports, religious ritual, "consumption" of mass communications).
	↕	↕
SOCIAL BELIEF SYSTEMS	7. Beliefs aimed at social control (e.g., business "ethos," dogma, doctrine, policy, syllabus). ⟷	8. Beliefs that express some insight or ascription of "value" (e.g., "Science" as a sub-culture, Economics).
	↕	↕
INDIVIDUAL CREATIONS	9. To operate on the physical and social environment (e.g., tools, persuasive documents). ⟷	10. To express personal values or idiosyncratic views about the environment (e.g., novels, poems, paintings).
	↕	↕
PERSONAL BELIEFS	11. How to survive. ⟷	12. Why to survive.
↓ PRIVATE DIMENSION		

say, specific symbols may be traceable to specific social structures, but the symbols in turn affect the social structure so that, by self-conscious manipulation of symbols, it is possible to alter social structure.

Her starting point is the work of Basil Bernstein in socio-linguistics. Dia-

DIAGRAM 2

(i) cardinal virtues
(ii) cardinal sins
(iii) the idea of the self
(iv) art forms

Speech
Socially Restricted

A   C

(i) piety, honor (respect for roles)
(ii) formal transgressions against social structure
(iii) self, passive, undifferentiated element in a structured environment
(iv) primitive: structural elaborations upon social categories, humans as cardboard allegorical figures

(i) sincerity, authenticity
(ii) sins against the self, hypocrisy, cruelty, acceptance of frustration
(iii) internally differentiated agent, attempting to control unstructured environment
(iv) romantic: triumph of individual over structure (escape, brief happiness, etc.)

Family Control System

Positional   *Personal*

(i) truth, duty
(ii) cardinal sin is failure to respond to demands of social structure
(iii) active agent, internally differentiated, responding to roles
(iv) classical: triumph of structure over individual

(i) personal success, doing good to humanity
(ii) generalized guilt, individual and collective
(iii) subject alone
(iv) professionalism: overriding concern with techniques and materials of creative process

B   D
Speech Elaborated

gram 2, evolved by Mary Douglas[10] in discussion with Bernstein, locates general cosmological ideas in terms of the social experience of the individual. Although notions of social class are irrelevant to this model, so-called "working-class culture" would predominantly be found in segment A—where socially restricted speech codes are combined with a positional system of family control. This picture of general cosmological ideas is of the most intense interest in providing a link between mass entertainment and religion—and, of course, through Bernstein's other work, with education. Popular drama, for example, is filled with representations of formal transgressions against social structure—A(ii), particularly in comedy, which can almost be defined in those terms. Again, football, as an art form—A(iv)—is a structural elaboration upon social categories, with humans as cardboard allegorical figures. And, insofar as religion involves all four ideas—cardinal virtues, cardinal sins, the idea of the self and art forms—it can be perceived as partially or wholly interchangeable with these other symbolic elements of culture.

In *Natural Symbols*, Mary Douglas propounds two social variables of elemental simplicity, whose interconnections with symbolic forms she examines. *Group* is the experience of a bounded social unit; *Grid* refers to rules that relate one person to others on an ego-centred basis.[11] Grid and Group can be found separately or in combination. Where they are found together, the quality of social relations is orderly and clearly bounded. If Group alone is experienced, a man recognizes very strong allegiance to a social group but does not know how he relates to other members of the group or what his expectations should be. Where Grid alone is strong, a man is constrained not by group loyalties but by a set of rules that engage him in reciprocal transactions.

Mary Douglas suggests, drawing upon an immense quantity of anthropological fieldwork, that these two variables are intricately related with the type of symbolic expression favored by individuals.[12] For example, the man who experiences closed social groups associates boundaries with power and danger; the better defined and the more significant the social boundaries, the more bias there would be in favor of ritual. By contrast, if social groups are weakly structured and their membership is weak and fluctuating, low value is likely to be put upon symbolic performance. Doctrinal differences too appear connected with these variables. With weak social boundaries and weak ritualism, emphasis is likely to concentrate on internal emotional states—sin becomes more a matter of affect than of transgression, sacraments and magic give way to direct unmediated communion, even to the valuing of states of trance and bodily dissociation.

Using these two variables to modify the schema shown in Diagram 2, Mary Douglas offers a theory of the middle range linking symbolic systems with social structure. The interest of her theory is that it is not culture dependent; comparisons between different periods of time and between different countries become possible. She is somewhat imprecise about how Grid and Group are to be defined; however, her theory of the middle range offers the possibility of putting the study of mass entertainment into perspective—illuminating its links with religion and with education, and providing, as we devise systematic ways of exploring individuals' experience of Grid and Group, a potent link between first-order theories and an agenda of grand unifying theory.

NOTES

¹Goodlad, A *Sociology of Popular Drama*, Chapt. 2.
²Wilson, p. 40.
³*A Sociology of Popular Drama*, p. 180.
⁴*Op. cit.*, Chapt. 5.
⁵Argyle and Beit-Hallahmi, Chapt. 8, review many studies in this area.
⁶Goodlad, "Approaches to Popular Drama."
⁷*Theatricality*, p. 149.
⁸Goodlad, "On the Social Significance of Television Comedy."
⁹Goodlad, *Conflict and Consensus in Higher Education*, p. 52.
¹⁰*Natural Symbols*, p. 29.
¹¹Douglas, p. viii.
¹²Douglas, p. 14.

REFERENCES

Argyle, Michael, and Beit-Hallahmi, Benjamin. *The Social Psychology of Religion*. London: Routledge & Kegan Paul, 1975.

Berger, P. L., and Luckmann, T. *The Social Construction of Reality*. New York: Doubleday, 1966.

Bernstein, Basil. "Social Class and Psychotherapy." *British Journal of Sociology* 15 (1964): 54–64.

Bernstein, Basil. "A Socio-Linguistic Approach to Social Learning." In *Penguin Survey of the Social Sciences*. Ed. by J. Gould. London: Penguin, 1965.

Bernstein, Basil. "A Socio-Linguistic Approach to Socialization." In *Directions in Socio-Linguistics*. Ed. by J. Gumperz and D. Hymes. New York: Holt, Rinehart & Winston, 1970.

Burns, Elizabeth. *Theatricality: A Study of Convention in the Theatre and in Social Life*. London: Longman, 1972.

Caillois, Roger. *Man, Play, and Games*. Tr. by Meyer Barash. London, 1962. (Chapter 3, "The Classification of Games," is reprinted in *The Sociology of Sport*, ed. by F. Dunning. London: Frank Cass, 1971).

Coles, Robert W. "Football as a 'Surrogate' Religion?" In *A Sociological Yearbook of Religion in Britain* 8. Ed by Michael Hill. London: SCM Press, 1975.

Douglas, Mary. *Natural Symbols: Explorations in Cosmology*. London: Barrie & Rockcliff, The Cresset Press, 1970.

Edgell, Stephen, and Jary, David. "Football: A Sociological Eulogy." In *Leisure and Society in Britain*. Ed. by Michael A. Smith, Stanley Parker and Cyril S. Smith. London: Allen Lane, 1973.

Goodlad, S. "Approaches to Popular Drama Through the Social Sciences." In *Western Popular Theatre*. Ed. by David Mayer and Kenneth Richards. London: Metheun, 1977.

Goodlad, S. *Conflict and Consensus in Higher Education*. London: Hodder and Stroughton Educational, 1976.

Goodlad, S. "On the Social Significance of Television Comedy." In *Approaches to Popular Culture*. Ed. by C. W. E. Bigsby. London: Edward Arnold, 1976.

Goodlad, S. A *Sociology of Popular Drama*. London: Heinemann Educational Books, 1971.

Hamilton, P. *Knowledge and Social Structure*. London: Routledge & Kegan Paul, 1974.

Herberg, Will. *Protestant, Catholic, Jew*. New York: Doubleday, 1955.

Huizinga, J. *Homo Ludens* (1938). London: Paladin, 1970.

Loy, J. W. "The Nature of Sport, a Definitional Effort." In *Sport, Culture, and Society*. Ed. by J. W. Loy and G. S. Kenyon. New York: Macmillan, 1969.

Murdock, G., and Phelps, G. *Mass Media and the Secondary School*. London: Macmillan, 1973.

Pickering, William. "Religion—a Leisure-Time Pursuit?" In A *Sociological Yearbook of Religion in Britain*. Ed. by David Martin. London: SCM Press, 1968.

Spence, L. *Myth and Ritual in Dance, Game, and Rhyme*. London: Watts, 1947.

Wilson, Bryan. *Religion in Secular Society*. London: Watts, 1966.

David C. Chaney and Judith H. Chaney:

The Audience for Mass Leisure

☆ IT IS USUAL TO ASSUME that the term "audience" is a category fundamental to the study of mass leisure activity. Yet looking at the way in which audiences have been conceptualized in different studies and the impasse into which so many of them have seemed to lead, one may question the extent to which the concept of "audience" has been a significant object of sociological study at all.

The dictionary definition of an audience is "assembly of listeners." The passive role thus attributed to audience members is an implicit theme in audience studies, where the nature of audiences is usually seen as dependent on either the content of the performance and/or the social context in which it takes place. A major focus of study has been the transition from the audience as a restricted community to the audience as a mass market. Like contrast conceptions of community, the idea of a mass audience gains force by contrasting it with that which is deemed to have been eroded. In this case, the key element is seen to be the particular relationship that can arise between producer and audience when audience membership is restricted by physical or social factors. A situation in which producers and audience members consciously draw on a common set of referents, where the performance is for both parties a cultural text providing commentaries on community life. Such a performance carries many meanings and—in the act of observing—the audience plays a creative part. "What we are studying in this context are the ways in which experience is worked into understanding and then disseminated and celebrated."[1] Descriptions of folk rituals in anthropological studies provide the clearest examples of audiences as communities but, in a similar vein, one might cite performances for highly specialized audiences.

This type of audience experience is contrasted with a situation in which

▶ This is a revised version of a paper first given at the British Sociological Association Conference in 1967. David C. Chaney is Lecturer in Sociology at the University of Durham, England. Judith H. Chaney is Lecturer in Sociology at Sunderland Polytechnic, England.

economic, technical and social changes have structured the context of leisure in industrial societies. Baumann (1972) suggests that the effectiveness of the media of mass communication in making culture a mass culture (and by implication creating a mass audience) is dependent on the degree of universalization of three components. The first is the movement away from an environment within which there was a closed circle of undeveloped exchange toward a universal dependence on the market based on mass and serial production. The second component is the dependence on organization and the third is the dependence on technology. When increasingly elaborate ranges of technical goods and amenities are available for leisure use, activities can be large scale, standardized, simultaneous and unconstrained by geographic or social barriers. The mass market defines at a simple level three roles of producer, distributor and consumer. This use of mass implies passivity to those in the role of consumers, which in turn suggests a vulnerability to exploitation and manipulation by distributors and producers, narrowed possibilities for creative participation by audience members and a consequent debasement in the quality of leisure experience. Where there is a potentially large market, there also lies a profitable field for market research, and a vigorous bookkeeping tradition in audience research has developed as the media themselves expanded. This production of market profiles means that at one level there is a great deal of information about those who use the mass media. We know which magazines they buy, their television channel changing patterns, whether they are married, have children, washing machines or mortgages, but we know little about the role these media products play in their understanding of their own experiences.

It is clear that the concept of mass is crucial in the study of audiences both in its technical, organizational sense and as a description of a particular quality of experience. However, it is not clear that these two elements are necessarily in any kind of contingent relationship to each other. The gemeinschaft-gesellschaft dichotomy in audience experience revolves less around the technical and organizational factors structuring the context of any particular performance than around the degree of involvement of the participants. By using a transitional framework, the study of audiences has become stuck on the question of ideological status of participation and neglected the processes by which individuals develop and express their taste in a mass context. It is the aim of this paper to develop a way of analysing this process. It has been asserted rather baldly that gross characterizations of audience participation are inappropriate, and this claim is supported in the next part of this paper by a discussion of some of the literature relating to studies of participation and response. Before embarking on this discussion, it should be noted that our reading of source material has been structured by a commitment to the argument that taste is a social characteristic that develops through time and that the process of development occurs through interaction with others. In other words, taste is a medium of social communication and the display of a certain form of taste is a mode of symbolic action that tends to be shared by others in similar circumstances. Thus, participation in a particular activity can have meaning for an individual or group beyond the manifest meaning of the activity itself. The implications of this approach are elaborated in the succeeding paragraphs.

Some of the associations inherent in the concepts of mass and audience have already been explored; in order to develop the argument, it may help to bring out another aspect of these concepts. This is that a common use of mass is to refer to leisure (non-work time) as it is defined by the distinctive part played by mass communications. When people are entertained by performances available through media of communication, such as newspapers, radio, television and the cinema, then they constitute a mass, a heterogenous social conglomeration unknown to each other. Mass media are not only leisure goods in themselves and therefore analogous in social significance with all other types of leisure goods and activities, but they are also the principal medium for diffusion of information about other available activities. The suggestion that there is a central interdependence between contemporary public communication and contemporary leisure has important implications. First, if there is a degree of interdependence between the development of mass communication and contemporary leisure, then there may be grounds for believing that the concept of an audience is only comprehensible in the context of changes in the social organization of different types of experience—be they work or play. The second implication is methodological in directing us to an inspection of the literature on the social implications of mass communication for material relevant to understanding audience taste.

In relation to the first point, both leisure and mass communication are inextricably entwined with the categorizations of property in industrial societies. The growth of free time in this century is meaningful only in contrast to the preceeding century of industrialization; the pre-industrial working week was probably considerably less arduous a (for more precise illustration of this see Clayre). The retrieval of adequate time for self-expression has been won by a combination of the working-class struggle to restrict hours of employment allied with a gradual change from explicit exploitation of the work force to the encouragement of capital mobility through high consumption of commerical products. Both aspects of changing relationships of work underlie an understanding of leisure as something that is owned rather than something that is made. Leisure has therefore come to be seen as something that the individual or group can keep to themselves, it is "free" time and therefore private. Paradoxically, the use of such a possession is demonstrated through patronage of a wide range of pursuits and activities provided by a very diffuse leisure industry. The consequent circulation of resources is functional for the economy as a whole, while the purchase of individual leisure choices encourages the feeling that the articulation of such tastes is the expression of a property right:

> The range of possible pursuits out of working time is arguably much wider than it was for any previous generation than ours. The point to be made is that these pursuits are wholly secular, organized for a commercial market, or at least for a user public, and, by and large, limited to what can be so organized.[2]

Thus leisure is not defined as a range of activities or as a particular period of time. Instead, leisure is seen as a mode of engagement with time; it is a period in which the individual can feel in control of time as a capital resource and can therefore "spend" it as he wishes. This approach allows us to account for such variations as those between people who spend no money on leisure pursuits and those who invest large amounts in equipment for various hobbies. It also allows us to override the sometimes ambiguous distinction between work and leisure in that while being employed some people may appropriate time for their own purposes. A further reason for developing this approach is that precisely because we conceive leisure as an opportunity for participants to invest their activity with a distinctive significance, so we envisage our analysis being concerned with the expressive implications of being a member of different audiences, and with the ways in which such memberships may enable people to further other social concerns. For example, the work of Bernstein has shown how the means available for the organization of meaning are a function of types of social relationship. The form of the relationship will act selectively on the mode and content of communication; closely shared identifications and affective empathy may remove the need for elaborate verbal expression. The language of some mass leisure goods (for example: song lyrics, teenage love comics and confession magazines) approximates in many respects the distinguishing characteristics of Bernstein's "restricted code" as a language of implicit meaning. In a culture where skill in the verbal expression of profound feeling is not a general trait, nor a readily accessible public love, poetry becomes functional as a vicarious means of conversation about feelings.

To return to the second implication of the relationship between leisure and communication, the suggestion that attendance at a particular performance may be related to other aspects of an individual's social life has also been made in studies of the implications of mass communication for other social institutions. For example, in a survey of information-seeking during an election campaign, it was found that potential voters were more likely to seek out material setting out candidates' views if they (the voters) expected to talk about the election with friends.[3] This type of report encourages a feeling that we search for material that is relevant to our interests and that enables us to develop and substantiate a certain social style or character. Chafee goes on to cite another study with which he was concerned in which it was found "that the media predominate in disseminating information about 'news' topics such as population problems, but more personal sources are used when a personal 'consumer' topic is involved, such as birth control."[4] The difference in medium of communication, and thereby the type of relationship engaged in, is explained by an argument that "public" affairs are seen by these respondents to be the province of impersonal communicators, but when one is concerned with matters that intimately relate to "one's social self," then face to face relationships are important and members of reference and membership groups consulted. This argument leads straightforwardly to a consideration of the ways in which audiences are structured. If individuals are influenced by others in their social milieu, then mass communicated messages will be mediated by the social structure of the several levels of "influentials."

The basis of the structural perspective was the discovery of the limited success of mass propaganda. Research on the diffusion and social availability of any relevant activity has been dominated by the "two-step flow" theory, a hypothetical model of communication flow in which material from the media is filtered through opinion leaders to relevant publics. In subsequent research, this process has been elaborated to include several groups of opinion leaders, sometimes conceived as a hierarchy, and studies have demonstrated that opinion leaders are relatively specialized in their sphere of influence. Three characteristics have been found to distinguish such leaders: a social position that is perceived to give them a special competence in the relevant subject, social accessibility and gregariousness and contact with relevant information coming from outside their immediate circle. These opinion leaders therefore monitor sources of information, reinforcing suitable ideas and values. Opinion leader research has proved to be a productive field for mass communications, not only because it has focussed attention on the social processes of reception and the rejection of simple stimulus-response theories, but also because it draws on and is compatible with sociological research in fields such as educational socialization. In a brief summary article, Katz has shown how studies of consumer behavior, the adoption of new drugs by doctors, the diffusion of new seeds in rural communities, changing hygiene practices in South American towns and comparative anthropological studies of westernization can all be seen to share a common structural frame of reference. The significance of this perspective for a more general theory of audience membership can be seen most clearly in the relevance of structural analysis to mass communications in third-world societies.[5] The impossibility of ascribing a blanket power to new forms of communication becomes apparent when appreciating the roles of new technology in settled rural communities.

The central criticism of the structural perspective is that it is essentially descriptive, a static analysis of audience organization that is not very useful for interpreting changes in taste (this use of "structural" is not to be confused with a "structuralist" approach to mass communication).[6] It is not surprising, therefore, that a complementary analytic perspective had developed in which the concern with the social implications of membership is extended by considering the uses and gratifications that a member of an audience might derive from participation. Theoretical emphasis is laid on the rewards of audience membership, so that the problems of their cohesion are translated into problems of discovering and classifying the types of reward they receive. "The scheme attempts to comprehend the whole range of individual gratifications of the many facets of the need 'to be connected.' And it finds empirical regularities in the preference for different media for different kinds of connections."[7] A shift in emphasis of this sort should, if successful, lead to a rewarding analysis of the cultural and social relationships embodied in the mass communications process.

A study that illustrates the overlap in interests between a "uses" approach and structural studies is Johnstone's study of television use by adolescents and their changing affiliations to parents and peers. The study draws on material collected as part of Coleman's research on adolescents and schools in the late 1950s and a report of it is included in the best recent collection of work in this area.[8] Johnstone argues that as adolescents mature, they attach relatively greater significance to their friendships with peers and particularly with members of the opposite sex, and that, therefore, as television is something watched at home with the family, the gross amount watched will decline and the type of programs enjoyed will change. More specifically, he argues that those adolescents who are relatively unsuccessful in the eyes of their peers will cling to the security of the family environment more than their more socially sophisticated peers. To cite two results, the first is that as hypothesized, the amount of television watched declines as children mature and become adolescents: "the results suggest that when significant others change, patterns of mass media exposure are also likely to change so that they fit better within the milieu in which one interacts with significant others."[9] Secondly, a relatively crude measure of sociometric status is found to correlate with differences in television watching so that "while this does not establish directly that television viewing functions to reduce tensions generated in the social world, it does at least suggest that felt deprivations emanating from the social environment do lead people to turn to television to seek out emotional restoration."[10] This style of analysis is characteristic of an approach oriented to the uses that members of an audience can derive from the performance. Other features of the social context that may underlie audience needs are a desire to ease problems, a desire for information about problems, a desire to overcome structural inequality, a desire to reaffirm fundamental values and, finally, a desire to keep up with the conventional knowledge of other members of an audience.[11]

The uses and gratifications approach is open to serious criticism. In this approach, a *social* theory is offered to explain communications behavior, but in effect the majority of research has used an *individualistic* frame of reference, with the result that the terms "function" and "use" are being used to refer to the satisfaction of individual needs. This means either that a theory of uses is little more than a restatement of utilitarian principles or that it has to explain the relevance of imputed needs as much as their functional satisfaction. "It is inescapable that what is at issue here is the long-standing problem of social and psychological science: how to (and whether to attempt to) systematize the long lists of human and societal needs."[12] It is because such a task is Sysyphean, and because in any case there may be more than one "need" operative in particular circumstances, that functional theorists have had in effect to choose between 1) assuming that a form of normative homogeneity is induced through socialization—a solution sometimes employed by macro-functional sociological theorists, although attempts to apply system concepts to processes of mass communication have largely been abandoned in recent years and 2) making functional theory irrelevant by crediting actors with the creative individuality to perceive their own relevances in terms of all possible situations, aims and rewards. The impasse between these choices has in practice been resolved by an implicit assumption that "average" and "social" are interchangeable so that correlational hypotheses that impute *reasonable* motives to collections of actors in *typical* situations become the substantive mode of analysis.

Such a mode of analysis, which turns on commonsense generalizations about stereotypical personality dynamics, is particularly inappropriate for studies of the audience for mass leisure. The quasi-functional analyses that replace studies of the effects of mass media on audiences by imputing more-or-less conscious needs to individuals have failed to seize their opportunity. They have retained the static features of structural analyses so that the researcher is concerned with taste in the past, and have failed to explore the modes of social experience and types of relationship that members of an audience are actually constituting and articulating through their participation in the social milieu of a performance.[13] In order to understand the actions of others, social theorists must go beyond external characterizations to grasp the subjective meanings for those concerned. Subjective originality enters biographies through individual definitions of situations, through the stock of expressive resources to hand and through intersubjective relationships with others.

Initially, the reason for placing our perspective on audiences under the rubric of sociology of taste was the desire to stress the ways in which membership of an audience expresses choice and taste, but secondly, we wanted to outline an approach in which the range of leisure activities characteristic of an individual or a group are understood as a social style. Toward this end, we suggest that differences in group selectivity and factors affecting that selectivity can be analyzed within a framework consisting of four foci: accessibility, conception, involvement and aspiration. The basis of this analysis is the idea that selectivity can define a group, that is, that any given group will exhibit consistent and stylized preferences within a range of possible choices. Audiences may formalize their common interests to the extent of founding an organization that concentrates on a topic (for example, a film society), but such a degree of organization is not characteristic of audiences in contemporary popular culture. We are more likely to find a situation in which memberships are recognized within social circles and marked by the significance they have for other social commitments rather than for the fact of membership itself. Another point is that while any research study in this field must utilize a structural perspective, such a perspective is not an independent focus, because each level can be characterized independently in terms of the same framework. Finally, although the uses and gratifications approach has reduced pessimistic fears about the power of the media, more weight should be attached to the interpretive resources that members of an audience utilize in developing their taste. Some groups are more vulnerable than others. Intention is not a separate focus of study because it is seen neither as a cause nor as an effect of the factors that this framework utilizes. In the same way that motives are shared means of making sense of actions,[14] intention is the medium through which these factors interact to articulate individual membership of different audiences.

Accessibility

Physical inaccessibility is an obvious negative factor to be included in any study of factors affecting consumption in the field of leisure. Social accessibility also acts as a limiting factor on audience behavior in several interesting ways. One possibility is that the social organization of knowledge in a society has developed in such a way that certain decoding skills are not available to members. It has been reported that some African societies are not "film-literate" in the sense that they cannot read photographic images.[15] In a study with related concerns, Lerner has reported that "traditional respondents occasionally found electric media incomprehensible because they could not conceptualize communication outside an interpersonal context." These findings suggest that media literacy is a social skill that is developed through opportunities for practice. Another aspect of accessibility is provided from a different field of research by the finding that the majority of heroin addicts in Britain and America had smoked marijuana before graduating to heroin. Instead of asking what it is in marijuana that predisposes its users to further drug experimentation, a number of researchers have thought it more useful to explore why membership of an "audience" for marijuana is likely to make heroin considerably more accessible. From this perspective, the researcher asks in what situations and among which social groups do different types of drugs become accessible?

The concept of accessibility is therefore intimately related to the idea of availability, but not synonymous with it. Availability is more usefully confined to those cases in which there is some restraint on the distribution of performances. This covers a range of situations from the conservatism of local retailers (for example, the programming policies of small stations in America will usually operate to "screen out" more controversial performances) through more explicit censorship (such as the controls that used to be imposed by the Hays Office in Hollywood, or the pruning practiced by commercial sponsors, or the institutional vulnerability of the "entertainment industry" to the type of witch-hunt associated with the McCarthy era in America). Availability thus refers to factors that influence the development of the conventions that guide producers in deciding what sort of performances to make available to what sort of audiences. Accessibility as an element in the organization of audience taste takes account of both the structuring effect of conventions governing availability and the technical and normative factors in any given context that help to structure audience response to performances. Accessibility is therefore concerned with what might be called the development of institutionalized competence within the social stratification of audience tastes.[16]

Conception

Conception refers to the processes by which audiences place performances within what they feel to be appropriate contexts. It is a sociological truism that an essential basis for social interaction is the ability of people from different backgrounds to recognize symbols of role and status so that they can engage in an appropriate style of interaction. Media performances possess their own style, which will be used by audiences as guides to appropriate responses. This includes not only characteristics of performance content but other elements, such as the people by whom the performance is usually viewed or heard; the perceived status of other members of the audience for a particular performance; the financial, temporal and social expense involved in being a member of the audience; and the relevance of this performance to other favored or disfavored performances of which the individual is aware—in other words, the whole social context of reception. Conception is a normative concept in that it is concerned with the values people use in interpreting their activities, and conceptions of particular performances will have implications for the way individuals see other aspects of their environments. A stereotype is a closely related concept referring to the simplification of a confusing profusion of impressions, thus Lippman said of stereotypes that "they may not be a complete picture of the world, but they are a picture of a possible world to which we are adapted." Although McQuail's survey of research reports on the influence of television is obviously more specific than our concern with contemporary leisure, he does discuss, inter alia, the influence of television in defining social reality. He notes that although this approach does not lend itself to conventional social science research techniques, there is sufficient evidence to argue that the media structure understanding through "the provision of a consistent picture of the social world." They structure understanding also because they are centrally concerned with "knowledge" in its broadest sense.

Survey research is not a particularly sensitive research tool with which to investigate audience conceptions; however, one such study can be used to illustrate the argument. The study, in which over three hundred convicted delinquents and two control groups were interviewed about their television watching and favorite programs, is more fully reported in Halloran *et al.* Although few significant differences were found between the samples in terms of crude indices of enthusiasm for television, there were differences in orientation to television. The first was that male probationers consistently looked for excitement more than their peers. It was also found that male probationers remembered and liked the heroes in television programs more than the control groups did. The same type of finding characterizes probationers' attitudes to television as a source of information. All respondents were divided into two intelligence groups and, as expected, those with higher intelligence scores were significantly more likely to mention the informational benefits of television. However, the differences between probationers and their peers ran counter to what would be predicted on the basis of their intelligence scores. Group attitudes toward preferred types of programs and toward educational television supported the thesis that probationers consistently undervalue television as a source of information. This finding points to the possibility of identifying consistent underlying orientations toward or conceptions of the potential benefits of television entertainment. Relevant to this point is the study by McLeod and Becker, in which, although they are substantively concerned with testing the validity of gratifications measures, they argue that in formulating a theory of response, it might be more appropriate to use the concept of orientation because audience members seek to avoid as well as gratify, and because performances are organized for audiences through cognitive restructuring.[17]

Involvement

It is important to distinguish analytically between involvement and conception to accommodate the importance that audience members attach to their understanding of experiences. Conception was described as a mode of organizing experience. Involvement as a focus for analysis refers to the process of ranking experience; what is emphasized now is the differential significance of elements of experience in maintaining stylistic consistency. However, as with the other analytic foci, the heading is meant to apply to social ascription as much as individual achievement. A related example comes in Matza's rather idiosyncratic use of a concept of signification. Matza sees three senses of signification in relation to deviant behavior: labeling, the authorized ordaining of deviants so that they can be distinguished, surveyed and controlled; stigmatizing, in which the label acts as negative identification; and making meaningful, in the sense that actor and act become identified as integrated social type. Therefore, the significance of deviance is generalized to encompass the individual's self-conception of his social world, "more potent than that, the spell of signification capitalizes on the subject's essential *incapacity*: he is *unable not to* see or glimpse himself as he appears in the eyes of another."[18] Functionalistic theory in mass communications has been criticized for its assumption of the prior existence of needs in society so that communication behavior is a selective adaptation to meet these prerequisites. The criticism of this theoretical assumption takes the same form as Mead's attack on the Darwinian arguments that language and gestures developed in order to express preexistent emotions and other states of consciousness.[19] Mead argued that consciousness emerged from the social act rather than vice versa. A recognition of the creation of social meaning through experience analytically distinguishes the concept of involvement in studies of audience behavior, and thus provides an historical context for the process.

Involvement provides a tool with which to study specialized enthusiasms within a mass activity. In recent years it has become quite common to point to situations in which the "stars" of specialist subcultures have become discovered by national audiences and have achieved a much wider following. In such situations, the total audience can be stratified by their degree of involvement with the subcultural values the star initially articulated (examples of the sort of stars we are thinking of here are "underground" musicians, gymnastics champions and working-class club comedians). A related phenomenon is the politicization of groups organized to assert the autonomy of their members—for example, Gay Liberation Front or Women's Liberation. It is not intended to be trivializing to suggest that such groups are leisure organizations (the control of leisure will continue to grow as a central focus for political emancipation), but the implications of such an observation is that the activities of such groups will attract increasingly heterogeneous audiences for whom differences in degree of involvement in the initial struggles will be an important distinction. Those who are highly involved in a particular audience are likely to develop their commitment through time in significant social relationships; such commitments are likely to swamp other relationships and be publicly affirmed through reenactments and retellings of rituals and/or myths.[20] Shibutani's study of rumors is an illustration of the role of communication as it emerges from an interaction between beliefs and other features of situations. His emphasis upon rumors as collective transactions that provide plausible solutions to problematic situations is both a useful corrective to functionalist accounts of rumors as responses to needs and a useful discussion of the reasons why groups find particular beliefs plausible. Shibutani directs attention toward situations where the intensity of collective excitement radically restructures the appropriate symbolic frame of reference. He suggests that performances may be important because they facilitate audience redefinition of social situations. In this approach, importance is not defined by behavioral "effects" but by the dynamic role performances have in the mutual creation of the reality of experience, "the product of communication is not merely the modification of the listeners' attitudes and behavior through stimulation, but the establishment of some measure of mutual understanding."[21]

Aspiration

The last focus of our framework, aspiration, is closest in spirit to the concept of gratification in uses and gratifications theory. The difference turns on a point well formulated by McQuail and Gurevitch in their survey of three approaches to the explanation of audience behavior. They note that "a significant problem arises in devising techniques to obtain information about an individual's motivation for *future* behavior, since, ideally, motivation for future behavior and past experience should be separated."[22] The focus of aspiration is concerned with future behavior rather than extrapolation from past experience. This does not mean that historical materials cannot be utilized, but that we draw on such materials to understand the significance of what was being accomplished through activities rather than what we might deduce caused their accomplishment. The argument should be clarified by an illustration from a paper by Carey and Kreiling. They discuss critically functionalist accounts of pornography and argue that a more useful approach is to consider pornography in the historical context of the development of the novel as a mode of bourgeois expression and to see the social relations of pornographic accounts as versions of the social relations of other popular cultural fictions.

> Pornography, then, is not solely or perhaps even largely about sexuality. It is an exploration of the grammar of human relations. It is a fantasy, a fiction, something made, but it is a making of collective images of men, women, classes, races and ethnic groups.[23]

This perspective can be developed by discussing some other aspects of a culture of mass entertainment. A central feature is the role of stars as individuals who seem to embody qualities admired to the extent that they attract audiences apart from those who attend their performances. People who have never seen Raquel Welch in a film can still be avid followers of her activities as depicted in newspapers and television talk shows. (It is surprising that few entertainment stars have successfully shifted their charismatic appeal to other kinds of institutional leadership, such as party politics). A functionalist account of the phenomenon of stardom could either stress their role as models for members of the audience or as fantasy substitutes for grim reality. This may be true at an individual level, but stars can also be located as a social category for making sense of structural tensions. "The girl who dresses like Elizabeth Taylor is not trying to display wealth or to testify to her membership of the leisure classes. She is expressing her membership, along with innumerable girls all over the country, of a world to which Elizabeth Taylor also belongs."[24] To feel oneself sharing a common reality with more privileged individuals may occasion jealousy and frustration if there are reasons for doubting the legitimacy of their privileges, but stars are typically not a sufficiently stable group to constitute a class—rather they are an exaggerated enactment of personal biographies. As such, their accessibility makes them into commodities for the mass market, but the uncertainty of their aura provides for dramatic tension.

> The specific function of . . . activities and events usually associated with the term 'leisure' . . . has to be assessed in relation to this ubiquity and steadiness of excitement control. . . . In the form of this class of leisure events our society provides for the need to experience the upsurge of strong emotions in public—for a type of excitement which does not disturb and endanger the relative orderliness of social life.[25]

The further implication of this mode of analysis is that in our society, leisure becomes a spectacle for itself. If the world that we aspire to make and participate in through our membership of leisure audiences is dramatically stimulating, then we come to judge our leisure by the quality of experience it provides.

> The data of cultural experiences are somewhat fictionalized, idealized, or exaggerated models of social life that are in the public domain, in film, fiction, political rhetoric, small talk, comic strips, expositions, etiquette and spectacles. All tourist attractions are cultural experiences.[26]

The initial impetus for the paper was provided by a dissatisfaction with the dominant traditions in studies of the audience for mass leisure. We felt it important to emphasize the ways in which membership of such an audience does not preclude creative enthusiasm or a discriminating self-consciousness about the aesthetics of leisure activities; nor does it preclude a desire to relate leisure enthusiasms to other aspects of life in such a way as to make a style of life consistent and comprehensible. In making these points, this paper would seem to form part of a "positive" view of mass culture in contrast to more "pessimistic" views, which stress exploitation.[27] In fact, we regard this opposition as largely irrelevant because it attempts too schematic a contrast. Though a common criticism of positive viewpoints is that they lack an historical consciousness, we do not think this could be made in relation to this analysis. We have tried to show that the institution of leisure is an historical phenomenon intimately related to the development of industrial capitalism, in which leisure, as a way of spending time, is functionally related to the circulation of commodities and the organization of productive relationships. In setting out the framework for the analysis of differences within and between audiences, we have, therefore, tried to show that the development of taste is a complex social process and that the constitution of taste works through the implications of structural relationships.

A further implication of these arguments leads to a reconsideration of the character of the distinction between work and leisure. If the common issues in studies of mass communication and contemporary leisure are subsumed under a general heading, such as the study of popular art, then this raises the question: How should popular art be defined? In a way that is consistent with the arguments set out in this paper, one of us has argued elsewhere[28] that the most fruitful method of discriminating between popular and "high" or "folk" art is in terms of their methods of production. That is, popular art is typically made by a team of workers for an anonymous audience in return for cash recompense. In the terms of this definition, leisure, as entertainment, is always work, and thus the activities that constitute leisure occasions are "works" (performances) for which there are audiences. There cannot, therefore, be a distinction between work and leisure in terms of type of activity, particularly when we bear in mind amateur enthusiasts who recreate others' works as leisure for themselves and others (e.g., steam train enthusiasts). Both work and leisure tend to merge in the staging of spectacles or experiences:

> In the place of the distinction Marx foresaw is an arrangement wherein workers are displayed, and other workers on the other side of the culture barrier watch them for their enjoyment. . . . Work in the modern world does not turn class against class so much as it turns man against himself, fundamentally dividing his existence.[29]

MacCannell has been quoted before and it is a pity that there is no space in this paper to provide a more detailed examination of his theory of a leisure class, but we can note now that studies of audiences for contemporary leisure are impoverished if they remain content with describing the social patterning of taste. The significance of processes of audience formation and change lies in their implications for class stratification based on property relationships. It is possible that the social alliances of leisure affiliation will provide the grounds for a changing politics of social stratification.

NOTES

[1] This quote from Carey is taken out of context but provides an apt summary.
[2] Burns, p. 46.
[3] Cited in Chafee, p. 98.
[4] *Ibid.*, p. 102.
[5] See, for example, Rogers and Shoemaker.
[6] See, for example, Morin.
[7] Katz *et al.*, p. 23.
[8] Blumler and Katz.
[9] *Ibid.*, p. 39.
[10] *Ibid.*, pp. 41–42.
[11] This list adapted from Katz *et al.*, p. 27.
[12] Chaney, *Processes of Mass Communication*, p. 24.
[13] This approach to popular culture, is more fully developed in Chaney (forthcoming), especially in Chapter 4.
[14] Cf. Blum and McHugh.
[15] J. R. and L. Forsdale.
[16] Cf. the work of Gans for a thoughtful exploration of levels of cultural style.
[17] McLeod and Becker, pp. 141–42.
[18] Matza, p. 174.
[19] Mead, pp. 18–19.
[20] For an interesting illustration of this approach to myth-telling as a process of membershipping, see Sykes.
[21] Shibutani, p. 170.
[22] McQuail and Gurevitch, p. 296.
[23] Carey and Kreiling, pp. 241–42.
[24] Alberoni, quoted in Burns, p. 48.
[25] Elias and Dunning, p. 6.
[26] MacCannell, p. 23.
[27] Rosenberg and White.
[28] Chaney (forthcoming).
[29] MacCannell, p. 37.

REFERENCES

Bauman, Z. "A Note on Mass Culture: On Infrastructure." In *Sociology of Mass Communications*. Ed. D. McQuail. London: Penguin, 1972.

Blum, A. F., and McHugh, P. "The Social Ascription of Motives," *American Sociological Review* 36 (1971): 98–109.

Blumler, J., and Katz, E., eds. *The Uses of Mass Communications*. London: Sage, 1974.

Burns, T. "Leisure in Industrial Society." In *Leisure and Society in Britain*. Ed. M. Smith *et. al.* London: Allen Lane, 1973.

Carey, J. "Mass Communication Research and Cultural Studies." In *Mass Communication and Society*. Ed. J. Curran *et. al.* London: Edward Arnold, 1977.

Carey, J., and Kreiling, A. "Popular Culture and Uses and Gratifications." In *The Uses of Mass Communications*. Eds. Blumer and Katz. London: Sage, 1974.

Chafee, S. H. "The Interpersonal Context of Mass Communication." In *Current Perspectives in Mass Communication Research*. Eds. F. G. Kline and P. J. Tichenor. London: Sage, 1972.

Chancy, D. *Fictions and Ceremonies: Transforming Popular Experience in Industrial Society*. London: Edward Arnold, forthcoming.

Chaney, D. *Processes of Mass Communication*. London: Macmillan, 1972.

Clayre, A. *Work and Play: Ideas and Experience of Work and Leisure*. London: Weidenfeld and Nicolson, 1974.

Elias, N.,and Dunning, E. "The Quest for Excitement in Unexciting Societies." B.S.A. Conference Paper, 1967.

Forsdale, J. R., and Forsdale, L. "Film Literacy," *Teachers College Record* 67 (1966).

Gans, Herbert J. *Popular Culture and High Culture*. New York: Basic Books, 1974.

Halloran, J. D., et al. *Television and Delinquency*. Leicester: U. P. Leicester, 1970.

Johnstone, J. W. C. "Social Integration and Mass Media Use among Adolescents." In *The Uses of Mass Communications*. Eds. Brumler and Katz. London: Sage, 1974

Katz, E. "The Diffusion of New Ideas and Practices." In *The Science of Human Communication*. Ed. W. Schramm. New York: Basic Books, 1963.

Katz, E., *et. al.* "Utilization of Mass Communication by the Individual." In *The Uses of Mass Communications*. Eds. Blumler and Katz. London: Sage, 1974.

Lang, K., and Lang, G. E. *Politics and Television*. New York: Quadrangle Books, 1968.

Lerner, D. *The Passing of Traditional Society*. New York: Free Press, 1958.

Lippmann, W. *Public Opinion*. New York: Harcourt Brace, 1922.

MacCannell, D. *The Tourist*. London: Macmillan, 1976.

McLeod, J. M., and L. B. Becker, "Testing the Validity of Gratification Measures." In *The Uses of Mass Communications*. Eds. Blumler and Katz. London: Sage, 1974.

McQuail, D. "The Influence and Effects of Mass Media." In *Mass Communication and Society*. Ed. J. Curran *et. al.* London: Edward Arnold, 1977.

McQuail, D., and Gurevitch, M. "Explaining Audience Behavior: Three Approaches Considered." In *The Uses of Mass Communications*. Eds. Blumler and Katz. London: Sage, 1974.

Matza, D. *Becoming Deviant*. New Jersey: Prentice-Hall, 1969.

Mead, G. H. *Mind, Self and Society*. Chicago: Chicago UP, 1934.

Morin, E. *New Trends in the Study of Mass Communication*. Birmingham: Centre for Contemporary Cultural Studies, 1968.

Reid, D. A. "The Decline of Saint Monday 1766–1866," *Past and Present* 71 (1976).

Rogers, E. M. and Shoemaker, F. *Communication of Innovations*, rev. ed. New York: Collier-Macmillan, 1972.

Rosenberg, B., and White, D. M., eds. *Mass Culture Revisited*. New York: Van Nostrand, 1971.

Shibutani, T. *Improvised News: A Sociological Study of Rumor*. New York: Bobbs-Merrill, 1966.

Sykes, A. J. M. "Myth in Communication," *Journal of Communication* 20 (March 1970).

Stefan R. Melnik

The "Uses and Gratifications" Approach in the Study of "Entertainment" and Leisure Use

☆ MASS COMMUNICATION research is plagued with concepts with little or no precise meaning, concepts that are difficult or impossible to use in an operational context, at least within reasonable limits. This is not a peculiarity of a field wherein systematic study is of relatively recent origin. Indeed many such concepts, *high culture* and *popular culture* for instance, have their origins in more traditional academic disciplines.

Entertainment is such a concept. What is entertainment; what is it to entertain or to be entertained?

The "entertainment function" consists of so many sub-functions, each of which appear in different constellations and different relative magnitude, according to the medium, the environment, the content and the personal predispositions at hand. This being the case, one must ask the following question: Why not look at these "sub-functions" in turn and forget entertainment, at least insofar as research is concerned? Indeed this is a conclusion that is implicit in much academic work, as I will illustrate.

Many authors, playwrights, scriptwriters and producers, however, frequently talk about and discuss entertainment, and because they do so, it is not a concept that one can altogether dismiss. Some go so far as to argue that the concept is necessary, at least for the purposes of planning. For such people, the concept of entertainment seems to be something very concrete. After all, they are involved in its production. But at the same time, it is a term that they find extremely hard to elucidate.[1] In the last resort—in the case of television, for instance—entertainment is simply that which entertainment departments produce, which is mainly program material that conforms with stereotyped notions, however inadequate they may be.

▶ This is an original article written especially for this book. Stefan R. Melnik, M.A., is a research student at the Department of Journalism and Communication at the Ruhr-University, Bochum, West Germany.

At the same time, the concept seems to function as a barrier, preventing such communicators from perceiving that a documentary is or can be entertaining (whatever this term may mean). The televised exploits of the ocean biologist, Jacques Cousteau, are a good example of such documentaries. The same, of course, applies to news broadcasts, educational programs and various other items presented on television. Conversely, entertainment can be informative and can influence. Many would argue that this is always the case. This is also widely overlooked by those involved in entertainment production. Institutional barriers help to cement this state of affairs in encouraging departmentalized thinking. Getting rid of the concept and institutional barriers could result in the production of radically different programs and thus help to counter some of the problems television organizations are presently faced with, the most important perhaps being the following: how can one attract a larger audience when the usual is not resorted to (e.g., variety shows and soap operas)?[2] The talk show, a relative innovation in West Germany, which traverses institutional barriers in combining interviewing of important personalities with conversation in a relaxed, intimate and sometimes light-hearted atmosphere, demonstrates that it is possible to attract a large audience using non-conventional means.

The concept that the mass media had a limited number of functions to perform (e.g., to inform, to comment and to entertain)[3] was one that proved fruitful for organizational purposes but barren for research. Such an approach can perhaps only be seen in the context of a mass communication research paradigm—still much in existence—concentrating attention on what the media do to people rather than what people do with media.[4] But it proved increasingly difficult to draw the lines between these functions. They seemed to overlap and sometimes not to operate where they should. Information, for instance, didn't seem to inform nor did it seem to comment as far as the recipient was concerned.[5] The concept of entertainment seemed to contain a number of very disparate elements. One way out of such dilemmas was to try to subsume various functions of mass media under one single function, a *ludenic* or *play* function, as Stephenson did,[6] or a *socius* function as Prakke did.[7] The other approach, also taking the recipient as its starting point, involved doing precisely the opposite (i.e., postulating a number of different functions). Here I am referring to the *uses and gratifications* approach. This approach does not necessarily contradict a macro-approach such as Stephenson's. The latter, I would suggest, operates at a different level. For the purpose of my argument, however, only the uses and gratifications approach is relevant.

According to this approach, media content, exposure to the media *per se* and the social context of media exposure (e.g., watching a film with friends) fulfill a variety of functions in accordance with recipient needs.[8] Furthermore, a recipient will use the medium that is most suitable for fulfilling a particular combination of needs.[9] These functions have been variously categorized as the three following classification systems show:

1

1. Diversion
   (a) Escape from the constraints of routine
   (b) Escape from the burdens of problems
   (c) Emotional release

2. Personal Relationships
   (a) Companionship
   (b) Social utility

3. Personal Identity
   (a) Personal reference
   (b) Reality exploration
   (c) Value reinforcement

4. Surveillance   McQuail (et al.)[10]

To these functional categories, the BBC Audience Research Department recommends adding a fifth:

5. Social Action[11]

2

1. Information, knowledge and experience
   (a) Mass media provide information about current events, contribute to a feeling of being up-to-date
   (b) They serve to broaden the individual's sphere of experience (new people, places and things)
   (c) They provide practical or personal information for use in daily life

2. Feeling of freedom from obligations and "duties," pleasant expectations and memories
   (a) Mass media provide entertainment and pleasurable amusement
   (b) They satisfy general curiosity
   (c) They provide a contrast to everyday realities
   (d) They permit physical and emotional passivity

3. Temporary retreat or shelter from the immediate environment
   (a) Consumption of mass media provides a "legitimate" shelter from the environment and allows freedom from role demands

4. Compensation for perceived failures, weaknesses—more or less deep-rooted and abiding—in the personality or social spheres
   (a) Mass media nullify consciousness of real ego-relations, allow identification, escape from reality
   (b) They provide substitutes for friends and acquaintances (parasocial interaction)

5. Maintenance and/or improvement of relations with the environment
   (a) Exposure to the media as social activity contributes directly to goal fulfillment
   (b) Mass media give guidance with respect to behavior and traits, provide topics of conversation
   (c) They themselves denote status, success, group membership and such on the part of the receiver

6. Individuality—to distinguish oneself from the masses
   (a) Mass media provide impulses and guidance
   (b) Exposure to the media and media consumption habits contribute to the goal

Lundberg and Hulten [12]

3

1. Improvement of information, knowledge and understanding
   (fulfillment of cognitive needs)

2. Increase aesthetic, pleasurable and emotional experience
   (fulfillment of affective needs)

3. Increase credibility, confidence, stability and status
   (combination of both cognitive and affective elements—fulfillment of integrative needs)

4. Strengthen contacts with family, friends and the world
   (also fulfillment of integrative needs)

5. Weaken contacts with self and one's other social roles
   (escape or tension release)

adapted from Katz and Gurevitch [13]

A closer look at the three categorizations I have chosen reveals that there is a measure of agreement as to what the media's functions are. For instance, 1.4 closely corresponds with clusters 2.1 and 3.1; the elements in cluster 1.1 with those in 2.2,3,4a and 3.2,5; 1.2,3 with 2.4b,5,6 and 3.3,4. As one can see, the information function has remained intact—although it can be further subdivided according to the specific requirements of each research project undertaken. The functions of entertainment and comment, on the other hand, have been replaced by a differentiated spectrum of functions. Companionship and escape, for instance, which are sometimes subsumed under a so-called entertainment function, are considered to be separate functions. The opinion function has similarly been split up into such functions as value reinforcement, provision of guidance, increase of status. The category of social action, only included under 1., represents an empirically backed observation that recipients can be motivated to functional or dysfunctional action,[14] a category which can probably be further subdivided. If such a category can be included, it would go a long way toward countering the criticism that the "uses and gratifications" approach involves the assumption that the audience manipulates the media and is not manipulated by them.

Such differences of categorization show that this approach, despite the fact that one can draw up a long history,[15] is still in its infancy. Lundberg and Hulten drew up their categories on basis of some sixty studies, with the result that they have probably included most functions presently conceivable. The Katz and Gurevitch categorization is derived from "(largely speculative) literature on the social and psychological functions of the mass media."[16] Mc-Quail's list of functions is the result of systematic interviewing, preceded by unstructured small-group discussions on the basis of which the interview material was constructed.[17] The different classification systems may be the result of these different approaches—but it is not the object of my essay to discuss the pros and cons of the categories themselves or the way in which they arrived at these categories. What seems to be far more important is the fact that the authors, all using different means, have been able to supply us with a large number of functions about which there seems to be some measure of agreement. This is a basis upon which one can build. However, the mistake must not be made in thinking that we are in a position to assess all media's functions (or that this is necessary) or that individual functions as they are defined will prove to be of lasting value as conceptual tools in tackling the social phenomena we are trying to explain.

What is needed in research is an agreed basic categorization of functions that will allow comparability of results and further research on the basis of what has already been achieved. This requires conceptual unanimity as to what various terms used denote, but doesn't mean that the results of such research are to be interpreted in any particular way: they can be used by most if not all theoretical approaches.[18] Over and above such a basic categorization, functions can be further subdivided according to the needs of each individual study. It is up to the latter to define the limit to the meaningfulness of further differentiation.

Why is such a paradigm necessary?

The functions that the uses and gratifications approach has supplied us with have far greater heuristic value than relatively undifferentiated concepts such as entertainment, as I now propose to demonstrate:[19]

First, it is possible to bypass the problems one faces in trying to define what is meant by entertainment (or commentary for that matter). An arbitrary and simple definition cannot be considered as an alternative because 1) it is difficult to separate a concept from its tradition and 2) it would only obviate the need for a delineation of further functions. For instance, if one were to define entertainment in terms of "escape from the constraints of routine," a separate function would have to be created for the "companionship" that media apparently provide. The controversy and/or lack of clarity that the use of a concept of entertainment would imply only serves to hinder an advance within mass-communication research (or indeed within social science as a whole). Whenever a function can be shown to contain disparate elements, and where this is of significance within the context of one's work, the best strategy I would suggest is to split the function up and see what happens.

Second, the uses and gratifications approach supplies us with means whereby we can *proceed* or *begin* to compare and discuss mass media activity in its various forms and the relationships between these various forms and other activities in a systematic manner. The research process doesn't stop at this point, however. This, I suggest, is necessary in view of the lack of research beyond the scope of simple stocktaking (e.g., media statistics—which are of course necessary in themselves) and also in the context of investigation into leisure-time activity. Leisure scholars, for instance, have made little attempt to investigate the relationship between active and passive leisure activity,[20] perhaps because they lack the conceptual tools with which to do this. Researchers in the field of mass communication, for their part, are probably too concerned with mass media "activity" and regard other forms of activity to be beyond their competency.

The significance of the kind of questions that need to be answered in this context are easy to see. A few examples will serve to illustrate the variety and extent of research that still has to be undertaken. A beginning can be made using such a pretheoretical approach. At the same time these examples suggest that the functions mass media fulfill are an alternative for other activities.[21]

The interaction between different kinds of work and different ways of spending leisure is a question, for instance, about which we know relatively little. An interesting study on this subject can help to illustrate the point I am trying to make:[22] it established that three factors during work were especially significant in determining the way in which leisure is used: work-rhythm (whether one was on shiftwork or not, for instance), degree of monotony at work and the kind of interpersonal communication the work allowed. Railway workers on shift work need a long time to recover from their strenuous and monotonous work, with the result that the relative time at their disposal for recreation is limited. In contrast, the nursing and sanitary personnel at a hospital have many breaks during the course of a working day and find time to talk with colleagues about matters not directly related to work. The number of such people actively engaged in cultural and social activities was exceptionally high. Among miners, recreation involving individual and social activity was equally observable. Close contacts during work are maintained after work. The use of the concepts of *monotony, social interaction* and *routine*, for instance, apply to both this particular example and to the uses and gratifications approach, which supplies us with functions that take these into account. Furthermore, there seems to be a direct relationship between these factors during work and leisure activity—including media consumption. Thus, for instance, is heavy media consumption the result of tiring work, little companionship, drab routine? Or from a different angle: Do particular forms of leisure activity increase efficiency at work? These are only a few of the possible questions within this context.

If we concentrate our attention on one particular mass medium and compare its use with other media and non-media activities, a similar wealth of questions presents itself. Television, for instance, is first by a long way in the list of most-favored leisure activities.[23] It is a leisure activity in which the vast majority of people in industrialized countries participate[24] and are prepared to spend a lot of money on.[25] But this is no more than simple stocktaking. Noelle-Neumann assesses that it was not the time spent reading newspapers and magazines that suffered as a result of the introduction of television but those hours devoted to active leisure activities—social activities such as playing cards, sports and gymnastics, individual activities such as model building, sewing, knitting, writing letters—although at the same time the wish to spend time on leisure actively grew. Indeed, recently, active leisure activity has shown some increase.[26] The questions present themselves, what functions does television fulfill that other activities cannot fulfill, at least to the same extent? What has the medium replaced and why? Can one deduce that the functions television fulfills are more important than other functions? What is it that leads people away from an active to a passive leisure activity or vice versa? A lot of statistical data is available that demonstrates trends (e.g., steady increase in the number of television viewing hours and decline in the number of cinemas or the average number of cinema visits *per capita* p.a.) but very little shows how film and television viewing are related to one another (for instance, what the two media have in common; which are the functions of film that television has replaced). Further interesting questions present themselves when one discovers that television sets often seem to be switched on when people are not looking or are doing other things at the same time.[27] Supplying part of the answer and laying the foundations for further study is within the scope of the uses and gratifications approach. The questions posed can be tackled by using various interviewing techniques, as has hitherto generally been the case. However, there is scope for imagination (e.g., controlled experiments in which subjects who usually watch television have no access to a television set for a number of weeks. How do they compensate for the lack of a television set?)[28]

Despite what I have said above, the term "entertainment" can still serve one important purpose: It points to an area of mass communication research in which there is an enormous deficit. I am referring especially to mass media products that attract a large audience, such as television serials (including soap operas), pop records, comics and mass-circulated magazines. Such neglect was (and still is) perhaps due to the stigma attached to such products, a lack of awareness as to their possible functions and far-reaching significance and a lack of adequate and common conceptual tools (at least until fairly recently). The uses and gratifications approach supplies us with a starting point. An ensuing debate as to its usefulness, after a certain amount of experience with the approach, can only result in the creation of better conceptual frameworks.

This approach, I have argued, allows us to analyze mass media reception as well as its relationship to other activities, particularly during leisure, in considerably greater detail than a single heterogenous function—entertainment—could. I have given examples of the variety and kind of important questions that could be tackled within the framework of the approach. The functions of the mass media, furthermore, are equally the functions of leisure in general.

To return to the communicator, appreciation of the variety of functions mass media perform may assist him in the production of content (e.g., content that meets specific requirements better than is perhaps presently the case). The concept of entertainment, as I have shown, tends to desensitize rather than sensitize. Answers could be supplied to the following question, for instance: What is it that attracts a large audience to a crime series, a variety show, a sports program? The elements that attract could perhaps be incorporated into other types of programs, or new program forms that would please the audience could be created. Or insights could be supplied with regard to the question as to what functions various mass media perform inadequately or not at all, functions for which there is a need.

NOTES

For an extensive review of the uses of gratifications approach, I would like to recommend the collection by Jay G. Blumler and Elihu Katz, eds., *The Uses of Mass Communications* (London, 1974).

1 Cf. Arthur Hofer, "Den Mond für die kleine Verkäuferin," *Süddeutsche Zeitung*, nr. 42 (20th February, 1978): 19 (based on his book, *Unterhaltung im Hörfunk* (Nürnberg [West Germany], 1978); Wolfgang R. Langenbucher and Walter A. Mahler, *Unterhaltung als Beruf?* (West Berlin, 1974).

2 See especially the hitherto unpublished papers by Schardt, Rölz, Neudeck and Hickethier presented at the *3rd Marler Fernsehforum*, Marl (West Germany), 20th–24th March, 1977; Zweites Deutsches Fernsehen (ZDF), *Mainz bleibt Mainz. Die Unterhaltungssendungen im Zweiten Deutschen Fernsehen*. Mainz (West Germany), 1965, for examples with respect to the two paragraphs above.

3 Cf. e.g., Walter Hagemann, *Grundzüge der Publizistik*, rev. ed. by Henk Prakke, Winfried B. Lerg and Michael Schmolke (Münster [West Germany], 1966), pp. 34–37; Wilbur Schramm and Donald F. Roberts, eds., *The Process and Effects of Mass Communication*, rev. ed. (Urbana, 1971), pp. 34 ff. Schramm distinguishes between the informational, instructional, persuasive and entertaining functions. In West Germany, all broadcasting organization statutes explicitly refer to information, education and entertainment as the areas in which their responsibilities lie, for instance (commentary is included in the first of these categories). The major divisions are accordingly named Entertainment Department, and so on. This is the case in other countries also.

4 Cf. Denis McQuail, *Toward a Sociology of Mass Media* (London, 1969), pp. 58–78.

5 Cf. Herbert H. Hyman and Paul B. Sheatsley, "Some Reasons Why Information Campaigns Fail," *Public Opinion Quarterly* 11, no. 3 (1947): 412–23. A recent study ascertained that an average 1.2 items out of an average total of 19.8 news stories per network broadcast were recalled (unaided). See W. Russell Neumann, "Patterns of Recall among Television News Viewers," *Public Opinion Quarterly* 40, no. 1 (1976): 115–23.

6 Cf. William Stephenson, *The Play Theory of Mass Communication* (Chicago, 1967).

7 Hendricus Johannes Prakke, "Die Soziusfunktion der Presse," *Publizistik* 5, no. 6 (1960): 556–60.

8 A good summary of the uses and gratifications approach is to be found in the IPC Sociological Monograph No. 11 (The Mass Media—Uses and Gratifications) prepared and published by the central Marketing Research and Services Department of the International Publishing Corporation (IPC), London, in June, 1975.

9 Elihu Katz and Michael Gurevitch, *The Secularization of Leisure. Culture and Communication in Israel* (London, 1976), pp. 215–43.

10 Denis McQuail *et al.*, "The Television Audience: A Revised Perspective," in *Sociology of Mass Communication*, ed. Denis McQuail (Harmondsworth, England, 1972), p. 155.

[11] British Broadcasting Corporation (BBC), *Annual Review of BBC Audience Research Findings*, No. 2 (London, 1976), pp. 47–48.

[12] Dan Lundberg and Olof Hulten, *Individen och Massmedia* (Stockholm, Sweden, 1968), Chapt. 7–10. A short unpublished English summary is to be found at the Centre for Mass Communication Research, Leicester, England.

[13] Elihu Katz et al., "On the Use of the Mass Media for Important Things," *American Sociological Review* 38, no. 2 (1973): 166–67; also Katz and Gurevitch, *op. cit.*: p. 219.

[14] BBC, *op. cit.*, p. 48.

[15] Cf. David Chaney, *Processes of Mass Communication* (London, 1972), pp. 25–29.

[16] Katz and Gurevitch, *op. cit.*, p. 219.

[17] McQuail *et al.*, *op. cit.*, p. 144 *ff.*

[18] Cf. Jay G. Blumler, "The Role of Theory in Uses and Gratifications of Research." Unpublished paper presented to the Annual Conference of the International Communication Association, West Berlin, 29th May–4th June, 1977.

[19] One can criticize the precision of most concepts used in mass communication research: cf. e.g., David L. Swanson, "Political Communication Research and the Uses and Gratifications Model: A Critique." Unpublished paper presented to the Annual Conference of the International Communication Association, Berlin, 29th May–4th June, 1977, p. 2 *f.* I believe, however, that the concepts one should adopt instead of entertainment are *relatively* more precise.

[20] Cf. e.g., Michael Smith and Lizbeth Stanley, comp., *Directory of Leisure Scholars and Researchers 1977*. England: Dept. of Sociological and Political Studies, University of Salford, 1977. Out of a total of 487 scholars, there are only 9 listed whose interests include research into mass media use.

[21] In this context, the work of Karl Erik Rosengren and Swen Windahl, "Media Consumption as a Functional Alternative," in *Sociology of Mass Communication*, ed. Denis McQuail (Harmondsworth, England, 1972), pp. 166–94, for instance, is of considerable interest.

[22] Battelle-Institute e. V., *Auswirkungen von Arbeitsbedingungen auf das Freizeitverhalten* (Frankfurt–Essen [West Germany], 1977). Project sponsored and commissioned by the Siedlungsverband Ruhrkohlenbezirk (SVR), Essen.

[23] Elisabeth Noelle-Neumann, ed., *Allenbacher Jahrbuch der Demoskopie 1976–1977* (München [West Germany], 1977), pp. 44–45.

[24] Ninety-six percent of West German households, for instance. *Media Perspektiven*, Daten zur Mediensituation in der BRD (Frankfurt, 1977), p. 16.

[25] Ifak Institute für Absatzforschung (Wiesbaden), Spiegel-Dokumentation. K(auf), K(onsum und) K(ommunikationsverhalten der Bundesbevölkerung) '76. Commissioned by the Spiegel-Verlag, Hamburg, West Germany, p. 106 *ff.*

[26] Elisabeth Noelle-Neumann, "Macht Fernsehen träge und traurig?" in *Frankfurter Allgemeine Zeitung*, Bilder und Zeiten, No. 186 (13th August, 1977).

[27] EMNID-Institut (Bielefeld, West Germany), *Spiegel-Umfrage. Freizeitverhalten.* Commissioned by the Spiegel-Verlag, Hamburg, in July, 1972. Table 22.

[28] Cf. e.g., Gesellschaft für rationelle Psychologie (München, West Germany), Fernsehpanel '71 (unpublished extracts of findings). This study on dependence on television and the influence of TV on personal and family life was carried out within the framework of a research project on leisure behavior, needs and expectations.

Nikolai Sergeyevitch Mansurov:

The Study of the Mass Communications and Cultural Establishments in the USSR. Some Results of Sociological Research

I

☆ IN THE SOVIET UNION much attention is devoted to the development of the mass communications and cultural establishments. This is confirmed, in particular, by the report of the General Secretary of the CPSU Central Committee to the 25th Congress. According to Leonid Brezhnev:

> In the period under review, much attention as given by the Central Committee to various questions pertaining to the raising of the ideological level, co-ordination and efficiency of the *mass media*. As a result, their impact on the development of the economy, science and culture and on the whole life of society has grown still more.[1]

The study of the activity of the mass communications and cultural establishments in the Soviet Union is conducted by a number of research centers. Among them we may mention the Academy of Social Sciences, the Institute of Sociological Research (Moscow) and the Institute of Socio-Economic Research (Leningrad), all three institutes belonging to the system of the Academy of Sciences of the USSR. In addition, studies are conducted at the Journalism Faculty of Moscow University, the Siberian Branch and Urals Scientific Centre of the Academy of Sciences of the USSR, the Moscow and Leningrad Institutes of Culture, the Research Institute of Culture of the Ministry of Culture of the Russian Federation, and at a number of university faculties.

During the past ten years of intensive research in the field of mass communications and cultural establishments, Soviet researchers have obtained a wealth of material, which has been repeatedly discussed at various symposiums and presented in many publications, such as a series appearing under the headings "Theory and Practice of Mass Communications" (Mysl Publishers), "Books and Reading in the Life of the Soviet Village" (published by the Lenin

▶ This is a hitherto unpublished paper. Dr. N. S. Mansurov is Professor of Sociology at the Institute for Sociological Research, Academy of Sciences, Moscow.

State Library), and "Problems of Journalism" (published by Leningrad University).

On the basis of research into various aspects of the activity of the mass communications and cultural establishments, a large number of these for the degrees of Candidate of Sciences and Doctor of Sciences have been presented and defended.

II

One of the topical questions studied with particular thoroughness in the Soviet Union at the first stage of research into the activity of the mass communications and cultural establishments was the structure of audiences: readers of newspapers and books, radio listeners, TV viewers, club members and theatregoers, and so on. These studies may be divided into three groups.

1. Theoretical studies of the audience of one channel of mass communications (e.g., newspapers) or any particular cultural establishment (say, a club). These studies were usually conducted on the initiative of research collectives and were not always representative; they embraced a wide range of questions that sometimes lay outside the framework of the mass communications and cultural establishments (e.g., questions such as the effect of club attendance on labor activity or the relationship between the press-reading and social activity of the respondents).

2. Empirical research into the mass communications and cultural establishments conducted by arrangement with a particular publishing house or ministry. As a rule, they were representative empirical studies of a comparatively narrow scope. These included analyses of the readership of the newspapers *Pravda* and *Izvestiya*, and the journal *Ogonyok*. The results of these studies have had important practical significance.

3. Theoretical studies of a systematic nature dealing with the main mass communications and routine cultural establishments. These studies were conducted on the initiative of research collectives and were aimed at analyzing fundamental problems (e.g., elucidating the relationship between various channels of the mass communications, the character of information exerting the greatest influence on the personality and changes caused by it, and so on). Studies of this latter type have been carried out in particular at the Institute of Sociological Research of the USSR Academy of Sciences.

III

Without dwelling in detail on the specific features, advantages and shortcomings of the three indicated types of sociological studies, let us cite some results.

To begin with, it should be pointed out that, as a result of the cultural policy pursued by the Communist Party and the Soviet state, a broad network of the mass communications and cultural establishments has been established in the USSR. In 1974, the Soviet Union published 86,000 book titles in a total printing of 1,731 million copies (the figures for the period from 1918 to 1974 are 2.7 million titles and 43.2 billion copies). In 1974 there were 8,172 newspapers and 7,123 magazines published in the country (the annual printing of newspapers reaching 37 billion copies, and of magazines, 3 billion copies).[2] Recently more than 400 newspapers and 113 journals and magazines have begun publication.[3]

In 1975, over 110 million radio sets and radio receivers and 55 million TV sets were in use in the country.[4] In 1974, there were 154,800 cinemas and film projecting facilities in operation in the country; 130,700 libraries (at the end of 1971, the total number of libraries of various types—public, scientific, college, technical and other specialized libraries—was 360,000, with a book stock running into 3.3 billion books); 134,300 clubs; 1,259 museums (in 1974, they were visited by 128 million people); 564 theatres (with a total audience in 1974 of 116,000,000).[5]

At the same time, it is important to stress the accessibility of the output of the mass communications and cultural establishments for the population, for, in contrast to the capitalist countries, books, journals and magazines are low-priced in the Soviet Union, as are also tickets for the cinema and theatre and other types of entertainment. All the different groups of the population have equal access to the mass communications and to the various cultural establishments.

Sociological studies confirm the fact that the mass communications and cultural establishments are within reach of the Soviet people and are actively used by them. For a comparison, let us cite the results obtained by various investigators.

These data show that the overwhelming majority of the population engaged in industry actively use the main mass communications and cultural establishments (the slight differences in Table I are due to the fact that, firstly, studies were conducted in different cities and, secondly, that they were carried

Table 1 USE OF THE MASS COMMUNICATIONS (in percentage to
the total number of the respondents)

	Grushin[6] 1967	Ladodo[7] 1969, Moscow	Ledovskaya[7]		Mansurov 1974–1975 (summary data for four cities)
			Moscow	Kuibyshev	
Newspaper readers	90	87	94 ± 4.15	92 ± 7.19	82
Book readers	75	53	92 ± 8.56	85 ± 16.9	92
Magazine readers	67	64	92 ± 4.8	86 ± 5.12	78
Film viewers	76	—	91	91	81
Radio listeners	76	78	96 ± 2.46	95 ± 3.97	87
TV viewers	—	95	95 ± 4.59	93.2.65	88
Theatre goers	—	—	—	—	73

out at different periods of time). These data give grounds for believing that in the country as a whole there is an upward trend in the workers' use of the mass communications and cultural establishments.

The above studies also show that in some regions of the country, various groups of the population use the mass communications and cultural establishments to different degrees. This can be illustrated by the data obtained by Ladodo (see Table 2).

Ladodo's data testify that there are differences between working men and women in their attitude to the mass communications. Thus, young people prefer radio (men) and television (women); radio and television rank first and second on the scale of preferences among young people, while older people prefer newspapers (first place) and television (second place). Among women of the middle-age group, television is again in the first place, while among men it holds second place, coming after newspapers. Young people prefer television and radio to newspapers, whereas this is not true of people in the other age groups.

Thus, the equal opportunities afforded by society in relation to the mass communications and cultural establishments are used to a different extent by different groups of the population. The way in which they are used is shown by special studies.

An analysis of the various data on the use of the mass communications and cultural establishments makes it possible to divide the population of the country into three groups:

One group embraces those who show an interest in all kinds of mass communications and often visit cultural establishments. This group is the most numerous, comprising upwards of 85 percent of the adult employed population in big cities.

The second group embraces people who make minimum use of the available opportunities (for example, they read little and either do not go to cinemas or else do so seldomly).

Table 2 PREFERRED MASS COMMUNICATIONS AMONG
DIFFERENT AGE AND SEX GROUPS IN MOSCOW
(1966–1968)

Rank of Preference	Men			Women		
	Age Groups			Age Groups		
	19–24	25–40	41–55	19–24	25–40	41–55
1	radio	newspaper	newspaper	TV	newspaper	TV
2	TV	TV	TV	radio	TV	newspaper
3	newspaper	radio	radio	newspaper	radio	magazines
4	magazines	magazines	magazines	magazines	magazines	radio
5	books	books	books	books	books	books

The third group consists of people who are known as film fans, book-worms and so on. They give preference to one particular channel of mass communications (or cultural establishment) and neglect other channels.

Eight to ten years ago we conducted a large-scale study in thirteen towns and rural settlements of the country: Moscow and the Moscow region, Leningrad, towns and villages of the Centre, South and North of the Russian Federation, Western and Eastern Siberia, the Urals and Sakhalin. Altogether, 7,218 people were polled. Using computers, we singled out groups of book readers according to the categories: "do not read," "read one or two books in two months," "three to four books," "five to six books," "over 6 books." Similarly, we grouped filmgoers: those who do not go to cinemas at all, who do so once or twice in two months, three to eight times, nine to twelve times, thirteen to sixteen times, and more than sixteen times in the same two-month period. Similar scales were formed for TV viewers, readers of newspapers and magazines, radio listeners, and those who go to clubs or theatres. Then we compared the groups:

Figures One and Two present the results of the comparison of book readers in towns and rural settlements. Figure One gives summarized data for towns and Figure Two data for rural settlements. The graphs clearly show that those who do not read books are also infrequent viewers of TV programs or films at a club or cinema and read fewer newspapers.

The same, in principle, may be said about filmgoers. Table Three shows fluctuation in the number of radio listeners in groups of people who are moderate filmgoers (three to eight times in two months) or who only occasionally go to films (once or twice in two months) and also fluctuation in the number of TV viewers in groups seeing films moderately, often or seldom.

It can also be seen from the table that a rise in cinema attendance is accompanied by a rise in the frequency of use of radio and TV (with regard to TV programs, this tendency is not so distinct, since remote areas of the country were not covered by the TV network eight to ten years ago).

A measure of dependence was also observed in relation to reading among the urban population. In towns, moderately frequent filmgoers read more books, magazines and newspapers than those who seldom go to cinemas. This tendency is not, however, in evidence for rural inhabitants who, with the increase in the number of films seen, read somewhat less.

It is interesting to note that the rule "everything or nothing" applies not only to an individual's attitude to the mass communications and culture, but often sums him up as a personality. Thus, the people who make greater use of the mass communications and cultural establishments display a higher degree of social activity and more often take correspondence courses than those who make insufficient use of the mass communications and cultural establishments.

Let us cast a brief glance at those in the third group of "consumers" of the mass communications and cultural facilities. Take, for example, film fans (i.e., those who often—twice or more times a week—go to a cinema). They are mostly people below eighteen years of age with a secondary (ten-year) or partial

Figure 1, showing the rate of attendance of cultural establishments and the use of mass communications as a function of the intensity of fiction reading (in percentage of
the total number of respondents in each group of
readers):

URBAN RESIDENTS

——————— never reading books
— — — reading one or two books
—.—.—.— reading two or three books

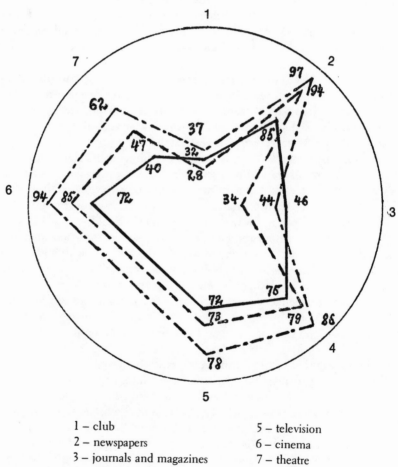

1 – club
2 – newspapers
3 – journals and magazines
4 – radio

5 – television
6 – cinema
7 – theatre

Figure 2, showing the rate of attendance of cultural establishments and the use of mass communications as a function of the intensity of fiction reading (in percentage of the total number of respondents in each group of readers):

RURAL RESIDENTS

_____ never reading books

_ _ _ _ reading one or two books

_._._._ reading two or three books

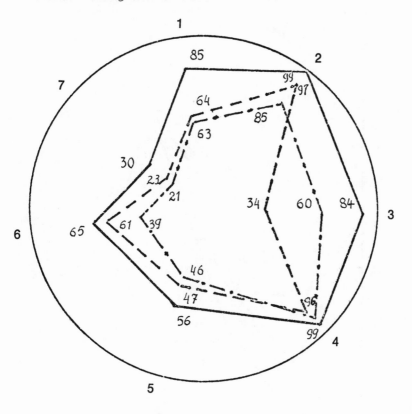

1 – club
2 – newspapers
3 – journals and magazines
4 – radio

5 – television
6 – cinema
7 – theatre

secondary education. In contrast to their coevals, they are not so active in social life and there are 16 percent fewer book readers among them (compared with those who often see films, but less often than they) and 8 to 9 percent fewer radio listeners and newspaper readers. But then film fans more often attend concerts and go to theatres and clubs.

Figure 3, showing the rate of attendance of clubs and theatres and the attitude to radio and television as a function of cinema attendance rate (in percentage of the total number of respondents in each group of filmgoers):

—·—·—·— regular filmgoers
— — — — occasional filmgoers
———— non-filmgoers

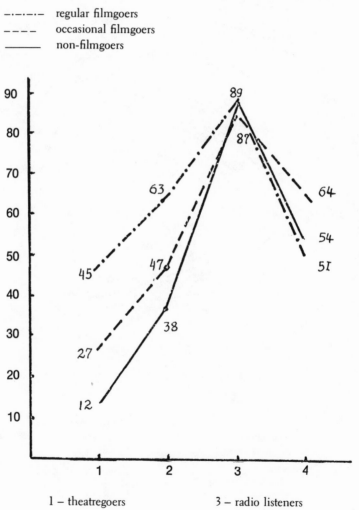

1 – theatregoers   3 – radio listeners
2 – those going to clubs   4 – TV viewers

TABLE 3 THE PROPORTION OF RADIO LISTENERS AND TV
          VIEWERS IN GROUPS VIEWING FILM MODERATELY,
          OFTEN OR SELDOM (in percentage to the total number
          of the respondents)

Investigated Towns and Areas	Number of Radio Listeners		Number of TV Viewers	
	In groups viewing films moderately or often	In groups viewing films seldom	In groups viewing films moderately or often	In groups viewing films seldom
TOWNS:				
Moscow	91%	−11%	87%	− 1%
Leningrad	72%	− 3%	68%	− 7%
Towns of the Centre	87%	− 3%	71%	+ 7%
Towns of West Siberia	91%	− 5%	43%	+16%
Towns of the Urals	85%	+11%	87%	− 2%
Towns of East Siberia	87%	− 3%	61%	−10%
Towns of the South	92%	−17%	63%	−29%
VILLAGES:				
Moscow region	96%	—	70%	—
Centre	97%	+ 3%	60%	+17%
Siberia	91%	− 2%	20%	+ 4%
South	100%	− 8%	89%	− 7%
SETTLEMENTS:				
North	100%	− 8%	52%	− 5%
Sakhalin	90%	−18%	28%	—

IV

A generalized picture of the use of the mass communications and cultural establishments may give an idea of the sources and rate of the cultural development of the population, but it is not conclusive enough to show how particular kinds of information spread among diffrent groups of the population. And so, jointly with Ladodo, we carried out a special study, asking respondents not just whether they were informed about international political events and the domestic policy of the state, but concretely establishing the channel of their first-hand information about the murder of Martin Luther King, the Soviet Law on the Family and Marriage adopted shortly before, or about an interesting film or sports event. Polling workers in Moscow, we obtained the following picture (see Figure 4).

The graph shows that information about the murder of Martin Luther

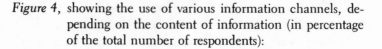

Figure 4, showing the use of various information channels, depending on the content of information (in percentage of the total number of respondents):

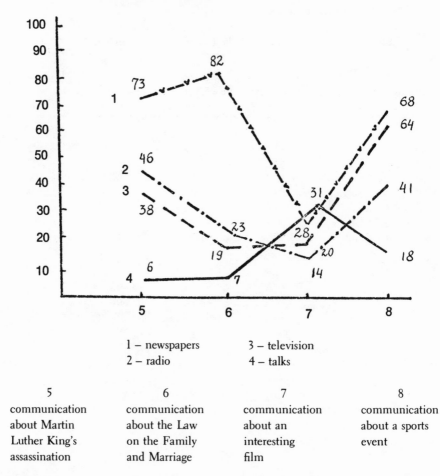

1 – newspapers　　　3 – television
2 – radio　　　　　　4 – talks

5	6	7	8
communication about Martin Luther King's assassination	communication about the Law on the Family and Marriage	communication about an interesting film	communication about a sports event

King and the Soviet Law on the Family and Marriage was obtained from newspapers and radio broadcasts; about an interesting film, they had learned from interpersonal communication and from newspapers; and about a sports event, mostly from newspapers and TV broadcasts. In other words, the channel of information depends on its content. In the course of the study, we also established the dependence between various kinds of information received and the age and sex of the respondent. Figures 5 and 6 show when and how differences arise.

Does the spread of information depend on its content? The answer is given in the work of V. Dulikov carried out in 1971–1972 under our guidance. One of the questions was: "Where would you like to hear a lecture on the interna-

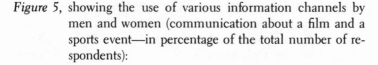

Figure 5, showing the use of various information channels by men and women (communication about a film and a sports event—in percentage of the total number of respondents):

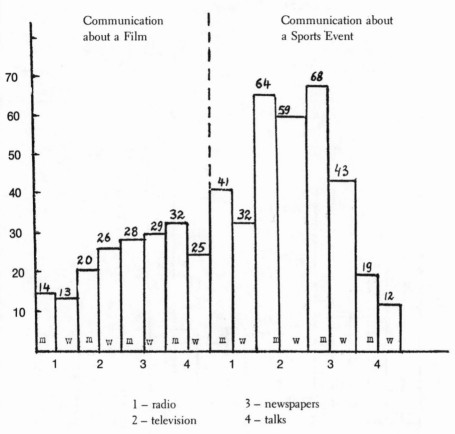

1 – radio   3 – newspapers
2 – television   4 – talks

tional situation?" The answers of workers polled in Moscow, a suburban township, and the agglomeration are presented in Figure 7.

Now, after all that has been said, an interesting and theoretically important question may be asked: What is the relationship between different mass communications and cultural establishments? On a general plane, the answer is: They may compete with one another, supplement one another or interact with one another.

As is well known, competition (in the capitalist countries) is a means of winning over an audience (this means not only booking-office receipts, but also recognition of particular bourgeois, liberal or reactionary ideas); emulation is a desire to win prestige and recognition (which is again manifested in the size

Figure 6, showing the use of various information channels by men and women (communication about the assassination of Martin Luther King and about the Law on the Family and Marriage—in percentage of the total number of respondents):

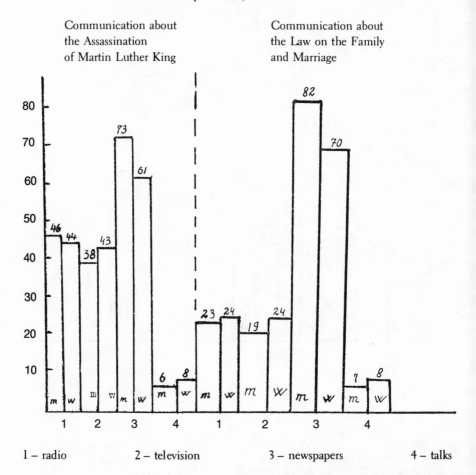

Communication about
the Assassination
of Martin Luther King

Communication about
the Law on the Family
and Marriage

1 – radio   2 – television   3 – newspapers   4 – talks

and structure of the audience); supplementing and interaction "share out" the leisure of people and the audience, since all the mass communications and cultural establishments are made use of during people's spare time, promoting or hindering the formation of public opinion or mood, the spread of knowledge, and so on.

Under socialism, competition between the mass communications and cultural establishments is ruled out and their financial position depends on a single source (the state). But emulation is a different matter. It may take place between newspapers, radio and television on the basis of general ideological, aesthetic and moral principles. They may, for example, emulate for preparing better material and presenting it more effectively.

Figure 7, showing the preferred channel of information about international affairs in the form of a lecture (in percentage of the total number of respondents):

——————— Moscovites
— — — — — inhabitants of a small town near Moscow
------------ rural inhabitants

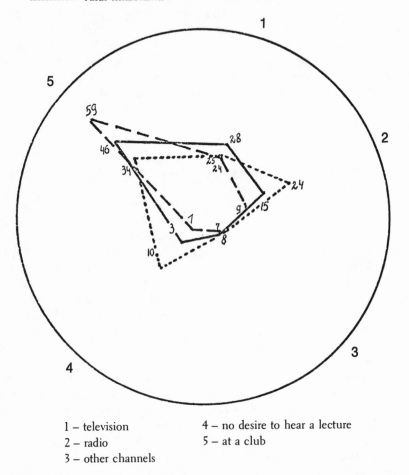

1 – television   4 – no desire to hear a lecture
2 – radio   5 – at a club
3 – other channels

As a rule, the Soviet mass communications and cultural establishments interact on the basis of the already mentioned ideological, moral and aesthetic principles, though there is a definite "division of labor" between them: *Pravda* carries more material about the general activity of the Communist Party, *Izvestiya* covers the work of state bodies, *Trud* deals with the activity of trade unions, and so on.

The interaction also exists because specific mass communications and cultural establishments have their own ("technical") features: radio supplies oral information at short notice and does not require any special expenditure of time on its reception, while the cinema provides audio-visual information in artistic form and requires outings, expenditures of one's time and money.

Table 4 below gives specific features of the mass communications and cultural establishments:

The "intrinsic" distinctions of the mass communications and cultural establishments often make them mutually supplementary. Interaction between them may be positive (when it strengthens them) and negative (when it weakens them). For example, the TV broadcasting of a film sometimes increases the cinema audiences viewing it; the success of a screen version of a work of fiction depends on its popularity and other factors. Whether interaction between various mass communications and cultural establishments is positive or negative depends in large measure on the content of distributed information.

In the Soviet Union the rule "everything or nothing" has at its basis a common ideological foundation through the interaction of mass communications and cultural establishments, provided that the personality itself is intrinsically active.

Let us demonstrate, for example, the relationship between participation in amateur art activities at clubs and attendance at cinemas, threatres and music concerts and book reading. Figure 8 shows two curves, one characterizing amateur art performers with a record of less than one year and the other those with a record of amateur art activities in excess of five years (a study carried out by I. Goncharov, a post-graduate student, in the Voroshilovgrad region in 1971).

As can be seen, the more actively one participates in amateur art activities, the better the use made of the mass communications and cultural establishments as a leisure pursuit. On the other hand, the data of the graph make it clear that the mass communications and cultural establishments do not affect one another negatively ("do not stand in each other's way").

In the light of the foregoing, Soviet sociologists have devoted much attention to analyzing the mass communications and cultural establishments in connection with the question of leisure. This question has been dealt with in a number of investigations. For example, A. Khmara has established that in 1965–1966 the adult population of Leningrad devoted its leisure to the following pursuits (in the decining order of preference): newspaper reading, radio listening, TV viewing, the reading of books, the reading of magazines, visits to theatres, museums, exhibitions, cinemas, libraries, Houses and Palaces of Culture, talks with colleagues at work and in the family circle.[8] In 1974–1975, we carried out a study among workers in four cities: Vilnius, Kishenyov, Minsk and Moscow. The picture of spare-time pursuits in this case differed somewhat from that given by A. Khmara.

In the first place, we arrived at the conclusion that none of the channels of the mass communications or cultural establishments was absolutely first, second and so on in the hierarchy of workers' leisure pursuits. Out of the fourteen types of leisure pursuits, the first place went to book reading, TV viewing, the reading of newspapers and magazines; the second place to meetings with friends, filmgoing and household work; the third place to radio listening and

Table 4 SPECIFIC FEATURES OF THE MASS COMMUNICATIONS AND CULTURAL ESTABLISHMENTS

Type of the Mass Communications and Cultural Establishments	Character of the Distribution of Information		Forms of Presentation			Time Expenditures on Receiving Information			Type of Information		
						No need to leave home		Going out and time expenditure required			
	at short notice	at longer notice	audio	visual	audio-visual	special time required	no special time required		Information	Documentary report	Artistic production
Radio	+		+				+		++	+	
TV	++	+			+	+			+	++	+
Newspapers	+			+		+			+		
Magazines		+		+		+				+	+
Books		+		+		+					+
Cinema		+			+			+		+	++
Club		+			+			+			+
Theatre		+			+			+			+

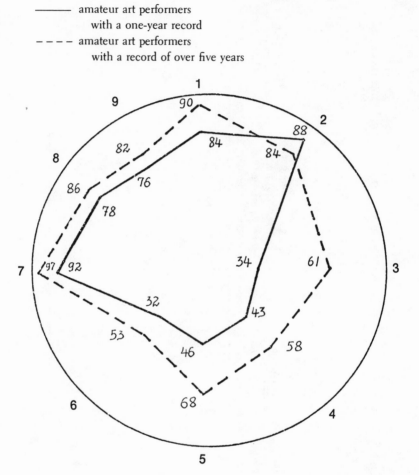

Figure 8, showing the attitude of amateur art performers at clubs to some cultural establishments and cultural pursuits (in percentage of the total number of respondents):

———— amateur art performers with a one-year record

– – – – amateur art performers with a record of over five years

1	2	3	4
listening to classical music	listening to jazz music	reading of classical literature	reading of modern prose

5	6	7	8	9
reading of modern poetry	reading of classical poetry	filmgoing	theatregoing	going to a circus

going to theatres; the fourth place to time spent with children and meetings with relatives; the fifth place to public work assignments; and the sixth place to club visits and amateur art activities.

This is a summarized list of leisure pursuits for the four cities. Naturally, there are differences from city to city, but one tendency has been established: People devote their attention primarily to those media and cultural institutions that provide fresh information, often in an entertaining (artistic) form, and that require a minimum of time (i.e., participation at home). Another tendency is that workers acquire an urge (after receiving fresh knowledge) for communication, for personal contacts, be it at home, in a cinema or a club. And a further tendency is that people strive to find extra time for bringing up their children and for maintaining ties with relatives.

All this led us to investigate another important theoretical question, namely what people like and dislike about the mass communications and cultural establishments. But before proceeding with its examination, let us look at another interesting aspect of the distribution of information.

Besides the mass communications and cultural establishments that may be described as official sources of information, a big role in the life of people is played by other sources (e.g., talks with colleagues at work, with acquaintances, and in the family circle). Figures 9 and 10 give data (obtained by I. Ladodo) showing the types of information received from such (non-official) sources. The data give an insight into the channels of information used by men and women and also indicate where this information is discussed.

It has to be admitted that the findings differ somewhat from those already published. Thus, the book *Political Information* contains the following table:

Table 5 CHANNELS OF INFORMATION[9] Study Conducted in
Moscow (in percentage to the total number of the
respondents)

| | Channels of Information | | | | | | | |
| | Official | | | | | Non-official | | |
Content of Information	newspapers	radio	television	magazines	documentary films	talks at work	friends	relatives
Political life of the country	79	52	45	14	11	17	10	8
Economic life of the country	33	21	20	9	6	5	3	4
International events	47	31	29	9	7	13	8	7
Science and technology	10	7	13	20	7	4	4	3
Moral questions	13	8	11	7	2	6	4	6

According to the source giving this table, only an insignificant number of people obtain information from unofficial sources (from talks); the character of information covered by the study is not clear either.

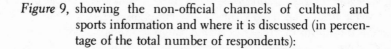

Figure 9, showing the non-official channels of cultural and sports information and where it is discussed (in percentage of the total number of respondents):

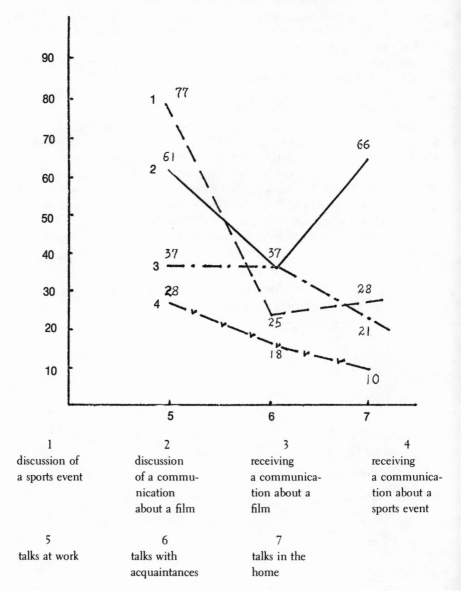

1	2	3	4
discussion of a sports event	discussion of a commu- nication about a film	receiving a communica- tion about a film	receiving a communica- tion about a sports event

5	6	7
talks at work	talks with acquaintances	talks in the home

Figure 10, showing the place where international (external) and
internal information is discussed (in percentage of the
total number of respondents):

———————— communication about a new Law on.
the Family and Marriage
– – – – communication about Martin Luther
King's assassination

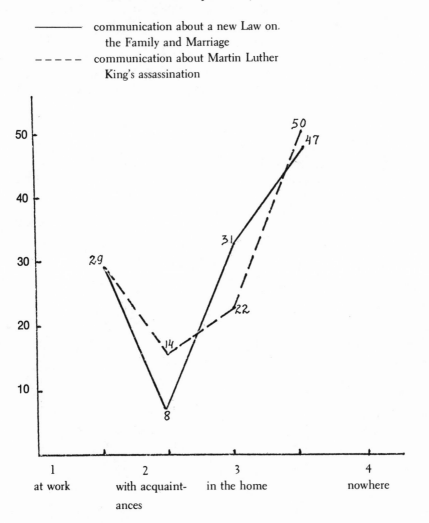

V

What kind of information do people like? What information do they select
in the first place? Naturally, the answer to this question will help answer other
related questions: What is the audience for particular information? What is the
educational effect of information and how can it be enhanced? The extensive
material at our disposal enables us to formulate a number of criteria showing
what people like and why:

1. People like those elements in the flow of information that add to the *knowledge they already have*. Let us illustrate this with a table compiled on the basis of the data obtained by V. Ledovskaya, a post-graduate student who has made a special study of the matter (see Table 6). The data obtained in Moscow are borne out by data for Kuibyshev. They clearly show that man's cognitive urge prevails over the entertainment motive, the desire to take some rest or to spend one's spare time with one's friends. This cognitive urge of Soviet people comes out quite distinctly from what they said they would like to see on the screen (see Table 7, investigation was conducted in Moscow and Moscow region).

Table 6 THE ATTRACTION OF THE MASS COMMUNICATIONS AND CULTURAL ESTABLISHMENTS FOR THEIR USERS (in percentage to the total number of the respondents)

	radio	newspapers	magazines	television	museums	lectures	exhibitions	books	films	theatre	clubs
They attract because they help people:											
to know life better	41	54	7	21	8	15	17	11	19	3	—
to acquire new knowledge	14	20	52	10	18	15	42	10	2	1	—
to learn about other people	18	10	30	45	—	—	—	11	6	2	—
to learn more about the country and its history	4	2	1	1	18	2	6	9	—	—	1
to emulate positive heroes	—	—	1	—	—	—	—	9	7	1	—
to relive together with the heroes	1	—	—	1	—	—	—	31	27	9	—
to see actors or performances by sportsmen	—	—	—	1	—	—	—	—	17	27	—
to rest	2	—	—	10	—	—	—	8	20	11	8
to fill spare time	—	—	—	5	—	—	—	2	5	1	1
to be with friends	—	—	—	—	—	—	—	—	2	1	10

Table 7 TYPES OF FILMS APPEALING MOST TO VIEWERS IN MOSCOW AND THE MOSCOW REGION (in percentage to the total number of the respondents)

	Muscovites	Inhabitants of the Moscow Region
Screening of works of fiction	47	37
Screening of theatrical productions	46	38
Documentary films	66	32
Opera films	56	40
Comedies	34	40

The table shows clearly an urge for knowledge shown by nearly one half of those polled, which goes to corroborate the thesis advanced earlier. At the same time, this fact puts one on guard with regard to data on film attendance (see Figure 11), which at times reflects not the viewers' perferences, but what is made available by the film-hire organizations.

2. Attention is drawn by something unusual and garish. This principle is used in advertising. However, the interest shown in the unusual does not mean that this "unusual" (resulting, for example, in high booking-office receipts) will be liked. Therefore, there is a divergence between the use of available opportunities (many readers of a book and such) and the attitude to them (whether the book in question is liked or not), but this divergence should not be misleading to the researcher.

It has to be remembered that the deliberate use of an unusual form or content may give rise to unjustified expectations. In this case the reader, viewer or listener is left dissatisfied.

3. One likes that which is *closer to one's way of life and thinking*. This has been established on the basis of a large number of facts. For instance, in 1965–1966, we conducted a series of studies which showed that readers like books that are set in the present day (see Table 8).[10] This applies to films, and music and the like.

4. *Emotional state*. It has been established experimentally that the effect of "liking" or "disliking" depends in a certain measure on the emotional condition of the audience. If, for example, prior to a film showing the audience is put into a mood opposite to the one that may be created by the film, the film will be liked 15 to 20 and even 30 percent less. In the course of the experiment, we succeeded in creating such an emotional mood in a cinema (before a film showing) and in a lecture hall (if printed matter was read before). The effect was always the same.

Figure 11, showing the various film genres preferred by men and women (summarized data for thirteen regions of the country—in percentage of the total number of respondents):

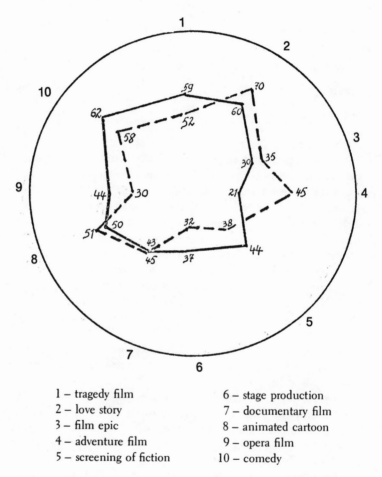

1 – tragedy film
2 – love story
3 – film epic
4 – adventure film
5 – screening of fiction

6 – stage production
7 – documentary film
8 – animated cartoon
9 – opera film
10 – comedy

5. *"The effect of co-participation."* This term implies the mental activity of the respondent as he watches a film, listens to a lecture, reads a book or an article. In the process, the respondent does not give any outward signs, but still he "is with it," perceiving, comparing and analyzing what he sees or hears (i.e., *"working" emotionally and intellectually*). The investigation revealed that the higher the mental activity of listeners, the greater the effect of learning and the stronger the impact of a film, lecture, book.

Table 8 TYPES OF LITERATURE LIKED BY READERS (in
percentage to the total number of the respondents)

	Moscow	Towns of the Centre
Russian classics	17	10
Foreign classics	17	7
Modern Soviet literature	43	50
Modern English literature	3	2
Modern American literature	4	2
Modern French literature	1	2

Of interest in this respect are the experiments conducted by L. Pavlova, a post-graduate student. Two clubs were selected in Moscow and a suburban village. At both clubs the same functions were organized: a university of musical culture and a "club of music lovers." For the sake of comparison, the investigators selected three groups of people who resided in the given localities and worked at the same enterprises, but who did not attend the functions at the club.

L. Pavlova investigated these three groups according to a single program: some listened only to radio broadcasts, others were drawn into an active form of musical education (evening university of musical culture), and still others had an opportunity to listen to and discuss musical pieces in a most active form. The investigation showed that the effect of aesthetic education was directly dependent on the activity of the individual in the process of perception, and this activity was ensured by organizing hearings of music.

This conclusion leads us to believe that it is necessary to create such forms of the activity of the mass communications and cultural establishments as would promote the activity of the audience. Such are some theoretical and practical results obtained from the study of the relationships between respondents and the mass communications and cultural establishments.

VI

Thus, the respondents' attitude to the mass communications and cultural establishments is determined not only by their world outlook, interests and views, and not only by the form of presentation of information material, but also by certain socio-demographic features, and depends directly on their way of life.

For example, people who are going to school and are less than eighteen years of age have no time for frequent visits to cinemas, clubs and dancing parties. As a rule, in this case, the use of the mass communications and cultural establishments is directed by parents. Young people of this age devote more time to reading, viewing TV programs and listening to radio.

At the age of between nineteen and twenty-four, young people acquire a certain measure of independence. At this age they more often go to clubs, theatres and dances. In other words, they strive to satisfy their urge for communion.

Young people twenty-five to thirty years of age devote again more time to reading and TV and radio programs, and visit cinemas and clubs infrequently. This is because by now they have their own families and children to look after and new obligations.

Then comes an "upsurge" in the attendance at cinemas and theatres (when their children are grown up), but with age, new tendencies appear in the attitude to the mass communications and cultural establishments, in particular, a drop in the level of reading (generally for the population as a whole).

Without going into concrete details of the attitude to the mass communications and cultural establishments, we have to note, however, that there are also sex, regional and national specific features, which have been already mentioned in passing. Their explanation and a compilation of the "portraits" of various groups of readers, listeners, filmgoers and such is the task currently engaging the attention of Soviet sociologists.

VII

The study of the attitudes of various groups of the population to the mass communications and cultural establishments has brought us inevitably to the need to elucidate questions relating to the social functions of these media and cultural institutions. This is a very important and interesting question, which has a direct bearing on a number of other things, such as leisure, the molding of the personality, the distribution of information in society, and so on. As we see it, the mass communications and cultural establishments perform the following social functions in society:

1. *Information function.* The distribution of information, facts and such. However, this distribution in a "pure form" occurs very seldom. By distributing information, the mass communications and cultural establishments at the same time perform a number of other functions.

2. *Educational function.* Information that is distributed is usually explained and commented on and thereby popularized as positive or negative.

3. *Ideological and educational function.* The mass communications and cultural establishments in Soviet society have the task of disseminating Communist ideas in society and educating the population. This is one of the most important functions.

4. *Integrative function.* By spreading ideas, views, judgments and knowledge, the mass communications and cultural establishments bring about a situation in which the greater part of the population [11] begins to share these ideas and views. In this way, the moral and political unity of society is achieved.

5. *The function of molding the personality.* By spreading knowledge, ideas and images, the mass communications and cultural establishments help to

mold a materialist world outlook, and to form Communist convictions, values, views and traditions desirable to society.

6. *Activating function.* By spreading information and by educating and rallying the people, the mass communications and cultural establishments may appeal to them and mobilize them for various tasks, fostering a readiness to do something.

7. *Function of molding social mood.* This function helps to form among the population a definite emotional enthusiasm, the readiness to undertake tasks needed by society and the like.

8. *Hedonistic function.* The mass communications and cultural establishments provide entertainment, helping people to rest and recreate.

9. *Function of filling spare time.* The mass communications and cultural establishments act mostly during people's leisure, helping to fill it. As a rule, a person using a specific channel of the mass media or opportunities afforded by cultural establishments has to redistribute his spare time.

10. *The function of carrying on traditions, developing new customs.* Without the mass media and cultural establishments, many traditions and customs wane. This is because traditions and customs cannot exist without human communion and are the result of the transfer of various kinds of information.

11. *Teaching function.* The mass communications and cultural establishments contribute to the spread of scientific knowledge and of skills required by people in this age of scientific and technological revolution. They are now being increasingly used as a means of instruction for secondary and higher schools.

VIII

It is impossible to enumerate in one article all the problems involved in the development of the mass communications and cultural establishments that have been dealt with by the Soviet sociologists. But enough has been said to show that the study of the mass communications and cultural establishments in the Soviet Union is being carried out on a broad scale.

A distinguishing feature of these investigations is that they are conducted on a single methodological scientific foundation—the philosophy of dialectical materialism—and study the totality of fundamental, theoretical and applied aspects of important and complex problems whose solution is essential in present-day society.

NOTES

[1] L. I. Brezhnev, *Report of the CPSU Central Committee and the Immediate Tasks of the Party in Home and Foreign Policy* (Moscow: Novosti Press Agency Publishing House, 1976), p. 93.

[2] *Narodnoye khozyaistvo SSSR v 1974 godu (The National Economy of the USSR in 1974)* (Moscow: Statistika Publishers, 1975), pp. 705–23.

[3] Quoted from L. I. Brezhnev, *Report of the CPSU Central Committee and the Immediate Tasks of the Party in Home and Foreign Policy* (Moscow: Novosti Press Agency Publishing House, 1976), p. 93.

[4] *Sovetsky Soyuz. Politiko-ekonomichesky spravochnik (The Soviet Union. Politico-Economic Reference Book)* (Moscow: Political Literature Publishing House, 1975), pp. 281–348.

[5] *Narodnoye khozyaistvo SSSR v 1974 godu (The National Economy of the USSR in 1974).*

[6] See B. Grushin, *Svobodnoye vremya. Aktualniye problemy (Spare Time Topical Problems)* (Moscow: Mysl Publishers, 1967), p. 81.

[7] Studies carried out under the guidance of the author of this paper as theses for scientific degrees.

[8] See A. Khmara, *Mesto televideniya v sisteme massovykh kommunikatsiy (The Place of Television in the System of Mass Communications)* (Moscow, 1966), p. 23.

[9] *Politicheskaya informatsiya. Nekotoriye voprosy teorii i praktiki (Political Information. Some Questions of Theory and Practice)* (Moscow: Mysl Publishers, 1974), pp. 88–9 (figures rounded off).

[10] See also N. S. Mansurov, "Obshchestvennaya psikhologiya i politicheskaya propaganda" ("Social Psychology and Political Propaganda), in *Voprosy teorii i praktiki partiynoi propagandy (Questions of the Theory and Practice of Party Propaganda)* (Moscow, 1971).

[11] It should be pointed out that in society there are always groups of people (children, the sick and such) that do not allow one to speak of the entire population.

Part Four

☆☆☆☆

SOCIAL AND POLITICAL RELEVANCE OF ENTERTAINMENT

Klaus Mäding:

Popular Literature in Dependent Society: The Case of Colonial Hong Kong

☆ A DEPENDENT SOCIETY, as in the case of Hong Kong, is ridden by severe structural conflict, which in turn produces sociopsychological strain. Although the industrial techniques and organizational setup of international companies seem to promise progress and well-being for Hong Kong's inhabitants, in some people's view more so than in most dependent societies, the actual state of affairs is characterized by exploitation and backward social conditions for the overwhelming majority of its Chinese population. The veneer suggesting splendid progress hides the vulnerable social structure underneath. Many elements of industrial enterprise in Hong Kong are the direct consequence of foreign economic and political interests, testifying to the degree in which they dominate internal social processes.

As in other dependent societies, only a small minority enjoys the benefits of this unequal relationship. The forces of international dependency, as they make their way into the structure of Hong Kong's society, entail that the minimal needs of the working population, its aspirations to better living conditions and to greater participation in society's affairs are repressed.

Is the voluminous and colorful stream of popular literature in Hong Kong a medium through which interests transcending the constraints of dependency can be expressed, and could authentic interests of the underprivileged be expressed in such a medium and perhaps challenge the existing social order?

A Closer Look at Popular Literature in Hong Kong

The many images of hope and conflict to be found in the popular literature of Hong Kong cannot of course be presented in any detail within this paper's scope. For a more direct impression as to the contents of such literature let us look at a summary of the short story, *Love, Love:* [1]

▶ This is an original article written especially for this book. Dr. Klaus Mäding is presently engaged in research on the sociopolitical development of China between the mid-nineteenth century and the present day.

A girl from a rich family loves a poor office boy. Twenty-six people live crammed together in his family's wooden house. The house has to be roped to the ground during a typhoon in order to prevent it from flying away. This big family literally lives in bunk-beds. The cooking utensils, the most essential possession, are stored underneath the beds. The young couple will be offered a lower-level bed after marriage and the bride's mother-in-law and younger brother-in-law will sleep above. The rich girl is frightened at the thought of living in such conditions and gives up her intention of marrying the office boy.

This is one example from the 219 short stories and novels in Chinese analyzed by the author.[2] They were all written in Hong Kong,[3] enjoy high circulation figures and are published either in journals, newspapers or cheap book series. A systematic analysis of this kind of popular literature had not been attempted to date in the case of Hong Kong. The reading of such mass circulated literature constitutes an important cultural activity for the four million people living in the colony, 98 percent of which are Chinese.[4]

In terms of the number of newspapers per inhabitant, Hong Kong ranks second in Asia, after Japan.[5] Of the two hundred newspapers and periodicals in Hong Kong, sixty-two are dailies—mostly in Chinese, only four being in English. The high interest in mass media shown by Hong Kong's Chinese population cannot be explained just by attributing it to the calculating interest of a commercial city in information from all parts of the world. Concern with emotional needs, the problems encountered in improving one's well-being, moral conflicts, strife within the family—such topics are not suppressed in the reading matter consumed by the masses. Entertainment in the form of stories, photographs and caricatures occupied an average of 20 percent of the total space in the daily newspapers included in this study, definitely more than the amount in their Western equivalents!

Our analysis is based on a sample of mass-circulated literature[6] that was balanced according to the information available on the socio-economic status of the readers.[7] Fortunately for the sociologist, commercial advertising interests ensured that readership surveys were carried out.

The Functions and Relevance of Mass-Circulated Literature

To apply standards of art to this kind of mass-circulated literature would be totally inappropriate. Similarly, an attempt at dissociating the forms of mass consciousness expressed in such literature from the social structure within which it was produced would be futile. Rather than allow the content of the texts under study to absorb our attention exclusively, the tools of mass-communication research should be applied in such a way that its social relevance is brought to light.

For readers in Hong Kong, entertainment is an outstanding quality of such literature. But as functional analysis has taught us, it is not likely that just one apparent social need will be served, but a multitude of them. I propose to study the functions of such literature in the light of the basic needs of the actors who constitute this particular society. The orientation interests of a society's actors, which define the substance of social constraint and which project the avenues along which needs can be satisfied, are of primordial relevance here. They bear the impression of the dominant economic, political and social forces that structure a certain social totality. However, human imagination and activity are not wholly determined by socio-economic conditions. Orientation interests, in my approach, are also a liberating force, propelling members of society toward the defiance of social constraints.

The functions of mass-circulated literature in Hong Kong are thus embedded in this society's historically determined mode of production and receive their specific relevance examined from the perspective of orientation interests.

Dependency, Exploitation and Legitimatory Processes

Export growth rates are used in Hong Kong to demonstrate the economic progress made by the colony. However, such an index, indicating an impressive performance, is highly misleading in that it does not reveal the economy's extreme vulnerability. Proof of this was offered again by the world slump in demand experienced in Hong Kong from mid-1974 to mid-1975. The British Governor, MacLehose, himself explicitly referred to "the total dependence of the prosperity of Hong Kong on external markets"[8] as the reason for the Colony's difficulties during the recession. In material terms, Hong Kong is not only dependent on the world's advanced industrial states but also on the People's Republic of China, the main source of its raw materials and foodstuffs. This is an unremitting feature of the Colony's economy throughout the recent decades. This dependency is used by the Government to legitimate the restraint on meeting the basic needs of the Chinese population. MacLehose innocently admitted that it was "the work force which bore the brunt of the recession."[9] Who else should—the employers, or the high-income groups in general, benefiting from extremely favorable tax progression rates in Hong Kong, or perhaps the Government?

Recent data bear out the author's observations for the period 1964-68 in that they show quite clearly that opportunities within Hong Kong's social structure are unfairly distributed and, furthermore, that there has been no substantial progress within this field. Between 1973 and early 1975 the exorbitant level of housing rents in the crowded city and consumer prices were responsible for a reduction of 18 percent in real terms in the wages of Hong Kong's hard-working labor force. At the same time, according to government statistics—which are rather too optimistic—9 percent of the labor force was unemployed (with no unemployment benefit to fall back on!), a total which the Government claimed had leveled off to 5.6 percent by March, 1976. Even according to the liberal *Far Eastern Economic Review*, "the central problem of wages, accidents and security remains to be resolved."[10]

Thus, the blows of depression are instantly passed on to the already underprivileged Chinese workers in Hong Kong. On top of the exploitation by foreign and Chinese capitalist enterprise, Hong Kong is fettered by an unequal colonial relationship, whereby vast financial reserves are deposited in British banks, the pensions of the British who have served in the Colony have to be paid and substantial contributions are made to the British defense budget.

Popular literature in Hong Kong, its entertainment function and the orientation interests of its readers, cannot be divorced from the characteristics of this society's structure. Processes that legitimate the existing power structure conflict with the authentic orientation interests of a vast majority of the Colony's population. Mass culture has to be understood within the framework of such social contradictions.

The statements of employers' organizations, of the government, some newspaper editorials and the views expressed in private conversation in commercial circles in which the author was present—all reflecting official opinion—used the arguments briefly outlined below in defense of the unequal distribution of wealth and opportunities: The Chinese population of Hong Kong was either born under the colonial system or entered the Colony as immigrants, often as refugees from the People's Republic of China. Its main concern lies in profiting from a capitalist system based on an unfettered exchange of talents and goods. —Because the territory is export-oriented and has no resources apart from human labor, wages have to be kept low in order to maintain competitiveness on the world market.—Traditionally, the Chinese prefer harmony, order and the *status quo.*—The geographical proximity of the People's Republic of China on the one hand and the rival government in Taiwan on the other forbids political participation and debate beyond the established channels of consultation under colonial auspices. Such involvement would only invite outside powers to use Hongkong as an arena for their own conflicts.—Necessarily, Hong Kong's situation doesn't allow the application of standards accepted elsewhere.

Such arguments attempt to legitimate the *status quo.* Does popular literature do no more than embody such legitimatory concepts of which examples were quoted above or does it, on the contrary, mischievously deride the existing order? Do authentic needs in a dependent society find expression in the literature published for its masses?

The Confrontation of Popular Literature with Social Reality

Such questions sensitize us as to the imprint left by social forces on popular literature and make it difficult to revert to a concept of "pure entertainment." Yet such awareness is not enough. Frequently, in a "self-fulfilling" approach, content elements are selectively borrowed from popular literature and rather directly interpreted as expressions of certain functions or interests.

Instead, I suggest that elements of social reality should be used as a yardstick for conclusions as to the social functions of specific literary products. In cases where elements of social reality are being distorted or suppressed in such literature, they constitute areas of "problematic reality." Dominating social forces tend to reduce psychosociological strain[11] either by legitimating power and wealth,[12] by controlling variant interests, or by offering escape from social pressure.

Martel and McCall's[13] concept of "realism" as applied to popular literature, which they used in their valuable study of American mass periodical fiction between 1890 and 1955, represents a rare attempt at defining the criteria of analysis clearly. Their concept does not correspond with what is usually termed the "realism" of literature but, in its stringent adherence to the requirements of social science research, more precisely with "ethnographic validity"—as they themselves explain. Clearly, they must conclude that "fiction is likely to make very poor ethnography."[14]

In my view, such standards tend to be too restrictive and not totally adequate in characterizing literary production because 1) we cannot expect literature to present us with a comprehensive reflection of social reality fulfilling the requirements of social science research; literary production has to be selective and 2) literary production, even in its most popular form, does not reflect reality directly. It recreates reality as a "second world" of imagination. In effect, "realism" as defined by Martel and McCall can almost always be rejected as one progresses to using more precise instruments either for content analysis or control data.

I suggest that the opposite approach can do more justice to the quality of the process of literary production. We should dissociate ourselves from the endless search for more or less adequate images of reality in popular literature and concentrate on the more tangible frame of reference embodied in the "distortion" of reality or, in the case of some essential structural elements, the "suppression" of reality.

The subject matter popular literature avails itself of is so inexhaustible that it will do little harm if we concentrate on a limited sample and, at the same time, one that is more precisely defined. The variables I have selected are either situational, e.g. aspects of work or housing, or valuative. If writers use subject matter of the kind we are looking for, we can examine the literature for verifiable differences between the presentation of reality and what we know about social reality. Further subject matter can of course be included—as long as it can be matched with the control data at our disposal. Control data were chosen from some of the results of comprehensive surveys conducted by R. E. Mitchell.[15]

Areas of "problematic reality" will emerge during the course of analysis. In this way popular literature will be related to its wider social context.

The Evasion of Political Analysis

The demonstrations of 1966 and 1967 in Hong Kong represented a challenge to the political establishment. Whereas in 1966 protest over the issue of transportation costs served as a vehicle for the expression of more general social discontent, especially among the Chinese youth, demonstrations against deplorable working conditions during the following year led to a politically motivated upsurge of activities in the British Colony connected with the Cultural Revolution on the Chinese mainland.

These later demonstrations are "reflected" in one of the stories analysed through the person of "Mr. Wang:" [16]

Wang is a member of a leftist trade union. In reality he ignores the differences between leftism and rightism. . . . When people said that imperialism is not good and they wanted "the east wind to win over the west wind," he joined and said that imperialism is not good and we want "the east wind to win over the west wind." . . . A trade union secretary told Wang: "If you write posters and hang up slogans you will receive a hundred Hong Kong dollars a day. If you persuade a work mate to go on strike, you will receive two hundred dollars. If you set the offices of a reactionary newspaper on fire, you will receive two thousand dollars. If you throw stones at buses whose crews are not on strike or at policemen—these all have a fixed price. If you injure somebody with a stone, you may get a reward of a few hundred dollars."

These and similar politically motivated "observations" are made by authors with *Kuomintang* inclinations. [17] My own observations indicate that the example presented above, for instance, is not an adequate reflection of the political realities these demonstrations gave expression to. It constitutes an attempt at reinterpreting outbursts of political discontent in terms of the money-making motives fostered by the Colony's dependent structure itself.

On the other hand, short stories in leftist daily newspapers stressed that the British Government was trying to enslave the Chinese inhabitants of Hong Kong through means of the educational system. Pressing political issues are rarely tackled in novels and short stories. But when references are made, they are usually full of aggression and bitter irony.

The legitimatory arguments official circles use in defense of colonialism—outlined above—are only employed in passing and are not expounded at any length. The unmitigated exertion of political power ensures that dependency is accepted as a firmly established fact. Persuasive techniques do not have to be used in justifying this central issue of colonialism. The colonial government practically never censors popular literature directly. The mechanisms of control are indirect—informal censorship by the publishers, self-censorship by the authors.

Economically, the authors are in a highly insecure position. Because there is a large surplus of Chinese intellectuals in Hong Kong, immigrants from South China, the Shanghai region and North China who came seeking refuge from war and revolution, novelists can easily be dismissed and replaced. Paid very low rates according to the number of words they write, their status is little different to that of the piece-workers they sometimes describe in their stories employed in factories manufacturing plastic flowers. As a result, many of the authors write daily installments to several serialized novels at a time. If an author is dismissed, his successor assumes responsibility for the serial and writes the following installments. As a last resort, the colonial government can always deport undesirable persons—a threat which certainly produces some measure of allegiance.

Such stories have to be popular with their readers—another factor militating against the incorporation of explicitly defined political standpoints and encouraging authors to move on safer common ground with regard to controversial issues. Certainly, there are data on the different readership groups in Hong Kong to draw upon and authors generally know whether they are writing for young female shop employees, Cantonese businessmen or high school students. But they cannot afford to lose readers—whether they are refugees from the Chinese mainland or young leftists—just for the luxury of being allowed to draw precise political conclusions.

Where channels for the direct expression of political dissent are closed, the contradictions to be found in real life are transformed, repressed and reappear at a personal level. The literature under examination is full of diffuse sentiments of alienation and sadness or of internalized aggression: "We are like drifting water plants without stalks. What can we do but to swallow our tears?"[18] "I am an unsuitable person. Society doesn't want me and I myself don't want society."[19] It would be a fruitless and naive exercise, I believe, to devote one's entire efforts—as is often the case—to a search for accurate images of the social structure in literature. Intellectually, authors as well as readers, rather than attempting to recreate social reality accurately, are trying to cope with the sociopsychological strains they experience.

A comparison with other major South-East Asian cities has shown that some forms of sociopsychic strain are most acute in Hong Kong.[20] This applies to the pressure of long working hours, low prestige connected with certain forms of employment, pessimism about one's chances of personal success, weakness of family ties, lack of interest in discussing problems with others, and so on. The structural pressures generated by colonialism and by dependency under the capitalist system thus shape personal experience. Do orientation needs remain unfulfilled in popular literature? Does entertainment merely provide escape?

The Restriction of Emancipatory Interests

Systematic content analysis and comparison of its results with the control data at our disposal as well as qualitative examination of the material lead to the conclusion that social reality had not altogether been distorted or suppressed in areas such as the following:

- the effects of housing conditions
- attitudes toward depressing working conditions
- the state of delinquency
- conflict between generations

Firstly, as a result, we can dismiss the notion that the colonial society's popular literature presents nothing but a "dream world." The findings can be explained instead by using the following "bridge hypothesis:" certain issues with which the reader is familiar are adequately covered in order to induce him to enter the world the story presents and to soften the defensive posture he may possibly have adopted. Later on, however, the author may go on to deplete these issues of any of their real meaning in society. In my approach, I have concentrated on the distortion and suppression of social reality so as to be able to analyze the conflict between processes of legitimation and orientation needs.

Authors emphasized middle-class educational values through the kind of characters they presented. Comparison with control data established that such emphasis was out of all proportion to the incidence of these values in real life. This example of distortion, not originally postulated but discovered during the course of content analysis, can be interpreted within the framework of deeply rooted social conflict to be found in Hong Kong: In a situation in which conflict between the interests of a majority of workers and capitalist interests embedded in an international structure of dependency is endemic, persuasive techniques are employed with the intention of orientating the middle classes toward cooperation with the privileged minority. Social control is disguised as praise: While interest in educational achievement is lauded and, what is more, the right to upward social mobility is acknowledged, the adoption of such a strategy by the middle classes implies a forfeiture of immediate rewards. Exams and degrees thus become retarding mechanisms as far as upward mobility is concerned.

The presentation of the woman's role in Chinese society is another area in which legitimatory pressures in popular literature could be established, in this case militating against the interests of emancipation. Two interrelated distortions of reality were found:

Firstly, when "appreciating good service," the relevant stories misrepresent women's orientations toward work. The stories avoid suggesting the professions as a possible source of satisfaction for women. The authors would have us believe that manual and simple clerical work or, of course, prostitution are the only occupational avenues open to women. The restrictions women face in this respect are definitely overemphasized. Surprisingly, even escape, involving illusion, fatalism and hedonism, is presented as a less acceptable outlet for women than for men. Their positive orientation toward "personal choice" and "Western cultural forms" is also exaggerated. In this context, a glimpse is offered of the pleasures awaiting women if they break with tradition requiring devotion to family and husband. Here one draws close to emancipation from the former roles of "merchandise for marriage" and the "exploited wife." But such an orientation is obstructed, rendered ambivalent, useless and unrewarding as soon as the stories disclose "what happens as a result. . . ." Colonial society, here in alliance with traditional Chinese mechanisms of social control, will deal a crushing blow to daring women, compelling them to commit suicide or condemning them to poverty and misery—so beware!

Secondly, the entertainment offered doesn't usually take the form of consolation employing the pacifying symbols of family harmony and peace—as in the case of particular types of novels to be found in advanced industrial societies. To begin with, a lot of space in the novels included in the sample is devoted to descriptions—which are quite often obscene—of love and sexuality. Here, independent women constitute a threat to the emotional rewards men seek and to male superiority. A meaningful distinction, however, can be drawn between the sword-swinging heroines of the widely read traditional novels such as *Erh-nü ying-hsiung chuan*[21] and the blood-sucking female demons to be found in *Liao-chai chih-i.*[22] Distortion of reality in modern Hong Kong novels in this case reflects the menace felt at a psychological level. Ultimately, when mechanisms of social control are firmly established, such fear-producing dangers are resolved. Suppression is not openly presented as a necessity. Rather, it is introduced in a clandestine manner through the notion that "they will be happier if they adjust." Entertainment, in the environment we are looking at, can be aptly described as being a circle in which menace is followed by relief.

Entertainment as a Means of Fulfilling Orientation Needs?

An analysis of mass-circulated literature can supply us with an insight into the legitimation processes operating in a dependent society. Such literature avoids presenting its readers with a *critique* of the political system. At the same time it bears the imprint of the dependent society within which it is produced in the way it contributes toward upholding the *status quo*. Further critical study along these lines is needed. In shunning comprehensive and detailed analysis of the sources and meaning of the sociopsychological strain which readers experience, popular literature disregards and even deflects authentic orientation needs. A thorough examination of Hong Kong's colonial status is avoided. Entertainment tends to assume a form that deprives emancipatory interests of their meaning. It doesn't necessarily have to function in such a way, as the popular literature of a number of struggling cultural and ethnic groups elsewhere shows.

At the same time, however, we can conclude that the structure of the popular literature produced in Hong Kong tends to be loose. Readers can recreate their own negative experiences when they read about characters facing similar social constraints, even though the author, at a later stage, endeavors to satisfy them with some glossy compromise or other. Popular literature does not constitute an all-embracing mechanism of legitimation and control as is sometimes suggested. The dialectical nature of the world of imagination has to be understood. There is room for the reader to decide at which point he is going to identify with the characters presented in the story he is reading. He can thus creatively use the clefts in the "images of reality" he is presented with and thus to some extent negate their restrictive function.

NOTES

[1] Author: "Ah-ying," in *Novel World* (1965).

[2] Thanks are due to Paul Ng Chun-ming, himself a Hongkong author, for his valuable assistance.

[3] They were published between 1964 and 1968.

[4] Figures for 1968.

[5] The two dailies with the highest circulation in Hongkong are included in this study: *Sing Pao* (circulation: 170,000; political orientation: "independent") and *Sing Tao Man Pao* (160,000; "independent-rightist"). "Leftist" papers have a lower circulation in Hongkong, e.g., in this sample, *Ching Pao* [70,000].

[6] The author estimates that during his stay in Hong Kong, 1964–68, the years for which the sample was taken, 1,000 novels and 700 short stories were·published p.a., a figure certainly worth consideration.

[7] For details, see App. 1 in the full German version: Klaus Mäding, *Massenhaft verbreitete Literatur in einer Gesellschaft mit hohen soziopsychischen Belastungen.* (Wiesbaden [West Germany], Harrassowitz: 1975).

[8] "Focus Hong Kong '77: The Money-Spinners," in *Far Eastern Economic Review* (18th March, 1977): 37 *ff.*

[9] *Loc. cit.*

[10] *Loc. cit.*: 47 *ff.*

[11] See C. Geertz, "Ideology as a Cultural System," in *Ideology and Discontent, People Society and Mass Communications* ed. D. E. Apter (London, 1964), pp. 47–76, for more details on this concept.

[12] Cf. H. D. Lasswell's early formulation (1948).

[13] M. Martel and G. McCall, "Reality-Orientation and the Pleasure Principle," in eds. L. Dexter and D. M. White, *People, Society and Mass Communications* (New York, 1964), pp. 283–334.

[14] *Loc. cit.*

[15] *Family Life in Urban Hongkong*, 2 vols. (Hongkong, 1969); *Pupil, Parent and School*, 2 vols. (Hongkong, 1969).

[16] Chang Ou-ping, "The Family of Mr. Wang," in *Literary Examination Hall* (1967).

[17] The ruling party in Taiwan (Republic of China).

[18] Mo Shou-ping, "The Trap," in *Chinese Students' Weekly* (1966).

[19] Yang T'ien-ch'eng, *Under the Eaves of Hong Kong* (1967).

[20] Here I am indebted to R. E. Mitchell *et al.* for the material they collected and presented in *Levels of Emotional Strain in Southeast Asian Cities*, 2 vols. (Hong Kong, 1969).

[21] "The Gallant Maid" by Wen Kang (1821–50).

[22] "Strange Tales of Liao-chai" by P'u Sung-ling (1630–1715).

Luis Ramiro Beltrán S.:

TV Etchings in the Minds of Latin Americans: Conservantism, Materialism and Conformism

☆ THE IMAGE OF THE WORLD that exists in our minds is the result of the interaction of every individual with his physical and social environment. What are the images of the world that the mass media communicate? This is the question to which the present essay is addressed. The question appears germane for it would be grossly unrealistic to pretend that the media have no influence in the formation of "the pictures of the world." These pictures that our minds host are: 1) acquired from experience with nature and society gained through interactive exchange based on communication, 2) determinant of our behavior and 3) highly influenced by the mass media, which tend to communicate to the many the ideologies of the few.

How do these conceptual guidelines relate to the Latin American mass communications reality? The rest of this paper will attempt to present answers in the specific terms of some television images, and their negative influence on audiences, as reported in research conducted in this region.

The Composite Imagery

Television research in Latin America is at such an early stage of development that it is not possible yet to safely and broadly generalize from the studies that have been done. Many more and even different studies will have to be carried out—particularly in the area of direct measurement of actual behaviors over time as they relate to assumed media effects—in order to gauge, with increasing reliability, the actual negative impact that messages have on people.

However, the available studies dealing with television images do already

▶ This is a shortened version of a paper presented at the *International Association for Mass Communication Research Conference* in Leicester, England, 1976, supplied by the author. Dr. Luis Ramiro Beltrán S. is a communication specialist and Representative for Latin America of the Division of Information Sciences at the International Research Centre in Bogotá, Colombia. The opinions expressed in this paper are solely the responsibility of the author, not of the institution for which he works.

provide reasonably valid indications that this medium is attempting to induce in its audience an adherence to a number of beliefs[1] about human life and destiny, which several critics rate as noxious. From study to study, there is a remarkable similarity in many of the observations. Conducted in different settings and at different times, with varying foci and using diverse procedures, the studies, nevertheless, demonstrate regularities suggesting patterns. In fact, a composite of the images the studies detected is essentially made up of the following frequently-found elements:

individualism	conformism
elitism	self-defeatism
racism	providentialism
materialism	authoritarianism
adventurism	romanticism
conservantism	aggressiveness[2]

Illustrations of "conformism" and "conservantism" may be found in a study done by two Argentinian researchers, Walger and Ulanovsky. Part of their study includes the story of Fabiana Lopez, a Buenos Aires girl from the slums, who experienced the "fairy godmother" role television may at times assume. Her story really begins on the day when her boyfriend abandoned her after having won three hundred million pesos in a softball score prediction game. The authors of the study report that television rescued Fabiana from this predicament and "introduced her to a new, almost magic world" in which she was "civilized" at the expense of being "publicly destroyed" by having to disclose before the cameras every intimate detail of her origins, existence and tragedy.

Once the dream and the nightmare were over, the same analysts note, Fabiana humbly returned to her everyday life, and the media covered her with praise because she had understood that her home was to be the slums.

The analysts claim that behind this conformity-inducing mechanism lies the will of the ruling class, represented by the media, "to fix each human being in his position within society, immobilizing him ideologically in the place where he belongs . . . it will only be possible to leave this place through the magic proposals the media offer. Thus, the magic solutions appear as a corollary of a harmonious society in which contradictions do not exist. The shantytown from which the Fabianas emerge are a natural fact, and are accepted as such . . ."[3]

Closely related to this idea of conformism is the notion of the necessary resignation of the masses that is propagated by television. A Colombian analyst of "soap operas" stresses a basic dimension of this gender: the notions of the immutability of the established order and the inevitability of each man's fate. Referring to the soap opera protagonists, Bibliowicz, the analyst, asserts: "They demonstrate how human beings are conditioned from the moment of birth to a social role and how this is unavoidable; whatever one does, the son of a nobleman will be a nobleman, the son of a worker will be a worker, and the son of a peasant will be a peasant. One class will be the dominant one and the other will be dominated. Some will be masters, others slaves. The world of the "soap opera" offers but one road: RESIGNATION."[4]

Another study by the Peruvian analyst Gorki Tapia, focuses on the images of individualism and materialism present in the TV cartoon *Los Picapiedras.* (*The Flintstones*). This is a translated United States serial program that is eminently addressed to children. It is set in a primitive community of cave-men, which is modernized to match the characteristics of present-day highly developed capitalist nations. Tapia perceives the following patterns as clearly and sustainedly present in the program:

1. The environment is that of a consumer society plentiful in material well-being and assumedly free of contradictions and conflicts. This set-ting is not accidental for the consistent intention of the series is to suggest, through such imagery, that the only natural course of human-ity is capitalism.
2. One central value proposed is selfish individualism coupled with rugged competitiveness. Opportunities may, in principle, be equal for all human beings, but the best places in life belong to the best individ-uals (i.e., those who excel over the others in competition).
3. Success and happiness in life consist of being on top of others in terms of material well-being expressed in an ever-growing possession of goods and enjoyment of services. This presents prestige and power.
4. Society rewards those who win this game and punishes the losers.
5. Those who remain losers must accept their lot as a product of "fate," "the will from above" and of their own incompetence and inferior en-dowment. Conformity and resignation should characterize their behav-ior, not rebelliousness and aggressiveness. For such is the natural order of things, and it should not be altered.

Tapia argues that this *pro-status quo* persuasion scheme operates on the audience, in this case children, as an early "social vaccination." The injection is given through the apparently innocuous cartoons into the children's con-sciousness, building defenses against different value propositions, new beliefs and opposite visions of life and development "that would imperil the individ-ual's psychic consonance with capitalist ideology."[5]

Potential Research Areas

The limited sample of the available research presented here offers suf-ficient evidence to show that there is genuine reason for concern about the images of the world provided by Latin American television. It would appear that these images are not unidimensional, but rather, include concommittant sub-images like cluster formations of stereotyped beliefs. For instance, "materi-alism" seems to include 1) "hedonism," 2) "Adonism," 3) "consumerism" and 4) "mercantilism." If these beliefs can, in fact, be classified as "central" and "peripheral," then it could be proposed that the central ones are likely to be "conservatism," "materialism" and "conformism."

If, in fact, the basic categories are clusters and if, furthermore, they are indeed closely interrelated, then they may amount to a sub-system of beliefs within the general belief system,[6] each person is assumed to carry in his mind. And if they are systemic—that is, jurisdictionally defined and functionally connected—their impact could be expected to be such that it is in fact able to instill in people a "general style of life" or an "ideology." The serious implications of it lead one to think that research ought to tap these possibilities for, if they hold through initial verification, this would suggest that the study of mass media images should also be *systemic in the sense of seeking to trace constellations of beliefs rather than isolated units of them.*

Another possible area for research would be based on differentiation by the main types of psychological stimulation TV is assumed to utilize: "narcotic-analgesic" and "exciting-energizing"—that is to say, either hypnotizing or stimulating the TV audience with the images. Whichever of these negative or positive stimuli is used, the purpose of the communicators would be to render the communiquees highly amenable to manipulative persuasion. Ultimately, such stimuli should result in the impairment of critical ability, the numbing of creativity and in compliant submissiveness. If something really effective is to be done one day to help people defend themselves from all these socio-cultural barbiturates handed out by the media, research must move beyond the identification of explicit and implicit images in messages. It must seek to find out what really happens in the inner world of the persons reached by those images in terms of *concrete behaviors produced by such stimulation.*

The Roots of the Imagery and Some Facts and Figures

Finally, there is another very important element to be mentioned: the origins of the images surveyed. For, without this element, this review would be seriously lacking in realism.

The answer to the question, where do the images identified come from? is not a difficult one to find. It is overwhelmingly clear that they are predominantly North American in origin or in influence. The facts plainly reveal this. On the average, close to one third of one week's television programming in eighteen cities of Latin America was found to directly originate in the United States.[7] Latin America spends close to eighty million dollars per year in importing TV canned material from the United States.[8]

However, programming and sales are not the only indications of United States influence in Latin American television. As a result of the control the United States exercises over technology, materials, technicians, and capital in Latin American television, most of the television programs produced in Latin America itself can hardly be distinguished from United States programs. This occurs because Latin America receives not just U.S. TV technology, but also a large amount of its ideological input.

Direct United States investments in Latin American television have decreased since 1970 due, perhaps, to the fear of political intervention. But United States industry has far from subsided, since indirect investment has safely and advantageously filled this vacuum through programming and advertising sales.[9] 83 percent of Latin American TV channels are privately owned commercial ones.[10] United States advertising firms clearly dominate Latin American advertising business. For instance, the first five advertising clients in Colombia, are Colgate-Palmolive, Lever Brothers, American Home Products, Lotteries and Raffles, and Miles Laboratories; over 50 percent of television advertising in this country is devoted to cosmetics, non-essential food stuffs, and detergents, most of which are produced by United States multinational companies.[11]

What are the consequences of this situation? Brazil's Minister of Communications offers an answer:

> Commercial television is imposing on youth and children a culture which has nothing to do with the Brazilian one . . . . 57 percent of current programming is made of imported materials . . . 'in the tribal village the world has become today, communication media are cornerstones,' but this evolution is a two-edged weapon. On the one hand, it widens the scope of individuals, it brings them together, and it informs them. On the other, it is capable of casting collective patterns of behavior, conditioning men to pre-established models, forcing alterations and not even allowing evolution.[12]

It becomes clear then that, as Mattelart puts it, "the message is not the medium: the message is society."[13] A British analyst condenses the critical perspective as follows:

> The commercial character of television has then to be seen at several levels; as the making of programs for profit in a known market; as a channel for advertising; and as a cultural and political form indirectly shaped by and dependent on the norms of capitalist society, selling both consumer goods and a "way of life" based on them. . . .[14]

Evidently, this situation is not one created by the "tropical imagination" of Latin Americans. As many other crucial things in their life, the intoxicating TV images that assail their minds indeed are, to a large extent, "made in the USA."

NOTES

[1] Rokeach (p. 2) defines beliefs as "interferences made by an observer about underlying states of expectancy."
[2] This sequence implies no ranking.
[3] Walger and Ulanovsky, p. 28.
[4] Bibliowicz.
[5] Tapia Delgado, p. 64.
[6] "A belief system may be defined as having represented within it, in some organized

psychological but not necessarily logical form, each and every one of a person's countless beliefs about physical and social reality." (Rokeach, p. 2.)

[7] Kaplun, p. 32.

[8] Mas.

[9] Mattelart.

[10] Kaplun.

[11] Beltrán and Fox de Cardona.

[12] Oliveira, p. 46.

[13] Mattelart, p. 195.

[14] Williams, pp. 41–42.

REFERENCES

Beltran, Luis Ramiro, and Fox de Cardona, Elizabeth. *Latin America and the U.S.; Flaws in the Free Flow of Information*. Bogotá, 1976.

Bibliowicz, Azriel. *Plaza Sésamo; Producto de la Industria Cultural*. Bogotá: Universidad Jorge Tadeo Lozano, s.f.

Kaplun, Mario. *La Communicación de Masas en América Latina*. Educación Hoy No. 5, Bogotá: Asociación de Publicaciones Educativas, 1973.

Mas, Fernando. "La Televisión Contra la Cultura," in *Visión* (Mexico, Octubre 10, 1969): 32–42.

Mattelart, Armand. *El Imperialismo en Busca de la Contrarevolución Cultural; Plaza Sésamo: Prólogo a la Telerepresión del Año 2.000*, no. 1 (Chili: Comunicación y Cultura, 1973): 146–223.

Oliveira, Euclides Quandt de. *A Televisao Como Meio de Comunicaçao de Massa*. Brasilia: Ministerio das Comunicaçoes, Coordenaçao de Comunicaçao Social, 1974.

Rokeach, Milton. *Beliefs, Attitudes and Values; a Theory of Organization and Change*. San Francisco: Jossey-Bass, 1969.

Tapia Delgado, Gorki. *"Los Picapiedra," Aliados del Imperialismo; Ideología y Medios de Comunicación de Masas*. Textual Revista del Instituto Nacional de Cultura, no. 8 (Perú, 1973): 63–66.

Walger, Sylvina, and Ulanovsky, Carlos. *TV Guía Negra; una Época de la Televisión en la Argentina en Otra Época*. Buenos Aires: De la Flor, 1974.

Williams, Raymond. *Television; Technology and Cultural Form*. New York: Schocken Books, 1975.

Charles Husband:

Some Aspects of the Interaction of the British Entertainment Media with Contemporary Race Relations

☆ IF WE ARE TO UNDERSTAND the function of the mass entertainment media in Britain, it is essential that the context in which they operate should first be discussed. Britain in 1977 is a multiracial society in as much as the demographic data indicate a significant ethnic minority population, the most visible of whom, both literally and politically, are those of Asian and West Indian origin. While an estimated 43 percent of the black population is British born, the settlement of significant numbers of Asians and West Indians has occurred within only the last twenty years.[1] Although the ethnic balance of a country may be significantly modified within such a short time, national culture and institutions are not so malleable, and indeed continuing economic and political forces may inhibit any such accommodation. Hence, although multiracial in demographic terms, the dominant culture is unequivocally white. Nor is this culture merely an artifact of culture lag; the culture reflects the continuing white hegemony in the political economy of Britain. The truth is that the mass media operate within a society where racial discrimination is widely practiced and where the dominant culture is suffused with racist assumptions. It will be one of the purposes of this chapter to assess the contribution of the entertainment media to sustaining that dominant culture.

First let us look at the culture that shapes the expectations and values which the majority white audience bring to their use of entertainment media. The most striking aspect of this culture is the remarkable historical homogeneity of the Englishman's image of the black man. The black man started with a disadvantage in that even the English language was, and is, against him. Thus by the sixteenth century the meaning of black in the English language included: "Deeply stained with dirt; soiled, dirty, foul . . . having dark or deadly purposes, malignant . . . atrocious, horrible, wicked . . ."[2] The importance of biblical imagery in determining the connotations of blackness is noted by

▶ This is an original article written especially for this book. Charles Husband is Senior Lecturer at the School of Social Analysis, University of Bradford, England.

Isaacs in that "the Bible's central theme of good and evil is constantly represented by the symbolism of 'black' and 'white' and 'dark' and 'light'."[3] More recently the "power of blackness" has been identified in the works of Hawthorne, Melville and Poe.[4] Powerful though linguistic connotations are,[5] the image of the black man in English culture has had a more substantial base.

Hunter has pointed out in an article of considerable erudition that by the sixteenth Century in England Shakespeare was able to rely upon the well-established stereotype of the Moor as a lascivious barbarian. Lines such as "an old black ram is tupping your white ewe" could be relied upon to echo the prejudices of the audience, prejudices which, as Jordan notes, predated contact with the black cultures of West Africa. Indeed, he notes that many of the accounts of these early contacts included much that was purely fictional elaborations of these preconceptions.

British involvement in slavery generated legitimating ideologies that stressed the inferiority of the blackman; while the wealth so accrued financed the industrial revolution, which gave the British an economic pre-eminence, which further legitimated their conviction in their own superiority.[6] From sixteenth-century involvement in slavery through colonial land grabbing in the late nineteenth century, the inferiority of the non-white has been an unchanging assumption of British culture. Sometimes the justification for the belief has been biblical and sometimes scientific, but though the legitimating arguments have varied, the essential belief has not. The history of British contact with black societies has been one of white domination; economic domination, political domination and, where it could be enforced, cultural domination. It can be no surprise then that in a survey carried out in the latter part of the 1960s, 58 percent of the respondents considered the British, on the whole, superior to Asians and 66 percent thought the British superior to Africans,[7] and that in an interview with all the demands of social desirability. More recent survey material, though, interpreted from different ideological perspectives, continues to tap contemporary attitudinal indicators of this cultural legacy.[8] Nor do we have to rely only upon attitudinal data, since there are those who would argue that such data is of questionable value.[9] Evidence of the racism of white Britain can be found in accounts of the experiences of the West Indian and Asian communities in Britain, where discrimination in housing, education, employment and at law is made vividly apparent.[10] Since some of these accounts may be felt to be partisan, telling confirmation of the reality of racial discrimination in Britain is provided in the independent documentation provided in the recently published *The Facts of Racial Disadvantage.*[11]

Extensive though this evidence of racial discrimination is, the total picture can only be achieved when it is understood that the British Government has itself provided exemplary models of racial discrimination though its immigration legislation.[12] The successive Acts have progressively discriminated against black immigrants rather than immigration per se; and the rationale for this has been political expediency based upon an acceptance of popular feeling. For example, Richard Crossman, a Labour Party cabinet minister, in an article in

The Times (6 October, 1972), provided an account of the Labour Cabinet's behavior in rushing through the 1968 Commonwealth Immigrants Act:

> As progressives we were opposed to capital punishment, persecution of homosexuals and racial prejudice, whereas a large section of our working-class supporters regard such ideas as poison. What they hate most is our softness on color. It nearly cost us the election of 1964—particularly in the West Midlands—and it was widely felt that our improved majority of 1966 was due to our new tough line on immigration control. That is why as a Government we were panicked in the autumn of 1967 by top secret reports predicting a mass expulsion of Asians from East Africa and began to make contingency plans for legislation which we realized would have been declared unconstitutional in any country with a written constitution and a supreme court.

Harshly discriminatory though the immigration legislation has been, its implementation has been positively draconian,[13] and it has reinforced the black community's perception of their rejection while helping to legitimate the racial myths and antagonism of the white majority

Large though this introduction bulks in a comparatively brief chapter, and still failing to provide an adequate review, it is justified in that an appreciation of the mass of historical precedent ossified in contemporary culture and the extent of contemporary racial discrimination is a fundamental prerequisite to any analysis of the function of the entertainment media in contemporary Britain.

Interestingly, it is appropriate to start a discussion of the entertainment media by briefly reviewing the literature on the news media in Britain, since the news media have contributed to the definition of the race relations situation—and more specifically have provided substantive issues for incorporation in entertainment programs, whether in characters and plots for drama or foci for comedians. The news media have defined race relations as largely a *problem* of immigration and they have habitually emphasized the symptoms of racial hostility rather than analyzed the underlying causes.[14] In doing this they have not only reflected habitual journalistic news values, they have also reflected the white consciousness of the media personnel. In 1975 it was estimated that 0.09 percent of journalists working on British newspapers and magazines were nonwhite,[15] this when the black population in the country as a whole was approximately 3 percent.

The impact of this staffing was reflected in the frequent white bias, and even in hostility, which was visible in the press and in television news.[16] Since the entertainment media of television, radio, cinema and publishing may be expected to present comparable staffing ratios, this alerts us to the possibility of comparable consequences. If white journalists produce news reflecting white concerns and white sensibilities, surely we must anticipate that an entertainment industry staffed by whites will reflect white interests and white aesthetics.

Some preliminary insights are provided in relation to broadcast radio and television in two recent government reports, one the *Report of the Committee on the Future of Broadcasting* (HMSO 1977), "Annan Report" after its chairman, and the other the report of evidence on "The West Indian Community" given to the *Select Committee on Race Relations and Immigration* (HMSO 1977). What becomes apparent in the evidence given by both the BBC and the Independent Broadcasting Authority is that neither saw fit to voluntarily provide explicit estimates of staffing ratio's to these government committees, while at the same time, it is the case that very, very few blacks are in production, let alone management. Indeed, concern in both committees is more directed to the visibility of blacks in the media. However, even here the prevailing assumptions do not augur well for black recruitment, for although the BBC evidence to Annan claimed that "they supported and practiced integrated casting according to the spirit and the letter of the Race Relations Act," they qualified this by stating that "they had to find the 'best available talent' and, within the open competitive system and the other personnel policies which they pursued, there was little room for special procedures."[17] Could it be that the BBC anticipates having to invoke "special procedures" in recruiting black actors?[18]

In their Memorandum to the Select Committee on Race Relations, one of their two qualifications to their position on "integrated casting in television drama" does say that "good acting must be the overriding priority. The BBC does not regard it as proper to cast, across the whole field of its drama output, for the primary purpose of changing social attitudes towards race."[19] The issue is made more explicit by Mr. Robin Scott, Controller–Development–BBC Television; in evidence to the same committee in speaking of the difficulties in using non-white actors he says:

> I am talking here about professional standards, because in the end, of course, professional standards have to prevail. We do not want to lean over so far backwards that, for the sake of keeping good relations with the actors' union and this particular group of actors, in fact the quality of productions visibly diminishes.[20]

If the evidence of Mr. Scott's colleague, The Hon. K. H. L. Lamb, Director Public Affairs–BBC, is to be taken seriously, then it seems that recruiting a black news reader to the BBC is a similarly fraught experience.

> No one would be more pleased than the BBC, and in particular in the news and current affairs field, if someone came forward who had the professional qualifications or potential to fill the role, and certainly there would be no reluctance to employ him. The difficulty is to find the right person, even after making it known as widely as possible.[21]

Thus the general impression gained from reading these reports is that not only is it accepted by both BBC and IBA that there is a need to recruit more blacks into the mass media, there is also evidence that prevailing attitudes may inhibit this, particularly as managerial zeal appears somewhat lacking.

As a highly pertinent aside, it is interesting to note that being a major government review of broadcsating, the Annan Report represents an unobtrusive measure of the white establishment's sensitivity to the media needs of ethnic minorities. In the section on "Program Standards," the treatment of racial minorities takes up less space than "bad language" and considerably less than "sex" or "violence." A comparable weighting of priorities is found in that while accepting that the Welsh language "is at the heart of the preservation of Welsh culture"[22] and therefore "a fourth television channel in Wales broadcasting in the Welsh language" should be established for the half-million Welsh speakers as soon as finance can be found, the recommendations for the large Asian population whose linguistic need is acknowledged is much more piecemeal.[23] A natural system of priorities you might say, but symptomatic none the less.

Though both the Annan Report and the Select Committee Report record concern about the visibility of blacks on television, they report no current empirical data. However, in 1972 the BBC. produced a report entitled *Non-Whites on British Television*, which was a content analysis of the output of BBC1, BBC2 and the Independent Television channel over a period of one week. The dramatic output of all three channels over the week contained 648 white characters and only 35 "non-whites"; and 56.8 percent of white characters had speaking parts, while only 25.7 percent of the "non-whites" had speaking parts. These parts included a black African waiter, a West Indian messenger boy, a West Indian school teacher-spy, a West Indian bus conductor and nine Hawaiians in various professional, semi-professional and laboring capacities. In this sample, 42 percent of the "non-whites" seen on British television drama appeared in programs imported from America.[24] This is a situation that is unlikely to have changed dramatically with the current diet upon British television of, for example, *Kojak, Starsky and Hutch, Star Trek, The Fantastic Journey, The Six Million Dollar Man, Bionic Woman* and *Hawaii Five-O*.

The findings of this 1972 report were confirmed in 1974 in a study carried out by the Equity Coloured Artists' Committee. (Equity is the trade union of actors and variety performers in Britain.) Their analysis of drama on all three channels over a week showed that of 641 characters seen only 11 were black artists and 4 of these (36 percent) appeared in programs of foreign origin. None of these 11 characters were classified as having a leading role, though 4 had supporting roles and the remaining 7 had small or walk-on parts. This report noted that in some of the very popular "soap operas," such as *Coronation Street, Crossroads* and *General Hospital*, the relative absence of black actors was particularly marked, as the settings for these stories were locations where in contemporary Britain one would anticipate the presence of black characters.

Since that time there has been an improvement in the "visibility" of black characters in such soap operas and indeed in, for example, *The Angels*, a series following the careers of young nurses, one leading part was given to a black actress with a British regional accent, a characteristic that challenges the prevalent assumption among the white audience that all blacks are "immigrants." This is a useful reminder that visibility is not all, the nature of the characterization is also significant, for drama provides a splendid opportunity for non-purposive learning.[25] Though the manifest function of viewing is enjoyment, facts can be assimilated and beliefs modified, since in the context of such programs the audience is more concerned about the credibility of the facts than about their validity. We may anticipate that this effect will be maximized where the "facts" presented are congruent with pre-existing attitudes. In this respect it is disconcerting that the probability remains that the majority of black characters seen on British television are in foreign programs, thus helping to sustain the notion that "Britain at least" is still a white society.

Similarly it seems to be the case that the sensibilities of television drama producers have not kept in touch with the implications of their actions. In 1974 it was noted:

> A further feature of British television that needs to be mentioned is the tendency to accept the definition of the situation provided by the news media as the basis for the production of entertainment. Those themes that have been central to news coverage of race are fastened into and elaborated in dramatic form so that the picture of reality provided by the news is reinforced and cemented in the public mind through drama. This is true particularly of the conflict/threat image of the colored population that we noted in news output. Thus, in the past few years *The Saint, Softly Softly* and *The Strange Report* have all had episodes in which the story line concerned illegal immigration. [26]

This dubious policy has continued with perhaps the most recent florid example being BBC's serial *The Gangsters*, which was transmitted in 1976. In this lurid confection, the West Indians were controlling prostitution and the Asians were involved in drugs and illegal immigration. Thus, though it is true that improvements have been consciously introduced, as for example in the soap operas and in B.B.C.'s series of thirty-minute plays by black writers on the minority B.B.C.2 channel, there remains a remarkable capacity for insensitivity.

Viewed in the context of television as a whole the portrayal of black people is more disturbing for, as both the BBC and Equity studies showed, blacks are much more visible in variety programs. Thus the "Sambo" image of the musical, all dancing, all singing Negro survives, woven into the relative visibility he is accorded in different areas of television programming, thereby reinforcing the assumptions of the white audience and sustaining the assault upon the sensitivities of the black audience. At a time when current affairs programs on British television are reflecting a new confidence in attacking racism, it is all the more depressing that *Tarzan* and *The Black and White Minstrel Show* should continue to carry forward the banner of white liberal ethnocentrism, and worse.

One area of television entertainment programming where white racial values have been most clearly manifest is that of comedy, wherein, following the pioneering success of *Till Death Us Do Part*, race has been a valuable commercial ingredient. Johnny Speight, the author of this series, justified giving a platform to outspoken bigotry by arguing that the series was intended to attack the racism he portrayed. In presenting this justification Speight was fortunate in that it was congruent with two dominant beliefs in British society. One belief is the acceptance of humor as therapeutic and cathartic, as, for example, encapsulated in the saying "People who can laugh together can live together." The other potent belief is the ubiquitous acceptance among the white audience of Britain as a tolerant society. Despite the reality of British treatment of Jews from the eleventh century,[27] of blacks in Britain from the sixteenth century,[28] and of other Europeans over the past seven centuries,[29] it is the myth of "British tolerance" that has consensual validation.[30] These two beliefs bonded together produce a powerful ideological entity in the acceptability of racial humor as a manifestation of tolerance.

It is probable that this dubious alliance has helped to sustain *Till Death Us Do Part* in the face of criticism from the black communities. In fact, research carried out by the B.B.C. indicated that the series may well have reinforced prejudice in its audience,[31] as there are indications of the selective exposure and selective perception discerned by Vidmar and Rokeach and Tate and Surlin in their studies of *All in the Family*. Also it is difficult to see how a program like *It Ain't Half Hot Mum*, transmitted in 1976, could have been conceived without this prevalent ideology. In this series, stereotyped images of 1940's India serve as a background for a military situation comedy wherein the main Indian protagonist, played by a blacked-up Englishman, is a hybrid mixture of Mowgli and Gunga Din, at once wily and innocent, wheedling and occasionally wise.

Recently, in a variant on *Good Times*, the British audience has been provided with a family comedy based upon a West Indian family, *The Fosters*. This program has an all-black cast and appears to be very popular with many blacks for this reason; it represents a unique experience. Yet even in the black audience there are criticisms where, for example, one black reviewer, while accepting the casting breakthrough, has asked: But what of the "heavy racist undercurrents. The most obvious is the image that we all are 'jive niggers' and that all Black fathers act like Mr. Foster or his eldest clown of a son, Sonny."[32] Clearly, with the different perspectives brought by the various black and white audiences, selective perception will always operate. However, in television there is still program content that unnecessarily sustains racist assumptions and denies the integrity of the black viewer.

Radio at a national level has shown itself to be largely incapable of responding to the ethnic heterogeneity of its audience. However, the B.B.C. local stations and the Independent (commercial) Local Radio Stations in dealing with more clearly defined audiences in specific cities have been able to respond to the entertainment needs of minority audiences.[33] These local stations have been able to acknowledge the geographical distribution of differing ethnic groups and, for example, provide programs in the majority Asian language in their area. They have also responded to the need for music programs that provide the distinctive preferences of each ethnic group, rather than the homogenized "pop" available on the national channels. As both Annan and Khan acknowledge, these are services that have yet to explore their full potential, or indeed be fully exploited by the black communities. While the current concern of the B.B.C. and I.B.A. to develop the local radio service to ethnic minorities is to be applauded, although there are also clear commercial considerations, it would be very wrong if this effort was seen as sufficient to in some way counterbalance the continuing white hegemony in broadcast radio and television management and production.

Local radio cannot become a media Bantustan, a reserve for servicing the ethnic minorities of Britain. The black communities in Britain expect the national media to reflect the reality of Britain as a multiracial society; this is necessary as much to starve the latent racism of the white British audience as to meet the legitimate demands of the black audience. In the light of current evidence, there is much that remains to be done.[34]

NOTES

[1] Accounts of the migration and settlement of West Indians and Asians in Britain can be found in Deakin (1969), Peach (1968), Krausz (1971) and Lomas (1973).

[2] Jordan, P. 6.

[3] Isaacs, p. 75.

[4] Levin.

[5] Cf. Burgest, Fanon, Searle.

[6] Cf. Bolt, Davis, Jordan, Walvin.

[7] Lawrence, p. 62.

[8] C.R.C., *Some of My Best Friends*; Little and Kohler; Marsh. The emergence of this cultural legacy can also be found manifest in contemporary novels, comics and textbooks. Milner (1975); Dummett (1973); Laishley (1975); Hill (1971); Children's Rights Workshop, (1975); Glendenning (1971); Stewart (1970); White (1971).

[9] Deutscher, Schuman and Johnson, Wicker.

[10] C.R.C., *Urban Deprivation*; Coard; Humphry; John; Morrison, *As They See It*; Select Committee on Race Relations; Smith and Whalley.

[11] Smith.

[12] Dummett and Dummett, Humphry and Ward.

[13] Akram, Moore and Wallace.

[14] Critcher *et al.*; Hartmann and Husband, *Racism*.

[15] Morrison, "A Black Journalist's Experience."

[16] Critcher *et al*; Downing; Evans; Hartmann and Husband, "Mass Media and Racial Conflict" and *Racism*; Runnymede Trust; Wood.

[17] Annan Report, p. 441.

[18] Maddy (1975) offers pungent personal comment and Khan (1976) provides a well researched account of the current experiences of black actors.

[19] Select Committee, p. 380.

[20] *Ibid.*, p. 392.

[21] *Ibid.*, p. 394.

[22] Annan Report, p. 412.

[23] *Ibid.*, p. 487.

[24] This same report, *Non-Whites on British Television*, noted that 67 per cent of the 'non-white' characters seen in feature films on British television were in American films. This is a situation which is likely to be continued as not only is television heavily dependent upon old films (Annan, 1977) but with the rising unit costs of television

production there has been a tendancy to also import American produced 'television movies'. With the decline in the indigenous British cinema industry the cinema networks are similarly dependent upon American production. Hence critiques of the American cinema industry are pertinent to a significant element of British mass entertainment. (Hartmann and Husband, 1974:189–195; Friar & Friar, 1972; Leab, 1975; Pines, 1975; Bogle, 1974) One exception in the British cinema industry is the growth of Asian cinemas. One report estimates that there are at least 40 full time Asian cinemas in Britain (Khan, 1976) and cinema attendance is a major leisure, and social, activity in the Asian communities.

[25] Krugman, Krugman and Hartley.

[26] Hartmann and Husband, *Racism*, p. 202.

[27] Garrard, Johnson, Sharf.

[28] George, Moore, Walvin.

[29] Bethel, Foot, Johnson.

[30] Husband, "Racism in Society."

[31] Husband, "The Mass Media."

[32] Shabazz.

[33] Khan, Select Committee.

[34] Since this article was originally written there have been positive developments: the BBC has successfully recruited some ethnic minority staff into news reporting and they have experimented with a comedy/drama series, *Empire Road*, which more directly than in previous series, sought to reflect the real tensions of a multi-racial community. The presence of multiple, and different, audiences has not left this series without its ambiguity in relation to audience response. Significantly the discussions at the 1978 *Edinburgh International Television Festival* indicated the awareness of many television production personnel of the important responsibility television has in generating material relevant to a multi-racial society. An element which emerged forcibly in this discussion was the assertion by production personnel that it was the management who constituted a significant restraint in controlling the development of more critical and socially challenging material.

REFERENCES

Akram, Mohammed. *Where Do You Keep Your String Beads*. London: Runnymede Trust, 1974.

Annan Report. *Report of the Committee on the Future of Broadcasting*. H.M.S.O., 1977.

BBC *Non-Whites on British Television*. London: BBC. Audience Research Department, 1972.

Bethel, N. *The Last Secret*. London: Futura Publications, 1976.

Bogle, Donald. *Toms, Coons, Mulattoes, Mammies and Bucks: An Interpretative History of Blacks in American Films*. New York: Bantam Books, 1974.

Bolt, Christine. *Victorian Attitudes to Race*. London: Routledge, 1971.

Burgest, David R. "The Racist Use of the English Language." *The Black Scholar* 5., no. 1 (Sept. 1973): 37–45.

Children's Rights Workshop. *Racist and Sexist Images in Children's Books*. London: Writers and Readers Publishing Cooperative, 1975.

Coard, Bernard. *How the West Indian Child Is Made Educationally Sub-Normal in the British School System*. London: New Beacon Books, 1971.

CRC *Some of My Best Friends*. London: Community Relations Commission, 1976.

CRC *Urban Deprivation, Racial Inequality and Social Policy: A Report*. London: Community Relations Commission, 1977.

Critcher, Charles; Parker, Margaret; and Sondhi, Ranjit. *Race in the Provincial Press*. In *Ethnicity and the Media*. Paris: UNESCO, 1977.

Davis, David Brion. *The Problem of Slavery in Western Culture*. Pelican Books, 1970.

Deakin, Nicholas. *Colour Citizenship and British Society*. London: Panther Books, 1969.

Deutscher, Irwin. *What We Say/What We Do*. Glenview, Illinois: Scott, Foresman & Co., 1973.

Downing, John. "The (Balanced) White View." In *White Media and Black Britain*. Ed. by C. Husband. London: Arrow Books, 1975.

Dummett, Ann. *A Portrait of English Racism*, Harmondsworth: Penguin Books, 1973.

Dummett, Michael, and Dummett, Ann. "The Role of Government in Britain's Racial Crisis." In *Justice First*. Ed. by Lewis Donnelly. London: Sheed & Ward, 1969.

Equity Coloured Artists' Committee. *Coloured Artists on British Television*. London: British Actors' Equity Association, 1974.

Evans, Peter. *Publish and Be Damned*. London: Runnymede Trust, 1977.

Fanon, Frantz. *Black Skin White Masks*. London: Granada Publishing Ltd., Paladin Books, 1970.

Foot, Paul. *Immigration and Race in British Politics*. Harmondsworth: Penguin Books, 1965.

Friar, Ralph, and Friar, Natasha. *The Only Good Indian: The Hollywood Gospel*. New York: Drama Book Specialists/Publishers, 1972.

Garrard, John A. *The English and Immigration 1880–1910*. London: O.U.P., 1971.

George, M. Dorothy, *London Life in the Eighteenth Century*. London: Kegan Paul, Trench, Trubner & Co, Ltd., 1930.

Glendenning, F. "Racial Stereotypes in History Textbooks." *Race Today* (Feb. 1971).

Hartmann, Paul, and Husband, Charles. "The Mass Media and Racial Conflict." *Race*, XII, no. 3, (1971).

Hartmann, Paul, and Husband, Charles. *Racism and the Mass Media*. London: Davis-Poynter, 1974.

Hill, Janet. *Books for Children: The Homelands of Immigrants in Britain*. London: I.R.R., 1971.

Humphry, Derek. *Police Power and Black People*. London: Granada Publishing, Panther Books, 1972.

Humphry, Derek, and Ward, Michael. *Passports and Politics*. Harmondsworth: Penguin Books, 1974.

Hunter, G. K. "Othello and Colour Prejudice." *The Proceedings of the British Academy* LIII, pp. 141–63. London: Oxford University Press, 1967.

Husband, Charles. "Racism in Society and the Mass Media: A Critical Interaction." In *White Media and Black Britain*. Ed. by Charles Husband. London: Arrow Books, 1975.

Husband, Charles. "The Mass Media and the Functions of Ethnic Humour in a Racist Society!" In *It's a Funny Thing: International Conference on Humour and Laughter*, Ed. by Anthony J. Chapman and Hugh C. Foot. London: Pergamon Press, 1977.

Isaacs, Harold R. *The New World of Negro Americans*, Chap. 3. London: Phoenix House, 1964.

John, Augustine. *Race in the Inner City*. London: Runnymede Trust, 1970.

Johnson, Paul. *The Offshore Islanders*. Harmondsworth: Penguin Books, 1975.

Jordon, Winthrop, D. *White Over Black*. Harmondsworth: Penguin Books, 1969.

Khan, Naseem. *The Arts Britain Ignores*. London: Community Relations Commission, 1976.

Krausz, Ernest. *Ethnic Minorities in Britain*. London: MacGibbon & Kee, 1971.

Krugman, Herbert, E. "The Impact of Television Advertising: Learning Without Involvement." *Public Opinion Quarterly* 29, no. 3 (Fall 1965).

Krugman, Herbert E. and Hartley, Eugene L. "Passive Learning from Television." *Public Opinion Quarterly* 34, no. 2 (Summer 1970).

Laishley, Jennie. "The Images of Blacks and Whites in the Children's Media." In *White Media and Black Britain*, Ed. by C. Husband. London: Arrow Books, 1975.

Leab, Daniel J. *From Sambo to Superspade: The Black Experience in Motion Pictures*. London: Secker and Warburg, 1975.

Levin, Harry, *The Power of Blackness*. London: Faber and Faber, 1958.

Little, Alan, and Kohler, David. "Do We Hate Blacks." *New Society*, 27 (Jan. 1977): 184–85.

Lomas, G. *Census 1971: The Coloured Population*. London: Runnymede Trust, 1973.

Maddy, Yulisa Amadu. "Creating a Black Theatre in Britain." In *White Media and Black Britain*, Ed. by C. Husband. London: Arrow Books, 1975.

Marsh, Alan. "Who Hates the Blacks." *New Society*, 23 (Sept. 1976): 644–52.

Milner, David. *Children and Race*. Harmondsworth: Penguin Books, 1975.

Moore, Robert. *Racism and Black Resistance in Britain*. London: Pluto Press, 1975.

Moore, Robert, and Wallace, Tina. *Slamming the Door: The Administration of Immigration Control*. London: Martin Robertson, 1975.

Morrison, Lionel. "A Black Journalist's Experience of British Journalism." In *White Media and Black Britain*, Ed. by C. Husband. London: Arrow Books, 1975.

Morrison, Lionel. *As They See It*. London: Community Relations Commission, 1976.

Peach, Ceri. *West Indian Migration to Britain—A Social Geography*. London: O.U.P./I.R.R., 1968.

Pines, Jim. *Blacks in Films*. London: Studio Vista, Cassell and Collier MacMillan, 1975.

Runnymeade Trust, *Race and the Press*, London: Runnymede Trust, 1971.

Schuman, Howard, and Johnson, Michael P. "Attitudes and Behavior." *Annual Review of Sociology* 2, (1976), pp. 161–207.

Searle, C. *The Forsaken Lover*. Harmondsworth: Penguin Books, 1973.

Select Committee on Race Relations and Immigration. Session 1976–1977, The West Indian Community, Vol. 2. London: Evidence, H.M.S.O., 1977.

Shabazz, Menelik. "The Fosters from Embarrassment to Insult." *Grass Roots* V 4, no. 8 (Sept.–Oct. 1976): 10.

Sharf, Andrew. *The British Press and Jews under Nazis Rule*. London: Institute of Race Relations/O.U.P., 1964.

Smith, David, J. *The Facts of Racial Disadvantage*, London: P.E.P., 1976.

Smith, David, and Whalley, Anne. *Racial Minorities and Public Housing*. London: P.E.P., 1975.

Stewart, I. "Readers as a Source of Prejudice." *Race Today* (January 1970).

Tate, Eugene D., and Surlin, Stuart H. "A Cross-Cultural Comparison of Viewer

Agreement with Opinionated Television Characters." Paper given to International Communication Association, Intercultural Communications Division, Chicago, Illinois, April, 1975.

Vidmar, Neil, and Rokeach, Milton. "Archie Bunker's Bigotry: A Study in Selective Perception and Exposure." *The Journal of Communication* 24 (1974): 36–47.

Walvin, James. *The Black Presence*. London: Orbach and Chambers, 1971.

White, Lydia. *Impact: World Development in British Education*. London: Voluntary Committee on Overseas Aid and Development.

Wicker, A. W. "Attitudes vs. Actions: The Relationship of Verbal and Overt Behavioral Responses to Attitude Objects." *J. Social Issues* 25 (1969): 41–78.

Wood, Wilfred. "Black Voices in the Media." In *White Media and Black Britain*, Ed. by C. Husband. London: Arrow Books, 1975.

Heinz-Dietrich Fischer:

From Cooperation to Quasi-Congruency—
Interdependencies between the
Olympic Games and Television

☆ THE INTERDEPENDENCIES that exist between sports and mass media are relatively new. One only has to bear in mind the attitude the press used to maintain toward extensive coverage of sporting events: it was regarded with considerable misgiving to say the least. Indeed, it wasn't until the beginning of the twentieth century that sports and the communications media embarked on a policy of closer cooperation. Sports events became regular features of mass communication, in newspapers and in the emerging new medium, film, only after the First World War and during the 1920s with the introduction of radio.[1] "It was the age of jazz and (the) Charleston, of the flapper and raccoon coats, of speakeasies and bathtub gin," say the social psychologists, Tannenbaum and Noah, along with the following observations:

> Among members of the sporting fraternity, the Roaring Twenties had another claim to fame: it was the "golden age of sports," when the American populace, flush with post-war prosperity, flocked to the arenas and stadia. Not only was this the heyday of the more conventional sports (boxing, baseball, football) but of the "fringe" sports (e.g., jaialai and six-day bike racing) as well. Whether partially responsible for this upsurge in sports interest, or a result of it, or merely coincidental with it, there also arose a new brand of sports writing and reporting during the twenties. The change-over was almost as dramatic as the difference between a present-day account of a cricket match in a staid British daily and a Big Ten college paper's eulogy of last Saturday's football upset. Informality of style, originality of composition and a new jargon blossomed on the sports pages—but accompanied by a tendency toward verbosity, triteness, and shopworn cliches, synonymns and analogies. The golden age of sports was matched by a slightly tarnished silver age of sports writing. This situation has undoubtedly been altered somewhat in the past few decades, possibly for the better. . . . The effect of the twenties, however, is still evident on today's

▶ This is an original article written especially for this book. Dr. Heinz-Dietrich Fischer is Professor of Journalism and Mass Communication at the Ruhr-University, Bochum, West Germany. The article was translated by Stefan R. Melnik, M.A.

sports pages. The sports writer still has a greater freedom of expression than most of his newspaperman colleagues.[2]

The more communications media gave coverage to sports events, the stronger the symptoms of audience or readership identification with top athletes, for instance, became (on the same level as identification with film stars). As soon as international competition between single athletes and teams became an established part of sports, success in the stadium or arena frequently began to go hand in hand with political objectives. This applies especially to the so-called "Olympic Movement." The Olympic Games, revived in 1896 by the French baron, Pierre de Coubertin, after a lapse of almost two thousand years, have almost always been accompanied by political ambitions of one kind or another, though to claim that the Games represent a "public symbiosis of positivism, fetishism, capitalism and technocracy"[3] is undifferentiated and superficial to say the least. Coubertin idealistically wanted to see the Olympic Games play an integrative role in international relations through the creation of equal opportunity, the encouragement of cooperation and the promotion of understanding between nations at least at the level of sporting activity.[4] Hackforth establishes, however, that the modern Olympic Games, ever since their initiation in Athens in 1896 (and especially the Olympics in Berlin in 1936), "had little in common with Coubertian concepts and ideas."[5] In 1900 and 1904, the Olympics were organized as relatively unceremonious supplementary attractions at the world exhibitions respectively held in Paris and St. Louis. In 1908, the Olympics, staged over a period of seven months, seemed to be more a fairground than a sporting event. After the 1924 Olympics, which for the first time saw competition in winter sports, Coubertin resigned as president of the International Olympic Committee (IOC). It was only after his retirement, with the remarkable success—as far as spectator interest is concerned—of the summer Olympics of 1928 in Amsterdam, that he could experience the first fruits of his work.[6]

Parallel with—or not long after—this increase in popularity, the mass media started to show a marked interest themselves in covering the events at the Olympics. This applies to radio as well as the press. Kurt Wagenfuhr informs us that the Olympics in 1924 were not given live coverage by radio, although radio programs were already being transmitted both in Switzerland, where the Winter Games were staged (in Chamonix), and in France, where the Summer Games were staged (in Paris). Radio was still in its infancy and simply didn't possess the resources with which to accomplish such a task. Four years later, on the eleventh of February, 1928, Radio Bern was already in a position to transmit the opening ceremony of the Winter Olympics live from St. Moritz. But only this event was broadcast. Similarly, the Dutch AVRO only gave live coverage to the opening ceremony of the Summer Games. All other news from the Olympics was bought up for exclusive use by the radio station from a Portuguese reporter. The following Olympic Games in Lake Placid (winter events) and Los Angeles (summer events), both in the United States, were undoubtedly given some radio coverage. What is more, powerful short-wave transmitters were already in existence, enabling transmission to Europe. It wasn't until 1936, however, with the Winter Olympics at Garmisch-Partenkirchen, Germany, that radio gave full live coverage of the events in which nineteen nations participated.[7] Forty nations took part in the competitive events at the Summer Olympics in that same year in Berlin. The National Socialists had been quick to grasp the opportunities offered by such an internationalized event in terms of propaganda, and had accordingly made extensive preparations. They spared no effort in trying to ensure that as many people as possible all over the world could follow the Olympics. A high-ranking National Socialist official bluntly admitted that "German radio has been given a task of the greatest cultural and political importance. . . ."[8] Radio commentators from a total of nineteen European and thirteen non-European countries ensured that a worldwide audience of hitherto unknown dimensions could now listen in to the sporting events in Berlin.[9]

Besides radio, the National Socialists used a whole range of other media for their gigantic propaganda effort—to the consternation of wide sections of foreign public opinion.[10] In addition to extensive use of the press,[11] who had been instructed to avoid reporting on any internal matters that might serve to damage Germany's image abroad,[12] film, for instance, was enrolled for the propaganda drive. Leni Riefenstahl, who had made a name for herself with her film on the National Socialist Party Congress, *Triumph of the Will*, was officially assigned the task of producing a two-part documentary on the Olympics.[13] Cigarette cards and their complementary albums depicting the Berlin Olympics, chauvinistic in terms of selection and presentation of subject matter, were also issued, albeit for domestic use, as part of the general operation (which is an example of how the simplest, and seemingly innocuous, of media could effectively be used).[14] The National Socialists were quick in seizing the opportunity of employing a further medium, a novelty which had made its debut just in time for the Olympics. An American researcher wrote the following with regard to this new medium:

> Independently from Leni Riefenstahl's project there were other, far more bulky cameras being set up at the sporting complexes. Some looked like long, white cannons. Some rode with their crews atop heavy vans containing whining electrical generators. All this photographic apparatus was intended to channel electronically devised pictures into eighteen new television halls (*Fernsehstuben*) in Berlin, seating, in all, three thousand. There was also a receiver at the Olympic Village.[15]

The Paul Nipkow Television Station in Berlin had resumed its regular transmission of programs on the fifteenth of January, 1936,[16] after a temporary closedown during which—on the twenty-third of December, 1935—control over operations was transferred from the Ministry of Posts to the Ministry of Propaganda.[17] With the initiation of regular transmission—programs were transmitted between 8 and 10 p.m. on a daily basis—television was overtly celebrated as "a noble product of German inventiveness, German technology and of the German Reich's will to propaganda."[18] Television had thus been established on a regular basis in time for the start of the Winter Olympics in Garmisch-Partenkirchen. However, live television broadcasting of the Winter Games was impossible at this stage because of the non-availability of picture transmission facilities. Television film material was thus sent to Berlin via the quickest route.

In the summer of that year things were different. There was live coverage of the festive inauguration of the eleventh Summer Olympic Games by the Führer and Reichs-Chancellor, Adolf Hitler; it was the first test transmission of its kind in the world. This live transmission of the opening festivities, propagandistically exaggerated by the National Socialist Regime, marked the beginning of live television in Germany and of live coverage of the Olympics.[19] Although an estimated total of some 150,000 people managed to get at least a glimpse of the televised coverage of the Olympics in the twenty-five television halls in Berlin—broadcast daily between 10 and 12 a.m. and 3 and 7 p.m., together with a round up of the day's events during the evening transmission[20]—it is still too early to speak of the existence of a mass television medium.

Because of the war, the Olympic Games planned for 1940 and 1944, in Helsinki and London respectively, had to be cancelled. For the same reason, television was given low priority and next to no advances were made in the field of television technology until the immediate post-war period. The 1948 Olympics at St. Moritz (winter) and London (summer), in which neither Germany, Japan nor the USSR participated, were covered for the worldwide audience mainly by the press and radio, as had hitherto been the case. In London and surrounding areas, however, those who had a television set in their household could also enjoy television coverage of the events (a bare two years after pilot television transmission had been recommenced).[21] The first attempt at television coverage for an international audience was made at the following Winter and Summer Olympic Games in 1952 (held in Oslo and Helsinki respectively), albeit in recorded form. Because there were no television links at the time, programs recorded on the spot had first to be transported to the recipient country, using conventional means. A limited live international link-up could already be engineered during the following Winter Olympics at Cortina d'Ampezzo in 1956. The Summer Olympics staged in Melbourne, however, could not be televised live because of the technical problems involved in intercontinental link-ups and the astronomical costs they would have entailed. As a result, there was little television coverage of these games. Similarly, the Equestrian Olympics in Stockholm were not given live coverage, although filmed reports were fed into the Eurovision network from the television studios in Hamburg. Again there was no direct link-up with European countries for the 1960 Winter Olympics at Squaw Valley, in the United States. During the summer of that year, on the other hand, the Rome Olympics were given extensive live coverage and transmitted via Eurovision to most European countries. The same was the case for the 1964 Winter Games at Innsbruck. The first intercontinental link-ups as far as the Olympics are concerned were engineered during the following Summer Games in Tokyo. Japanese and American audiences were also able to watch the whole event in color.[22] The television viewers overseas were "spectators in Tokyo via satellite," as one commentator put it.[23]

For Mass Communication Research, the Tokyo Olympics are of especial interest because for the first time a large-scale survey of the television audience watching the Games was undertaken. The Japanese National Television Company (NHK) conducted this research program with a view to assessing audience reaction with regard to the nationwide preparations for the Games, and actual broadcasting and especially television coverage of the contests taking place in the stadia, as well as ascertaining its evaluations and impressions after the Games. In other words, the NHK survey was designed to discover something about the nature and degree of Japanese audience involvement in the event as a whole.[24] The report ascertains that during the two-week period from the tenth to the twenty-fourth of October, life was centered on the Olympics. In post-war Japan there had never been an event that had united the entire Japanese people in the same way. The coupling of the Olympics and television in the minds of the people had already become quite firm early in 1964. For example, in the Prime Minister's Office II survey conducted in March, 84 percent nationwide and 89 percent of those interviewed in Tokyo (degree of awareness was 97 percent and 100 percent respectively) answered that they wanted to see the Olympic Games on television. In the NHK's pre-Olympic survey conducted in June, 90 percent of the people interviewed in Tokyo and Kanazawa expressed the hope of viewing and hearing television and radio relays from the Olympic Stadia without fail. Thus the basis for saying that the Tokyo Olympics were the "Olympics made by television" has already been formed long before the actual event took place.[25]

How was television used during the Olympics? The report goes on to say that the number of sets in use during the two-week period was slightly higher than normal, although no marked singularity was evident during morning, noon and evening when the viewing rate is usually high (see following graph). The most conspicuous phenomenon was the rise of the number of sets in use by more than 20 percent between 2 and 4 p.m. on Sunday and weekday afternoons. This is the real basis for saying that television viewing increased greatly during the Olympics.

The data suggest the following two points: firstly, it is necessary to consider the differences between the ratings for sets in use and those for individual viewing behavior. With regard to peak viewing hours (between 7 and 9 p.m.), the ratings are very similar. Other data, however, indicate that there was an enormous increase in the number of viewers per set. Secondly, the number of sets in use during the late morning and afternoon increased considerably during this period, suggesting that many people were watching more television than usual.[26]

According to the NHK survey immediately after the Olympics, 99 percent and 98 percent of those interviewed in Tokyo and Kanazawa respectively said

Figure 1 TV Reception Rate During the Olympics (Weekday)
(Nielsen TV Index)

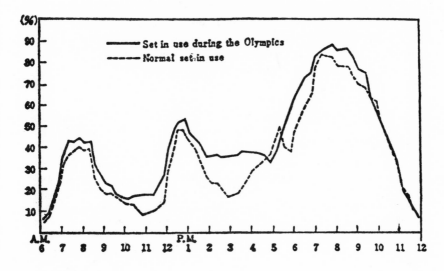

that they had watched Olympic events on television. According to the survey undertaken during the Olympics, 61 percent of those who watched the Olympics on television watched frequently. 55 percent said that they watched any program related to the Games. 51 percent said that they would watch the Games even at the sacrifice of other activities. In the surveys conducted during the Olympics and immediately after, the question "Do you think television is (was) adequate for viewing the Olympic contests or do you think it is (was) not of much interest unless you saw the contests on the spot?" was posed to those who answered that they were watching or had watched the contests on television. More than 50 percent of those questioned in Tokyo thought that televiewing was enough (both surveys). In Kanazawa (survey immediately after) 74 percent thought that televiewing was enough. What should be noted here is that those who replied that televiewing was not enough were not necessarily the same people who were dissatisfied with television. A desire to come into contact with the real contests seems to have been aroused by the medium. In short, what was important was the arousing of a feeling of participation in actuality.[27]

Eight hundred items of programming from Tokyo were fed into the Eurovision network, a similar amount to that from America covering the events during and after the Kennedy assassination in autumn, 1963.[28] The 1968 Winter Olympics at Grenoble (France) and the Summer Olympics in Mexico City were given similarly extensive worldwide coverage on television. In both cases, a high proportion of the transmissions was already in color: about 56 percent in the case of Grenoble[29] and about 85 percent in the case of Mexico City. An impression as to the size of European television operations during the Summer

Games can be gained from the size of Eurovision and Intervision's operations group, which consisted of 160 staff members recruited from nearly all the European member organizations and in Mexico City itself. The European television organizations received, for selection and further distribution, 136 hours of sporting events from Mexico City. [30] The following graph demonstrates the importance the international television system gave to coverage of the Mexico Olympics in comparison with other important events: [31]

An official of the French National Television Service (ORTF) gave the following detailed account of the various problems encountered in transmitting the Winter Games from Grenoble as well as the scale of the operations:

> Transmitting the different events over radio and television called for a considerable effort on the part of the ORTF for three main reasons: a) the venues were widely dispersed; b) this was the first introduction of large-scale outside broadcasts in color; c) the American Broadcasting Company (ABC) was provided with separate facilities. As in Innsbruck in 1964, a whole region was involved (in the television operations). . . . Since these Olympic Games coincided with the launching of color in Europe, the ORTF made a live color transmission of the following events: the opening and closing ceremonies, the ice hockey matches, the figure skating and Alpine ski events, the men's and women's downhill races and various slaloms, and the 90-metre ski jump. In addition, a 15-minute film summary in color was shown on Eurovision every day from 8:20 to 8:35 p.m. The ORTF also provided facilities for the American Broadcasting Company, which had obtained transmission rights for a sum of two million dollars. We had to set up a separate color network, which practically doubled the plant and equipment to be installed, since the ABC uses a definition of 525 lines instead of 819, an electricity supply at 60 Hertz instead of at 50 Hertz as used in Europe, and the NTSC color system, which is different from SECAM. Four year's work went into the installation of all this equipment. The ORTF had already sent observers to Innsbruck, and the director-general then set up a working group composed of the best specialists in the ORTF, engineers and senior staff, who met regularly. They planned and installed the equipment, after frequent journeys to Grenoble and numerous contacts with the representatives of the Organizing Committee of the Olympic Games and the municipality. . . . The television technical center was spread over three floors. It comprised both a vision and a sound-distribution center, a master control room, ten television tape-recording positions (four others were set up at the ice stadium), one laboratory for film processing (color and monochrome), three monochrome television studios and their control room, one color studio and its control room, seventeen film-cutting rooms, four screening rooms (two of them equipped for dubbing), twenty-five commentary cabins for film summaries and off-tube positions, and offices allocated to organizations from abroad. . . . We had to provide services for thirty-two television and forty-six radio organizations, which were represented at Grenoble by 731 journalists, engineers, cameramen, producers, and others. . . . In France, the programs were spread over the two channels more or less equally: about sixty hours each. We wished to avoid imposing too many sports sequences on the public, which would not have been well received; so we en-

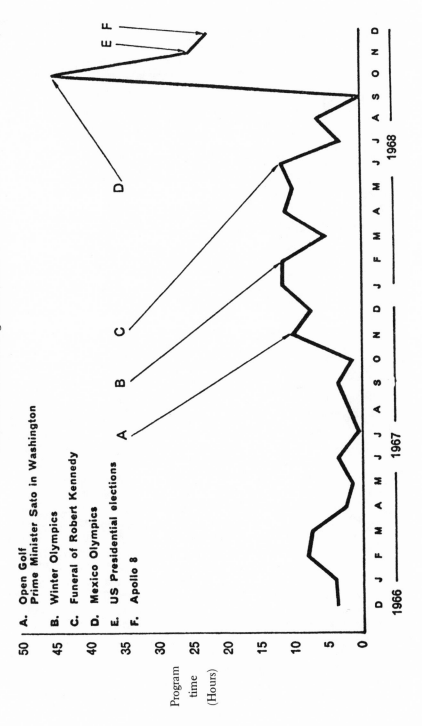

Figure 2 Trend of Satellite Telecasts with Major Events Indicated (Pacific Region)
December 1966 through December 1968

50

45

40

35

30

Program
time
(Hours)

25

20

15

10

5

0

A. Open Golf
    Prime Minister Sato in Washington

B. Winter Olympics

C. Funeral of Robert Kennedy

D. Mexico Olympics

E. US Presidential elections

F. Apollo 8

deavored to allow sufficient free time during the evenings for the broadcasting of some other programs. We seem to have achieved our aim, since our en- quiries have shown that more than 65 percent of the public were satisfied with our coverage of the Olympic Games. Some other points are worth mention- ing. We were surprised by the extent of listening devoted in the mornings to sports relatively unknown in France; the cross-country ski runs and the speed- skating events. The proportion of (television viewers watching these events) was around 10 percent (more than three million viewers), which proves that there is a potential audience at that time. Moreover, ice hockey, also a sport very little practiced in our country, scored an incontestable success. During the course of the Games, 173 hours 28 minutes of live television was offered to the various Eurovision and Intervision organizations, including 95 hours 41 minutes in color and 23 hours 27 minutes of programs alternating between two events. Furthermore, 166 unilateral broadcasts were produced, represent- ing 79 hours 30 minutes. . . . As regards film material, 100,000 metres in color and 70,000 metres in black and white were developed. For the foreign television services alone, 220 hours of editing were necessary.[32]

The graph on pages 218 and 219 gives an indication of just how important the 1968 Olympics at Grenoble and in Mexico were internationally in terms of European program exchange.[33]

As one can gather from the following account by Ernest P. Braun, Head of the European Broadcasting Union's Operations Group for the Mexico Olympics, the amount of planning, the scale of operations, as well as the mag- nitude of the problems encountered were, if anything, even greater at Mexico City than at Grenoble:

(The four years leading up to the Olympics were) filled with planning, coor- dination, the selection of personnel, specification of equipment and, finally, its installation. Actual operations lasted only a fortnight, but those four long years of preparation proved invaluable, since in 1968 Europe had the fullest and highest-quality television and radio coverage of any Olympic Games to date. Despite the lateness of the transmission times, some 300 million viewers watched the opening ceremony and most of the outstanding finals. Television coverage of the sports events totalled 136 hours, and eight television services together produced a further 40 hours or so of interviews, statements and com- mentaries on a unilateral basis. Actual output by the individual European television services varied widely; according to the information available at the time of writing, it ranged between 70 and 100 hours in most cases, with peaks of up to 140 hours for the First and Second Programs of the Office de Radio- diffusion-Télévision Française. . . . The nerve center of the whole operation was on four floors of the Mexican Government's brand new Telecommunica- tion Tower. So brand new it was, indeed, that some of its essential services were not yet ready as the opening ceremony drew near, and tremendous efforts were required from all concerned in order to get on the air by D-Day. The period leading up to the Games was strewn with all kinds of hazards: frequent changes in the management of the Organizing Committee, the South African question, the failure of the Intelsat III satellite launch and, last but not least, the student riots. However, the heavy machinery of the Olympic Games had such an initial momentum that only one outcome was possible: the obstacles were overcome.[34]

Braun also comments on an aspect of international cooperation with regard to program exchange:

> The presence of colleagues from so many countries was a constant reminder to each and every individual that he was working for the European community of broadcasters, and successfully ensured that he would not think in purely national terms. Compared with other types of Eurovision operation entrusted to one member organization, even where the latter does its job with the best will in the world, the principle of a multi-national operations group offers the best guarantee that the interests of all member organizations will be respected and that the coverage will be of a genuinely international character.

Further serious problems were encountered in the purchase of televising rights for the Olympic Games, which had progressively become more and more expensive, reaching an initial all-time high in 1968. Such problems, however, have to be seen in perspective, as an official of the European Broadcasting Union's Department of Legal Affairs attempts to show:

> One is tempted to think that it (i.e., the legal aspect of the purchase of televising rights) merely involves signing a contract after preliminary soundings and negotiations and agreement between the parties on a fee. Even the drafting of the contract may appear to the uninitiated to be a very simple matter: after all, a sporting event is not the work of the intellect, and thus does not involve copyrights or performers' rights. One may be excused for thinking that the legal departments of broadcasting organizations are faced daily with far more difficult problems. The transmission on Eurovision of an opera staged by an outside promoter, for example, may involve both the originating organization and the other broadcasters in sometimes highly complex preliminary enquiries regarding copyright protection of the opera in a given country, ownership of the copyright and the manner of its remuneration. . . . Audience interest in sports programs was apparent from the very start of television. A football match between world-famous teams is a social phenomenon which excites public opinion with the same intensity, if not in quite the same way, as any other newsworthy event. Thus, almost since Eurovision came into being, broadcasters have been under strong compulsion to provide their television audiences with coverage of these events, just as much as with that of the outstanding events of international affairs, such as the journeys of heads of state. What they have also had to contend with, however, has been the hostility of sporting interests, and the first point on which the lawyers were called to intervene was in asserting the broadcasters' right to information, that is to say, their right of access to a sporting event. When sports broadcasting became a day-to-day reality, broadcasting organizations felt the need to normalize their relations with sports promoters. A model contract for purchase of the right to televise an event on an international basis was therefore drawn up and has been widely applied, especially as the basis for the contracts respecting the Winter and Summer Olympic Games, the world football championships and

Figure 3 Eurovision Program Statistics

Key to Organizations

RTA — Radiodiffusion-Télévision Algérienne (Algeria)
ORF — Österreichischer Rundfunk GmbH (Austria)
BRT — Belgische Radio en Televisie (Belgium)
RTB — Radiodiffusion-Télévision Belge (Belgium)
DR — Danmarks Radio (Denmark)
YLE — Oy. Yleisradio Ab. (Finland)
ORTF — Office de Radiodiffusion-Télévision Française (France)

ARD — Arbeitsgemeinschaft der Öffentlich-Rechtlichen Rundfunkanstalten der Bundesrepublik Deutschland (Federal Republic of Germany)
DFP — Deutsche Fernseh Pool (Fed. Rep. of Germany)
ZDF — Zweites Deutsches Fernsehen (Fed. Rep. of Germany)
RUV — Rikisútvarpid (Iceland)
RTE — Radio Telefís Éireann (Ireland)
TVI — Israel Broadcasting Authority
RAI — Radiotelevisione Italiana (Italy)
CLT — Compagnie Luxembourgeoise de Télédiffusion (Luxembourg)
RMC — Radio Monte-Carlo (Monaco)
RTM — Radiodiffusion-Télévision Marocaine (Morocco)
NTS — Nederlandse Televisie Stichting (Netherlands)
NRK — Norsk Rikskringkasting (Norway)
RTP — Radiotelevisão Portuguesa (Portugal)
TVE — Dirección General de Radiodifusión y Televisión (Spain)

SR — Sveriges Radio (Sweden)
SRG/SSR/TSI — Schweizerische Radio und Fernsehgesell-schaft / Société Suisse de Radiodiffusion et Télé-vision / Società Svizzera Radiotelevisione (Switzer-land)
RTT — Radiodiffusion-Télévision Tunisienne (Tunisia)
BBC — British Broadcasting Corporation (United Kingdom)
ITV — Independent Television Authority and Independent Television Companies Association Ltd (United Kingdom)
ITN — Independent Television News (United Kingdom)
JRT — Jugoslovenska Radiotelevizija (Yugoslavia)
CBC — Canadian Broadcasting Corporation (Canada)
NHK — Nippon Hoso Kyokai (Japan)
ABC — American Broadcasting Companies, Inc (USA)
CBS — Columbia Broadcasting System, Inc (USA)
NBC — National Broadcasting Company, Inc (USA)
USP — U.S. Pool (USA)
BT — Bolgarskoe Radio i Televidenie (Bulgaria)
CST — Ceskoslovenska Televize (Czechoslovakia)
DFF — Deutscher Fernsehfunk (east Germany)
MT — Magyar Televizio (Hungary)
TVP — Polska Telewizja (Poland)
TVR — Radiodifuziunea și Televiziunea Rômînă (Romania).
TSS — Televidenie Sovietskoio Soiuza (USSR)
IV — Intervision
UN-TV — United Nations Television
Div — Various other organizations

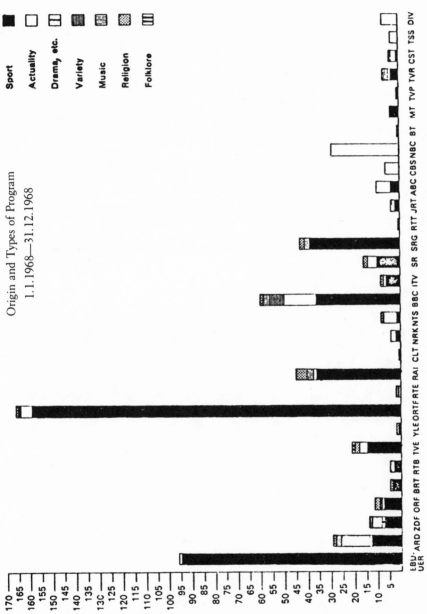

Origin and Types of Program
1.1.1968—31.12.1968

Sport
Actuality
Drama, etc.
Variety
Music
Religion
Folklore

170
165
160
155
150
145
140
135
130
125
120
115
110
105
100
95
90
85
80
75
70
65
60
55
50
45
40
35
30
25
20
15
10
5

EBU·
UER
ARD ZDF ORF BRT RTB TVE YLE ORTF RTE RAI CLT NRK NTS BBC ITV SR SRG RTT JRT ABC CBS NBC BT MT TVP TVR CST TSS DIV

The first column refers to transmissions from Mexico coordinated by the EBU international championships in various sports. The representatives of sporting interests have seen no difficulty in allowing reporters from the written press inside sports venues, nor have they objected to the presence of sound radio reporting teams (with certain restrictions in some countries, especially regarding football matches). What is more, the written press and sound radio have as a general rule been granted access to sporting events without any preconditions of a financial or other nature. The point was that press reports subsequent to the event could have no influence whatsoever on live attendance; the same was true even of live radio coverage, because the visual element was missing. On the other hand, the growth of television gave rise to the gravest apprehensions in sporting circles. Promoters felt that television coverage of an event was calculated to cause a serious reduction in gates and hence in the legitimate profits anticipated from ticket sales.[35]

Long before the next Winter Olympic Games in Sapporo, Japan,[36] and Summer Games in Munich, West Germany, in 1972, legal and financial questions were already in the forefront of discussion. The legal expert, Krause-Ablass, made the following observations:

As the most monumental sporting spectacular, the Olympic Games, also in the case of television, have worldwide viewing appeal. This viewing appeal is an income factor as far as the Olympic Games enterprise with its large investments is concerned. The legal question centers on this point: what rights does the enterprise have with regard to the televising of such an event with such viewing appeal? Television transmission of the Olympic Games . . . is also governed by the legal norms protecting the public's interests in the field of information, and the principles of public order. The legal questions that have to be answered concern the "performing" rights covering the events at the Olympic Games; the admission of broadcasting organizations for the purpose of recording events in the Olympic Stadia; broadcasting organizations' recording rights; and the television ban on transmitting advertising slogans (outside allocated advertising time). In the context the question of exclusive televising rights is also important.[37]

German television avoided some of the legal and financial problems they might otherwise have encountered by deciding to set up a special joint company for both television organizations (ARD and ZDF) "whose management will be responsible to a shareholders' meeting (comprising both ARD and ZDF) composed on a parity basis and a supervisory board made up of representatives of both organizations. All concerned are determined that the prestige of individual broadcasting organizations shall play no part whatsoever in filling the company's key posts."[38]

An impression as to the enormous expenditure that goes into the production and transmission of television coverage of the Olympics can be gained by looking at the figures given by the two West German television organizations. In the case of the Mexico Olympics in 1968, around 50 staff members were dispatched to Mexico City (producers, reporters, cameramen and other technical staff). In all, 100 hours of programming were produced for transmission.

The venture cost DM 5,000,000 (approx. US $2,000,000), of which DM 3,400,000 went to the European Broadcasting Union for its services (including royalties), DM 720,000 were paid for the use of transmission facilities and DM 400,000 consisted of staff expenses (travel, meals, hotels, and such). The rest consisted of expenditure on various items of software—e.g., 35,000 metres of 16 mm color film used for the production of 90 three- to eight-minute films complementing the coverage of the Olympic events themselves. [39]

The responsibility for all technical and organizational aspects of the preparations for broadcast coverage of the twentieth Olympic Games in Munich was transferred to the *Deutsches Olympia Zentrum* (DOZ), a company that had been established jointly by the ARD and ZDF in May, 1968, for the duration of the operation. The DOZ was also granted exclusive rights with regard to actual radio and television coverage of the Games and were therefore expected to provide the necessary technical facilities required at home and abroad. [40] This involved the provision of areas reserved for reporters, TV and film camera areas, commentator stands and facilities, areas reserved for mobile TV units, and such. DOZ plans specified that a) full radio and television coverage of all sporting events was to be provided; b) all coverage was to be in color, using the same transmission system as in West Germany, PAL; c) electronic and film coverage was to be provided for television; d) that, in order to rationalize the technical side of production, one type and brand of film would be used (Gevachrome 16 mm color film). The DOZ's program schedule foresaw daily television transmission between 900 and 2300 hours (Central European Time) for worldwide use, the items for this purpose being chosen in accordance with generally accepted journalistic criteria; a daily twenty-minute film summarizing the most important events of the day; and, furthermore, the possibility of producing unilateral programs. [41] The 380 stands for the many foreign and domestic commentators were all fully equipped (including television monitors). Nineteen contest areas out of a total of thirty-five were to receive full live coverage. The equipment required for this venture included 27 mobile TV camera units, 130 electronic television cameras, 80 TV film cameras, 83 videorecorders (69 stationary, 14 mobile), 11 slow-motion units (6 stationary, 5 mobile), 20 film- and slide-transmission units, 850 commentator units and 550 sound-recording units. [42]

As the director of the DOZ ascertained, the extremely detailed technical planning that went into the Munich Olympics proved its worth; 1,198 journalists and 464 assistants from many television and radio organizations all over the world were accredited for the purpose of reporting and providing commentary on the events in Munich and Kiel between the twenty-sixth of August and the eleventh of September, 1972. Lembke informs us that, overlooking a few exceptions, the inclusion of the camera areas in the original construction plans had achieved its objectives. Foreign broadcasting organizations had praised the pictures they received, especially from the swimming stadium and the rowing events. As expected, there were differences in the quality of cameramanship, but as the Games progressed, considerable improvements were to be seen throughout. At the same time, it must be remembered that Munich saw the most unpunctual Games in the recent past. This applies especially to the swimming events, and also to the volleyball and basketball events, where the timetables were seldom adhered to, which led to considerable difficulties, above all with regard to prearranged satellite transmission bookings.[43]

A ZDF official recounts some of the problems that journalists were faced with:

The "national" assignment all West German radio and television stations took upon themselves before and during the Olympics inevitably put a strain on personnel resources. A compromise had to be made between the responsibility for providing the world with pictures of high quality and the egoism involved in putting all one's effort into supplying the home audience. . . . The DOZ in its role as supplier for all television services worldwide was also the source of our domestic picture material. . . . Just like every other producer in the world, we could choose (for ourselves) what to include in our domestic transmissions from a wealth of live material available between 8 a.m. and after midnight. . . . This involved selecting sequences from the 45 to 50 hours of live coverage available every day so that one ended up with 14 hours of daily programming, also including summaries, studio interviews and own film production. Decisions from the producers were required within a matter of seconds.[44]

The murder of the Israeli Olympic team on the fifth of September, 1972, cast a deep shadow over the Munich Olympics, which had promised to offer so much in the way of entertainment for many millions all over the world—— "heitere Spiele" ("the merry Games"), as one public relations campaign put it.[45] The media, quickly adjusting themselves to the new situation, focused their attention on the relationship between politics and sports, a subject which had long been avoided and little discussed by the IOC officialdom.[46] After a short break, the Munich Olympics were continued, but things weren't as they were before. The tragedy marked a turning point in the history of the Olympic Movement, showing how unrealistic some of its aims were.

No reliable estimates as to audience size worldwide during Olympic television transmission are available. But perhaps a ZDF audience survey can give us some impression as to the scale of audience involvement in the event: 12 percent of all television sets on weekdays and 26 percent on Saturdays were in use before noon. For afternoons, the respective figures were 24 percent and 35 percent; between 6 and 8 p.m., 41 percent and 36 percent; and between 8 and 10 p.m., 40 percent and 36 percent. After 10 p.m., an average of nine percent of all sets were in use. The average for all Olympic transmissions during the two-week period (excluding the opening ceremony and the intermission on the fifth and sixth of September as a result of the attack on the Israeli team) was 25.7 percent.[47]

The frequent observation that the Olympics of 1972 were held "in the living room"[48] led the philosopher, Lenk, to speak of an age of "telecratic sport"[49] and to make the following comment: "The Olympics and television—these are giganticisms which today complement each other: records are broken by both, one after another."[50] A German media critic writes that the 1972 Olympics as shown by television constituted, without doubt, the greatest electronic spectacle to date, not only in terms of presentation but also in terms of reach. But he goes on to ask:

> So what? Whenever one reflects upon the omnipresence of television at events or in covering achievements commanding worldwide interest—for instance, the Olympics, space flights or significant national events (above all in political life)—it is surely less important that the size of the audience should be regarded as one's starting point than that the following points be considered: firstly, whether and how such thinking in quantitative terms affects the quality of the event or achievement, and secondly, whether that which is being portrayed on television is something different or is purposely being made into something different from that which is happening in real life (i.e., something different from the reality television claims to reflect). . . . Let us take the example of Munich again. The viewer will only experience a fraction of the reality encompassed by the Olympic Games: namely, that (which) is happening in a particular part of a particular stadium as seen by a camera.[51]

Another television critic touches upon a further problem that has to be faced with regard to the Olympics: the extent to which the Olympics have been turned into a show contracted by television. The very fact that, at great expense, the stadia were designed so as to do justice to television underlines the point he is trying to make.[52]

The general director of the ZDF at the time, Professor Karl Holzamer, in reply to such and similar criticism, made the following comments:

> After having heard so much about "total television" and "the 1972 television Olympics," during the weeks and months before, during and after the Games in Munich, many must have started to believe in what was being said. In fact, nothing of the sort existed, even in rudimentary terms. And it doesn't seem as if it (i.e., total television) can be realized either in the immediate or in the foreseeable future. . . . Those who sat in front of the monitors at the heart of world production at the Olympic Center . . . may perhaps have had an idea as to what "total television" means. The television pictures being taken at the many contests taking place in various stadia were simultaneously fed into this center. If it had been possible to transmit all these pictures simultaneously to the millions of viewers watching television—something which is conceivable in the eyes of some futurologists—one could then have spoken of something approaching total television: the viewer would have been involved in the totality of the events taking place in various localities. But, of course, technically this was impossible. . . . The viewer could only receive one picture at a time from the production rooms; selection and editing was necessary. . . . Priorities and emphases had to be set. The viewer at home didn't watch a multitude of events side by side; for him the Olympics were a series of visual extracts. . . . No doubt millions of television viewers saw more of the Olympic Games, and in greater detail, than those who were spectators on the spot—but this doesn't consistute "total television." . . . (What one saw was) the greatest possible display television is capable of.[53]

Dr. Fritz Hufen, another television functionary, also came to the defense of the way in which the Olympic Games were presented:

> The 1972 Olympics can be regarded as one of television's greatest achievements. Although memories of the Games themselves . . . may fade, the technical achievements of international and national television organizations will continue to live in our minds . . . just as much as the achievements of those who supplied the commentary to the sporting events day after day. The other media, above all the press, didn't spare any effort in criticizing; it was they that coined the term, "television Games." . . . The suspicion that the 1972 Olympic Games, more than any other similar event, were staged for or even by television was frequently cast, either explicitly or between the lines. The Olympic grounds as television studios, swimmers who broke world records as television extras—sporting reality was turned into television reality. . . . Those on the spot, however, will have perceived that television was more a requisite than a master of ceremonies. . . . Television without doubt made use of its capabilities and doubtlessly also came up against the limits to the things it could do. . . . It has learned from the event, not only as a result of outside criticism, but also because it tried to understand itself and its capabilities from the very first moment. Its greatest achievement, at the same time its most sobering experience, cannot be forgotten so easily.[54]

The controversy surrounding the question as to television's role with regard to the Olympic Games proved to be more than a cursory matter judging by the critical comments made during the 1976 Olympics. Whereas the scale of television operations during the Winter Olympics at Innsbruck could still be considered "normal," the Games at Montreal were severely criticized on this count in particular by European journalists. Curiously enough, the same giganticism and perfectionism so harshly criticized even after the Olympics at Munich were suddenly found to be missing. Feelings were voiced complaining about the boredom engendered by the way in which the Olympics at Montreal were being covered and lamenting the ostensible frugality.[55] On the other hand, there were some who thought that Montreal did not represent a catastrophe in terms of television.[56] Such defendants included television functionaries, a strange change of roles one might think. The director of the ARD Program Division even went so far as to say that "if anything, too much rather than too little of the Montreal Olympics was shown on television."[57] The head of the ZDF Sports Department made the following observations, which neatly summarize the mood prevalent in Germany and the reasons for the difficulties which helped to foster it:

> The transmissions from Montreal were met in Germany with somewhat mixed feelings. Bitter criticism predominated, especially during the first week. The search for the reasons behind this continues. . . . Forty countries with television all received the same program schedule, a schedule which was drawn up carefully and conscientiously but which, as events were to prove, couldn't satisfy everyone. Eurovision and Intervision, which for financial reasons had pooled their resources, found themselves carrying out their assignments in

Montreal literally under the same roof. As a result, it was hardly surprising that at the planning sessions every morning opinions as to what should be transmitted differed so widely. When necessary, differences were put to the vote. Of course, this being the case, the stronger party would win.[58]

The Norwegian Head of the Eurovision/Intervision Operations Group during the 1976 Summer Olympic Games also joined in the discussion that took place after Montreal (which centered on the role television coverage should play during the event) with the following sobering comments to make:

> A common element of this discussion is the question (of) whether one contributes too greatly to the inflated interest which is created in advance, whether the Games themselves take up too much or too little transmission time, whether the coverage—especially on television—is satisfactory from a purely professional point of view, whether it steals too much interest and absorbs too high an investment at the expense of the real sports movement, which faithfully and regularly works day after day throughout the year. Finally, the question is asked whether the media commit themselves too one-sidedly to the events that can be measured in centimetres and seconds that take place in the competitive arenas while other interesting aspects of this fantastic spectacle are neglected. The discussions often begin and end with the same question: How long can it continue? The underlying assumption is that unless the Olympic movement kills itself, or is stifled by the primary sports organizations and federations, the Games will be politically or economically impossible some time in the near future. And even if this should not be so, then they will be practically impossible to arrange. Who can undertake to stage the next? We have been hearing this question at least as long as I have been working with sports for radio and television. But the Games are going on. . . . There is every reason to assume that the Olympic Games will also be organized in the foreseeable future. After the almost happy ending of the Montreal Games, they have already lowered their voices—many of those who earlier prophesied that nothing would ever come of Lake Placid and Moscow. Both hosts, both organizing committees and both nations have difficult years ahead of them. We are going to read many a pessimistic account before the opening ceremonies are witnessed by a billion people.[59]

After making his general position clear, he goes on to tackle various criticisms leveled at television coverage of the Olympics in greater detail and from a broadcaster's point of view:

> It may be said—and many people have done so—that our job is to transmit the Games as they are, not to take part in staging them. But there are those who also maintain that one should study individual aspects of the development more closely. The most negative critics pose questions which may be summarized as follows: Is this extremely expensive enterprise—staged under antiquated rules which do not take into consideration the political, social, economic and medical realities and facing a constantly expanding commercial influence and a rising number of cheating athletes—worth all this attention? Transmitting the Olympic Games is already expensive, despite the fact that the coverage that was carried out was very simple. If the production—

especially on the part of television—is to keep pace with the rapid development and sophistication of broadcasting at a national level, the expense would
be considerably higher. It is not unlikely that EBU member organizations
might wish for more modernized coverage of future Games. . . . If this is the
case, an even greater share of the annual budgets will be allocated for this purpose. A question which may then be raised is whether so great an investment
will lead to one-sided coverage of sports in general, because one must save in
other areas. Is this in tune with the general policy vis-à-vis sport as a social factor? [60]

In answering the critics, he also discusses the financial dependence of the
Olympic Games on television:

The organizations pay for the right to transmit the Games on television. To a
certain extent, the staging is based on this income, and the existence of the
IOC to an even greater extent. The American investment, of course, is larger
than that of Europe, but this is a question of principle for broadcasters
throughout the world. . . . When one goes in as such a significant investor,
one must also be regarded as a co-organizer. Is it not natural, then, that one's
voice should be heard? Some people would say at once: Television does not
wish to assume any responsibility as a co-organizer. Others would reply: If the
Games could not take place without the participation of television, this is
merely playing with words. [61]

The importance of the Olympic Games in Eurovision's operations can be
gauged from the following table. Apart from 1956 and 1960, each Olympic
year coincides with a considerable upward deviation from the norm both in the
number of programs and in the number of hours transmitted via the Eurovision
network: [62]

If one looks at more detailed statistics, however, a slightly different picture
emerges. For instance, the following breakdown of the annual number of contributions offered for Eurovision transmission shows that the programs offered
under the category of sports constitute 80 percent of the total number, with
very little fluctuation either way throughout the years 1971 to 1976, with the
exception of 1974 (a non-Olympic year, but the year of the World Cup Football Championships). [63] The only difference between "normal" and Olympic
years is that the average number of television organizations transmitting the
Eurovision programs during the latter was higher for the simple reason that the
Games command the interest of all European countries.

The most important conclusion that can be drawn from these statistics is
that the question as to whether the Olympics are staged primarily with sporting
or with television interests in mind is more than just a hypothetical one, as
many television functionaries would like one to believe. Moreover, it is a question that applies not only to the Olympics, especially when one looks at the
sheer volume of sporting events transmitted via Eurovision.

With certainty it can be established that, because of developments and
improvements in the field of transmission technology, the show effect of such
important sporting events has become much more pronounced. The sportsman

Table 1

Year	Total Number of Programs Transmitted	Total Number of Hours Transmitted
1954	55	73
1955	91	115
▶1956	250	273
1957	207	261
1958	203	259
1959	292	339
▶1960	500	440
1961	679	606
1962	1,427	586*
1963	3,110	3,610
▶1964	3,717	4,497
1965	3,115	4,053
1966	3,790	5,212
1967	3,387	4,092
▶1968	6,240	8,251
1969	5,363	6,809
1970	4,501	6,582
1971	4,573	7,153
▶1972	7,396	12,189
1973	4,028	6,681
1974	5,609	8,312
1975	4,530	6,504
▶1976	7,114	10,254

* until 1962: without news transmissions

has thus been given greater opportunities of creating an image for himself, even of marketing himself, which extend beyond his active sporting career.[64] The more the Olympics Games have been adapted for the purposes of television and the greater the spectacle, the more they become part and parcel of the entertainment demanded of the medium, whether the sportsman likes it or not.[65] Furthermore, as another points out, the Olympic Games are a lucrative indirect source of income:

> It is impossible to calculate the amount of advertising done for the host country's economy. . . . As advertisements, the newspaper articles and radio and television reports printed or broadcast throughout the world in the years before as well as during the Games would have cost thousands of million (German marks).[66]

The potential of the Olympic Movement in political terms is a factor that is given insufficient attention in the debate outlined above. Schelsky, who considers the Games to be fundamentally political in nature, would like to see them fulfilling the following function: "Making mankind, nations and states

Table 2
Type of Eurovision Programs Offered for Transmission: Number and Percentage

	1971 No	1971 %	1972 No	1972 %	1973 No	1973 %	1974 No	1974 %	1975 No	1975 %	1976 No	1976 %
Sport	515	77.8	553	78.0	535	80.7	660	87.1	634	83.1	634	83.9
Actuality/* current affairs	81	12.2	92	13.0	67	10.1	51	6.7	76	10.0	67	8.9
Light entertainment	38	5.7	36	5.1	36	5.4	27	3.6	17	2.2	24	3.2
Religion	17	2.6	17	2.4	15	2.3	11	1.4	18	2.3	20	2.6
Music, Jazz	6	0.9	9	1.3	7	1.1	4	0.5	9	1.2	6	0.8
Folklore/ Drama/opera/ ballet	5	0.8	2	0.2	3	0.4	5	0.7	9	1.2	5	0.6
Total **	662	100.0	709	100.0	663	100.0	758	100.0	763	100.0	756	100.0

* as distinct from Eurovision news exchange
** the number of programs offered for transmission multiplied by the average number of TV organizations adopting each program offered supplies us with the figures given in the previous table. For instance, in the case of 1972, 709 programs multiplied by 10.4 approximately equals 7,396 (i.e., total number of programs transmitted via Eurovision for that year).

more fully aware of the central political task facing them, something for which the Olympics are more suited than the actions, institutions and conflicts of everyday political life." But he also sees the obstacles facing the movement in its aim of creating a forum where peoples can meet freely and at least temporarily set aside their differences. There is hardly any point for instance, if, as in the case of international conferences, they can only be staged after stringent security measures have been enforced, and if athletes and spectators are subject to constant surveillance.[67] To what extent the constant presence of television cameras are is also responsible for turning the Olympics into a forum for political demonstrations—ranging from murder (as in Munich) to attempts to exclude certain nations from participation at the Games—is a question that cannot be answered easily. But it is fair to say that attention is almost exclusively paid to the camera lens and not to the spectator present at the stadium, not to speak of the changes that considerations of national prestige have wrought with respect to the *de facto status* of the athletes participating in the various events.[68]

During the course of the last twenty years, modern technology has made full television coverage of large-scale sporting events possible.[69] In the words of the Head of Eurovision's Operations Group for the Mexico Games, television has turned the Olympics into "a living reality for many millions of people throughout the world. . . . The present audience for the Olympics is a worldwide one, and the live attendance at the Games is a microcosm of it. This fact must be borne in mind and measures taken accordingly."[70] What measures, one may ask? Perhaps the kind that Josef Hackforth recommends:

> Precisely during the Olympics Games, which owe so much of their popularity and continued existence to television, the medium should attempt to pay more attention to the individual athlete: The loser, those who came in fourth, sixth, eighth. . . . Is it necessary that only the winner should be filmed at the finishing post? Backgrounds, the fortunes of single athletes, experiences outside the arena should be given greater coverage. Television will only be in a position to brush the criticism aside that it creates heroes (just as it creates heroes through its entertainment programs) if it fulfils such criteria.[71]

Another author is apparently thinking along the same lines when he says:

> Sports commentary is the almost exclusive province of those who come from the world of sports. They still think of sports exclusively in terms of attempting to break records, coming first (*Leistungssport*). Entertainment is not regarded as one of its functions. . . . (The commentator must) obtain the ability to present sport in its social context as entertainment, put sporting sensations into perspective, present questions which extend beyond the field of competition.[72]

From another critic:

> If everything went the way the "high-performance fanatics" among sports commentators would like, the Olympics of the eighties would have to have the whole world as their arena: each single competition would have to be staged in that part of the world in which conditions were best suited for breaking records

(e.g., "We will now switch to the Kenyan Highland for the high-jumping event"). The camera-to-satellite link threatens to tear sport away from its home, the arena. We are threatened by an electronic dictatorship in which the television viewer bent on seeing new records reigns supreme. Television can become the great doping agent in sport. It is time that we consider the dangers—before the medium irreversibly becomes the message and sport only its gladiator." [73]

Has television been successful in conveying the Olympic message in its coverage of the Games, bringing peoples together and encouraging mutual understanding? Perhaps a cynical commentary to be found in the German weekly news magazine, *Der Spiegel*, supplies us with the most plausible answer:

> The television Olympics unites ARD and ZDF, Western Europe's Eurovision and Eastern Europe's Intervision, communists and capitalists, Hamites and Semites, Mongolians and Monegassians, Old, New, Third World. The Games unite mankind—in front of the television set. [74]

Hardly more.

NOTES

[1] For a short international overview on the history of sports and the press, cf. Siegfried Weischenberg, *Die Aussenseiter der Redaktion. Struktur, Funktion und Bedingungen des Sportjournalismus* (Bochum, 1976), pp. 118–63 (*Bochumer Studien zur Publizistik- und Kommunikationswissenschaft*, Vol. 9).

[2] Percy H. Tannenbaum and James E. Noah, "Sportugese: A Study of Sports Page Communication," *Journalism Quarterly* 36, no. 1 (Iowa City, 1959): 163.

[3] Hans Lenk, *Werte—Ziele—Wirklichkeit der modernen Olympischen Spiele*, 2nd ed. (Stuttgart, 1972), p. IX.

[4] Cf. Pierre de Coubertin, *Der Olympische Gedanke* (Stuttgart, 1967).

[5] Josef Hackforth, *Sport im Fernsehen* (Münster, 1975), p. 139.

[6] *Ibid.*, p. 140.

[7] Kurt Wagenführ, "Olympia-Berichterstattung," *Rundfunk und Fernsehen* 16, no. 4 (Hamburg, 1968): 414.

[8] Cited from Heinz Pohle, *Der Rundfunk als Instrument der Politik. Zur Geschichte des deutschen Rundfunks von 1923/38* (Hamburg, 1955), p. 416.

[9] *Ibid.*, p. 417 f.

[10] Cf. Arnd Krüger, *Die Olympischen Spiele 1936 und die Weltmeinung. Ihre außenpolitische Bedeutung unter besonderer Berücksichtigung der U.S.A.* (Berlin–Munich–Frankfurt/Main, 1972), pp. 227 ff.

[11] Cf. the National Socialist-oriented Ph.D. diss. by Gerhard Stabenow, *Die Olympiaberichterstattung in der Deutschen Presse* (Halle/Saale, 1941), pp. 15 ff.

[12] Cf. William L. Shirer, *The Rise and Fall of The Third Reich. A History of Nazi Germany* (New York, 1960), pp. 232 ff.

[13] Cf. Hajo Bernett, "Leni Riefenstahls Dokumentarfilm von den Olympischen Spielen in Berlin 1936," in *Untersuchungen zur Zeitgeschichte des Sports* (Schorndorf bei Stuttgart, 1973), pp. 115 ff.; ef. also David Stewart Hull, *Film in the Third Reich* (Berkeley–Los Angeles, 1969), pp. 135 ff.

[14] Cf. Gerhard Zwerenz, ed., *Die Nazi Olympiade, unveränderter Nachdruck des offiziellen Olympia Albums von 1936* (Frankfurt/Main, 1972); cf. also Heinz-Dietrich Fischer, "Olympia-Sammelalben als massenmediale Politica—eine aussagenanalytische Studie," in *Die politische Funktion der Zigarettenbilder-Sammel-Alben in den zwanziger und dreißiger Jahren*, ed. Ernst Horst Schallenberger (Trier, forthcoming).

[15] Richard D. Mandell, *The Nazi Olympics* (New York, 1971), p. 138.

[16] Cf. Anon., " 'Paul Nipkow-Sender, Berlin' wieder in Betrieb," *Presse-Mitteilungen der Reichs-Rundfunk-Gesellschaft*, no. 489 (Berlin, 24th January, 1936): 2 f.

[17] Anon., "Olympia wird ferngesehen," *Berlin hört und sieht—Die reich illustrierte Funkzeitschrift*, no. 1 (Berlin, 5th January, 1936): 7.

[18] Gerhard Duvigneau, "Seit 15. 1. wieder regelmäßig Fernsehen," *Funk-Stunde*, no. 4/36 (Berlin, 26th January, 1936): 159.

[19] Josef Hackforth, *op. cit.*, p. 150.

[20] *Ibid.*, pp. 15, 151 f.

[21] *Ibid.*, p. 148.

[22] Kurt Wagenführ, *op. cit.*, p. 414.

[23] khm (= Karlheinz Mose), "Giganten auf Gegenseitigkeit, 1936 bis 1972—Wie das Fernsehen auf die Tribüne kam," *Hör Zu*, no. 37/72 (Hamburg, 9–15th September, 1972): 5.

[24] Akira Fujitake, "Tokyo Olympics and the Japanese Public," *Studies of Broadcasting* (Intl. ed.) 5 (Tokyo: NHK, March, 1967): 50.

[25] *Ibid.*: 81 f.

[26] *Ibid.*: 81 ff.

[27] *Ibid.*: 89 f.

[28] Cf. the graphs in *EBU Review*, no. 90 B (Geneva, April, 1965): 13.

[29] Josef Hackforth (*op. cit.*, p. 149) is completely wrong in assuming that there was no color TV transmission from Grenoble, France!

[30] Cf. Heinz-Dietrich Fischer, "The Contribution of Eurovision and Intervision to Global Television," in *International and Intercultural Communication*, 2nd ed., eds. H.-D. Fischer and J. C. Merrill (New York, 1976), p. 361 ff.

[31] *EBU Review*, no. 116 B (Geneva, July, 1969): 15.

[32] Raymond Marcillac, "The 1968 Winter Olympics in Grenoble. How the ORTF met the challenge," *EBU Review*, no. 110 B (Geneva, July, 1968): 19 f.

[33] *EBU Review*, no. 115 B (Geneva, May, 1969): 28.

[34] Ernst P. Braun, "Mexico 68: In Retrospect," *EBU Review*, no. 113 B (Geneva, January, 1969): 12–14.

[35] Madeleine Larrue, "Sports Programmes and International Television: The Legal Aspect," *EBU Review*, no. 110 B (Geneva, July, 1968): 52 ff.

[36] Cf. Kentaro Hiro, "Japan Prepares for the 1972 Winter Games. Plans for Complete Radio and Television Coverage at Sapporo," *EBU Review*, no. 110 B (Geneva, July, 1968): 25 f.

[37] Günter B. Krause-Ablass, "Die Rechtslage der Fernsehübertragungen von den Olympischen Spielen," in *Rundfunk und Fernsehen* 20, no. 2 (Hamburg, 1972): 159.

[38] Robert E. Lembke, "The Footballer in the Living Room. Sport and Broadcasting in Germany—Outlook for the 1972 Olympic Games," *EBU Review*, no. 110 B (Geneva, July, 1968): 23 f.

[39] Kurt Wagenführ, *op. cit.*, p. 413.

[40] Walter Schwarz, "Die Olympischen Sommerspiele 1972 in München—rundfunk-

technisch gesehen," in *Zweites Deutsches Fernsehen. Jahrbuch, 1971* (Mainz, 1972), p. 128.

[41] *Ibid.*, pp. 128 *ff.*

[42] *Ibid.*, pp. 130, 135.

[43] Robert E. Lembke, "Die Lokalrunde. Die Berichterstattung in Hörfunk und Fernsehen von den Olympischen Sommerspielen München/Kiel 1972," in *Arbeitsgemeinschaft der öffentlich-rechtlichen Rundfunkanstalten der Bundesrepublik Deutschland. ARD–Jahrbuch, 1972* (Hamburg, 1972), p. 1 f.

[44] Willi Krämer, "Die Olympischen Sommerspiele 1972 in der Sportberichterstattung des ZDF," in *Zweites Deutsches Fernsehen. Jahrbuch, 1972* (Mainz, 1973), p. 63

[45] Cf. Klaus Commer, "Nicht mehr heiter, aber: weiter. Versuch einer subjektiven Bilanz nach der Fernseh-Olympiade," in *Funk-Korrespondenz* 20, no. 37 (Köln, September, 1972): 13–17.

[46] Cf. the journalistic report by Thilo Koch, *Piktogramm der Spiele/Pictogram of the Games* (München, 1973), pp. 50 *ff.* (German ver.), pp. 128 *ff.* (English ver.).

[47] Willi Krämer, *op. cit.*, p. 64.

[48] Josef Hackforth, *op. cit.*, p. 150.

[49] Hans Lenk, "Im Brennpunkt des Lebens," in Deutsche Sporthilfe (ed.), *München, '72* (Zürich–Oberrieden, 1972), p. 55.

[50] khm (=Karlheinz Mose), *op. cit.*, p. 5.

[51] Manfred Delling, "Die gespielte Wirklichkeit," in *Abteilung Information und Presse des ZDF. Augenzeuge in Olympia. Reflexionen über ein Fernsehereignis.* (Berlin, 1972), p. 11.

[52] Klaus Commer, *op. cit.*

[53] Karl Holzamer, "Am Rande der Realität," in *Abteilung Information und Presse des ZDF, op. cit.*, p. 35 f.

[54] Fritz Hufen, "Chancen und Grenzen," in *Abteilung Information und Presse des ZDF, op. cit.*, p. 8 *ff.*

[55] Cf. Ferdinand Ranft, "Das grosse Gähnen. Olympia als Sparprogramm," *Die Zeit* 31, no. 32 (Hamburg, 30th July, 1976): 9.

[56] Cf. Hanns Joachim Friedrichs, "Wirklich eine Fernseh-Katastrophe? Olympia darf auch nicht zu wichtig genommen werden," *Die Zeit* 31, no. 32 (Hamburg, 30th July, 1976): 12.

[57] Cf. Anon., "Eher zuviel gebracht als zuwenig." (Interview mit ARD-Programmdirektor Hans Abich über die TV–Olympia–Berichterstattung), *Der Spiegel* 30, no. 32 (Hamburg, 2nd August, 1976): 99–101.

[58] Hanns Joachim Friedrichs, "Olympiaberichterstattung 1976," in *Zweites Deutsches Fernsehen. ZDF–Jahrbuch, 1976* (Mainz, 1977), pp. 71 f.

[59] Jarle Høyaeter, " 'The Games Must Go On!'—But with What Kind of Radio and Television Coverage?," *EBU Review* 27, no. 6 (Geneva, November, 1976): 6, 9.

[60] *Ibid.*: 7.

[61] *Ibid.*

[62] *Internationales Handbuch für Rundfunk und Fernsehen 1973/75* (Hamburg: Verlag Hans-Bredow-Institut, 1974), p. E 104; *EBU Review* (Geneva) 25, no. 3 (May, 1974): 45; 26, no. 3 (May, 1975): 69; 27, no. 4 (July, 1976): 40; 27, no. 4 (July, 1977): 37.

[63] *EBU Review* (Geneva) 23, no. 3 (May, 1972): 36; 24, no. 3 (May, 1973): 45; 25, no. 3 (May, 1974): 44; 26, no. 3 (May, 1975): 68; 27, no. 4 (July, 1976): 39; 28, no. 4 (July 1977): 36.

[64] Cf. Heinz Harder, *Unternehmen Olympia* (Konstanz, 1970), p. 53.

[65] Cf. Brigitte Tümmler and Siegfried Tümmler, "Sport, Olympische Spiele und das Fernsehen. Zu einigen Aspekten des Verhältnisses der Massenmedien zu Körperkultur und Sport," in *Theorie und Praxis der Körperkultur* 22, no. 9 (East Berlin: Sportverlag, September, 1973), pp. 811–16.

[66] Heinz Harder, *op. cit.*, p. 16.

[67] Helmut Schelsky, *Friede auf Zeit. Die Zukunft der Olympischen Spiele* (Osnabrück, 1973), pp. 7, 37.

[68] Cf. K. Heinilä, "Citius–Altius–Fortius. Der Olympische "Beitrag" zur Professionalisierung des Sports?," in *Ommo Grupe: Sport in unserer Welt—Chancen und Probleme* (Berlin–Heidelberg–New York: Springer-Verlag, 1973), pp. 383–88.

[69] Siegfried Weischenberg, *op. cit.*, p. 154.

[70] Ernst P. Braun, "Television and the Olympic Games," *EBU Review*, no. 110 B (Geneva, July, 1968): 10 f.

[71] Josef Hackforth, *op. cit.*, p. 190.

[72] Siegfried Weischenberg, *op. cit.*, p. 190.

[73] Alexander Rost, "Der Sport und die Medien oder Weltrekord als Ware," in *Sport— kritisch*, ed. Alex Natan (Bern–Stuttgart: Hallwag Verlag, 1972), p. 139 f.

[74] Anon., " 'Knall, Schuß, bumms, raus, weg'–Olympia–TV: Die größte Schau der Welt," in *Der Spiegel* 26, no. 36 (Hamburg, 28th August, 1972): 24.

Peter Kaupp:

The Misunderstood Best-Seller: The Social Function of Entertainment Literature

The Terminological Jungle

☆ FROM THE VERY OUTSET, the term "entertainment literature" ("Unterhaltungsliteratur") brings to mind a whole range of associations, all of which bear the stamp of some definite point of view and almost all of which imply some form of evaluation. To take an example: The problem with the very widespread concept "trivial literature" ("Trivialliteratur") is that it involves a clear a priori value judgment. However, if, in the course of research into "trivial literature," "popular literature" or "best-seller literature," we wish to achieve genuinely objective results, we must forgo any kind of a priori evaluation.

In this respect it has been suggested that the concept "trivial literature," which implies some kind of value judgment, should be replaced by the term "commercial literature" ("Gebrauchsliteratur")—or better still by "mass produced self-confirming literature" ("Bestätigungsliteratur in Massenproduktion"), since the identical pattern of events within the plot allows the reader to find, through identifying with the characters, a continual confirmation of his own personality.[1] Yet, in the last resort, is it not true to say that "high-brow" literature is also written and printed to be consumed and that these works can also offer opportunities for identification (although admittedly for a numerically smaller audience)? And while it is usually entertainment literature that fills the best-seller lists, this is by no means exclusively the case. The Bible was printed in enormous numbers for popular consumption and yet no one would for one moment suggest that, in consequence, it should be placed in the category of "entertainment literature." Even the term "kitsch" does not do justice to the complexity of this branch of literature. For, what from an aesthetic point of

▶ This article is a shortened version of a much longer article published in *Bertelsmann Briefe* (No. 85, January, 1976) specially prepared by the author. Dr. Peter Kaupp is a senior officer at the Federal Statistical Office in Wiesbaden, West Germany. The article was translated by Andrew Hurrell, B.A.

view appears as "kitsch," can—as will later be pointed out in detail—be considered to be an integral part of entertainment literature because of its sociological function and its socio-psychological effects. Moreover, the use of the term "kitsch" in relation to "entertainment literature"[2] can be viewed as the expression of a definite prejudice on the part of the dominant arbiters of taste in each generation.

The same thing applies in the case of the term "popular literature" ("Populärliteratur"), which—even on a linguistic level—evokes a whole stream of associations of a hermetic, undemanding literature, aimed exclusively at entertainment and deemed to be the sole preserve of the "people." It is significant that the dictionary of the Académie Française[3] links the word "populaire" with the lower social classes; in other words, it relates it to a social class which has nothing in common with the nobility and with "noble" things. Moreover, the distinction between "littérature savante" and "littérature populaire" is problematic for the very reason that it involves the comparison of an intellectual with a social quantity.[4]

Finally we come to the questionable dichotomy between "fringe literature" ("Marginalliteratur") and "esoteric, high-brow literature" ('Kunstliteratur'), questionable because it only becomes meaningful when it is related to some concept of a "central literature" ("Zentralliteratur") and this, in turn, represents a value judgment based upon some firm standpoint, fixed and agreed by a given social group.

What Is "Entertainment"?

The term "entertainment literature" involves less of a value judgment, is more widespread and encompasses all the various levels of literary entertainment. The dichotomy between an intellectually demanding "high-brow literature" ("Hochliteratur") intended for a small élite and an "alternative literature" ("zweiten Literatur"), which satisfies the legitimate literary needs (above all the need for entertainment) of a less demanding audience unconcerned with any conceptions of aesthetic value, is, however, no less problematic. This is primarily because "high-brow" literary works can also have an entertainment value (even if for a different category of reader). People have justly pointed to a phenomenon that has only become apparent in recent times whereby any attempt to entertain the reader seems to have been banished from "high-brow literature" and in particular from German "high-brow literature."[5]

Another reason for the dubious nature of the dichotomy outlined above is that even for those members of the higher social strata who tend to read more intellectually demanding books, there is a basic human need for entertainment (even if this is not generally admitted), which is satisfied by these self-same books. In this context it should be noted that many "high-brow" literary products have their roots in extremely "trivial" material. In addition, there are books that one generation may classify as "high-brow" but that a succeeding generation—with a changed system of values—will consider "only" as "enter-

tainment literature," and vice versa. There are many examples of books originally classed as "entertainment literature" that have "risen" to achieve "high-
brow" status. "High-brow literature" can be conceived in terms of market-effec-
tiveness just as "trivial literature" can owe its existence to some inner creative
impulse and can possess a high degree of artistic self-consciousness.[6]

In the face of the social-psychological functions of "entertainment literature" (which remain to be more fully explored), it is questionable whether one
can rightly claim that such literature lacks "real depth."[7] It is more probable
that "entertainment literature," however each individual reader may choose to
interpret this term, satisfies a set of human needs that are different from those
satisfied by other types of literature but that are no less vital to the individual.
Finally, the assertion that authors of "entertainment literature" are "fundamentally unconcerned with the aesthetic perfection of their material,"[8] can also be
applied to a large proportion of "high-brow literature," particularly modern literature.

It seems hardly possible to discover a way out of this terminological
jungle. "It has been impossible to find a term which would fully emphasize the
particular character of this newly discovered material for literary research. . . .
The problem of finding a methodology for researching into the role of the trivial in the history of art and literature . . . is insoluble in the context of any
evaluation based upon formal or aesthetic values."[9]

In the rest of this article we will mainly use the term "entertainment literature" and throughout, this term should be seen against the background of all
the limitations outlined above; furthermore, out of purely practical considerations, we will understand the notion of undemanding entertainment to be the
central feature of this complex branch of literature.

Entertainment Literature as a Consumer Article

In October, 1973, the opinion-poll institute at Allensbach (Institut für
Demoskopie) established by means of a representative random sample that the
adult West German spends on the average 1 hour and 56 minutes each week
reading for entertainment and 1 hour and 8 minutes reading for his own further education.[10] Women read more for their entertainment than men (2.12 as
against 1.73 hours a week), young people more than old (2.19 as against 2.16),
and those with a higher school education almost twice as much as those with
less (3.05 as against 1.57).

What is understood as entertainment literature may vary greatly within
each individual socio-economic group. A more exact picture can be obtained
by examining more closely the exact composition of the readership of novelettes. In May, 1975, according to a survey carried out by the same institute,[11]
27 percent of the adult population of the Federal Republic read novelettes: 2
percent read between six and ten a month; 17 percent read five a month; 8 percent of those asked read less than twelve a year. 30 percent of the women read
them, only 23 percent of the men. The lower the academic standard attained,

the greater—according to this survey—the consumption of novelettes: 15 per-cent of those with a higher school education as against 32 percent of those with less.

Since novelettes, like weekly[12] and illustrated magazines,[13] have only a low social prestige, the number of readers (male and female) may well in reality be higher rather than lower, above all among those questioned who came from the higher socio-economic groups.

In any case, the sales of novelettes of all kinds run into millions. The 162 *Jerry Cotton Stories* alone have so far sold about 10 million copies. The same publishers regularly print 30 novelette series (mostly weekly) with sales figures of 1.8 million copies; the women's novelette *Silvia* achieved the highest number of copies sold. In addition, there are sixteen comic series, with each edition selling a total of 1.25 million copies as well as eight puzzle book series with sales of nearly 500,000.

Apart from occasional figures mentioned in publishers' advertisements for individual novels (claimed—rightly or wrongly—to be best-sellers), there are no reliable figures for the sales of all the various publications that can be classified as "entertainment literature." Certain figures can, however, give us a general indication of the sales of entertainment literature among subscription readers. Hans G. Konsalik, for example (*Der Arzt von Stalingrad, Wer stirbt schon gern unter Palmen, Liebesnächte in der Taiga*), achieved with twelve titles sales of around 2.3 million. The twenty-eight titles of Marie Louise Fischer (*Wilde Jugend, Küsse nach dem Unterricht, Liebe im* Grand Hotel, *Im Schatten der Vergangenheit*) sold 4 million copies. Willi Heinrich (sixteen titles, including *Schmetterlinge weinen nicht, So Long. Archie, Liebe und was sonst noch zählt*) also sold 6.5 million copies. All these successful authors are, however, over-taken by Johannes Mario Simmel (*Und Jimmy ging zum Regenbogen, Der Stoff aus dem die Träume sind, Bis zur bitteren Neige*), whose fourteen titles achieved sales figures of 8.5 million copies. Because all these figures deal with the number of subscription readers, the actual total sales of these authors may well be even higher. The total sales of the original editions of the 207 novels by Hedwig Courths-Mahler are estimated to be at least 30 million copies.[14]

These sobering figures are evidence of a very important fact: that the various types of entertainment literature play a very substantial role in the life of the average reader. One may question the quality of this reading material, but this does not alter the fact that the only contact that large sections of the population have with literature is almost invariably limited to the realm of en-tertainment literature.

The Beginnings of Interdisciplinary Research

Whoever poses the question as to the social relevance of literature should not limit himself to the socially binding canon of a narrow class composed of those more demanding citizens intent on their own self-education; in other words, he should not exclude the literature that is in fact read. The intrinsic value and importance of this literature was already recognized in the nineteenth century, although by only a few. As early as 1847, Robert Prutz believed that the traditionally negative aesthetic assessment of popular reading material missed the point and demanded that entertainment literature should be studied, however "tasteless, boring, old-fashioned these outdated, unsavory books may seem," the primary reason being that such books form "an organic part of public consciousness."[15] For him there existed, alongside the literature chronicled by the literary historians, another "perhaps very unaesthetic literature which stood in ill repute but which had the not inconsiderable advantage of actually being read." In 1889, Edmund Wengraf established that the "inferior" literature in society—above all that read by women—conveyed a falsified picture of contemporary life and for this very reason was an object worthy of study.[16] In this context, a real step forward was made in 1913 by Levin L. Schücking, one of the precursors of the sociology of literature, who showed that taste was the product of "temporal, cultural and sociological conditioning." According to him, "the main question for the literary historian" should be: "What do people of very widely varying educational backgrounds read at any given time?"[17]

This question could only be answered when the isolation of the various academic disciplines had been overcome. Nowadays there is widespread agreement that entertainment literature is a significant phenomenon that encompasses both literature and economics, social history and education theory, sociology and social psychology. Above all, one can observe that there has been a definite increase in the amount of academic work devoted to this subject since the 1960s. In the following pages we wish to deal more closely with an often neglected and underrated aspect of this problem: the social function of entertainment literature.

Rest and Relaxation

Despite the views of many critics, entertainment literature has always enjoyed much greater popularity among the broad mass of the population than any other reading material. This is the same today as it was in the time of Goethe and Schiller. The numerous condemnations that novels about knights, robbers and ghosts drew upon themselves only serve to confirm the suspicion that this literature was the only most eagerly "consumed" at the time. The reason for this is easily recognized: "Trivial literature owes its enormous popularity to the fact that it satisfies some of the elementary human needs of its consumers."[18]

The publisher Hubert Burda once appropriately described entertainment as "a primary need, essential to man's whole existence."[19] The need for rest and relaxation, a need for which entertainment literature provides one possible answer, plays a part that should not be underestimated in a society still characterized by the pressures of work and the problems of everyday life, problems which, if anything, increase with more free time. As Sigmund Freud has remarked: "The life to which we are condemned, is too taxing for us: it brings too much pain, too many disappointments, too many impossible tasks. Life is intolerable without some means of alleviating this pressure."[20] Whoever recognizes this need as legitimate cannot object to the idea that entertainment literature should offer a broad range of such palliatives covering all tastes.

Similarly, Wilmont Haacke has pointed to the "liberating effect" of entertainment: "People seek entertainment in order to relax from the total exhaustion caused by work or to free themselves from the monotonous routine of everyday life. Entertainment is not merely a source of distraction and of new life but also a liberating and humanizing agent." He, too, realizes that "entertainment, directed at the great mass of the population by all the media, definitely helps to relieve frustrations," and asks rightly: "Why not admit its psychotherapeutic value?"[21]

Entertainment brings relaxation and recovery from the continual pressure of having to compete in an industrial society. It breaks down pent-up aggressions and tensions by appealing to, and reawakening interests that would otherwise have remained dormant. Entertainment makes possible the regeneration of a person's strength ready for the next day's work—a decisive factor in a competitive society like our own—and achieves this by compensating for the sacrifices and failures forced upon the individual by the pressures of work and of life in general.

It alone makes possible and bearable the level of achievement demanded by society and the often disadvantageous position of the individual in that society. "Above all, however, it leads to a positive reconciliation of the individual with the unavoidable norms, demands and pressures of society by affirming and representing his actual world even through the construction of counter-images to that world."[22] The kind of entertainment offered on television, in magazines, in booklets and novels often seems fundamentally suspect to many critics because it is politically relevant in a way that has been recognized as wrong. "From a sociological standpoint, one distinct intellectual group in society takes upon itself the right of organizing the leisure time of others: this group demands a permanent level of achievement, continuing even beyond the realms of work and career. Against this, one must uphold the idea that, particularly today, the mass media also have a function as regards our free time, namely that they contribute to our relaxation from the demands of a competitive society."[23]

Escapism

Inseparably linked to the need for entertainment is a whole series of other primary human needs that are no less basic: the need to escape from reality, the need to confront reality, the need to identify with others and to dissociate from others, the need to be curious and finally the need to gossip with others. These needs are many and varied and often appear to contradict one another; basically they are not linked to any particular social system: the latter stages in the development of capitalism, for example.

First of all, we must mention that primary longing to forget the everyday world, at least temporarily, and the dissatisfaction with one's own fate; the longing to cut oneself free of the existing social norms, ties and duties: this we call escapism (Escape, evasion, "Ablenkung"). One can conceive of this escapism as assuming various forms. Entertainment literature can offer escape 1) into a real dream world but one that the normal reader could never achieve, 2) into dreams whose realization appears to be totally possible (visions of a better future), 3) into an unreal dream world, 4) into a counter-image of a world full of terror and horror.

However surprising it may seem, a fictitious world of horror and terror can distract just as well as the portrayal of paradise. For, "through the threatening, exaggerated fantasy world, reality gains a new security: escapism leads the reader—with a thankful sigh of relief—back to the reality from which he sought to escape. . . . The portrayal of a happier and more perfect world—usually pictured in terms of a higher social position—will have a similar effect. Such a portrayal also releases the reader from the spiritual bondage of everyday life. In his fantasy he can take part in something which would always be beyond his own everyday life. The more insecure reality appears to him—whether the threatening force is material, political or spiritual—the more he will long for the portrayal of a secure existence. The book becomes a dream factory which—for a short time—provides fulfillment beyond the limits of everyday life." [24]

As reflected in entertainment literature, the reader searches for a simulated and better "other world" (but one that is always imminent) in order to seek refuge from the misery of everyday life. Here he will not only seek to forget his social misery for a short while but he will also enjoy the fictitious defeat of this misery. "Mrs. Courths-Mahler made her living from the unfulfilled aspirations of stunted men, and her daughters followed her successful principle." [25] Various critics hold it against such undemanding entertainment literature and those who produce it, that such works—consciously or unconsciously—prevent social and political changes ("the effect which entertainment literature has in stabilizing the system [26]"). Some believe that the offer to escape in entertainment literature is so compelling that reality will be forgotten. Others are of the opinion that certain material presented in the media consciously projects such a one-sided and pleasant picture of reality that social change no longer appears at all desirable.

Confrontation with Reality

The mass media (together with entertainment literature) fulfill two distinct functions that are closely linked together and can be alternately fulfilled. On the one hand, escape from reality; on the other, confrontation with reality. The reader craves not only for escape stories but also for real-life stories. This is because people have a "psychological need to learn about their own existence. We want our life to be interpreted, explained and analyzed. All true-to-life fictitious representations of reality help people to solve their problems."[27] The German newspaper expert Robert Prutz recognized exactly what this statement meant when applied to entertainment literature over a hundred years before the American psychologist Ernest Dichter. "All the needs of the masses can be boiled down to this: They want to find a transfigured version of themselves in the books they read. They want to find their environment, the places where they live, the people they know and the circumstances with which they are familiar."[28]

However, there seems to be a direct contradiction between the notion of escapism and the desire for a portrayal of one's own area of experience ("Men like you and me"). Yet, as Marion Beaujean has rightly pointed out, the familiar can also entertain if the means of portrayal illuminates new aspects of a familiar reality. The critical factor is that we are here talking about a different kind of pleasure: "The joy of recognition which characterizes all encounters with the very well-known and the long familiar."[29]

According to this idea, entertainment should not merely be interpreted in terms of the need for fantasy worlds standing as counter-images to our own world. Besides the idea of reading for entertainment, we have the need for contact with our surroundings, for information. "Entertainment literature does not only fill the individual's narrow everyday existence with second-hand experiences, motives, feelings and emotions but it also enriches this existence with new information of all kinds. On the one hand, this is a natural corollary of the need to lend credibility to the fictitious world; on the other, it corresponds to a general need for education and knowledge."[30]

The distinction between a literature that entertains and a literature that informs is often hard to draw since each overlaps the other. The recipe for the success of "Gartenlaube" rests not least upon the way in which the man who thought it up, Ernst Keil, conveyed knowledge and information at the same time as providing entertainment.

Simple Patterns of Identification and Dissociation

The success of popular entertainment literature obviously rests upon the fact that, through the use of stereotyped characters, it provides the less educated and more undemanding reader with simple patterns of identification and dissociation; this is true both of the portrayal of fantasy worlds and of descriptions of everyday existence. Both sets of patterns contribute to behavioral security and to a confirmation of one's own personality. Without being personally involved, the reader can identify with positive heroes and plots and distance himself from negative heroes and plots. In the case of descriptions of personal, everyday experience, the identification with positive and the dissociation from negative heroes and plots gains a new and perhaps more direct attraction. Here we are no longer dealing with ideal heroes and plots that, by their very nature, are out of reach, but rather with a familiar and well-known reality in which we can immediately recognize our own opinions, feelings and wishes. Identification and dissociation occur more easily within a common area of experience.

However, both in the portrayal of fantasy worlds and in the descriptions of everyday existence, the habitual superiority of the hero within a predictable plot has one very important result: In the course of this identification and dissociation process, certain opinions, built up and predetermined through the use of stereotypes, receive continual confirmation. In consequence, Höllerer has suggested that the whole genre be classified as "the literature of self-confirmation."[31] A form of writing that is based on the confirmation of the reader's personal attitude and orientates itself to the needs of that reader—these two features have been put forward by various authors as being typical of what is understood as "kitsch."[32] "One can best define 'kitsch' by the term 'the literature of wish-fulfillment.' 'Kitsch' promises mass salvation but guarantees only the appearance of fulfillment."[33]

Curiosity and Gossip

The social need for entertainment is complex and corresponds to various unconscious drives, above all to the desire for communication (which may take the form of gossip) and to our instinctive curiosity. This instinctive curiosity to learn about anything strange and unknown and the desire to communicate have the same origin and are as old as the medium of language of which they both make use. This is because it is only through communication and assimilation that any real contact with one's environment can be achieved and the desire for knowledge, even in its simplest form, can be satisfied. One person may concern himself with the propagation of knowledge already acquired (since it is only through this process that it attains a personal significance). Another may be curious to learn about those things of which his own perception leaves him ignorant or those which he is unable to comprehend without further explanation.

Emotional curiosity appears to be one of the most important needs of the reader of entertainment literature. This curiosity results from a craving on the part of the reader to take part in events from which he is normally excluded. Entertainment literature thus satisfies one primary human need: curiosity. This curiosity is unquenchable and unconstrained. It diffuses itself over the whole range of human experience, encompassing both the heights and depths of existence. Very unfairly, the word curiosity has acquired almost exclusively negative connotations in everyday usage.

Arno von Blarer has summed up the role of curiosity and has conceded the following "positive" functions, which, in our view, can also be recognized in entertainment literature:

> In behavior dominated by curiosity, people provide themselves with an endless supply of new objects suited to "ersatz" fulfillment and sublimation. . . .
> This is why curiosity and behavior dominated by curiosity is so enormously

important for an understanding of the human desire to recognize, to know, to experience and to create.[34]

The socially isolated reader of entertainment literature is particularly characterized by a curiosity regarding the fate and fateful mistakes of other men. Moreover, curious people know more about human nature than others. This knowledge gives them a lead over others and an increase in their prestige.

In many respects, gossip can fulfill similar social functions. Psychologists have long known just how important chatting with one's neighbor can be. Gossip provides a form of relief and brings people closer together. As the psychoanalyst Alexander Mitscherlich has written:

> Even though gossip may be annoying and at times even dangerously poisonous (as when it reaches the level of character assassination), it is a safety valve without which people caught up in the web of society could not exist. . . . Embittered gossip is the means by which we seek to forget a little of the misery of the world in which we live. Slanderous rumor is the only power possessed by the powerless. . . . Everyone loves to experience, through slanderous rumors, a strengthening of his group consciousness ("We are better") and the possibility of relieving pent-up drives.[35]

Heinz-Jürgen Ipfling has similarly pointed out that gossip, both for the speaker and the listener, unconsciously aims at a strengthening of self-consciousness ("I'm not like that").[36] Commercialized and marketed as a "service," with all the trimmings of technology, gossip has for a long time been a basic ingredient of mystery and whodunnit stories as well as of magazines dealing with similar subjects. One can hardly hope that gossip will ever disappear from man's social life nor from the media, which have made it very much their own. "And, since we so much enjoy gossip, it is debatable whether we would ever want to be so mature as to want to manage without it; that would mean losing too much enjoyment."[37]

Is Entertainment Harmful?

Popular entertainment literature has always been subject to a flood of criticisms and doubts: uncritically adapting to "bad" taste and to the "base" needs of the masses, offering the appearance of fulfillment instead of providing actual help in coming to terms with life, misleadingly holding out the promise of unlimited opportunity for social advancement, denying the existence of social barriers and obstacles in the world, setting up false values and models for the reader, concealing or denying the existence of cause and effect in society, providing false solutions to social problems, which leads in turn to a resigned lack of interest in all social and political problems. Such criticisms of entertainment literature always give rise to the same ideological suspicions: namely that, by means of seemingly harmless entertainment, a minority bent on the maintenance of the existing power structure consciously manipulates the unconscious mass of the population according to their own ideas. As Walter Hollstein has tried to show by means of an analysis of present-day German illustrated novels, people are "manipulated by forces which are outside themselves and whose decisions flood over them merely offering powerful demonstration of their own powerlessness."[38] Thus the reader of entertainment literature becomes the victim of his own reading material.[39]

According to Rudolf Schenda, the whole range of popular reading material in the nineteenth century tended to form opinions and to determine behavior, and readers of popular books allowed themselves to be manipulated in many ways. Popular entertainment literature is thus made responsible for all the evils of the last century: submissiveness, nationalism, chauvinism and militarism. And, according to Schenda, what was true of the nineteenth century is basically still true of the present.

> Popular reading material avoids any critical examination of modern life. It is not equal to social and political problems. Its conservatism is sterile. Progressive forces are totally dismissed. . . . Popular reading material does not only avoid critical confrontation with current problems; rather it cements reactionary modes of behavior and opinions and establishes these as eternally valid. The content of such books is presented as an unchanging norm. These books are the reactionary dictators of public opinion.[40]

For Hermann Bausinger the factor that links all trivial literature is its essentially "conservative stance."[41]

Justification for this undoubtedly necessary criticism of what is offered as entertainment in no way requires this kind of "manipulation theory." After all, why shouldn't there be differences in the quality of entertainment literature just as in the case of other "goods"? Such manipulation of consciousness and behavior is moreover only possible (if it is possible at all) in authoritarian social systems, where the state rigorously suppresses certain media and certain items in the media and systematically demands the presence of others. But even when free competition within each branch of the media and between the differing material presented is safeguarded to a certain extent, the process by which opinions are formed remains extremely complex, involving the substantial participation of and interaction between many diverse groups. While it is true that the mass media and entertainment literature play an important part in the process by which opinions are formed, research into mass communication has shown this influence to be by no means decisive. Hence, there are definite limits to all hopes of using entertainment to spread knowledge; similarly, the same limits apply to all fears that entertainment might be used to stabilize a social system or to prevent reforms.

NOTES

[1] W. Höllerer, in *Studien zur Trivialliteratur*, ed. O. Burger (Frankfurt a.M., 1968), pp. 51, 55.
[2] Thus, e.g. J. Schulte-Sasse, *Die Kritik an der Trivialliteratur seit der Aufklä*rung

(München [West Germany], 1971), p. 12, note 4; W. Killy, *Deutscher Kitsch*, 2nd ed. (Göttingen [West Germany], 1962), p. 15.

[3] 17th ed., vol. 2 (Paris, n. d.), p. 456 f.

[4] R. Escarpit, *Littérature savante et littérature populaire* (Paris, 1965), p. 6.

[5] H. F. Foltin, in *Studien zur Trivialliteratur*, p. 243, note 1.

[6] G. Sichelschmidt, *Liebe, Mord und Abenteuer. Eine Geschichte der deutschen Unterhaltungsliteratur* (Berlin, 1969), p. 11.

[7] *Ibid.*, p. 11.

[8] *Ibid.*, p. 12.

[9] R. Schenda, *Volk ohne Buch. Studien zur Sozialgeschichte der populären Lesestoffe 1770–1910* (Frankfurt a. M., 1970), p. 24.

[10] G. Schmidchen, "Lesekultur in Deutschland," in *Börsenblatt für den Deutschen Buchhandel*, no. 39 (1974), table 1.

[11] Cf. *Börsenblatt für den Deutschen Buchhandel*, no. 71 (1975), p. 1165; *Media Perspektiven*, no. 9 (1975), p. 449.

[12] Cf. P. Kaupp, "Die Regenbogenpresse. Inhalt-Leserschaft-Wirkung," in *International Journal of Communication Research* 1, no. 2 (1974): 168–87; no. 3: 321–39.

[13] Cf. P. Kaupp, "Die schlimmen Illustrierten." (Düsseldorf [West Germany]–Wien [Austria], 1971), p. 17 ff.

[14] W. Krieg, "Unser Weg ging hinauf," *Hedwig Courths-Mahler und ihre Töchter als literarisches Phänomen* (Wien, Bad Bocklet [West Germany]–Zurich, 1954), p. 8.

[15] R. Prutz, in *Menschen und Bücher Biographische Beiträge zur deutschen Literatur- und Sittengeschichte des 18. Jahrhunderts*, Vol. 2 (Leipzig, Germany, 1862), p. 9.

[16] E. Wengraf, "Literatur und Gesellschaft," in *Neue Zeit*, no. 7 (1889), pp. 241–48.

[17] L. L. Schücking, "Literaturgeschichte und Geschmacksgeschichte," in *Germanisch-Romanische Monatsschrift*, no. 5 (1913), pp. 562, 564.

[18] G. Waldmann, *Theorie und Didaktik der Trivialliteratur* (München, 1973), p. 50.

[19] H. Burda, "Unterhaltungsillustrierte und Bedürfnisse." Speech at the annual meeting of the Organization of German Station-Booksellers (Verband deutscher Bahnhofsbuchhändler) in Garmisch-Partenkirchen, West Germany, on 21st May, 1974.

[20] S. Freud, *Das Unbehagen in der Kultur* (Frankfurt a.M.–Hamburg, 1963), p. 103.

[21] W. Haacke, "Die Spielgärten der Erwachsenen. Zur Soziologie der Unterhaltung in den Massenmedien," in *Kölner Zeilschrift für Soziologie und Sozialpsychologie*, no. 3 (1969), p. 543 f.

[22] Waldmann, *op. cit.*, p. 13.

[23] B. Frank, in *Das Parlament* (Hamburg, 3rd July, 1971), p. 4.

[24] M. Beaujean, *Der Trivialroman in der zweiten Hälfte des 18. Jahrhunderts* (Bonn, 1964), p. 15.

[25] F. Hodeige, ed., *Das werck der bucher. Von der Wirksamkeit des Buches in Vergangenheit und Gegenwart. Festschrift für Horst Kliemann* (Freiburg i.Br. [West Germany], 1956), p. 221.

[26] Waldmann, *op. cit.*, p. 10.

[27] E. Dichter, *Strategie im Reich der Wünsche* (Düsseldorf, 1961), p. 227.

[28] Prutz, *op cit.*, p. 26.

[29] Beaujean, *op. cit.*, p. 16.

[30] A. Klein, *Die Krise des Unterhaltungsromans im 19. Jahrhundert* (Bonn, 1969), p. 66.

[31] W. Höllerer, in *Studien zur Trivialliteratur*, p. 41, note 1.

[32] Thus, e.g. Schulte-Sasse, *op. cit.*, pp. 25, 47.

[33] Hodeige, *op. cit.*, p. 221.

[34] A. von Blarer, *Die Neugier* (Zürich, 1951). p. 138.

[35] A Mitscherlich, *Auf dem Weg zur vaterlosen Gesellschaft* (München, 1963), p. 404 *f.*

[36] H.-J. Ipfling, *Jugend und Illustrierte* (Osnabrück [West Germany], 1965), p. 39.

[37] Mitscherlich, *op. cit.*, p. 405.

[38] W. Hollstein, *Betrogene Sehnsucht. Das Menschenbild im deutschen Illustriertenroman* (Münster [West Germany], 1969), p. 192.

[39] Schenda, *op. cit.*, p. 487 *ff.*

[40] *Ibid.*, p. 439.

[41] H. Bausinger, in *Studien zur Trivialliteratur*, p. 26, note 1.

Part Five

☆☆☆☆

ECONOMICS AND PRODUCTION OF ENTERTAINMENT

Werner Zeppenfeld:

The Economics and Structure of the Record and Tape Industry: The Example of West Germany

☆ DURING THE COURSE of its more than one hundred-year history, the record—together with its later counterpart and competitor, tape—has progressed to become a mass medium of central and worldwide significance. The industry based on recorded sound[1] had an annual turnover in 1977 of over nine million dollars, non-Western countries excluded. As a key leisure medium, recorded sound overtook cinema long ago. The industry's products leave a decisive imprint on wide stretches of our accoustical environment, either directly or with the assistance of other channels of mass communication. Records and tapes have been and are omnipresent carriers of culture and agencies of socialization for whole generations of youth: rock music—which accounts for more than half the total world turnover in recorded music—can hardly be underestimated in its influence on the way a young generation perceives and understands itself.

The interest social science research has hitherto shown in this medium contrasts starkly with its indisputable importance. The deficit in knowledge on all its aspects is enormous. A reorientation of communication scientists' interest doesn't seem to be any less remote than it always has been, despite the occasional suggestion that music is a much more important component of youth's experience with mass media than television, for instance, which has been the subject of intense and wide-ranging research. In Germany also, the record and tape as a subject of research have been bypassed to a very large degree in favor of the following: the effects of broadcasting, the economics of the newspaper industry and speculation concerning the potential of new communications technology. No doubt sentiments against mass culture and incompetency in musical analysis have contributed to this state of affairs.[2] Areas that have suffered especially as a result of this far-reaching disregard for recorded sound are: 1) research into the psychological and sociological effects (not the object of inter-

▶ This is an original article written especially for this book. Werner Zeppenfeld, M.A., is a freelance journalist. At present he is researching into the mechanics and structure of the German recorded sound market.

est within the confines of this short essay) and 2) analysis of the economics and structure of the record and tape industry, which is fundamental if the contemporary phenomenon of recorded sound is to be understood. Before looking at the latter in greater detail, here are a few important facts and figures on the German recorded sound market:

Development of the Market [3]

The market for records and tapes in West Germany is one of the most important in the world, ranking behind the United States and equaling those of the United Kingdom and Japan. In 1977, records and tapes to the tune of almost DM 1,875 million were sold.[4] Approximately the same sum is spent each year on complementary hardware (i.e., stereo and hi-fi equipment. If the sale of blank tapes are included in the figures, the German market for hard- and software has an annual turnover of DM 5,000 million—equal to that of the national book market. The following breakdown gives some impression as to software production figures: in 1977, a total of some 176 million recorded sound units were sold. Of these, 40 million were singles, 97 million LPs and 39 million tapes of various kinds. The market for singles has been stagnant for years and is as such regarded as the most insignificant part of the recorded music industry as far as potential is concerned. The LP still dominates the market outright, despite ever increasing pressure of competition from the technologically more promising tape.

The dominant type of prerecorded tape marketed throughout Europe is the compact cassette, more commonly called "musicassette," pioneered by Philips (Netherlands) in 1963. The American cartridge never had a chance against this smaller and cheaper competitor. All German recording companies have long gone over to producing their LP repertoire simultaneously on musicassette. The enormous potential of the musicassette market can be gauged by the fact that between 1972 and 1977 the ratio of LPs to musicassettes fell from 9:1 to 7:3. Easy handling and transportability are the two major factors explaining the musicassette's present success. A third factor, quality of sound reproduction, which now more or less matches that of the Gramophone record, may indeed play *the* crucial role in completely replacing its rival in the not too distant future. The hardware position doesn't seem to present too great an obstacle to such a development. Although 80 percent of all West German households possess record playing equipment, 50 percent have already purchased cassette recorders. Furthermore, the proportion of hi-fi cassette decks within this percentage is constantly increasing. The traditional reel-to-reel tape has already suffered as a result of these factors.

Development of the Repertoire

Records and tapes are almost exclusively used for the reproduction of music. Non-musical categories can be dismissed without further comment because of their insignificantly small share of the market. In terms of value, the majority share of turnover is accounted for by light music. The recording industry includes everything within this category that is not "classical" or art music. (Incidentally, the percentage share of the German recorded sound market for "classical" music is the highest for any country in the West: 13 percent as compared with 7 percent in Great Britain and less that 5 percent in the United States.) In contrast with the stable proportions maintained by various genres (mainly symphonic music and opera) of "classical" music, those within the mass market for light music are always subject to heavy fluctuation as a result of taste and fashion trends.

Since the early 1960s, all new major trends (e.g., rock 'n roll, beat, rock) on the German market have been imported from Anglo-American popular cultural circles. West German impulses in the formation of both national and international musical innovations hardly exist. The preferences shown by German youth for Anglo-American pop has resulted in massive changes in the structure of the recorded sound market. Experience has shown that such preferences continue to operate even after youth, with the result that the share of Anglo-American pop on the German market is continuing to increase. Whereas typically German pop songs ("Schlager") still accounted for a 50 percent share in the 1950s, its present share consists of a bare 10 percent. Only every second record on the domestic market for recorded light music is a German production and even these are increasingly conforming to international standards of taste. The other half consists of foreign pop, at present almost exclusively "mainstream" and "pop rock." This continuing development is indicative of an increasing international homogenization of musical taste conforming with Anglo-American standards.

Structural Problems

German recorded sound production has enjoyed stable growth rates since the early 1960s, uninterrupted and unaffected by the ups and downs of the national economy. The last few years, however, have seen developments that mark a critical turning point in the fortunes of the industry. Despite rising sales, both quantitatively and in terms of value, profits have been severely hit.

This crisis is due mainly to the general price collapse on the inland record market. LPs are now selling for prices, despite rises in production costs, nominally below those ten years ago! The reasons for this are to be found in the abolition of resale price maintenance in 1972—as a result of which fierce competition broke out among retailers—as well as in the price differences within the European Community, especially between Great Britain and West Germany. In the former country, because of lower wage levels, lower royalty fees, differing exchange rates and such, records are sold to the consumer for the price usually paid in Germany by the retailer. As a result, more and more retailers have resorted to importing Anglo-American music products directly from Great Britain, and thus bypassing (and to the disadvantage of) domestic licensees. In promoting its products, the German recording industry inevitably promotes its rival British pressings of the same record. On top of this, sales are affected by numerous "pirate" pressings and "bootlegs."

The real danger for the recording industry, however, is posed by the so-called blank tape. 95 percent of such tapes are used for re-recording the music marketed by the recording industry, either directly off its products or indirectly off radio programs. In 1977, the German recording industry estimated that blank tapes had reached the annual turnover of approximately DM 1,000 million and, according to the information at their disposal, there were no signs that sales were leveling off. Besides resulting in direct losses in royalties (in 1977, in the region of DM 300 million), such trends, if they continue, could develop into a serious threat to the structure of the whole recorded sound market. If demand were to slacken for prerecorded records and tapes, the accompanying reduction in production levels would initially lead to severe cuts in the repertoire for minorities, which have to date been subsidized through the profits made by pop products. In response to the danger posed by blank tapes, the recording industry has begun to argue for the introduction of a copyright fee on each blank tape sold, a suggestion that is, of course, bitterly opposed by the manufacturers of such tapes.

The Suppliers on the Recorded Sound Market

As everywhere in the West, the recorded sound industry—completely in the hands of private enterprise—is in the hands of an oligopoly consisting of a few important producers who control the market. Although small-scale enterprise can also produce and market pop music, only large-scale enterprise can be relatively sure of long-term success. All large-scale recorded sound producers in some way have connections with the so-called communications combines (i.e., companies producing everything, e.g., from books to sophisticated electronics). Frequently these combines operate at an international level with their main business activities either concentrated in the electronics or the leisure sector.

In West Germany, the major firms supplying recorded sound products can be split into two categories: traditional European-based firms and their rapidly expanding competitors, the subsidiaries of United States companies. The core of the traditional European recording industry consists of three leisure combines. Thirty-two percent of the German market alone was controlled in 1977 by the Polygram Group. This international holding company is jointly owned by Siemens AG of Germany and Philips of the Netherlands. Polygram is the third largest music combine in the world, involved in music publishing, film, television and audivisual software as well as record and tape production. Total turnover in 1977: DM 1,919 million. Three Polygram subsidiaries compete independently of each other on the German market: the Deutsche Grammophon Gesellschaft (DGG) in partnership with Polydor International, Phonogram GmbH in partnership with Phonogram International B.V.; and Metronome Records GmbH.

EMI-Electrola GmbH of Cologne in 1977 had an approximate 18 percent share in total German market turnover. The company is a subsidiary of EMI in London, beside CBS the largest recorded sound producer in the world, which is also engaged in the electronics, leisure and television business. World turnover: DM 3,430 million (1977 figures). Finally, approximately 13 percent of the recorded sound market was controlled in 1977 by the only recording company fully owned by a German enterprise: Ariola-Eurodisc GmbH, a subsidiary of the publishing combine Bertelsmann AG. Bertelsmann's turnover for 1977: DM 2,885 million. The combine, however, is also expanding and internationalizing its activities (e.g., with the relatively recent establishment of Ariola America Inc. and the Interworld Music Group, both in the United States). Besides these three large recorded sound producers, mention has to be made of Teldec Schallplatten GmbH (6 percent of the total sales in 1977), which is jointly owned by the British Decca Record Company Ltd. and the German electro-giant AEG Telefunken. The above companies by and large monopolized competition on the German market until the 1970s. Numerous small-scale producers didn't pose a serious threat to their position.

The constantly growing success of Anglo-American music products in Germany since the mid-1960s was accompanied by a dramatic breakthrough on the German recorded sound market by non-European enterprise. American companies, which used to market their products through leading domestic companies, proceeded to establish their own subsidiaries. The first to take this step, in 1963, was CBS, the second-largest recorded sound producer in the world. Warner Communications Inc. followed suit in 1970 with the establishment of the subsidiary WEA; RCA followed in 1973. Eighty percent of the products marketed by these companies are simply European editions of recordings in the United States parent's repertoire. However, the European subsidiaries are also engaged in building up an extensive domestic repertoire. Because Ango-American rock and pop music are favored by trends in German musical taste, the sales figures of these companies show a higher annual average rate of increase than those of their European rivals. The following table gives an impression as to trends on the German market and also allows some insight into patterns of business concentration.

In 1977, the four leading companies between themselves controlled 59 percent of the total recorded sound market in Germany in terms of value. Ten companies controlled about 90 percent. The remaining nine percent was shared by two medium-sized companies and approximately ninety smaller firms. Comparable figures for 1974 show that the four leading companies shared 70 percent of the market and the first ten almost 95 percent. At first sight, when comparing these figures with those of other communications industries, especially the press, the trend with regard to concentration within this particular sector seems, remarkably, to have taken the opposite direction. No concentration has occurred during the recent past. Indeed, deconcentration seems to be taking place.

This development, however, cannot be taken as a sign that small, independent units have successfully established themselves and expanded their output, and that thereby the number of producers in a position to compete on

Figure 1 Annual Turnover of Recording Companies on the
German Recorded Sound Market as a Percentage of
Total Turnover (in terms of value)

Name of Company	% of Total Turnover (1974)	% of Total Turnover (1977)
Deutsche Grammophon Gesellschaft	20.0	18.0
EMI-Electrola	20.0	18.0
Ariola-Eurodisc	16.0	13.0
Phonogram	11.0	10.0
CBS	3.5	8.0
Teldec	14.5	6.0
K-tel and Arcade	—	5.0
WEA	3.5	4.0
RCA	1.0	5.0
Metronome	1.5	4.0
Other Companies	(9.0)	(9.0)
TOTAL:	100.0	100.0

equal terms has increased. To the contrary, the market is firmly in the hands of multilateral business organizations and small competitors do not have much chance of acquiring a significant portion. Only large-scale enterprise can hope to enter the market in a big way. The hitherto secure existence of small-scale enterprise is due only to the uninterrupted growth of the recorded sound market. No external pressures encouraging fusion exist at least with regard to demand.

Whereas in 1974 three European media combines (Polygram, EMI and Bertelsmann) together gained a 68.5 percent share of the West German recorded sound market, their share in 1977 dropped to 63 percent. On the other hand, three United States multimedia enterprises (CBS, WCI and RCA) managed to double their share within the same short space of time. If one adds the shares of these two groups of producers together, it can be seen that this limited number of enterprises control three-quarters to four-fifths of the German market.

The implications of the developments I have outlined are much greater than one can gauge from the picture drawn of the recorded sound market alone. They must be seen in the context of parallel developments, for instance in the field of hardware. Internationally oriented media combines were quick to establish themselves in all areas where prospects were promising (i.e., not only in recorded sound production, but also in the production of entertainment electronics [record players, hi-fi equipment, television sets, and such] and in the leisure industry in general). For a long time now, these large-scale combines have been attempting to achieve a market breakthrough for audiovisual equipment (video recorders, for example) and its complementary software. Because such "electronic and music marketers" outsize the press, no matter what measure one uses, the foreseeable future promises that the problem of concentration within the newspaper industry will be overshadowed by the same phenomenon within the recording, entertainment electronics and leisure industry.

In the medium or long term, it is not unlikely that the musical content of recorded products will be influenced to an even greater extent than at present by the oligopolistic nature of the national and international market (EMI and CBS share 20 percent of the latter). It is likely that the concentration of global production and marketing of recorded music in the hands of a few media combines with worldwide sales organizations and marketing strategies could supply significant and critical impulses for an international homogenization of musical culture. The signs that this will happen are already there. In the Federal Republic of Germany, Anglo-American music has already put the once flourishing national pop culture on the defensive. The same is likely to be the case in other countries.

The Communications Environment of the Record and Tape as Regulator of Supply and Demand

The promotions channels at the disposal of—and used by—the recording industry help to maintain the oligopolistic status quo. Moreover, they secure an influence for its products that reaches far beyond that which it could attain in relative isolation from the mass communication system. With this in mind, the above facts and figures can only give an incomplete picture of the significance of recorded sound in comparison with other mass media. Using other mass media, recorded sound (mainly recorded music) can claim an audience many times greater than the one reached through the purchase of records and tapes alone, one which potentially consists of the entire population.

Looking at the communications environment of recorded sound allows us to do two things: 1) to assess the indirect dimension of recorded sound diffusion (e.g., recorded music transmitted by radio stations) and 2) to estimate the advertising potential at industry's disposal (with which it can stimulate the purchase of the records and tapes themselves). In this context it must be mentioned that even less is spent in Germany on direct advertising for recorded sound products than in the United Kingdom and the United States, for instance.

The indirect dimension of recorded sound diffusion enables the market to function smoothly and without significant fluctuation. The concerted action of all mass media nowadays enables 1) rapid turnover rates, 2) high sales rates for many individual products through the homogenization of taste the mass media encourage and 3) the launching of innovative styles ("sounds") and stars according to the requirements of the producers of recorded sound. The diagram below supplies us with a rough idea as to the complexity of recorded sound's communications environment. The numerous feedback processes have not been indicated (e.g., the feedback gained from actual sales figures, through audience size, reviews, the choice of records and tapes in radio programs):

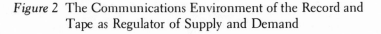

Figure 2 The Communications Environment of the Record and
Tape as Regulator of Supply and Demand

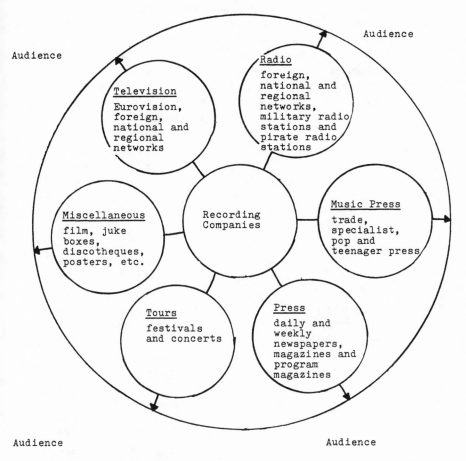

Note: Various feedback channels have been omitted in order to simplify the diagram (audience to
recording company through demand, audience to the electronic media through audience surveys,
letters to the press, electronic media to recording company through reviews, festivals to the press
through reviews, the press to jukeboxes through pop charts, and so on).

Within the scope of this short paper the interdependencies existing between all the media indicated in the diagram cannot be described. I will thus
restrict myself to casting some light on the two most important media for the
promotion of recorded sound: Within this system radio is probably responsible
for the initiation of approximately 40 percent of all record purchases in Germany.[5] Germans over the age of fourteen listen to the radio for an average of
two hours every day and mainly to light music programs. Such programs take
60 percent of their material from the recorded sound repertoire and 40 percent
from other sources (archives, live performances). The advertising effect for the

products of the recording industry is clearly enormous. Although the whole broadcasting system in West Germany is publicly owned and commercial activity is not allowed, radio is at least as dependent on the products of the privately owned recording industry as the latter is on the former. Radio could never hope to fill its music schedules by itself, let alone pay for the stars the recording industry can afford. For minimal royalties totaling DM 7.2 million p.a. radio stations can transmit as much commercially produced recorded music as they like. In comparison, DM 200 million have to be spent on the other 40 percent (i.e. live performances, own recordings). Put another way, the recording industry subsidizes the public broadcasting authorities.

The presence of pop stars on public television cannot be ascribed to such concrete financial considerations. Their appearance on the screen is nonetheless necessary if television is to achieve the audience ratings it wants in the case of some of its programs. The quantity of program time allocated to the recording industry's products is small in comparison with that allocated by radio but relatively more effective: TV accounts for the initiation of 30 percent of total record sales. The recording industry itself regards television as the better medium for launching new productions, stars or groups when compared with radio. It can be used more effectively for the creation of a "new image."

The recording industry, dependent on these two media to a large extent for the promotion of its products, doesn't have any means of institutionalized influence on the public broadcasting authorities—at least in theory—as to the number of times certain recordings are broadcast (as they do in the case of stations such as Radio Luxemburg). This doesn't however prevent recording companies from attempting to do so, for instance through the use of personal contacts between public relations experts and radio or television producers.

In the realm of television, a new breakthrough has been achieved by the recording industry. Not only are PR-men employed to maintain good relations with their counterparts but television material is now also being produced for television transmission by various recording companies themselves. The provision of "playbacks" has long constituted part of the "cooperation" between television organizations and the recording industry. Now, however, more and more finished products in the form of film clips are being supplied and accepted for transmission purposes, further evidence of the way in which the recording industry is taking control of the media available for promotion, a phenomenon which is more overt in the case of festivals and concerts (which is totally in the hands of industry) and the pop press (which is totally dependent on the industry for its advertising revenue).

Conclusion

During the course of this paper I have looked at trends in the structure and economics of the recorded sound market in the case of West Germany. It was established that recorded sound production is concentrated in the hands of a relatively small number of enterprises, all of which have ties with combines constituting the worldwide oligopoly on the recorded sound market. This situation has implications stretching far beyond the purely economic dimension, the most significant of which is cultural homogenization in the field of light music, something which is apparent in trends in German musical taste. Anglo-American music seems to be the common denominator in this development. Such trends are encouraged by the fact that the powerful competitors on the German recorded sound market compete with the same products (Anglo-American pop and rock music) and strengthen their position through the dependencies that exist with other media. The exploitation of such dependencies in the field of broadcasting is probably even more advanced in the case of countries without public broadcasting authorities. Moreover, it must also be stressed that broadcasting organizations themselves have to carry a large portion of the blame for such developments. On the other hand, one cannot get rid of the dependencies themselves. It is the outgrowths and distortions within the system that must be brought under control. Discussion and reform should start at this point.

NOTES

[1] The term "recorded sound" includes gramophone records and all forms of tapes.

[2] The following major publications, at least to a certain extent, present analyses of the West German recorded sound market: Werner Metzger, *Schlager. Versuch einer Gesamtdarstellung unter besonderer Berücksichtigung des Musikmarkts der Bundesrepublik Deutschland* (Tübingen [West Germany], 1975); Eberhard Werthmann, *Die Entwicklung der deutschen Schallplattenindustrie, ihre gegenwärtige Situation und Marktformen.* Diss. (Graz [Austria], 1958); Siegmund Helms, ed., *Schlager in Deutschland* (Wiesbaden [West Germany], 1972); Wolfgang Hamm, Wolfgang Kolneder and Stefan Paul, Popmusik. "Profite für das Kapital," in *Sozialistische Zeitschrift für Kunst und Gesellschaft*, no. 6 (Tübingen [West Germany], 1971); Kurt Blaukopf, *Massenmedium Schallplatte* (Wiesbaden [West Germany], 1977). The following book is recommended for those primarily interested in content and the use made of music by the mass media: Hans-Christian Schmidt, ed., *Musik in den Massenmedien Rundfunk und Fernsehen. Perspektiven und Materialen* (Mainz [West Germany]).

[3] The following sources were used for current statistical information on the German recorded sound market: Annual Reports edited by the Bundesverband der Phonographischen Wirtschaft (Katharinenstr. 11, 2000 Hamburg 11, West Germany), whose members constitute approximately 90 percent of the German recording industry in terms of production. Further information can be obtained from the annual reports of individual enterprises, although total turnover is not broken down so as to supply an insight into the performance of their various constituent companies (e.g., the annual reports of CBS, RCA, WCI, EMI, Polygram, Bertelsmann). The most important periodical for the recorded sound sector is *Rundy. Musik und Medien-Nachrichten* (Otto-Kämper-Ring 20, 6072 Dreieich 3, West Germany), published weekly since 1975, when it first appeared. A yearbook for this sector does not exist.

[4] US$ 1 approx. = DM 2.0.

[5] Cf. unpublished survey by the Institut für Werbepsychologie und Markterkundung in 1973. The study also claims that 30 percent of all records and tapes purchased are "initiated" by television.

Vincent Porter:

Television and Film Production Strategies in the European Community

The Relationship between Cinema and Television

THERE IS NO DOUBT that the massive decline in cinema audiences over the last two decades must be attributed to the growth in television. Even now, there is an inverse correlation within the European Economic Community between the frequency of cinema attendance and the ownership of television sets, as Table 1 shows. The relationship is only approximate since, for instance, car ownership also accounts for the use of leisure time. Nevertheless, the connection is clear and if allowed to continue, the future of the cinema as a place of mass entertainment is in jeopardy. This is not to deny a place in society for the cinema, it is to suggest that its future role can only be determined in the context of a combined policy for the cinema and television together.

The growth of television has enabled the cinema to provide alternative viewing opportunities, which were not previously available to the public. The nature and character of these alternatives have varied from country to country, but nevertheless a series of common factors emerge. The first alternative, launched by Hollywood in 1953, was the wide-screen spectacular. A combination of anamorphic projection systems, large budgets, spectacular subjects, exotic locations and, at that time, color, offered the cinema-goer delights he could not hope to experience on the small screen. The high production costs of the large-scale film and the economic and other advantages of runaway production led to the internationalization of film production or, more precisely, to the massive penetration of European and other world markets by the major American companies. The extent of this penetration is now quite staggering, not only in terms of the number of American films seen, but also in the percentage of the total revenues that accrue to American companies, not merely through production, but also through the distribution and finance of European production.

▶ First published in *Film in Europe*. Vincent Porter (ed). Polytechnic of Central London 1974. Vincent Porter is Principal Lecturer in Film at the Polytechnic of Central London.

Table 1 CINEMA ATTENDANCE AND TELEVISION OWNERSHIP IN
THE EEC (1971)

Country	Population (millions)	Cinema Tickets (millions)	TV Sets (millions)	Cinema Visits per Year	TV Sets per 1000 Population
Belgium	9.7	27.6	2.02	2.85	208
Denmark	4.9	22.1	1.26	4.51	257
France	51.3	177.0	10.97	3.45	213
Germany	61.7	152.0	16.67	2.46	270
Ireland	2.9	28.0	0.50	9.66	172
Italy	54.8	535.7	10.24	9.77	186
Luxembourg	0.3	1.31	0.08	4.36	266
Netherlands	13.1	25.7	3.07	1.96	234
United Kingdom	55.7	182.0	17.2*	3.26	285

* Estimates. Figure adjusted upwards because of artificially low figure due to industrial action.

The competition between the cinema and television did not only produce the international large-budget picture however, it had other effects; in particular, the growth in sex, nudity and violence on the cinema screens, since this type of viewing fare is not normally available on the television screen. The predominance of teenagers among cinema audiences led also to a growth in films tailored to their taste, with large helpings of either rock music or political protest. Finally, there has also been a growth in the serious study of film, of the specialized cinema and the art house. In short, the cinema no longer appeals to a mass audience but to a series of specialized audiences—the affluent audience, the youth audience, the intellectual audience and the voyeurs. These trends are, however, overlaid by other factors. The most significant of those affecting cinema attendance is the programming policy of the national television networks.

As can be seen from Table 2, the programming policy throughout the EEC is by no means constant. However, it is the fiction programs, particularly the feature films, which, on all television networks, attract the largest audiences. As Belgian television points out:

> The attraction, particularly of fiction films, is such that in a country such as Belgium, which is largely covered by neighboring programs, it is noticeable that a section of the public regularly switches to foreign stations that are showing cinema films. It is an important element of competition, especially since the extension of television transmission and RTB has to take this factor into account all the time in programming its transmissions.[1]

For those countries, such as France and Italy, where for reasons of politics and geography there is a state television monopoly, the frequency with which feature films are screened can be used as a weapon in balancing the competition between cinema and television. In Italy, only two feature films are

Table 2 TELEVISION PROGRAMMING IN THE EEC (1971)

Country	Weekly Program hours (total)	Light Entertainment		Arts, Letters and Science	
		hours	percentage	hours	percentage
Belgium	99h.29m	12h.50m	12.90	9h.33m	9.59
Denmark ('70)	38.00	4.00	10.53	9.00	23.68
France	153.21	40.10	26.19	17.55	11.68
Ireland ('70)	55.05	20.15	37.85	1.10	2.12
Italy	110.00	20.00	18.18	5.00	4.55
Luxembourg	39.00	26.45	68.59	—	—
United Kingdom (70)	198.19	57.15	28.87	21.05	10.63

Source: UNESCO

screened each week and one of them is Italian. In France, under the "Declaration Commune" signed between the director general of ORTF and the Minister of Cultural Affairs in 1971,[2] ORTF undertook to limit the programming of feature films to those days and times when cinema attendances were high, to refrain from transmission on Saturday evenings and to reduce their frequency on Sunday afternoons. The result was that in 1972, attendances in French cinemas increased by 4.7 percent. Significantly however, in the regions of Nancy and Strasbourg, where it is possible for the French viewer to tune in to programs from German television, the decline in cinema audiences continued by a further 4 percent.[3]

In the United Kingdom, where there is a geographical if not a network monopoly, the independent companies are restricted by the IBA to showing not more than six feature films per week, of which not more than two are British. For the BBC however, there is no such restriction and over all three channels some thirteen or fourteen films are screened each week in the London area.[4] In the United Kingdom, as in West Germany, it is inter-channel competition that is the key factor in attracting audiences. In these countries, the feature film is only one of the weapons in the ratings war that is fought every night, attracting audiences not only from the other channel but also away from the cinema.

The Television Economy

There are basically two types of economic system for deciding how limited quantities of capital and talent may be used to their best advantage. These are the command economy and the market economy. In a command economy, the decisions as to what to produce, when to produce, by whom and at what cost are taken by a central authority—usually the State or one of its agencies. In a market economy, these decisions are made in the marketplace by the laws of supply and demand.

While there is no doubt that the major advantage of television over the cinema is its use of electronic distribution instead of physical distribution, there are several other ways in which the television economy differs from the cinema economy. These differences stem primarily from the command nature of the television economy compared with the market nature of the cinema economy.

The first factor is the captive nature of the audience. As has been shown, the political and geographical situations of French and Italian television make it possible for ORTF and RAI to ignore the demands of its audiences by depriving them of feature films, which are popular viewing fare, and transmitting instead programs that are culturally or politically "better" for them. Even in the United Kingdom, where the BBC and the Independent Television Companies are in competition, the pull of market forces is restricted by limitations on the number of feature films that may be screened each week, by an 86 percent British quota for the ITV companies (which, somewhat surprisingly, remains unmodified by the accession of the United Kingdom to the EEC), and, according to Tesler, Director of Programs for Thames Television, "by the very large part the IBA plays in the shaping of the ITV companies schedules."[5] In scheduling minute-by-minute competition, the BBC and the IBA ensure that, to a large extent, the captive audience can only escape to a program of a similar nature. Feature film competes with feature film, current affairs program with current affairs program, and so on. The captive nature of the television audience does however make it possible for the television organizations to schedule a range of programs that are appealing to various sections of the population, to minority as well as majority audiences, to puritans as well as hedonists.

The command nature of the television economy has implications beyond

Table 3 TV PROGRAM COSTS AND AUDIENCES (1970)

Program	Type	Cost per Hour	Source	Audience (in millions)	Cost per Viewer	
British Film Night	Feature Film	£4,000	Bought	12.7	£3.1.	10^{-4}
The Virginian	Western Series	£4,000	Bought	11.3	£3.5.	10^{-4}
Blue Peter	Children's Program	£4,000	Produced	5.4	£7.4.	10^{-4}
Sportsnight with Coleman	Live Sports Program	£6,000	Produced	8.9	£6.7.	10^{-4}
Omnibus	Arts Program	£8–12,000	Produced	3.2	£25–37.5.	10^{-4}
Softly, Softly	Police Series	£25,000	Produced	10.9	£22.9	10^{-4}
The Dave Allen Show	Light Entertainment	£25,000	Produced	9.7	£25.8	10^{-4}
The Wednesday Play	Modern Drama	£25,000	Produced	5.8	£43.1	10^{-4}

the type and quality of programs available to the television viewer. The ability of the vertically integrated television organization to decide how its overall program budget is to be distributed between individual programs also gives it tremendous power in the allocation of resources. Table 3, drawn from a survey of British television in 1970,[6] illustrates the general principles.

Two clear conclusions may be drawn from these figures. First, it is the bought programs that are substantially cheaper than the produced programs and that command larger audiences. Second, of those programs that are produced by the television organization, it is those that are least efficient when analyzed on a cost-per-viewer-hour basis that have contributed most to the long-term cultural health of British film. The low cost to television of bought programs is an international phenomenon and is common to all countries of the European Community as Table 4, which is taken from a recent survey in the trade press,[7] shows.

The reasons for these low purchase prices for film material stems partly from the monopolistic bargaining position of the television companies, but it also arises because all of the product has already been "consumed," either worldwide in the cinema or on United States television. For the sellers of the product, the revenues are bonuses that accrue after recouping most, if not all, of their production costs from other markets. Conversely, no producer can afford to plan an independent production that aims to recoup its costs from the European television market alone. The low purchase price of film material for television does of course permit television organizations to produce their own material for their own market and to distribute the program costs according to their own internal policy. As Table 3 shows, the BBC, using this command of its own resources, was able to effectively subsidize programs such as *The*

Table 4 PRICES FOR FILMS ON TV (1973)

Country	Half Hour TV Series*	Feature Film
Belgium	$ 400– 600	$ 1200– 2000
Denmark	$ 200– 250	$ 1000– 1200
France	$ 2700–3000	$ 7000– 8000
Germany (West)	$ 3000–3500 (undubbed)	$ 4000–16000 (dubbed)
Ireland	$ 70– 75	$ 275– 300
Italy	$ 600– 900	$ 5000– 6000
Luxembourg	$ 160– 200	$ 175– 225
Netherlands	$ 550– 575	$ 1850
United Kingdom	$ 3500–4200	$18000–30000
TOTAL	$11180–$13300	$45500–$65575

* One hour episodes are approximately twice the price of half-hour episodes

Wednesday Play and *Omnibus* at some ten to fourteen times more the cost-per-viewer-hour than for the *British Film Night*.

The policy of producing new television plays and programs about the arts, such as *Omnibus*, is defensible however, not simply because they satisfy the tastes of a middle-class cultural elite, but also because they have been soil where much new cultural talent was nurtured and developed. The predecessor to *Omnibus* was *Monitor*, where talents such as John Schlesinger and Ken Russell learned and practiced their craft before making their film distributors substantial profits with films such as *Midnight Cowboy* and *Women in Love*. The *Wednesday Play* also nurtured talents such as Tony Garnett and Ken Loach, who went on to make *Kes* and *Family Life*. Programs such as those they made on television, although highly inefficient in terms of a market economy, are essential to the long-term cultural health of the industry.

The BBC strategy of using the financial benefits of the low purchase price of films and TV series for the benefit of long-term cultural development is employed all over Europe. However, it is not the only strategy available to a television organization. The others are the commercial strategy and the co-production strategy. The leading exponent of the commercial strategy in Europe is Associated Television and its film production arm, ITC. Three times winner of the Queen's Award for Exports, ATV has made television series such as *The Saint, The Avengers, Danger Man, Department S* and *The Persuaders*. The main world market for ventures of this nature is, of course, network United States television. The antithesis between culture and commerce, between the command economy and the market economy is starkly illustrated by comparing the approach of the BBC as outlined above with that of ATV. Whereas the command economy is able, to a large extent, to subsidize certain programs against the pressures of the marketplace, the market economy embraces these pressures willingly. Commercial success lies in giving the customer (i.e., the US television networks) what he wants. "The key factor is US agreement on the concept and the scripts for a successful and profitable global sale," writes Anthony Gruner of Talbot Television,[8] and again, "United States partners must be consulted on *all aspects* of production"[9] (my emphasis). Again, Larry Gelbart, who wrote and produced the *Marty Feldman Series*, an ATV comedy series, states: "No special British references are allowed in the scripts, and regional accents are discouraged. A censor from the American network sat in the gallery throughout the recording. She was not called a censor, of course. They are given some euphemistic title like Department of Continuity Practice, but censor she was. She blue penciled everything from long hair to bad language, but her chief concern was to avoid any excess of nudity or cleavage."[10] While, however, the public of middle America, of Omaha, Nebraska or of Peru, Indiana, may be disturbed by a little female flesh, its capacity for violence is stronger than that of the United Kingdom. Both *The Avengers* and *The Saint* have occasionally been toned down for *British* audiences according to one source.[11]

The alternative strategy to the commercial strategy is the strategy of co-production. This strategy, which is not, of course, confined to television, has been most popular in France, Italy and Spain with their similar backgrounds of romance culture and languages and the Roman Catholic religion. The co-production strategy was primarily a defense strategy against the mid-Atlantic WASP hegemony of Western culture. The co-production strategy has moved in two fundamental directions. The first between television and film, which we shall consider later, and the second, in the field of international television co-production. The most frequent partners have been ORTF in France, RAI in Italy, TVE in Spain and, occasionally, Bayerische Rundfunk in Germany. Television co-productions offer three advantages. They can be a source of revenue for additional sales, they offer a means of extending the sphere of influence of the producing network, and, of course, they reduce the production costs. Although the details of co-production contracts vary, a typical deal might be the "troika" system, where three networks nominate a program or series and each network would agree to take one or more programs from each of the other partners.

Despite the theoretical advantages of the co-production strategy, program quality and hence costs tend to be pushed upwards in order to satisfy partners. Ultimately, the co-producers look to recoup costs from sales, and naturally their eyes turn toward the lucrative markets of the United Kingdom and the United States. Because the statutory 14 per cent foreign quota of the independent Companies and the voluntary 15 per cent quota of the BBC is nearly all allocated to United States product, the United Kingdom market is virtually closed to this type of production. Only one European TV series that has not been made in the United Kingdom has so far been sold to United States network television—the RAI/ORTF *Leonardo da Vinci*—which achieved the distinction of being the first dubbed series on network television.

The financing of a television series is dominated by the outlet and there is no question that one or more major outlets are critical to commercial success. Another essential is an international distribution organization. It is not surprising therefore that in the field of the television series, the co-production strategy has combined with, or perhaps more correctly, yielded to, the commercial strategy. The limited foreign sales, and the impossibly high costs of making twenty-six or even thirty-two episode series for the United States market has led both ORTF and RAI to join ATV in co-production deals worth about £5 million. The Anglo-Italian ventures announced include *The Life and Times of William Shakespeare, The Origins of the Mafia, Space 1999* and *Moses the Lawgiver* (previously known as *The Ten Commandments*), while liaison with ORTF promises twenty-four 1-hour episodes of *Cabsmash*. According to Sir Lew Grade, head of ATV, "Our potential partners look at us and know they will stand an excellent chance of seeing our joint efforts on the screens in up to a hundred and twenty different countries. And also of seeing their national identities displayed."[12] A marvelous prospect indeed.

At a deeper level, however, the vision is slightly less rosy. Commercially there is little doubt that the series will be profitable. What is of concern is the cultural price that must be paid for commercial success. The final answer cannot of course be given until the programs are screened, but early omens indicate that despite the different subjects, the mixture will be as before. All of the co-productions will be shot in English,[13] but more than that, as Bernard Kingham, a director and General Manager of ITC makes clear, a typical European co-production might provide for "production to be in the hands of the British partner, the Continental partner having rights of consultation and also the right to contribute or nominate certain factors"[14] because "production must vest in him so that the series may qualify British quota."[15]

Although it is possible to recoup something like 40 percent of the finance for a television series from the United Kingdom market,[16] the series must still meet the demands of the United States network—or as Kingham puts it, "it would be most imprudent to mount such a series without a pre-sale."[17] Commercial strategy is dangerously close to being a commissioned strategy with United States television as the sponsor.

The Cinema Economy

In contrast to the television economy, the cinema economy is, at first sight, much closer to a market economy. Indeed, when the cinema economies of both the United States and the United Kingdom threatened to assume some of the characteristics of a command economy through the vertical integration of production, distribution and exhibition, the governments of both countries acted to introduce more free market competition into the system. Between 1938 and 1952, the United States Department of Justice sought to break the oligopoly of the major motion picture companies in the courts claiming that there was "a combination and conspiracy to restrain and monopolize interstate trade and commerce," which resulted in a series of decisions by the United States Supreme Court, the most famous of which was the decision requiring the major motion picture companies to divorce their production and distribution interests from their exhibition outlets. In the United Kingdom, the government requested the Monopolies Commission to report on the supply of films for exhibition in cinemas. When they reported in 1966, they found that "the introduction of a larger measure of competition into film exhibition . . . would be advantageous to the industry," although they stepped back from the logical outcome of their conclusion, which would have been to break up the exhibition circuits. Which they felt would be "a drastic step of which the results would be uncertain."[18]

The dilemma in which the Monopolies Commission found itself reflects the relevance that a free market economy has to the ideal form of the cinema economy. Although more than one-third by value of the films supplied to exhibitors in Great Britain were supplied to companies with the Rank Organization, which was clearly a breach of the Monopolies Act, it had to be recognized that in breaking up the Rank circuit, the financial rewards would most likely be spread more thinly, and "unless the number of admissions or the level of seat prices were substantially increased, the average return on each film would be lower than it is now. To that extent the financial incentive to additional British production would be reduced."[19]

The message is clear, economically, that the tendencies toward monopoly are more efficient in the short term, even though the choice of films may appear to be more restricted—and therefore, from an exhibitor's point of view, unduly limiting.

The contention that the divorcement of production and distribution from exhibition offers a wider consumer choice and gives the smaller exhibitor a chance to offer a better service than his bigger competitor is, however, open to serious doubt. The results of divorcement in the United States coincided with the growth of competition from television, but nevertheless there are strong indications that life for the small exhibitor in the United States was harder in the 1950s not only because of television but also because of divorcement.

The results of divorcement were criticized both by the exhibitors and the distributors and one of the results of the new practice of competitive bidding for product by exhibitors was "that small exhibitors who have relied for an adequate supply of films on some traditional friendly relationship with a distributor, may, when faced with competitive bidding, lose all the advantages of this relationship and become less instead of more able to compete with a large neighbor or circuit."[20] It was the small and medium-size exhibitors who were most vociferous in criticizing the system.[21] More time, and therefore more money had to be spent both by producers in "selling" pictures and by exhibitors in "buying" them. Small wonder then that the distributor assumed a role far more important than before. "Qui tient la distribution, tient le cinema." The French adage is even more true today. The growth of the distributor, particularly the American distributor, as distributor and financier for the majority of feature films made today is well known. The power wielded by the major distributors is so strong that in many ways the cinema has come to resemble a command economy in all respects except one—that of commanding the audiences to pay to see the film.

The root of the power of the distributor lies in the unique combination of distribution and finance combined with the very large sums of money involved. It is not possible to finance a series of films unless they are distributed to the cinemas. Equally, it is not possible to distribute films on a large scale unless a flow of product can be assured. Distributors that have given up financing of production, such as the Rank Organization, have ceased to be world film distributors of stature. Equally, production companies such as ABC, which in the six years from 1966 to 1972 invested some $80 million in film production, found that production without international distribution could be equally ruinous, as Table 5 shows.

For in a cinema economy, the distribution fees, and, some would claim, the print and advertising costs, do not represent the real costs. In a command economy, distribution is little more than the shipping prints from place to place. The distribution fee includes a substantial fee for handling the picture,

Table 5 36 ABC Films (1966–1972)

	$ Million	$ Million
Domestic Rentals	75.275	
Foreign Rentals	31.815	
TOTAL RENTALS	107.090	
Negative Costs		75.460
Bank Loan Interest		10.250
Participations		4.925
Distribution Fees		27.278
Prints and Advertising		36.250
TOTAL COSTS		154.433
NET LOSS		47.343

Source: *Variety*. 30 May 1973.

which can be reinvested in new production. Over a substantial investment program, the box office successes cross-finance the box office losses. The major distributors are slowly but surely taking over the cinema economy. The key to their success is in their size, and their policy of risk spreading is akin to backing all the horses in the race—that way film finance becomes less of a gamble. The only way to lose is if the racetrack closes down. Far from being a market economy, the cinema economy is almost a command economy. The cinemas depend on the distributor for product, the producer depends on the distributor for finance. The distributors do, however, have an Achilles' heel—the exhibitor. In the chameleon-like world of finance and asset-stripping, the cinema is not only a cinema, it is also a piece of real estate. Cinema owners continue to remain unsure of whether they are film exhibitors or property developers. Once it becomes more profitable to develop cinema sites for other uses, the distributors will start to lose a major percentage of their outlets—leaving only television to the main outlet.

The Stable State Economy

The energy crisis that now besets the indistrialized world and the commodity crisis that may soon accompany it, will almost certainly mean that filmmakers, like many other manufacturers, will have to cease thinking automatically about living in a growth economy and switch to considering their position in a stable-state economy. In this new state of affairs, television can be seen to have the crucial weakness of being extremely voracious in its consumption of product. The notion of repeating programs in television has until now been thought of as a weakness. It is a point of view that may well change.

The recycling of product may not simply lead to the replaying of old movies, it may lead to a new type of product. New product might be thought desirable, if it was not comprehensible on the first viewing, so that several reviewings were necessary in order to understand the film. Alternatively, imagine the creative possibilities of putting all the Hollywood films of the thirties onto a RAVE computer. The various compilations and re-edits that could be produced is beyond belief.

Whatever possibilities do emerge, however, one thing is clear. The copyright owners of all material, old and new, will receive a further bonus for their coffers. Indeed, it is questionable whether the principles on which all the International Copyright Conventions were based will continue to be observed, for the assumptions underlying the undertakings to sign the Conventions are all changing.

The relationship between cinema and television may also change. Not only has motoring become significantly more expensive as a leisure-time activity, but according to a recent report,[22] the decision to close cinemas and theatres in Rome at 11 p.m. sent people home and there was a rise in electricity consumption. The logical way to save power it would seem, is to limit television viewing hours and encourage people to go to the cinemas.

The Film Economy

The production of films can only be planned in conjunction with an analysis of how they are viewed. The traditional viewing outlets of the cinema and television are currently complementary outlets for product and competitors for the viewer's attention. Other outlets such as cable television and video-cassettes loom as future possibilities, but it is doubtful how far the technical possibilities of these systems will become economically significant. In the United States, the capital markets have become cautious with regard to the speculative risks of cable investment,[23] and the much talked about video-cassette boom is dependent on a general expansion of consumer affluence, which looks increasingly unlikely until the international energy and commodity crises have been resolved. Any film strategy therefore should continue to be conceived primarily in terms of the cinema and television.

The only film companies with a clear strategy toward *both* the cinema and television are, of course, the American majors. According to the MPAA/MPEA, its worldwide sales to television are about a third of the gross revenue derived from theatrical exhibition;[24] at the same time, they supply some 70 percent of the prime-time programming on the three national television networks.[25] This latter figure includes both television film series and feature films. The one revenue factor omitted from the revenue account in Table 5 is, of course, the sale of the films to television. ABC's own financial breakdown anticipated a flat $816,000 per feature ($960,000 less 15 percent expenses) for television network and syndication sales,[26] which, even if optimistic, indicates a revenue from the United States television market of the order of ten times that from the EEC market (see Table 4). Thus, although the cinema box office throughout the whole of the EEC is of the same order of size as that of the

United States ($1,000 million: $1,300 million), the free market price in films for television is lower in Europe by a factor of ten.

The result of the low TV market price for product in Europe has been the growth of film production for television, either by the television companies themselves or in co-production, effectively subsidized by the cheap market price of independent product, which has in turn boosted the audience ratings. At the same time, TV license fees have remained low, making television very competitive with the cinema. Also, film aid levies, entertainment taxes and indeed VAT have all pushed up the prices of cinema seats, making them less competitive with television. The dilemma of European production is that it is trying to operate a free market economy between the command economies of the European television networks on one side and the command economies of the American film distributors on the other. The only way forward is to set up a structure for European film production that has substantial elements of a command economy and that can compete as a genuine third force with its television and trans-Atlantic rivals.

The ways in which this third force may develop are many. Nevertheless, it is possible to outline a series of characteristics that would be desirable. First of all, such a force should be able to guarantee outlets for its product. These outlets might be in the cinemas or on television—or perhaps both. Second, the force should be able to finance its own product. This should not be carried out piecemeal, but on a scale large enough to spread the investment risk across several pictures. The finance might come from the private sector, or from the public sector, or indeed from a mixture of both. Third, the force should carry within itself a degree of competition—to avoid the complacency bred by monopolistic supremacy, but limited enough to prevent unnecessary waste of resources, and to ensure the maximum exposure of product. The nature of the competition within this force will be determined by its constituent groupings, and the nature of these groupings will in turn affect the type of product and perhaps the long-term success or failure of the enterprise. The two most obvious ways in which the competition might develop is either on a national basis between nations or between multi-national companies.

Although there are tendencies toward cultural nationalization in Italy where, for example, RAI pays substantially higher fees for Italian feature films than for foreign films and produces large numbers of "cultural" co-productions with private film companies, the move toward the development of a para-state film industry is most clearly formalized in France. The "Declaration Commune" between the Minister of Cultural Affairs and the Director General of ORTF makes provisions for ORTF to supply some ten million francs to the cinema. Approximately half of this is to be invested in co-productions with private French film companies, with ORTF as the minority partner. The other half is to be contributed to the film aid fund, in return for which ORTF is to have representatives on most of the consultative and deliberative committees of the Centre Nationale or of the Ministry, including the commission for advances against receipts. The Gaullist view that "la télévision c'est le Gouvernement dans la Salle à Manger" makes one fearful that ORTF may aspire also to be "le Gouvernement dans le cinéma." The real danger for Europe, in the nationalistic approach, however, is that the culture of the smaller countries will go to the wall. The economic power of Ireland or of Denmark can offer little competition against the larger members of the community. In Belgium, even though half of the country speaks the same language as France, there is a heavy dependence on the francophone market in France. In the field of television, as RTB makes quite clear, "the criteria and needs of ORTF are not those of Belgium."[27]

Not only is the path to nationalism economically unsound, leading to the balkanization of Europe, it also makes culture the pawn of the government, who, through their control of television, its funding and its senior appointments, may very quickly turn a national culture into a State culture. While television may legitimately concern itself with national needs, the cinema is international. The growth of the multi-national company is the obvious way in which internationalism in the cinema can grow. Indeed, such companies already exist in the film world, although most of them are United States controlled or dominated. The peculiar nature of the film industry, which basically requires no investment in property or factories, makes multi-national companies virtually impossible for governments to control. Whereas an oil company may be bypassed by direct government to government deals between supplier and purchaser, this is not possible for the motion picture multi-national. It may be possible to prevent revenues from leaving the country, but frozen revenues reinvested in new productions do not solve the problem, they simply postpone it, as post war experience in Europe showed. No government can afford to have its policies determined by companies over whom they have no control.

A more modest move toward internationalism has been made by the growth of international co-productions ratified by co-production treaties, particularly between member states of the Community. While these treaties may be able to generate the finance and the market necessary for a feature film of international stature, the system suffers from two main disadvantages. The legalistic red tape and bureaucracy necessary to decide whether any one film fulfills the nationality criteria of both signatories makes the integration of art and commerce subject to the obstacles of legalistic fine print and bureaucratic haggling. More seriously, all co-production contracts are conceived in terms of one film only rather than in terms of a program of films, thus ensuring that, for example, two sources of finance yield two Anglo-Italian films rather than one British film and one Italian which might recoup in both markets. Not only does such a policy stultify cultural adventure, but perhaps more importantly, it mitigates against the long-term diversification of risk taking, which has been one of the keys to the strength of the United States majors. More seriously again, the proposal for a multilateral co-production treaty, which is currently under discussion in the Community, is bogged down in international bureaucratic haggling by civil servants whose prime concern is to defend their own national interest and who are neither briefed nor expected to think on an international scale.

Various proposals have been made by CICREC and FIAD for setting up a European Film Finance Corporation and for setting up chains of European Film Distributors. Proposals have also been made for the harmonization of film aids and, more radically, for putting these aids into a Community pool. All of these if brought together could form the basis of a European film force. But there are other elements that should not be ignored. The cinemas too are part of the film world and they should be integrated with distribution and finance. Furthermore, it is questionable these days whether the film aid funds should continue to come from a tax on cinema seats as they do in France, Germany and the United Kingdom. Television has clearly built up its own production strategies on the basis of the low market prices of old feature films and American television series; the question should now be asked as to whether the time has not come for television to repay the debt it owes to the film producers of Europe by contributing substantial payments to a European film fund. Such a fund, if established, could be used as finance for a European Film Industries Reorganization Corporation, which could stimulate the mergers, cross-financing and vertical integrations necessary to build a European film industry with a healthy long-term future.

One caveat remains, however. The establishment of a European film force, which could clearly occupy the commanding heights of the cultural economy of Europe, and the injection of large funds from the public sector into this force must mean that private enterprise must be answerable to public authority. After all, if the constituent elements of the European force are to become the guardians of our cultures, then must we not also ask, "Quis custodit ipso custodes?"

NOTES

[1] Radiodiffusion–Television Belge, *Rapport d'Activite 71–72* (Brussels, 1972), p. 106.

[2] Centre National de la Cinematographie, "Declaration Commune Cinema—ORTF," in *Bulletin d'Information du CNC*. no. 133 (Paris, February 1972).

[3] Centre National de la Cinematographie, *Activite Cinematographique Francaise en 1972.* Supplement to *Bulletin d'Information*, no. 140–41 (Paris April–June 1973).

[4] E. Buscombe, *Films on TV*, SEFT/UNESCO (London 1972).

[5] B. Tesler, *The Art and Craft of Programme Control—ITV*, BBTA Bulletin 19 (London, May 1973).

[6] C. F. Pratten, *The Economics of Television*, PEP Broadsheet 520 (London, September 1970).

[7] *Variety* (4 April 1973).

[8] *Variety* (4 April 1973), p. 68.

[9] *Ibid*.

[10] *Quoted in N. Garnham, We Apologize for the American Interference on Your Screen*, Observer Colour Supplement (London, 15 June 1972).

[11] T. Green, *The Universal Eye*, Chap. 6 (Bodley Head, London, 1972).

[12] Quoted in Bill Hughes, "*Sir Lew Sets an Example and Leads TV into Europe*," *Cinema TV Today* (24 November 1973).

[13] *Ibid.*

[14] Bernard Kingham, *Financing the Production of a TV Series.* Film Finance no. 5 (London, May 1972).

[15] *Ibid.*

[16] *Ibid.*

[17] *Ibid.*

[18] The Monopolies Commission, *Films, a Report on the Supply of Films for Exhibition in Cinemas*, para. 261 (H.M.S.O., 1966).

[19] *Ibid.*, para 241.

[20] Ralph Cassady, Jr., "Impact of the Paramount Decision on Motion Picture Distribution and Price Making," in *Southern Californian Law Review 1958* 31: 150–80.

[21] *Ibid.*

[22] *Evening Standard* (London, 4 December 1973).

[23] Honourable Dean Burch, *Cable Television: The US Experience* (Paper read before the UK Standing Conference on Broadcasting, London, 17 November 1973).

[24] Motion Picture Association of America and Motion Picture Export Association of America, *1972: A Review of the World of Movies* (New York, 1973), p. 28.

[25] *Ibid.*

[26] *Variety* (30 May 1973), p. 5.

[27] Radiodiffusion–Television Belge, *op. cit.*

Graham Murdock and James D. Halloran:

Contexts of Creativity in Television Drama:
An Exploratory Study in Britain

Introduction

☆ THIS PAPER SETS OUT to throw some light on the factors affecting drama production in British commercial television, through an exploratory study of one of the major program companies—ATV Network Ltd.

Drama currently occupies a key place in the output of the commercial companies. In an average week, almost a quarter of the total broadcast time is taken up with plays and episodes from dramatic serials and series, making drama the largest single category of programming. This dominance also extends to the ratings. Most weeks, installments from the two major "soap operas," ATV's *Crossroads* and Granada's *Coronation Street*, provide half of the shows in the Top Ten, with episodes from successful series like *The Sweeney* and *Upstairs, Downstairs* usually contributing two or three more. These raw figures are corroborated by the findings of a variety of other audience studies, and all in all, there is little doubt that watching drama plays a central role in most people's television experience.

This fact has not gone unnoticed. On the contrary, it has been the subject of widespread comment and concern among politicians, commentators and moral crusaders. Indeed, the long-standing debate about the effects of television has frequently focused on drama programs, particularly those portraying acts of violence an aggression. A similar concentration of attention has also characterized research, producing a large number of studies mapping the values and social images caried by television fiction and an even larger number exploring audience responses. A great deal more work still needs to be done in both these areas, but at least the existing studies of content and response provide a departure point for future work. When we turn to questions of production, however,

▶ This is an original article written especially for this book. Graham Murdock is engaged in research at the Centre for Mass Communication Research at the University of Leicester, England. Professor James D. Halloran is director of the Centre.

the situation is rather different, since the number of studies can almost be counted on the fingers of one hand. The analysis of television production has always been the poor relation of broadcasting research, but even so, drama production stands out as one of the least developed areas in a generally under-developed field. Although the last five or six years have seen a revival of interest in questions of production among media researchers on both sides of the Atlantic, most of the resulting studies have concentrated on actuality television—on news, current affairs and documentaries. This work was certainly long overdue and it has added very considerably to our knowledge, but unfortunately it has not so far been matched by a comparable series of studies of fiction and entertainment production. Paradoxically then, we know least about the production of the very programs that are the most popular with viewers. This paper aims to contribute to redressing this imbalance. We would, however, stress the limited and exploratory nature of the study reported here. The aim was to indicate questions for future research, not to provide answers. Before outlining the project in more detail, however, we first need to situate it more generally by briefly outlining the kind of work that needs to be done in this area.

Basically we can distinguish four main types of research approach:

1. *Production studies*, which trace the progress of specific programs from initial idea to final transmission, looking particularly at the factors influencing the decisions made at various stages in the process. So far, the only British account of these processes come either from participants, usually scriptwriters, or from journalist observers.[1] As yet there is no sociological analysis of drama production to set alongside Philip Elliott's pioneering study of the making of a current affairs series.[2]

2. *Organizational studies*, as their title suggests, focus on organizational units beyond the production team. These range from particular departments or sectors, as in the present research, up to entire broadcasting organizations, as in Professor Tom Burns's well-known work on the BBC.[3] Unfortunately, however, there is no equivalent study of a British commercial television company.

3. *Context studies* focus on the interrelations between media organizations and the cultural, political and economic environments in which they are embedded, and attempt to trace the influence of these contexts on their operations and output.

4. *Occupational studies* go beyond the situation in particular organizations to examine production personnel in a cross section of contexts. The aim is the build-up of a social and professional profile of key occupational groups, such as producers, directors and writers. To this end, studies usually cover such things as social background, patterns of recruitment and career, work situation and views of the job. Muriel Cantor's study of Hollywood television series producers and Joan Moore's work on scriptwriters are well-known examples.[4] So far there is nothing comparable in Britain, although interviews conducted by journalists often provide valuable basic information.[5]

These various approaches are complementary. Each has its particular strengths and each offers essential information and insight into the dynamics of production. Consequently, in an ideal research situation all four levels would be incorporated. Usually, however, one has to compromise with contingency, and the study reported here is no exception.

The biggest problem was time. The study was originally undertaken at the request of the organizers of the Prix Italia as a contribution to the proposed research symposium on fiction production in television.[6] However, the time from the date the research was commissioned to the dedline for the final report for the conference was less than six months. This immediately ruled out certain research strategies on practical grounds. It would, for example, have been impossible to undertake either a full-blown occupational study or detailed production studies. After considering the remaining options, the most feasible appeared to be a case study of drama production in one particular company. Here we were fortunate to secure the cooperation of ATV Network Limited, one of Britains biggest and most successful commercial television companies, and one of the few to collaborate with academic researchers on a regular basis. They gave us every help with the study, arranging interviews with production personnel at a variety of levels and providing access to relevant company documents. Drawing on this material, the present paper attempts to outline the main contexts within which drama production operates and the pressures they exert; to suggest some of the ways in which these impinge on program making; and to point to the variations in the way that drama personnel perceive the situation and respond to it. In terms of the four approaches outlined earlier, the present study attempts to combine organizational and contextural analysis.

Contexts of Production

ATV is a commercial company, and as such its continued viability and growth depend in the last analysis on its ability to maintain and increase its level of profitability. Not surprisingly then, questions of cost and revenue figure prominently in production decisions at every level. As one producer put it:

> Everyone who works in commercial television has to be aware of commerce— of money . . . you can't go mad and overspend your budget three times in the name of art. I think that there will always be this kind of hedging—this uneasy balance between artistic considerations and commercial considerations.

Economic criteria are applied unevenly, however. By no means all programs are expected to be money-spinners or even to cover their costs. Some stem from the personal enthusiasms and commitments of creative and executive personnel, others from the desire to increase the company's prestige and professional standing among critics and fellow broadcasters, others still from a combination of the two. Occasionally, a prestige production will also command high ratings. ATV's dramatization of the life of *Edward VII* for example, attracted both widespread critical acclaim and a large popular audience. But this is comparatively rare. As one executive put it: "That's having your cake and eating it." More often than not, however, prestige productions are not success-ful commercially. ATV's adaptation of the Royal Shakespeare Company's pro-duction of *Anthony and Cleopatra* is a case in point. At the time it was made, this was one of the most expensive productions ever mounted by a British tele-vision company. It received very good reviews and was voted best single play of 1974 by the Society of Film and Television Arts, but according to one senior executive, it is highly unlikely that the program will ever recoup its costs. There are, however, certain intangible returns on these sorts of prestige produc-tions. They may, for example, make it easier to attract top-flight actors, writers and directors to the company in the future. They may also enhance the com-pany's general image and strengthen its bargaining power vis-a-vis the Indepen-dent Broadcasting Authority, the regulatory body in charge of renewing the franchises and overseeing the general operations of the commercial system. Al-though they are a commercial undertaking, ATV and the other independent program companies do not operate in a pure "free market" situation. They can-not simply pursue their own organizational goals; they must also satisfy the requirements of the Authority.

As the official custodian of the public interest, the IBA lays down certain guidelines designed to ensure the variety and balance of commercial pro-gramming. The large companies like ATV, for example, are required to pro-duce a certain number of single plays per year, although these are generally both more costly and less popular than series or serials. The companies are also expected to reflect the distinctive character of the regions in which they are based acrosss a range of programs. However, it is often possible to fulfill these requirements without jettisoning prior commitments to profitability or prestige. ATV's long-running and very successful soap opera *Crossroads*, for example, is set in a motel on the edge of the Birmingham conurbation, thereby neatly combining high ratings with a regional slant. Other examples include the com-pany's popular police series *Hunter's Walk*, which is set in a small Midlands town, and their prestigious serialization of Arnold Bennett's *Clayhanger* books, which are based in the area around Stoke-on-Trent, another of the region's major towns. In adition to satisfying the IBA, however, the company is also centrally involved in the network system, and this imposes a further set of con-straints and pressures.

There are two types of commercial television companies in Britain, the network companies and the regional companies. Network companies are based in the revenue-rich population centers of London (Thames Television and London Weekend Television), the Midlands (ATV), Lancashire (Granada) and Yorkshire and Tyneside (Trident). The regional companies serve the remaining areas, most of which have relatively low population densities and therefore less revenue potential. Consequently, they operate on an altogether smaller scale, since they have neither the capital nor the production resources to compete ef-fectively with the major companies. The smallest regional concerns mainly confine themselves to producing the regional news and current affairs programs required by the IBA. The larger companies offer a more ambitious range of programs and some have acquired considerable reputation in certain specialist areas. Anglia Television, for example, has achieved universal acclaim and regular national networking with its wild life documentaries. But these are exceptions. By and large, the bulk of the regional companies' schedules are made up of programs originated by the five largest companies. So, although these companies are based in particular regions, most of their major programs are produced for the national network, hence their title, network companies. Besides the influence of the IBA, therefore, the commercial television schedules are also the product of the complex bargaining between the network companies as each bids to ensure that their programs are given national exposure in favorable slots.

This system has repercussions for program planning within companies, since they are obliged to take account of the others' proposals when thinking about their future productions. Under the network system, for example, each of the major companies is expected to produce one thirteen-part drama series for network showing each year. However, their choice of theme is heavily influenced by what their competitors are planning. As one of our repondents explained:

> (Our) drama policy fits into the pattern of network requirements. Now what thirteen part series shall we do next year to fulfill our commitment to the network between such and such a date? Do we put in a police series? No, it's no good putting in a police series because Thames would have done *The Sweeney* the previous thirteen weeks. . . . What sort of anthology series shall we do? . . . You obviously would not want to do six plays about the life of a policeman.

Besides shaping program decisions in these kinds of direct ways, the competition between the companies impinges on production more subtly. Over the years, the various companies have evolved distinctive production philosophies that define their approach to program making and give their productions a stamp that distinguishes them from similar material produced by their competitors. ATV personnel, for example, experienced no difficulty in explaining how their police series, one-shot plays and so on differed from those of the other network companies. This kind of product differentiation serves two purposes. It helps to cement corporate identity and it avoids head-on clashes of interest between the major companies. It is a response to competition and also a way of regulating it.

To a large extent, these "house" program philosophies reflect the values and preferences of the companies' key decision makers and their accumulated responses to the various pressures on production. In the case of ATV, there is little doubt that the prevailing company philosophy bears the imprint of the Chairman, Sir Lew Grade. His views help to define the general parameters of production by specifying what is and is not considered appropriate to an ATV program. As he explained in a recent interview:[7]

> I'm against nudity and bad language. I'm vigorously against them on the screen in the home. . . . I'm shocked even now when I hear bad language on television. . . . I'm shocked every time I see a woman with her breasts ex-

posed . . . it won't be my show. My company understands how I feel about these things.

Judging from the interviews conducted for this study, employees did indeed understand these embargoes. While some accepted them as an inevitable fact of company life, others actively endorsed them and added excessive violence and heavy drinking to the list of things that the company generally avoided in its productions. These strictures are not enforced through the direct personal intervention of members of the higher echelons or by explicit censorship procedures; rather they are embedded in the company's overall drama policy and in the general ethos that prevades the organizations and informs production decisions at all levels. This ethos marks out the boundaries of acceptability and defines the overall framework of assumptions within which work proceeds. Becoming a member of the organization means learning to recognize the contours and characteristics of the company ethos and finding ways of working within it while still preserving and promoting one's own personal enthusiasms and commitments. As well as the exclusions, however, respondents also mentioned a number of positive features of the company's drama ethos. These included: a commitment to mass entertainment as an end in itself, an endorsement of social relevance as against the political tub-thumping they saw as characteristic of some of the other companies, a penchant for spectacular star-studded productions and an insistence on the highest standards of technical excellence in every aspect of program making.

The emphasis given to these various elements in specific situations varies considerbly, depending on the nature of the production and the specific commitments of the people involved. And as we shall see later, the possible combinations are often more complex than many commentators have made out. However, it is important to bear in mind that the mix, arrived at in particular productions, is shaped not only by the motivations of creative personnel, but also by the interplay of pressures exerted by the various contents in which production is embedded. Of these, we have chosen the economic context for special consideration in the present paper. There is a good reason for this. Other things being equal, commerial considerations are likely to increase in importance during periods of economic recession. As one respondent put it:

> . . . it is the ratings that matter in the end. They are honest businessmen here, but they are businessmen—businessmen first and artists very much second. In good times, when the money is flowing, it's nice to have prestige as well as the shekels . . . but when the chips are down, the businessman will argue—and he's absolutely right—that it's a fat lot of good me creating things that get prestige and the public don't view it.

At the time the interviews were conducted (in the spring and early summer of 1976), British commercial television was emerging from one of its periodic recessions in revenue. Hence, the situation presented an excellent opportunity to throw some empirical light on the much-discussed issue of "creativity versus commerce." Consequently, exploring the ways in which economic considerations impinged on program making became one of the main themes of the study.

Commerce and Creativity

Economic factors impinge on drama production at a variety of levels, from overall policy to the content and style of particular programs. The most general impact has been to reinforce the squeeze on one-shot plays and concentrate production on series and serials.

In its early days of operation, the company produced over twenty single plays a year. Over the years, however, this figure has been gradually whittled away until at the time of the study it was down to single figures. The reasons for this cutback are complex, but questions of cost and revenue have certainly been an important consideration. In the first place, single plays are relatively expensive to produce. Unlike serials and series episodes, each one requires a new set, and construction costs have been one of the fastest rising areas of expenditure in recent years. Nor have mushrooming costs been met with increased audiences. On the contrary, from a peak in the early sixties, the audience for single plays has generally fallen away. Several explanations for this have been suggested. Some commentators have argued that audiences have become bored with the "slice of life" plays that dominate the output. In the present harsh economic and social climate, the argument goes, people don't want to be reminded of how difficult and problematic things are. They increasingly want the kind of entertainment and reassurance that the series and serials provide. Moreover, they add, these forms have the added attraction of offering characters and situations with which viewers can empathize and identify on a continuing basis. In the absence of better empirical evidence on audiences, these arguments must remain speculative. But, whatever the underlying dynamics, the basic fact remains that one-shot plays are relatively unpopular with viewers. One response to this has been to move single plays nearer to the series format by grouping them into anthologies based around a common theme or location. At the time of the study, for example, ATV had a play anthology called *Cottage to Let* in production. Although each play remained self contained, with its own plot and characters, each was set in the cottage of the title. This device neatly combined a considerable saving on set costs with a potential means of increasing audience interest and involvement.

As well as helping to shape the overall balance of drama output, economic factors also affect the scope and content of production in other ways. To take single plays again: With the reduction in the number of available slots, there is an understandable tendency for producers and executives to play safe and go for established writers who they know will deliver a shootable script on schedule, and whose names are known to viewers. While this obviously reduces production problems and helps the ratings, it means fewer opportunities to experiment with the work of young untried writers. As one respondent explained:

> . . . if you in the old days were doing twenty-six plays a year, you could af-
> ford six of those to have been gambles, two or one of which might come off
> . . . but when you are doing six or seven plays a year and no more, you can't
> afford to gamble on any of them.

Established writers, too, are expected to recognize the parameters of the situation and to cut their cloth accordingly. This means turning in work that fits the dominant styles and is likely to attract audiences. Hence, they are also likely to play safe. As another interviewee explained:

> People very quickly find out that unless they have a pretty good knowledge of
> what is required at a particular time and the style of program that is being
> made, then they haven't a cat in hell's chance of getting anything accepted.

To a large extent then, demand conditions supply. Faced with the declining opportunities for risk and experimentation offered by the medium, writers have become less and less inclined to offer their more adventurous material to television, since they know that it is unlikely to be accepted. The result is an increasingly closed circle. As one person put it:

> It doesn't seem to me that it is a particularly attractive medium to those writers
> who want to do something different . . . in the sixties, when television was a
> slightly more vibrant medium, there was a feeling that things were happening,
> and I think that attracted a lot of writers who nowadays wouldn't think of offer-
> ing their material. . . . What talent there is tends not to offer its originality to
> television, it offers its craftsmanship . . . (they) do television for bread and
> butter.

Much of the more contentious and path-breaking dramatic material currently being produced finds its way into the "fringe" theatre, which has blossomed since the mid sixties—over the same period in fact as experimentation in television has declined. A few people like John McGrath, one of television drama's leading innovators in the sixties, have deserted television altogether and devoted their energies full time to fringe theatre. McGrath gave up a prestigious position at the BBC to run a radical drama company, "7:84" (the name refers to the famous figure for the distribution of wealth in Britain, whereby the top 7 percent of the population own 84 percent of the country's wealth). Most other radically committed writers, directors and producers, however, continue to divide their time between television and theatre.

The underlying economics of the situation have thus tended to reduce the areas available for experimentation and to concentrate resources on the tried and tested and already successful. This applies to themes as well as to writers. Once a theme has been a hit with audiences, there is a strong incentive to produce variations on it until the vein is mined out. The success of *Edward VII*, for example, has encouraged ATV to launch upon a series of dramatized historical biographies. In the words of Sir Lew Grade:[8]

> We had a tremendous success with *Edward VII*. Unbelievable. I thought,
> "What else should we do?" . . . So we thought of Disraeli. I'm going to do

Rasputin, too. . . . For a long time I've been considering George III, but I'm not finding George III easy.

In addition to shaping the choice of themes, economic factors have also affected forms of presentation. By altering the ratio of location to studio work, they have helped to shift television drama back toward traditional naturalistic modes. In the early days of the medium when production was studio-bound, television drama leaned heavily on the established theatre for material and styles, with the result that it tended to work with the naturalistic forms that dominated stage production. It was essentially a theatre of dialogue, of people talking in rooms. In Tony Garnett's somewhat sarcastic description:[9]

. . . people would occasionally walk in or walk out of a door, but while they were together they would sit around and have a conversation. Occasionally, because you wanted a bit of action, they would pour a drink.

Gradually, however, the dominance of naturalism began to break down. Using the new cameras and recording equipment, more and more people left the studios and took to shooting drama on location, drawing on the cinematic styles pioneered by documentary makers, the Italian neo-realists and others. As a result, the sixties saw a flowering of social realism in British television drama. Ken Loach and Tony Garnett's contributions to the BBC's celebrated *Wednesday Play* series and John McGrath's early episodes for the police series *Z Cars* are probably the best known examples, but there were plenty of others. Indeed, for a time social realism became the dominant form of television drama. With the worsening economic climate of the seventies, however, the wheel has begun to turn again in favor of naturalism.

Shooting on location is roughly twice as expensive as studio-based production. According to recent BBC figures, for example, it costs something over £25,000 to make a fifty-minute drama program in the studio as against well over £53,000 for an all-film production.[10] Given these kinds of cost differentials, television companies, including ATV, have become rather more stringent about the use of film footage. As one interviewee explained:

It comes down to economics—this money structure again. We're moving much too much to studio-based operations. We have the facilities to go outside. We don't because of cost effect and what have you.

Take for example, ATV's afternoon series *The Cedar Tree*, which follows the fortunes of a middle-class country family in the 1930s. Several years ago, a director might have expected to establish the atmosphere by intercutting studio sequences with film footage of the family driving into town, out riding or simply walking around the gardens of the house. Due to cost pressures, however, the whole series was shot in the studio and all the action concentrated in the house, thereby pulling the production decisively back toward the naturalistic conventions of the stage and away from cinematic realism.

Reactions to this general return to the studio varied considerably, depending on the respondent's general ideas about television drama. Some regretted the cutback in filming, arguing that it reduced flexibility, curtailed experiment and reintroduced an outmoded "stagey" quality to productions. Others, however, welcomed the resurgence of naturalism, since it corresponded with their conception of "good" drama. As one respondent put it:

> The economic crisis that has made filming such an expense and an extravagance is a blessing, because it's forced people inside into interior close-up drama. . . . I have always been a great believer in creating atmosphere through dialogue as you (do) in the theatre.

These divisions of opinion were linked in turn to much broader differences in the ways that respondents saw their situation and responded to it. But, before we explore these variations in more detail, we need to examine one other important dimension of the economic context surrounding production, namely the question of internationalization.

Internationalizing of costs and revenues makes good economic sense. Cooperation agreements with foreign companies help to spread expenses, while overseas sales considerably increase a program's profit potential. ATV has been in the forefront of British television's involvement in both these areas. It has been particularly successful on the sales side. It was the first British commercial television company to pursue an aggressive export policy and the first to make a significant dent on the all-important United States market. By the summer of 1969, ATV had more programs showing on prime time American network television than any other single company, except MCA-Universal. And in the period from then until January, 1977, program sales to America have grossed well over $238 million. Attitudes to this situation and to the company's general move into international marketing varied considerably among the people interviewed for this study.

Some were wholeheartedly in favor, arguing that internationalization opened up possibilities for programming that domestic financing and marketing was unable to support. As one enthusiast put it:

> . . . you need an overseas sale in order to spend a quarter of a million pounds above and below the line per play. . . . It really has to be America, because they are the biggest and the choosiest. They've got the most money . . . at the end of the day, it is really financial. . . . That's my view of the export thing. It is marvelous for us—the people who make the programs—because we are able to lavish affection all over the production.

Others were less enthusiastic, however, and pointed to ways in which production with an eye to exports imposed contraints on program makers. They argued that maximum overseas sales meant making programs that are easily intelligible to as many people as possible—which to them meant concentrating on the standard action/adventure formats. The result is a significant loss in variety. As one of these critics put it:

> . . . if you are going to sell to seventy-eight countries—if some Arab sitting in a tent watches a car chasing along and a man going bang, bang, he knows what it is about. So you get this terrible, simple, clockwork dialogue, no at-

tempt at character—it's something that could be seen by anybody and understood at this level. We do these mid-anywhere, mid-Atlantic programs because they have to sell all over the place and therefore lose the very form of English drama that is special to us.

Against this, supporters of the company's export orientation pointed out that some of British television's biggest overseas successes had been programs like *The Forsyte Saga*, *Upstairs, Downstairs* and *Edward VII*, which dealt specifically with English themes in a distinctively English way. Given the limited brief of the present project, it was not possible to explore these issues further, but the impact of internationalization is clearly an important area for investigation in future studies. Having outlined the main contexts of drama production and having suggested some of the ways in which they impinge on program making, we turn finally to a brief analysis of ways in which drama personnel perceive and respond to their situation.

Varieties of Response

As we have already noted, respondents were sharply divided in their responses to internationalization and to the cutback in location filming. But, are these variations related to more basic and deep-seated differences in the way they see their situation and their role within it? Previous research strongly suggests that the answer is "yes." Muriel Cantor, for example, found two basic views of the job among the Hollywood series producers she interviewed. Some saw themselves simply as providing well-made entertainment for a mass audience, while others saw their role as making programs with a "message," programs that would present contemporary social problems and force viewers to think again about things they usually took for granted. A version of this same division was also evident among our respondents. A number presented themselves primarily as entertainers:

I am there to entertain them, to tell them stories that will make them want to turn the page, exactly (as) in days back, when people used to run out and buy the next installment of *Pickwick Papers*.

I belong to the school that likes the theatre that makes you feel rather than the theatre that makes you think. . . . I want to make people laugh and cry and be anxious rather than spark off new ideas, new sorts of political or sociological thought.

Others however, argued for a more critical, challenging, socially committed drama:

I think it's important—probing, examining social things. . . . I think it's television's job occasionally to disturb and not just to reassure. . . . A notable example is *Cathy Come Come*—that sort of play that opens people's eyes.

Previous work in the sociology of occupations suggests that differing views of the job are strongly related to variations in work situation, and this was broadly confirmed in this case. People working on the high-rating serials and series tended to emphasize the entertainment function of television drama, while those involved with single-play production were more inclined to argue for critical drama. At the same time, however, this division was by no means clear cut.

In the first place, many of those who saw themselves primarily as entertainers were also committed to using their shows to put across social messages and public information to a mass audience. There are well-established precedents for this in British broadcasting. The long-running BBC radio serial *The Archers*, for example, started life in 1951, "to give farmers information and advice that would help them in their daily routines, and to give townsfolk a better idea of the farmers' problems. It was to be information presented as entertainment."[11] This idea of presenting information within an entertainment format was often mentioned by those involved with ATV's high-rating serials and series such as *Crossroads* and *General Hospital:*

> I'm entertaining, but I would like where possible to make people think a bit more in terms of message giving.

> We are very much concerned with making social comments and doing public service. When we are reaching fifteen million people nightly, we are giving them information that they need. . . . They will take from our people.

The relationship between entertainment and social commentary also connected those involved with single plays. On the one hand, they saw television as the most effective medium for reaching a large audience. As one person put it:

> It's no good writing wonderful plays about socialism for your well-heeled middle classes, who go to the Royal Court. . . . Television is a powerful thing, and if you've got something to say to the masses, then that's the place to do it.

But, at the same time they recognized that to command a mass audience, or even a sizable one, it was necessary to find ways of presenting social commentary in an entertaining way. As one respondent put it:

> I want to have a dig at something and not just fill an hour. But I think you should have a dig in an entertaining way—there's nothing worse than being bawled at.

These responses reflect the creative personnel's continuing attempts to accommodate to the crosscutting pressures on program making and to find ways of balancing institutional demands for ratings prestige and public service against personal commitments and convictions.

Conclusion

As mentioned at the outset, the present project was an exploratory study whose main aim was to raise questions and suggest directions for future research. Of these, two stand out as particularly important. Firstly, the study strongly suggests that the much talked about conflicts between creativity and control, art and money, and the responses to them are both more complex and more ambiguous than previous discussions have presented them. Secondly, it became evident in the course of the research that an adequate investigation of this complexity needs to look not only at the internal dynamics of creative organizations, but also at the shifting configuration of pressures operating on them from outside and to find ways of relating the two. This is certainly a daunting task, but we would argue that it is also a necessary one if we are to arrive at a more adequate understanding of the dynamics of television and of its role in contemporary cultural life.

NOTES

[1] Participant's accounts include Cecil.Taylor, *Making a Television Play* (Newcastle-Upon-Tyne: Oriel Press, 1970); John Elliott, *Mogul: The Making of a Myth* (London: Barrie and Jenkins, 1970) and *A Change of Tack: Making "The Shadow Line"* (London: The British Film Institute, 1976). The better journalistic accounts include John Russell Taylor, *Anatomy of a Television Play* (London: Weidenfeld and Nicholson, 1962); Charles Barr *et al.*, "The Making of a Television Series: 'Upstairs, Downstairs'," *Movie*, no. 21 (November, 1975): 46–63.

[2] Philip Elliott, *The Making of a Television Series: A Case Study in the Sociology of Culture* (London: Constable, 1972).

[3] Tom Burns, "Public Service and Private World" in *The Sociological Review Monograph No. 13*, ed. Paul Halmos (University of Keele, 1969).

[4] Muriel Cantor, *The Hollywood TV Producer: His Work and His Audiences* (New York: Basic Books, 1971); Joan Moore, "Occupational Anomie and Irresponsibility," *Social Problems* 8, no. 4 (1961): 293–99.

[5] See, for example, the interviews collected by Paul Madden in *British Television Drama 1959–1973* (London: The British Film Institute, 1976).

[6] The full text of the papers presented at the symposium, together with the comments of the other participants, can be found in *Organization and Structure of Fiction Production in Television*, Volume 1: *Introductory Reports* and Volume 2: *Interventions* (Torino: Edizioni Radio Televisione Italiana, 1977).

[7] Quoted in John Heilpern, "And Now a Word for the Bard's Sponsor," *The Observer Supplement* (8 May 1977): 46.

[8] Quoted in Heilpern, *op. cit.*: 42.

[9] Quoted in Roger Hudson, "Television in Britain: Description and Dissent," *Theatre Quarterly* 11 (June, 1972): 19.

[10] Figures quoted in *Broadcast*, no. 902 (7 March 1977): 4.

[11] Norman Painting, *Forever Ambridge: Twenty-Five Years of "The Archers"* (London: Sphere Books Limited, 1976), p. 14.

Gerhard Schmidtchen:

Light Music and the Radio Listener

☆ THE ERA OF EMPIRICAL RESEARCH into the mass media was introduced during the Second World War by a negative theory of human nature and by pessimistic expectations as to the role of the media in the development of society. For more than a decade, these neo-puritan theories provided the guiding principle for all investigations in this field. The major hypotheses were as follows:

1. The media have narcotic effect. They contribute to apathy and political inactivity. People spend their time in contact with the media instead of engaging in social activity. Knowledge about problems becomes confused with the actual treatment of those problems.[1] This thesis has given rise to a great many investigations into the function of the media and in particular into the function of the entertainment component as a stimulus for escapism.

2. The media contribute to social conformity. The existing structure of society is tendentially strengthened by the flood of news and entertainment emanating from the media. Implicit in the media is a loyalty to the given social structure. No one who is interested in change can rely upon them.[2] According to this thesis, it is particularly the way in which the American media are organized that has contributed to a reinforcing of the structure of society. The media may very well give expression to certain attitudes in the interest of achieving the greatest possible effectiveness, but they do not change these attitudes. Maximum effectiveness as a basic criterion for the media leads tendentially to the maintenance of the social structure rather than to social change.[3]

3. The media lower cultural norms. The increase in the media's capacity for dissemination proceeds much faster than the growth of the cultural preconditions for the absorption of what is offered. The larger the audience, the lower the average of cultural demand. If the media merely follow the principle of au-

▶ The article was originally published in the *Internationale Zeitschrift für Kommunikationsforschung* 1, no. 3 (Köln, West Germany; Wien, Austria, 1974), pp. 443–68, and is reprinted here with the kind permission of the author. Dr. Gerhard Schmidtchen is Professor of Psychology at the University of Zürich, Switzerland. The article was translated by Andrew Hurrell, B.A.

dience maximization, then the standard of the material offered must inevitably even out at a lower level. This, in turn, impairs the chances of achieving an improvement in the standard of culture. Toward the end of the Second World War, it was feared that the mass media were caught in a vicious downward spiral of ever lower standards. At the very best, it might be possible to keep the existing state of culture intact. For example, the attempts to replace soap operas with more demanding programs failed completely: the listeners merely switched off. One cannot raise the taste of millions by an improvement in mass-produced material. In 1946, Lazarsfeld and Merton noted:

> We know an enormous amount about failures in this field. If the discussion were to be reopened in 1976, then perhaps we could report with a similar degree of certainty about the positive achievements.[4]

Adorno has given a social-critical dimension to the idea that the mass media encourage a worsening of musical taste or receptivity. In an essay that appeared in 1945, he said that as a result of the possibilities for dissemination provided by the mass media, music has become a consumer article. The listener gives up all intellectual activity when he listens to music: he judges it in a purely gustatory way. This regress on the part of the listener, this preparedness to give up all insight into the inner coherence of a piece of music—Adorno calls this "atomistic" or "segmental" listening—leads to a complete transformation of the role of classical music. It now only functions as entertainment, although the listeners still maintain their belief that they are partaking of some great cultural product. Thus, it is serious music in particular which contributes to this delusion. Radio music, according to Adorno, prevents the listener from criticizing social reality.[5] The broadcasting institutions of the Federal Republic of Germany broadcast—if we disregard commercial advertising—70 percent entertainment music and 30 percent serious music. According to Adorno's analysis, this 30 percent of serious music is thus much more dangerous than the 70 percent of entertainment music.

4. The media represent harmful socialization influences. In 1950, Riesman declared his suspicion that the socializing function of light music consisted of setting up a definite image of American childhood and youth. According to the image, people were enjoying a time of unproblematic happiness in which they could dress and behave outlandishly; it was a time for dancing, of visits to the coke bar and of blues that were not really blue. In this way, the real problems associated with growing up were avoided. Riesman formulates four pessimistic socialization hypotheses:

a) The incoherent presentation of music on the radio generally strengthens the atomization of experience in modern urban industrial society?

b) Does indentification with pop stars lead to a lessening of social conflict?

c) Is it a characteristic of light music to tell people how to feel about their problems in much the same way as daytime serials (soap opera) package their social lessons?

d) Since light music is often dance music, it plays a part—both in terms of gesture and of overall behavior—in the formation of people's attitude to the other sex. Do not people assume the facial expression dictated by the music? Does not this music suggest a combination of smoothness and stylized spontaneity, a reserved pseudo-sexuality?[6]

In the face of these neo-puritan theories, one can only be amazed and wonder how, during the course of such earnest consideration of light music (and of serious music, whose function is even worse), we managed to survive in both social and biological terms. In terms of the research that they stimulated, these theories were not particularly productive, and where they did dominate research, they led nowhere. Reality did not fit in with these theories. It is now time to develop alternative concepts. However, I will expressly avoid speaking of counter concepts, since there would be no point in counterposing a pessimistic theory with an optimistic one. The formulation of value judgments does not represent the best way to approach reality. We should push aside our tendency to make normative judgments until such time as we understand the structure of reality. Analysis should have primacy. The following findings of the last twenty years directly contradict such pessimistic theories about the effects of the media:

1. The development of the media and the increase in the average per capita exposure to the media have contributed substantially to a psychological mobilization among the population. It can be shown that television increases interest in politics.[7] Large social groupings of people held together by a single set of opinions are being increasingly broken up, the number of "don't knows" is increasing, as can be seen from recent election results. In spite of being more engrossed in the products of broadcasting, the population spends its leisure time more actively, which is a result both of the increased possibilities for arranging one's leisure time that is offered by growing affluence and of the mental stimulus provided by the changes in the structure of society and concomitant political sensitization.[8] Interest in social problems—both as reading material and news content—is increasing rapidly.[9]

2. The media do not anaesthetize criticism but rather encourage it. The investigation relating to the German Diocesan Synod[10] showed that criticism of the church grew with increased exposure in the media. Contradictions between traditional institutions—and this applies not only to the church—and the demands of modern society are brought to life through the communication process.

3. The effect of the media does not necessarily lead to conformity with the existing system. It can be shown that the political magazine programs on television contributed substantially to the change in the power-balance in Bonn.[11]

All this, however, says nothing about the function of light music, only about the fact that we need new research concepts to replace those inspired by moral pessimism.

Towards an Understanding of the Importance of Light Music

It is only worth talking about the role of light music in the relationship between the listener and the radio station if light music does indeed possess a real importance. How important, in fact, is light music? The level of demand represents the only criterion by which this importance may be judged, and the data relating to the demand for light music does lead to a clear conclusion: The need to listen to light music and entertainment music is immense and so far has not been satisfied by any broadcasting corporation to the degree demanded by the listeners.

If one uses day-by-day audits to systematically inquire into what television viewers listen to when they turned on the radio instead of television, the reports are unequivocal: almost 80 percent listened to light music, 11 percent to serious music and 32 percent to news programs (a figure partly formed in combination with the other two groups).[12] If one then makes a general inquiry into the degree of interest shown by the listener, the same set of relations emerges again and again. One of the questions put to listeners of South-West German Radio (Südwestfunk) read as follows: "Think of the various types of radio programs and then explain which type of program represents exactly what you enjoy listening to and forms the reason for your owning a radio." A wide choice of possible answers was presented. At the top of the list of answers in 1968 was: good entertainment music or pop music with 72 percent; symphonies and chamber music with 11 percent.[13]

Among television viewers during the evening period, the various types of programs offered on the radio achieved the following cumulative weekly audiences: light music, 72 percent; serious music, 18 percent; political programs, 24 percent; plays and general educational talks, 12 percent each.[14] A breakdown of the music offered on the radio does not correspond to the results of this inquiry. Whilst 80 percent of the listeners wanted to hear light music, such music only accounted for 39 percent[15] of the total program output of the ARD (the consortium of the Broadcasting Corporations of the Federal Republic of Germany)—and this figure includes the music used in advertisements. There is constant and insistent criticism in listeners' questionnaires. Large groups of the listening audience complain that the number and range of the music programs offered are too limited or—what for them amounts to the same thing—the times of these music programs are unsuitable.

The Function of Light Music for Young People

Paul F. Lazarsfeld established as early as 1945 that it was particularly the younger generation that was interested in popular music. The data of this period showed that 72 percent of those between the ages of twenty-one and twenty-nine particularly enjoyed listening to light music, as against only 22 percent of those over fifty.[16] The pattern shown in these findings is repeated right down to the present day. It is young people who want hit songs and pop music and it is older people who show less interest (see Graph 1). The older generation prefers a more "folksy" kind of popular music and also tunes from operettas and operas: in other words, they enjoy light music insofar as it is composed of these elements.[17] They dislike new types of music that mean little or nothing to them and that they find hard to listen to.

Young people are not only interested in light music. They are interested (more so than other groups) in all types of dramatic material—in films, theatre and detective programs on the radio. Lazarsfeld, for his part, supposed that there was some kind of "vitality factor" behind this interest in light music and films. We should now view this conjecture far more in terms of how it conforms to the laws of development psychology. Young people have no fixed social identity; rather they remain impressionable for a long time. The question posed by Pirandello: "Who am I?" is *the* question facing young people. We know from investigations that young people take themselves more severely to task than older people. The thought "I would like to change the kind of person I am" is common among young people, but occurs to them less frequently as they grow older. During this phase, the personality is confronted by a particularly serious set of problems related to the control of their emotional makeup. And it is in this area that light music probably has a function.

DIFFERENCE IN MUSIC PREFERENCES BETWEEN GENERATIONS

Listeners' reactions to the program *Südfunk aktuell*. "I like this modern beat and pop music very much. They should carry on just as they are."

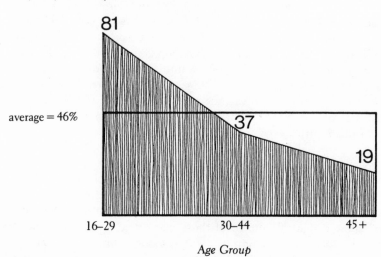

Age Group

Source: Institut für Demoskopie Allensbach: *IfD-Bericht* 1845/1, p. 80.

Light music can also contribute to the formation of social groups and to the development of new styles and fashions. Pop music and the city suit do not go well together. It is the social systems built up around the subcultures of the young that are heralded by a particular musical trend and it is around these new musical trends that opportunities for mutual understanding and identification emerge.

Hence music is not simply music, important cognitive and social structures are dependent upon it. Music—indeed the music that we would classify as popular music in its widest sense—has become the symbol of the cultural revolution that has taken place among young people. It is possible that the Beatles have contributed more to the "modern spirit" that was inspired by the younger generation and that has so affected our institutions than we are at present capable of recognizing. In any case, we feel entitled to say that this music has not contributed to any social anaesthetization but rather to its exact opposite.

Readers and Light Music

People who enjoy reading are very reserved when it comes to the idea of listening to music on commercial radio. Non-readers, on the other hand, candidly admit that this is something that they enjoy. This reserve confirms our image of the "ideal type" of intellectually demanding listener. The reader of books is interested, so we are led to believe, in everything that you find in journals, in science, art, education, classical music, even in jazz; yet he shudders at the idea of sentimental songs and light entertainment. This manifest rejection of the kind of musical entertainment offered by commercial radio clearly belongs to the self-projected image of the educated man. However, in daily audits of radio listening, during which this self-projected image hardly played any part, a clear conclusion was reached as if by the use of a statistical lie-detector: In reality, educated people, those who enjoy reading books, listen to more commercial radio and light music than do others.

How does it come about that the current image of the intellectual listener bears so little relation to reality? How does this distorted "ideal type" emerge? Our theories about the relationship of the intellectually demanding listener to the radio have up to now been apparently justified mainly by the results of normative thinking, and this thinking lies behind the criteria by which we decide just what constitutes an intellectually acceptable content and what does not, and which activities are intellectually "refined" and which are intellectually "coarse." In every case, a continual outpouring of light entertainment and sentimental songs is held to be intellectually "coarse." Strangely, the intellectually demanding listener does recognize his own wishes within this normative distortion. In fact, the large periods of time that the person who enjoys reading spends listening to light music do not stand in contrast to the intellectual content of that music, only to a system of values based upon intellectual criteria. If, however, those who enjoy reading books do tune in to commercial radio and do listen to light music to such a great extent (however much they might admonish themselves for so doing), then the need for light music must be intimately connected with the psycho-dynamic quality of our mental capacity for sustaining interest.

Intellectuals (who we here equate with those who enjoy reading books) cannot cultivate their rationality, cannot acquire knowledge and education without acquiring a very special relationship to their own inner world of thought. The intellectual does not only read and in so doing withdraw himself from social contact but also involves himself in a play of ideas and notions as they come to mind. Light music does not only meet the requirements of the situation, but also has a necessary compensatory effect and in addition makes more bearable the relative isolation to which the reader of books—as a skilled esoteric—has given himself up. The greater "nervous" capacity of intellectuals also certainly plays a role in the relationship of the reader to light entertainment. It is striking that people who do not often listen to the radio, do not read much either, whereas regular listeners tend to read a great deal. Thus, we are here faced with differences in the potential for assimilating one's environment. Generally the hunger for new impressions grows with intellectual accomplishment, with higher intelligence quotient or with more intensive education.

Entertainment in the Light of a Theory about the Activity of the Central Nervous System

The search for light entertainment, for pleasant sensory stimulation is so extensive, so strong and so persistent that its origins must lie within our drive nature. All drives are linked to some bodily organ. Recent psychological research ascribes to the brain—which is, after all, one of the most important human organs—its own drive tendencies. Experiments concerned with sensory deprivation have shown that stimulation and a variety of stimuli are the basic prerequisites for the normal functioning of the cortex. Thus, we may extend this line of thought and say that people engage in a restless, even aggressive search for suitable sensory stimulation when they find themselves living in quiet surroundings—in other words, when their capacity for assimilating stimuli of all kinds is not fully utilized. Any disproportionally large need for entertainment should tell us that, within the present social roles granted to the individual, we are making relatively little use of the total neurological capacity of the brain.[18] Measured against our capacity for assimilation, we are living in a world that is clearly too simply constructed.

This theory should be set against the theory of *Reizüberflutung* (sensory inundation). *Reizüberflutung* is produced less by the total quantity of stimuli than by their mutual incoherence. There is an observation made in England and Germany that is of great importance in this context. According to this observation, the demand for the entertainment function of television becomes greater as one goes down the social scale—in other words, as the possibilities for activity become less complex and culturally less demanding. Thus, the total quantity of the demand for entertainment may well vary in accordance with the structure of society.

On the other hand, the need for entertaining and aesthetic stimulation will not disappear with still more interesting social activities. Music, in particular, can have an important function during phases of relaxation and recovery in terms of the restoration of an optimal readiness for activity of the cortex. In spite of promising investigations in neuro-psychology, we still know too little about the way in which these factors interrelate to be any more than curious.[19] However, that there must be some kind of important interrelation between these factors is demonstrated by all the investigations into the behavior of the population in the face of the available entertainment, in which light music plays a very important role.

Just how often the personality can be less than fully occupied is demonstrated by the success among housewives of a program broadcast in the mornings by Stuttgart-based South German Radio (Süddeutscher Rundfunk). The program, *You Choose It . . . We'll Play It*, was introduced in 1967 and is broadcast between 11 and 12 every morning. Some time after its introduction, this request program achieved (as daily audits of listening show) a cumulative audience of 14 percent of those at whom the program was aimed. We are familiar with the general pattern of what happens to new programs. Usually a program reaches its audience, its circle of interested listeners, almost immediately after a relatively short initial period. This leads to a statistical evening out of the number of listeners at a fixed-average level. All previous experience of audience research shows that the number of listeners remains constant provided the program and the program structure remain unchanged. Comparable polls, carried out three years later in the autumn and winter of 1971, showed that the program *You Choose It . . . We'll Play It* had doubled its audience. The program was the same as it was when it started, nothing had been changed, yet the audience levels rose constantly. This situation was without parallel in previous German audience research. How can we explain why an established program continued to attract new listeners?[20]

These request programs involve social activity, an appeal to the listeners. Listeners—predominately female—are encouraged to send in their telephone numbers on a postcard. They are telephoned during the program and can express their particular choice of music, which is then played. The course of the program is thus determined by direct participation. One not only listens to the music and the announcer but also to the other listeners speaking on the telephone. By means of this form of participation the program opens up opportunities for social comparison and thereby triggers off psychic processes that are characteristic of man's group nature. The program offers a surrogate that compensates for a lack of human contact—something that affects housewives generally and older housewives in particular. Here they can join in with the activity of some respectable institution like the radio or at least listen to other people like themselves joining in. It is this opportunity for participation that was gradually discovered. Nor can we exclude the possibility that this program provides a stimulus for social contact: Neighbors may well discuss their choice of music together. This program provides empirical backing for the hypothesis that the mass media are in a position to activate forces in the personality that have up to this point lain fallow. At the same time, the success of this program can be seen as in some way symptomatic of the situation of many housewives.

Light Music and the Relationship to the Radio Station

People clearly consider light music to be an important matter, certainly as far as the seriousness of their demand for such music is concerned. What then happens if the broadcasting corporations—one of the basic sources of this entertainment material—fail to supply enough music of this kind? This interrelation was thoroughly examined for the first time by the Institut für Demoskopie at Allensbach (The Allensbach Opinion Poll Institute) in 1952.

If this happens, listeners begin to get annoyed with the radio station along the lines suggested by the theory of frustration and aggression formulated by Sears, Dollard, Doob, Miller and Mowrer.[21] The less satisfied the listeners are with the entertainment music offered, the more they become annoyed with the station.[22] In practice, it is of no consequence whether listeners are satisfied with the other programs offered: sports, news, plays or jazz. It is changes in the entertainment music offered that have the decisive influence over the attitude of the listener to the station. The greater the interest in entertainment music, the greater the frustration. Young people are more prepared to express their annoyance about the lack of entertainment music in terms of an overall negative judgment of the station than is the case with older people (see Graph 2).

The relation between the structure of the music offered and the reaction of the listener can be determined by a multi-levelled analysis. Here we compare radio stations that, according to the evidence of statistics of the ARD, offer a below-average proportion of light music with those that offer an above-average proportion. Listeners of those stations where light music occupies proportionately less of the total program output are far more critical and far less satisfied than those listeners of stations in which entertainment music forms a greater percentage of the total program output (see following Table).

Since 1953, South German Radio (Süddeutscher Rundfunk) has systematically utilized its knowledge of this interrelation. An extensive field experiment in 1953 proved that the audience levels of information programs can be increased by the use of an introductory piece of light music. Daily audits before and after the program showed that the number of listeners of political programs increased on average from 11 percent to 17 percent. During some weekends there was even a doubling of audience levels.[23]

Light music therefore seems, both psychologically and hence also physio-

LIGHT MUSIC AND THE RELATIONSHIP TO THE RADIO STATION

Young listeners sooner frustrated

All radio listeners (.39)

The correlation between quantitative music supply and judgment on the station's performance as expressed by four different age groups

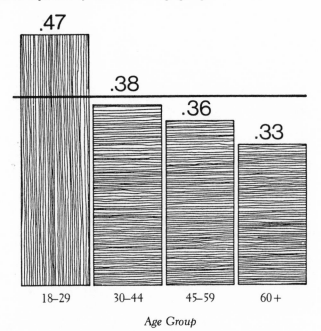

Age Group

Universe: Radio listeners from the age of eighteen. Area covered by South German Radio (Süddeutscher Rundfunk) based in Stuttgart. Sample = 4004.

Source: Institut für Demoskopie Allensbach: *IfD-Umfragen* 516, 520, 522 and 526.

logically, to be an important conditioning agent that makes possible the restoration of the individual's capacity to assimilate verbal material. Over the course of years, light music, although not actually increased in overall percentage terms, has created a better service and the impression of having more time devoted to it; this was achieved by skillfully interspersing light music with other material. More and more listeners explained that South German Radio did supply enough light music and the dissatisfaction receded. At the same time, the relationship of the listeners to the station improved.[24] South German Radio was not particularly popular among listeners at the beginning of the fifties, but by 1963 it had achieved the greatest popularity of all German radio stations and since then has always maintained a place in the leading group of stations.

Table 1 STRUCTURE OF MUSIC SUPPLY AND LISTENERS' REACTIONS

	Listeners in Areas Covered by ARD Radio Transmissions	
	Stations broadcasting less light music than average	Stations broadcasting more light music than average
Quantity of Light Music in Regional Radio Programs		
just right	36%	43%
too little	37%	24%
too much	10%	12%
undecided	9%	13%
rarely, do not listen	8%	8%
Satisfaction with Regional Radio Programs		
very satisfied, satisfied	57%	65%
not particularly satisfied, unsatisfied	33%	26%
don't know	2%	3%
rarely, do not listen	8%	6%

Source: Institut für Demoskopie Allensbach: *IfD-Umfrage* 2028, April/May, 1967. Universe: radio listeners during the previous month.

The Consequences of a Good or Bad Relationship to the Radio Station

What effect does the low popularity of a station have on broadcasting? The effect of declining popularity is not directly financial—except where it declines to such a point that people actually give up owning a radio. Such an extreme is hardly ever reached or, at least, is not discernible. Frustrated listeners who hold a negative opinion of a station avoid that station's entire output. They stop tuning in. If we compare the behavior of satisfied and dissatisfied listeners on a fixed day, we get a dramatic picture of the consequences of a programming policy that denies this legitimate need for entertainment. At best, the dissatisfied listener makes only half as much use of the programs offered as compared to the satisfied listener (see Graph 3). In most cases, listeners who stop listening to a particular station tend to give up listening to the radio completely. Although there is a certain observable tendency to switch to neighboring stations if one is dissatisfied with one's own regional station, this does not compensate for the decline in audience levels that comes about through dissatisfaction with the music programming. According to polls in 1971, listeners satisfied with South

SATISFIED LISTENERS MAKE GREATER USE OF
SOUTH GERMAN RADIO

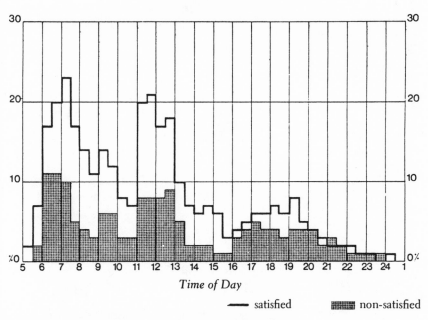

Time of Day

—— satisfied   ▦▦ non-satisfied

Sample: approximately 1,500 interviews from six fixed-day polls.

Source: Institut für Demoskopie Allensbach, Archiv-Nr. 561/1, 3–7 (October/November, 1971). South German License fee area.

German Radio (Stuttgart) listened to an average of 1.4 news broadcasts per day, those not satisfied, only to 0.4.[25]

The relationship of the listener to the station follows a series of psycho-economic laws: The greater the quantity of hedonistic material contained within the overall program output, the more positive will be the attitude of the listener to the entire range of programs offered by the station. When the emotion is positive, there will be a growing tendency to enter into a close relationship with an object. This will also be the case with parts of programs that, taken alone, would otherwise be far less popular. Vice versa, if the effect of a program is overwhelmingly non-hedonistic, negative emotions are built up that block any interaction with the broadcasting system. Dissatisfied, frustrated listeners are, for example, no longer in a position to turn to the news output of a station in the same way that a satisfied, regular listener would be. The dissatisfied listener makes only half as much use of the station's news output.

NOTES

[1] Paul F. Lazarsfeld and Robert K. Merton, "Mass Communication, Popular Taste and Organized Social Action," in *Mass Communications. A Book of Readings*, ed. Wilbur Schramm (Urbana, 1960), p. 501 *ff.*

[2] *Ibid.*, p. 503 *ff.*

[3] *Ibid.*, p. 512.

[4] *Ibid.*, p. 507.

[5] Theodor W. Adorno, "A Social Critique of Radio Music," in *Reader in Public Opinion and Communication*, eds. Bernard Berelson and Morris Janowitz (Glencoe, Ill., 1950, 1953), pp. 309–16.

[6] David Riesman, "Listening to Popular Music," in *Mass Culture. The Popular Arts in America*, eds. Bernard Rosenberg and David Manning White (Glencoe, Ill., 1957, 1959), pp. 411–12.

[7] Gerhard Schmidtchen, "Soziologische Funktionsstellung zwischen den Nachrichten," in *Hörfunk und Fernsehen*, no. 3 (Hamburg: Hans-Bredow-Institut, 1965); Institut für Demoskopie Allensbach (IfD) (Allensbach, West Germany), *IfD-Bericht* 1489 (1968).

[8] Gerhard Schmidtchen, "Gesellschaftlicher Wandel und Situation der Massenmedien," ZV + ZV, no. 29/30 (25th July, 1967): 1119–27.

[9] Institut für Demoskopie Allensbach, *IfD-Bericht* 1750, p. 25 *ff.*

[10] Gerhard Schmidtchen, *Zwischen Kirche und Gesellschaft* (Freiburg [West Germany], 1972, 1973).

[11] Elisabeth Noelle-Neumann, "Methoden der Publizistikwissenschaft," in *Publizistik*, eds. Noelle-Neumann and Schulz (Frankfurt [West Germany], 1971), p. 186.

[12] Institut für Demoskopie Allensbach, *IfD-Bericht* 1403, p. 20.

[13] *Ibid.*, *IfD-Bericht* 1547/II, p. 173.

[14] *Ibid.*, *IfD-Bericht* 1403, p. 22.

[15] *ARD Jahrbuch 72* (Hamburg, 1972); calculated on the basis of Table 4, pp. 264–65.

[16] Paul F. Lazarsfeld, "Audience Research," in *Reader in Public Opinion and Communication*, eds. Berelson and Janowitz (Glencoe, Ill., 1957, 1959), p. 340.

[17] Institut für Demoskopie Allensbach, *IfD-Bericht* 1606/II 2, p. 151.

[18] This hypothesis was first put forward by Gerhard Schmidtchen, "Über die gesellschaftliche Kraft der Massenmedien," ZV + ZV, no. 26/27 (September, 1962): 1332–44.

[19] Doris Soibelman, *Therapeutic and Industrial Uses of Music. A Review of the Literature* (New York, 1948). Cf. also the articles in the journal *Musiktherapie* and Harm Willms, "Physikalische und medizinische Aspekte der Wirkung Leichter Musik." Paper presented to the 2nd International Forum on Light Music Broadcast by Radio in München, West Germany, 15th May, 1973.

[20] Institut für Demoskopie Allensbach, *IfD-Bericht* 1845/I, Table A28.

[21] Sears *et. al.*, *Frustration and Aggression* (New Haven, 1939). Later, Berkowitz played a leading part in the discussion on the role of annoyance as a result of frustration: Leonard Berkowitz, *Aggression: A Social Psychological Analysis* (New York, 1962).

[22] Institut für Demoskopie Allensbach, *IfD-Umfragen* 516, 520, 522, 526.

[23] *Ibid.*: *IfD-Bericht* 333/III, p. 50.

[24] *Ibid.*: *IfD-Bericht* 1187/I & 1854/I, p. 16.

[25] *Ibid.*: *IfD-Bericht* 1845/I, p. 12.

Günter Rohrbach:

Why Television Entertainment, for Whom and How?

☆ ENTERTAINMENT IS NOT ONLY television's most loved but also its most despised program category. It is the ultimate quality and function of this particular mass medium. Although the majority of non-entertainment programs are watched by many millions of viewers, such numbers remain a minority. Only entertainment is able to attract a majority. While it is impossible to doubt the significance of television as a medium of information, a restriction of this function to other mass media, to radio and the newspaper, which to a considerable degree still cater to the demand for information, is conceivable. If entertainment were to be removed from television, however, serious—and for most people unbearable—crises would probably ensue.

With the purchase of a television set and a monthly payment for the license amounting to DM 10.50, we aquire not only the means but also the right to be entertained in the most comfortable way conceivable—that is, at home. All that you have to do is simply press the button. Hardly any other product of civilization has affected and changed life so fundamentally. This still applies today, despite the fact that the institution's novelty and appeal are showing signs of wearing off, as is only to be expected. Indeed, the more television becomes a routine part of the day's activities, the more entrenched its degree of indispensability.

Because television is primarily seen to be a medium of entertainment, the audience judges its performance by the reliability with which it fulfills this function (i.e., the audience shows considerable discontent when its demand for permanent entertainment is not met—either because one refuses to provide it or because the programs presented do not fulfill subjective expectations). A society in which the laws of supply and demand, the relationship between money

▶ This is an extract from a hitherto unpublished paper presented at the 3rd Television Forum in Marl, West Germany, between the 20th and 24th of March in 1977. It is reprinted here with the kind permission of the author. Dr. Gunter Rohtbach is former Director of the WDR (the North-Rhine Westphalian Broadcasting Authority) Television Entertainment Division, and is now General Manager of the Bavaria Atelier GmbH: München.

and goods function so smoothly naturally begins to have problems when in cer tain areas such automatic mechanisms fail to operate. Television is such a area, because the direct contact between the supplying broadcasting center an the paying audience is interfered with by "public control."

It can be taken for granted that in handling audience demand affirma tively, a private television authority would keep discontent at a lower level. Ir this respect, publicly operated television concerns have created difficulties fo themselves. This is mainly because of their failure to come to terms with enter tainment in an adequate manner.

According to the regulations governing West German broadcasting (*Rund funkgesetze*), entertainment is one of its main objectives, the other two being information and education. But it is no secret that there are considerable dif ferences in rank. The controversy surrounding communications policy, in which the public, the political parties and other important organizations are in volved, centers almost exclusively on information programs. This is hardly surprising, in view of the effectiveness attributed to opinion formation through television. If television is in fact decisive in determining the relative ratios of political power and attractiveness, whether an election is won or not or whether someone's political career is made or broken, the issues at stake are too impor tant to warrant concern with entertainment as well.

The present state of affairs within broadcasting organizations is to be seen more or less as the outcome of such public concern. A relatively large propor tion of program time—and, consequently, of expenditure—is allocated to en tertainment, but attention and commitment are focused upon other areas. This is even reflected in the manning of top posts: politicians, trained bureaucrats and, if need be, journalists. That a former manager of an operetta company could become general director (*Intendant*) of a broadcasting organization is a thing of the distant past and is remembered today only as a curiosity.

It is presumed that entertainment will somehow function smoothly and not cause any trouble. The number of staff in entertainment departments is very limited in comparison with that of other areas of broadcasting activity. But at the same time, the former are an object of considerable envy because of the large audiences they attract and the enormous funds placed at their disposal— although their products tend to be regarded with disdain. The average age of entertainment producers is relatively high; new recruits are practically nonexis tent. The prejudice against entertainment was particularly marked during the years of extensive personnel recruitment. Younger members of a broadcasting staff are reluctant to apply their talents to this specific field; at the very most, entertainment is chosen as subject matter for critical reviews!

The dilemma that entertainment faces regarding the framework of respon sibilities embodied in the statutory objectives of broadcasting is reflected in the uncertainty and indecisiveness governing bodies display and in the detachment shown by young producers. That we all require ways and means of occupying ourselves during leisure hours is undeniable. But does this justify making the

supply of entertainment on television a sole public responsibility? Isn't leisure—and therefore also its use—a private matter? Would it ever have occurred
to anyone to entrust a public authority with the supply of entertainment if
public control had not proved necessary in other areas of broadcasting activity—the supply of information and of commentary—and if television had not
been granted a monopoly in the latters' supply. Is entertainment a public institution because television is a public institution? Isn't entertainment essentially
commercial in nature?

There are many indications that this is how many view the issue of entertainment—also, for instance, the critical public. The discussion on the reform
of the ARD's structure during the last few months has shown this clearly once
more. It bore out the way in which it is taken for granted that a shifting of
resources away from information in favor of entertainment would constitute a
threat against adequate fulfillment of the organization's public responsibilities.
One can safely assume that the prospect of a development in the opposite direction (i.e., in favor of information) would not have been subject to such disapprobation.

Has television entertainment always been appraised in the way indicated
above, or are such attitudes justifiable in view of the condition that it is in at
present? Does entertainment suffer the criticism of commercialism because it
seems to have become so commercialized? Is there an alternative?

A short digression for the purposes of definition cannot be avoided. The
programs that are produced in the television stations' entertainment divisions
only constitute part of the output the audience perceives as entertainment. For
the viewer, television drama, feature films, theatre productions, operettas and
musicals are just as much a part of entertainment as shows, quizzes, crime and
family series are—quite apart from the fact that information programs evidently
possess some kind of value in terms of entertainment. Personality dispositions
and traits ultimately decide what individuals find entertaining and what they do
not. Because no definition is without a certain element of arbitrariness, I would
like entertainment to be understood in this context: as anything that provides
the *masses* with enjoyment. It is precisely such mass-oriented entertainment
programs that provide most cause for suspicion in terms of television's public
responsibilities—or so it seems.

In the case of opera, theatre and art exhibitions we have learned to live
with the incongruity between the subsidies paid out for such institutions and
the minority that makes use of them. What makes it so difficult to come to the
defense of performances that provide enjoyment for most, if not all? *Tristan
and Isolde*: yes—a musical: no? Because the former is a work of art, deeply experienced, rich in fantasy, conceived and created with the utmost effort and
self-discipline—which can only be understood by those who are sufficiently at-
tuned; whereas the latter—in the view of precisely such cultured persons—is an
untold mixture of labored clichés, a painful aberration of taste. Do the cultured
classes defend their privileges in the debate on the issue of television entertain-

ment by the very means of expressing contempt for those programs the masses love? Do producers support their cause by cynically producing programs that serve to convince the audience as to its lack of taste?

To view the problem from a different angle: Entertainment produced conforming with producers' and critics' standards of taste and intellect risks excluding the lower classes from its enjoyment—as is already the case as far as information programs are concerned. Entertainment thus cannot be legitimated in social terms on the basis of taste alone. What then legitimates entertainment?

Entertainment constitutes the environment within which information programs are presented, thus rendering the latter accessible to an audience that would otherwise show little inclination toward informing itself. This is evident especially in the case of popular morning and lunchtime radio programs (light music followed by an interview and such). Through entertainment, we increase the receptiveness for information that, for the purposes of life in society, takes precedence. It is conceivable that legislators could have placed information programs under public control while leaving entertainment in private hands. One suspects, however, that information programs in such circumstances would not have been able to withstand the kind of permanent competition that would have ensued.

The fact that entertainment has been placed under public control has a further reason, an ecological one. There are consequences, for instance, with respect to the portrayal of sex and violence on the screen; we are spared the inconvenience of advertising breaks during the course of a program; and it ensures that no content offensive to the eye and the ear is presented. Is this enough, however? Can't entertainment as a public responsibility legitimate itself on its own merits? Namely, through the various things it achieves?

What does it achieve? It helps one to relax, it distracts from everyday worries, it dissipates a bad mood, it makes one forget. It also pleases the senses, activates our feelings, allows our fantasy to roam freely; it initiates dreams. It liberates us, makes us carefree and high-spirited; emotionally it moves us, fills us with sorrow, makes us shudder; it frightens us and relieves us. But it also disappoints; it angers us, kills our time, makes us dependent, paralyzes us. It is our fortune and misfortune. Not infrequently it is both at the same time.

It would be a fruitless exercise to consider what we could do without television entertainment. It is there and we have arranged our lives accordingly. For most of us, it is the most important and dependable means of relaxation, for many, the only one. As a result, the way in which we accomplish our work, come to terms with our problems, cope with life, also depends on the quality of television entertainment.

It is precisely this aspect that has led Marxist critics to postulate a link between extraneously controlled television entertainment and alienation from work. Such a relationship of course exists, but one cannot at the same time draw the conclusion that entertainment should be abandoned and that something specifically different—that is, information—should take its place. Rather, an attempt ought to be made to improve the quality of entertainment just as our society aims to improve the quality of work.

If, on the other hand, there is a relationship between television entertainment and coping with life, if entertainment is in a position to contribute toward our understanding of ourselves, our spiritual equilibrium, our ability to communicate with others, it is high time that we take entertainment as a social responsibility seriously and on a par with the standing and importance that information already has. At the moment, we are still a long way away from this.

There is no doubt (and in this respect I do not wish to abrogate my own responsibility) that the issue as to how to improve entertainment must be tackled primarily by the broadcasting organizations themselves. Nevertheless, this can hardly be initiated, if it is to have any prospect of success, unless outside pressure is forthcoming. Above all, a counterweight should be introduced to the proposals on media policy made by the political parties. In their programs for reforming various aspects of media operation and control, entertainment is not mentioned. In their approach, however, regardless of their differing political positions, entertainment is reduced to its superficial characteristics. Their representatives all too readily and easily belittle. The legitimate need for entertainment is only mentioned as if it were a necessary evil. Suspicions are only aroused when entertainment also claims content matter for itself that is not only of personal but also of social import. In contrast, it seems that entertainment (devoid of food for thought, of course) is not unwelcome when economic difficulties are on the increase and social conflict comes to a head. Entertainment as a narcotic?

Entertainment can help one through life, encourage one to persist despite personal and social problems. Of course it can only do this if on the one hand it sticks to reality and, on the other, despite the former, it boldly presents concepts and utopias. It is in this area that the most far-reaching mistakes have perhaps been made: our films and television plays have probably rather too timidly avoided reality in the material they made use of, were rather too cautious in that they restricted themselves to the facts that program research had presented. We were too concerned with proof and too little with suggestions. We spent all our energy on analysis and restricted fantasy. We reproduced a lot of the usual but very little adventure. We spent too much time on people like "you and me" and too little on heroes. We were too concerned with recognizing ourselves in the things we watched and hardly ever with identifying ourselves with what we saw. Because we feared the dream factory, almost all our films soon began to resemble the news.

Entertainment's attempts to imitate the methods used in producing an information program are probably also a sign of lack of self-confidence. Although such means open up new possibilities for the field of entertainment, specific opportunities are lost. In future, we will certainly produce less films taking topical issues as their themes (alcoholism, social integration, problems at school and the like) and instead produce stories about people, their feelings, their dreams, their struggles, their victories and defeats. Reality will thereby present itself in a more sensual and imaginative manner than in so-called "realistic" television plays. These would be part of a self-confident and effective entertainment.

However, although feature films and television plays were subject to a certain amount of criticism during the course of the last fifteen years, their prestige was never really endangered. The "libel" of those who regularly despair at the entertainment presented on German TV is directed almost exclusively at shows and quizzes. Are things in this sector of entertainment really so bad, and if so, can change be brought about? And if things can be altered, do television organizations want a change? I do not want to pass judgment or to differentiate in qualitative terms in this context, but the following comment must be made: I believe I can stand up and defend those programs produced by the WDR in this field—not without a measure of self-criticism but also not without expressing a certain amount of pride in the achievements of my colleagues.

Back to the question: Can one change anything and does one want to? I have the impression that many broadcasting organizations see this sector of entertainment as a kind of testing ground involving trial and error that one has to accept, albeit a little shamefacedly, but nonetheless thankful that it doesn't spark off political protest. Bad conscience, insofar as it exists, is relieved by the apparent fact that there is a lack of alternatives. Producers themselves are not unaware of this. Many producers see themselves as lone fighters, abandoned but also left alone by their superiors to get on with what they are doing. They are glad to be able at least to keep current series going. They lack the energy and the time for new concepts. They have got used to the fact that their programs are loved by many but despised by the few whose recognition they would really like to have. They have resigned themselves to the fact that more colleagues from other divisions ridicule than stand up and defend their work in critical appraisals or discussions shown on television. Everywhere entertainment producers look, they are confronted by big industry, which, with an overpowering mobilization of capital and ideas, is able to decisively influence and prefabricate the form programs are to take or supply the finished product from which the producers can only passively choose.

The broadcasting organizations, apparently so powerful, are totally on the defensive in the sector of musical entertainment. They can decide which music to play and which not, which singers they want to present and which they don't, but they cannot provide their own alternatives, alternatives that can hope to compete with industry's products. This doesn't justify the fraternization that is occasionally noticeable and doesn't legitimate the way in which some stations allow themselves to become the vehicles of industry. On the other hand, the public should realize that a different course is only feasible if there is a considerable increase in the funds that are placed at our disposal. Is that what one wants? The WDR has come to the conclusion that for the time being it can only severely limit the time allocated to musical entertainment. But is this possible in the long term?

The most important issue for the broadcasting authorities relates to the so-called "grand entertainment" shown on Saturday evenings and designed for the whole family. For many years now, this variety of entertainment has been firmly in the hands of a few professional entertainers, who have proved their abilities during the course of thousands of "battles," who possess energy, self-confidence and personality of a kind that enables them to fill an evening practically on their own. Although some of them are still—to use an apt expression—"in business," their demise is near. What does one do when the personalities with such powerful and enveloping charm retire, dying out like dinosaurs? Who should replace them?

To my mind, this deficit opens up new opportunities. When we don't have the great personalities with which to fill a stage anymore, we will simply have to reduce the stage in size. The programs may perhaps lose their attraction, but they would gain in human terms instead. In any case, one has to ask whether entertainment that intimidates, creates a barrier of fearful admiration between the audience and entertainer, paralyzes rather than helps one to relax.

There is reason to hope that this form of playful entertainment will become less perfect, more direct, quiet, relaxed and cheerful than has hitherto been the case. A singer will no longer walk down the stairs with a wide smile on his or her face, hastily deliver a playback song and then make for the exit. We will meet him as a person, we will participate in the interpretation, we will be involved in the process of art. Entertainment won't consist primarily of presentation anymore, but of mediation. Such a development would leave what is being mediated intact.

Entertainment as a social responsibility—which criteria does one use in order to measure its success? Surely not a quantitative one alone—the number of viewers who watch! We must use this criterion. It is important that the entertainment provided by a public authority gains the acceptance of the masses. But this is only one of many. It is important that entertainment should convey messages of one kind or another, but it is not essential. Experience teaches us that pure or almost pure entertainment can also achieve certain aims.

Does entertainment need to be aesthetics? Of course, but it is not to be judged by this criterion as in the case of a work of art. Entertainment's aesthetic qualities are simple, obvious and naïve. The variety of means, the refinement of form increases its intensity but reduces popularity. The value of entertainment is measurable solely in terms of its effects: if it imparts new energy or if it paralyzes, if it liberates or not, if it encourages fantasy or hampers it, if it makes one more able to live or not.

István Petur:

Some Aspects of Entertainment Theory and Practice

☆ GRANTED MY HEART'S DESIRE, I would change the coordinate conjunction of the title into a contrasting one—and not only for its surprise effect. (Surprise whom? Well, certainly not the experts of theory.) Rather to draw attention to the distance—to put it moderately—that separates theory from practice in entertainment just as in numerous other spheres of life. In order to forego critical comments, let me stress emphatically that I am far from associating myself with all trends of anti-theoreticism. On the contrary, in accordance with my original inclination, I am attracted to a theoretical approach. Working at a certain point of the well-known process—practice–theory–practice—however, I arrived at the conclusion that in our field practice often renews itself from its own experiences while the intermediate phase, theory, though principally very important, has little effect on renewing practice. However, I restrict this remark to this present topic in the present tense. Interesting as it is, our two-year debate[1] on entertainment affected neither practice in a direct way nor did it achieve a much-desired clarification of concepts. Without wishing to bagatellize the complexity of theoretical work, I feel that a clarification—or shall we say a clarification fulfilling practical requirements—of the relevant basic concepts (entertainment, amusement, culture, and so on) ought to have been achieved. Obviously without this we cannot even begin to hope for any practical application.

On the other hand, proceeding from practice, it is fairly easy to arrive at—very important, though evident—conclusions that, when read in theoretical essays, provoke the question: Is that what all this fuss is about? For instance, the relationship between public education and entertainment; a clear differentiation between culture and non-culture and the necessity in understanding transitions between the two clearly; the divergence between programs whose func-

▶ This is a translation of an article that was originally published in the Hungarian journal *Rádió és Televízió Szemle* 5, no. 2 (Budapest, 1973): 51–58, and is reprinted here with the kind permission of the Hungarian Mass Communication Research Centre. The article was translated by András Héjj.

tion it is to entertain and what the recipients expect of entertainment. I devoured the literature of the debate and took pleasure in noticing that the views contrary to my own opinions have been disproved successfully with a reasoning corresponding with my own. I am thus able to choose any selection of views I like. However, I think that our topic is more objective in nature than to make such a personal approach decisive. Therefore, I am of the opinion that those concerned should see to it that our experts try and really *solve* the most important problems posed by our topic, thus providing practice with exact support and not just papers that allow the reader to feel justifiably that he is being confronted with interesting views rather than scientific truths.

On the other hand, there is a serious problem in the fact that even irresolute essays often forget to compare thoughts expressed with the practice required by society; no specific advice is required in preparing programs, but it should be considered to the extent that when the category of values is referred to in connection with entertainment (artistic entertainment and such), the consequences of the following reality are summarized: in entertainment in the present historical situation, cultural value and non-value inevitably exist simultaneously in regards to how the two are related to one another and how their conglomorate is related to the recipient. (As a man of practice I do not want to quote examples, but I think the reader may substitute in accordance with his taste—though it may be advantageous if even that were not governed by taste!) If we don't take the practice required by society into consideration, the result will be one of hopeless voluntarism and one that may lead to entertainment having to meet unjustifiable requirements. On the other side of the pole: no producer should work in the knowledge that his duty is the production of socially necessary refuse.

So, on the whole, practice develops independently of theory (which is not to be applauded), but its basis is provided by political and cultural policy decisions. The former and the latter, however, are not identical. In order to arrive at correct cultural policy decisions, a wide theoretical basis would indeed be desirable. Needless to say, the foregoing is not meant to provide an apology for practice. Practice is the way it is. Theory could play a better part in trying to improve it.

What Is Entertainment?

Let us point to a few aspects in which practice is in need of further theoretical clarification. The examples are drawn from the debate. To begin with, let us take our main concept: entertainment. This is a perfect case of lack of agreement as to what it should mean:

1. The transmission of certain defined contents.
2. The transmission of a certain genre.
3. The application of a certain form.
4. The application of effects such as to arouse the sensation of entertainment (functional approach).

I should like to refer to the fact that during the process of scientific examination, numerous attempts were made at grouping program categories according to their different aspects. These groupings enabled one to draw up interesting tables and facilitated the deduction of certain conclusions. The contentual and functional approaches were most often selected as the method of examination. As far as the category "contents" is concerned, the following, for instance, are to be found listed thereunder: current affairs, science, politics, literature, social affairs, serious music, light music, variety. The last two of these come into question when looking at entertainment (*mutatis mutandis*), but undoubtedly do not embrace the entirety of entertainment. I therefore find the application of the category "genre" justifiable, thus enabling the categorization of types of programs that cannot be described in terms of "contents." For instance, cabaret—is it to be subsumed under literature, politics, social affairs, current affairs? It is none of these (i.e., does it contain something of all)? Its specifics can be approached using genre as a criterion (thrillers and the like).

The functional approach (whether we consider the aims of the producer or the demands of the recipient) causes no problems. I consider it to be of prime importance that the formal approach also be included, by which I mean particular forms of programs (the unambiguously entertaining of which include quizzes, games and a number of programs with audience participation, for instance) and also such program elements that attract the audience and promote entertainment. At this point, the formal and the functional approach meet. I should like to stress that even the most precise differentiation cannot be perfect. Different approaches fade into each other at numerous points. I am convinced that all four types contain what we must call entertainment. The entity of our concept, therefore, can only be embraced by such a wide definition. Thus, entertainment programs must equally comply with the following requirements:

1. They allow the release of tension, are a means of recreation (functions).
2. By no means should they be purely artistic—thrillers, music and dance, cabarets (i.e., content-genre approach).
3. In terms of form, they should be easily accessible to (almost) everybody (quiz, audience participation, playful appearance).

The unification of these aspects is not impossible. The only problem would arise if an entertaining practice could be evolved within these very wide definitional possibilities that involved the whole of the institution, whose tasks were executed with the desired degree of efficiency. The answer to this must be an undoubted no, since everyone—individuals or boards of editors—should define freely within the given limits cultural policy allows. In reality, we must say that we do not have a unified practice of entertainment. We must say this in spite of our achievements.

In my view, a convergence of the means of definition is required in order to enable us to grasp what entertainment as an entity—with all its systems of relevance—is. At any rate, the practice of the Department of Entertainment indicates this and apparently not unrealistically.

Entertainment and/or Public Education

In the debate, it was clearly stated that our entertainment—regardless of the categorization of value of the particular entertaining elements—must, as a result of the character of our institution, be integrated within the system of public education. This remark is very practical and practicable and refers to the tendencies that must be strengthened. However, the question remains as to what we should do with entertaining elements that have no relation whatsoever to public education (blocking or offering no transition towards "real" culture). It is unlikely that, pointing to the public educational tasks of radio, one would refer to thrillers, folk music, dance music as vehicles to be recommended. At the same time, these are indispensable parts of the programs we produce. This does not imply that they are of no public educational importance—in fact: if only they were not! (To avoid misunderstanding: I think that some of the entertaining genres(?) that I normally accept and, what is more, enjoy, when consumed instead of culture, conserve an underdeveloped taste and standard of education).

Practice offers a "solution." Our recommendation is to advance from the basis of the satisfaction of demands, taking a few small steps at a time. But ought we not to examine how, parallel with each step forward, we mass produce the counter-affecting materials that might cancel the advance and could indeed reverse the process? I understand the extremely tight limits on the effectiveness with which mass communication can be used, but this does not exempt us from such worries. Entertainment as discussed in terms of public education is not always identical with that promoting public education, not only because of the qualitative reasons but also because of certain matters to do with genre and the social necessity of balancing program supply.

We cannot avoid facing the question of the theory of culture or that of the "two cultures." Some—depending on their points of view and their personal interpretation of the terms involved—stress the unity of culture and entertainment, others the necessity of a sharp differentiation (though the purpose may be the same in both cases). I know that I will be accused of elitism when I say that the first step should be to distinguish clearly between culture and non-culture, value (in terms of art) from non-value, programs that hinder development from those leading toward higher standards. Without this, we would produce a chaotic mixture, we would unjustifiably demand changes of function of products that are incapable of change, we would confuse the original with the lifeless copy. After such distinction, we can proceed to make use of the types of programs grouped under the weaker class, because we would have made sure that they would not be used dysfunctionally. We know that they (good if judged in themselves) may also represent certain values that, with their favorable psychically loosening effect, promote human recreation.

The second step enables us to start working on the Sisyphean task of constructing a bridge toward human culture as such, using elements implicitly containing value. At this stage, we do not have to fear confusion. In fact, our duty is to prepare the audience for the conquest of ever higher spheres of culture, paying due attention to the theory of graduality. This is the stage where art and entertainment come closest to each other and are interrelated but, let us add, cannot be substituted by any means. (It is obvious from the foregoing that our program practice inevitably requires a narrower definition of culture that does not allow the confusion of fundamentally different qualities and the over-rating of sub-cultural values. This schematic formula does not suggest that there is no transition between the two fields—on the contrary! But more about that later.)

What Makes Programs Entertaining?

Mention has been made of the possibilities of approaching entertainment from different angles: contents, form, genre and functions. Whichever we choose, we cannot avoid the following question: What is it that makes our programs entertaining? When praising entertainment, we use phrases such as: the witticisms were good, the compèring was pleasant, the audience was quick to react, lots of laughter was to be heard, it was light, it was gay, it was spectacular, it was funny and so on. Even if such expressions have their place, they are commonplace. Besides—*mutatis mutandis*—they apply to other types of programs.

What then is the special element that entertains? I have no answer to the question, although I should have one. All I know is that in its nature it imparts a sensation of pleasantness (and not of catharsis), it loosens up, it frees me of my inhibitions, it refreshens and it soothes. And knowing from practice the sort of programs that bring this effect about, we can create them. But that is too little. After all, is it not an effect of purely psychological character that can fit into any program? Interest? Style? Presentation? Packaging? One of the participants in the debate justifiably carried the chain of thought so far that he awaits entertainment from every program as a criterion of enjoyability. Within such a wide definition, however, the necessity of an independent construction of entertaining programs is to be questioned also.

The question may thus be put: Which element (formal, stylistic, structural, modal, psychical or the like) is it that characterizes entertainment. The examination of the effects inducing entertainment and the mechanisms by which they do so in correlation with recipient personality—these are the basic questions that ought to be answered.

What Entertains?

It is no good if we construct an entertaining program and the viewer is not entertained. It has often been said that it is highly accidental whether or not the recipient (depending on his education, his attitudes, his spiritual constitution, even his momentary mood, his emotional tuning, his habits) considers something to be entertaining. It has been suggested that in a favorable situation, the best entertainment is to be found in the highest form of art. Unfortunately, it is not a quality of the twentieth century that the ability to perceive and understand art has increased to such an extent that almost everyone finds delight in it. It is not a matter of certainty that delighting in the arts is the same as having "good fun" (again the uncertainty of the term!). Let us give an example:

Those who have recently seen Richter Schubert's play could experience lots of things: the opening up of a strange, deeply sad world; the infinite richness and loneliness of man; the opening up of entirety, its grasping and its unachievability; the thrilling pleasure of philosophical existence—everything that is specific save one: "the pleasurable" (i.e., "entertainment"). Attila József[2] said something of the following sort: a poem should not be heard by one in a cushioned easy chair, sitting back with one's eyes closed, but sitting up with one's eyes open and fully alert. Where does entertainment come into all this?

Let us expand our line of argument and say: "There is nothing more entertaining than thinking." We become uncertain as to whether our concept can embrace such a definitional statement and whether its meaning remains the same in all contexts. The resulting very broad definition is hardly applicable to practice. I suppose that it would not contradict this very direct way of putting the problem to acknowledge that a nice ballet, a light opera by Puccini, a funny play by Molière or a lively poem by Petöfi provide both artistic experience and pleasant entertainment. But by acknowledging the presence of art here, there and everywhere we cannot avoid having to define the quality inducing entertainment in terms of concepts outside art.

It follows from this acknowledgment that the element inducing entertainment is somehow capable of an independent existence and is not inextricably bound to certain values (artistic, philosophical and such) to be found in content. And, as all accept readily that entertainment has definite psychological functions in the process of the individual's recreation, we should also accept theoretically that: (1) entertainment in itself may be valuable even if it is realized in a valueless medium (outside the realm of culture) and (2) "pure entertainment" also exists whose contents are irrelevant. Here, all we can do is to see to it that its lack of content is neutral and non-destructive.

We must say that—practically regardless of their standard of education—people make use of numerous forms of entertainment that belong to the latter neutral sphere and have the ability of providing relaxation (cards, thrillers, adventure films, farces and the like). For our topic, it is irrelevant that originally they all had their historical (and sometimes class) determinants and are able to play the role of a means of manipulation. It is thus possible to imagine that the psychic and the cultural purposes of entertainment could be separated from one another. Without giving up our main aim of alloying the two, we can also see that this facilitates very practical consequences for program production and allows that "pure entertainment" also has certain values when fulfilling its own function.

If we study the recipient, we are confronted with a vast wealth of variation. A classification attempted on empirical lines would inevitably lead to the problem of stratified entertainment. In this matter we have made, so to say, no progress. Obviously, present-day stratification of entertainment is made in accordance with standards of taste, and its main characteristic is that it is bound to certain contents (genres). On the other hand, practicability would require that almost all material in which values are to be transmitted (and, of course, not only entertainment material) be cast in several variations in accordance with the intellectual stratification of recipients. In this context, it is easiest to refer to the great difference between village and city, between their living conditions and their systems of relations—differences that make it impossible for a certain (definite) production to be perceived and understood in the same manner (e.g., how a point fantastically made in a cabaret that would cause roars of laughter in a city would have no meaning whatsoever in a village).

However, the formula is even more complicated, since—still on the topic of humor—its system of reference is inevitably bound to a degree of factual knowledge and its understanding requires associative capacities. But are we ready to face the fact that the best ideas will not be understood by up to 70 to 80 percent of the viewers simply because of their lack of education? (Here I am referring to the frightening data of some TK surveys.[3])

It is just as unacceptable to think that stratified entertainment implies, let us say, dance music and folk music at the lower end and quizzes and political cabaret at the other end of a scale with beat and thrillers in between as it is to term programs of lower standard "entertainment." The task would have to be the compilation of intellectual cabarets and village cabarets, academic quizzes and competitions for unskilled laborers, for instance. Again let me explain: I am not suggesting that we should increase separation and thus help to conserve the stratification of present-day society with the help of wrongly selected titles. All I want to say is that it is not enough to proclaim the end of "programs for the whole of society." We should also act. Programming departments cannot do this alone. Only the initiative of the leadership, the development of taxation and other important measures can bring improvement. Until then, stratified entertainment only remains a slogan.

Solution to the Dilemma?

Wherever I have directed my thoughts, I have found extreme ambivalences both in concepts and in practice. I have shown that there is almost a possibility of editorial schizophrenia. Fortunately, however, in everyday work, our dilemmas are often resolved through means of a conscious or instinctive eclecticism, dwelling on—as one can interpret—all the possibilities of entertainment in terms of content, genre and form, though perhaps primarily proceeding from the entertaining function in the broadest sense of the term. This functional approach contains both what we may call entertaining in "genre" (cabaret, dance music, thrillers, lectures) and what we call entertaining in "form" (games, quizzes, programs with audience participation). We try to make use of everything within the limits of its respective potential.

Entertaining elements may be observed almost anywhere and they may be applied almost everywhere. It follows from our approach that our primary task is to pay especially close attention to investigating how values could be transmitted through means of entertainment. The first step is to show which instruments are incapable of providing a way toward culture ("pure entertainment"). The second, to take advantage of means of nurturing culture. A very wide borderland exists between culture and non-culture, one which we can plunder freely just as others do. It can be approached from both sides. Masses of people for whom efforts should be exerted live in this borderland. An infinite quantity of (mental) nourishment is to be found in this area, nourishment that can conduce movement in both directions. (In making this observation, nothing has been said about the immense complexity of the practical question as to the concrete judgment of the nourishment's quality! Put simply: how immensely difficult and responsible a task is the differentiation between art and non-art; how many think that they have experienced art when they are only scratching at its surface. And also how many do not realize that they have crossed the threshold!) If we work well and if we understand the issues involved, we will be able to devote the better part of our energy to making the most of entertainment serving the interests of public education. We laugh happily at a good cabaret. And our joy will be manifold if through this we enable even a single true thought to edge its way into the audience's consciousness.

NOTES

[1] The above article is the last of a series on the subject of entertainment published in the Hungarian journal, *Rádió és Televizió Szemle.*—The basic article of the discussion is Tamás Szecskö, "Szórakoztatás—müsorpolitika" ("Entertaimment—Programme Policy"), no. 3 (1971): 5–28.

[2] Translator's note: A. Jòzsef (1905–1937), poet and editor of the literary-political magazine *Szép Szó (Esthetic Word)*. He believed in realizing democratic freedom through the esthetic powers of the word (language).

[3] TK: Tömegkommunikációs Kutatóközpont (Mass Communication Research Centre).

Contributions include:

Békés, T. "Egy hozzászólás vázlata" ("The Blueprint of a Contribution"), no. 3 (1971): 29–30.

Bölcs, I. "A szórakoztatás más oldalairól" ("On Other Aspects of Entertainment"), no. 4 (1971): 45–50.

Boros, J. "Szórakoztatás—politika" ("Entertainment—Politics"), no. 4 (1971): 39–44.

Buda, B. "A szórakoztatás dilemmái" ("Dilemmas of Entertainment"), no. 4 (1971): 5–10.

Csapó, Gy. "Müfaj-e a szórakoztatás?" ("Is Entertainment a Genre?"), no. 3 (1971): 31–36.

Dozvald, J. "Milyen szinü a szórakoztatás?" ("What Color Is Entertainment?"), no. 4 (1971): 31–38.

Fellegi, T. "Másfél év után . . . Hozzászólás a szórakoztatásmüsorpolitika vitájához" ("After One and a Half Years . . . Contribution to the Discussion on Entertainment Program Policy"), no. 1 (1973): 44–48.

Halász, L. "Szórakoztatás, aktivitás, izlés" ("Entertainment, Activity, Taste"), no. 4 (1971): 21–26.

Hermann, I. "Szórakoztatás és szabad idö átstrukturálódás" ("Entertainment and the Changing Structure of Leisure"), no. 4 (1971): 11–20.

Liszkay, T. "Kezdeményezzünk!" ("Let's Initiate!"), no. 4 (1971): 51–60.

Lukácsy, A. "Esztétikai közfelfogásunk és a szórakoztatás" ("Our Aesthetic Public Conception and Entertainment"), no. 4 (1971): 27–30.

Zeley, L. "A szórakoztatás történeti tanulságai" ("Historical Lessons of Entertainment"), no. 4 (1971): 61–66.

Zentai, J. "Gondolatok a szórakoztatás vitájához" ("Some Thoughts to the Discussion on Entertainment"), no. 3 (1972): 63–72.

SELECT BIBLIOGRAPHY

Adorno, Theodor W. *Gesammelte Schriften* (*Collected Works*). Ed. by Gretel Adorno and Rolf Tiedemann. Vol. 13: *Die musikalischen Monographien* (*Monographs on the Subject of Music*). Frankfurt, West Germany: Suhrkamp, 1971.

Alderson, Connie. *Magazines Teenagers Read*. Oxford: Pergamon Press, 1968.

Altick, Richard D. *The English Common Reader*. Chicago: University of Chicago Press, 1957.

Barloewen, Constantin von, *et al. Talk Show. Unterhaltung im Fernsehen =Fernsehunterhaltung?* (*Talk Show. Television Conversation =Television Entertainment?*). München, West Germany: Hanser, 1975.

Beaugrand, Günter. *Fernsehmord für Millionen. Brutalität auf dem Bildschirm als Massenkonsum* (*Television Murder for Millions. Brutality on the Screen as Mass Consumption*). Hamm, West Germany: Hoheneck, 1971.

Beaujean, Marian, *et al. Der Leser als Teil des literarischen Lebens* (*The Reader as Part of Literary Life*). Forschungsstelle für Buchwissenschaft an der Universitätsbibliothek Bonn, Kleine Schriften 8. Bonn, West Germany: Bouvier, 1971.

Bigsby, C. W. E., ed. *Approaches to Popular Culture*. London: Arnold, 1976.

Bigsby, C. W. E. *Superculture: American Popular Culture and Europe*. Bowling Green, Ohio: Bowling Green Popular Press, 1975.

Blaukopf, Kurt, and Mark, Desmond, eds. *The Cultural Behaviour of Youth*. Wien, Austria: Universal Edition, 1976.

Blumler, Jay G., and Katz, Elihu, eds. *The Uses of Mass Communications*. London: Sage, 1974.

Bontinck, Irmgard, ed. *New Patterns of Musical Behavior*. Wien, Austria: Universal Edition, 1974.

Brecht, Bertolt. *Gesammelte Werke* (*Collected Works*). Ed. by Elizabeth Hauptmann. Vol. 18, pp. 121 *ff.: Radiotheorie* (*Theory of Radio*). Frankfurt, West Germany: Suhrkamp, 1967.

Burger, Heinz Otto, ed. *Studien zur Trivialliteratur* (*Studies on Trivial Literature*). Frankfurt a.M., West Germany, 1968.

Burns, Elizabeth, and Burns, Tom, eds. *Sociology of Literature and Drama*. Harmondsworth: Penguin, 1973.

315

Caillois, Roger. *Man, Play and Games.* New York: Free Press, 1961.

Campo, S. del. "La Television como Medio para la Inversion del Ocio" ("Television as a Medium for the Inversion of Leisure"). In *Revista Espanola de la Opinion Publica* (Madrid, 1966): 41–56.

Cazeneuve, Jean. *La Société de l'Ubiquité (The Omnipresent Society).* Paris: Editions Denoël, 1972.

Cazeneuve, Jean. *L'Homme Téléspectateur (Televiewing Man).* Paris: Editions Denoël, 1974.

Chaney, David. *Fictions and Rituals: Transforming Popular Experience in Industrial Society.* London: Edward Arnold, 1977.

Chapman, Anthony J., and Foot, Hugh C., eds. *Humour and Laughter: Theory, Research and Applications.* London: Wiley, 1976.

Chapman, Antony J., and Foot, Hugh C., eds. *It's a Funny Thing, Humour.* Oxford: Pergamon Press, 1977.

Clayre, Alasdair. *Work and Play: Ideas and Experience of Work and Leisure.* London: Weidenfeld & Nicolson, 1974.

Curran, James, *et al.*, eds. *Mass Communication and Society.* London: Edward Arnold, 1977.

Delling, Manfred. *Bonanza und Co. Fernsehen als Unterhaltung und Politik (Bonanza and Co. Television as Entertainment and Politics).* Reinbek, West Germany: Rowohlt, 1976.

Dexter, Lewis A., and White, David M., eds. *People, Society and Mass Communications.* London: Collier-MacMillan, 1964.

Dumazedier, Joffre. *Sociology of Leisure.* Amsterdam: Elsevier, 1974.

Dumazedier, Joffre. *Towards a Society of Leisure.* London: Collier-MacMillan, 1967.

Dumazedier, Joffre, and Guinchat, Claire. "La Sociologie du Loisir: Tendances Actuelles de la Recherche et Bibliographie (1945–1965)" ("The Sociology of Leisure: Current Research Trends and Bibliography"). In *Current Sociology* 16, no. 1 (La Haye—Paris, 1968): 1–127.

Dyer, Richard. *Light Entertainment.* BFI Television Monograph No. 2. London: British Film Institute, 1973.

Eberhard, Fritz. *Der Rundfunkhörer und sein Programm (The Radio-Listener and His Station).* West Berlin: Colloquium, 1962.

Elliott, Philip. *The Making of a Television Series.* London: Constable, 1972.

Ellwein, Thomas. "Freizeit und Massenkommunikation" ("Leisure and Mass Communication"). In *Fernsehen und Bildung* 5, no. 3/4 (München, West Germany, 1971): 161–71.

Friedrich, Hans, ed. *Politische Prägung durch Unterhaltung (Political Value Formation through Entertainment).* Politische Medienkunde Band I. Tutzing, West Germany: Akademie für Politische Bildung, 1973.

Fülgraf, Barbara. *Fernsehen und Familie (Television and Family).* Freiburg, West Germany: Rombach, 1965.

Gans, Herbert J. *Popular Culture and High Culture.* New York: Basic Books, 1974.

Geerts, Claude. "Le Divertissemente, Fonction Principale de la Télévision?" ("Entertainment—the Principal Function of Television?"). In *WACC Journal* 22, no. 4 (Geneva, 1975): 19–23.

Goldstein, Jeffrey H., and McGhee, Paul E., eds. *The Psychology of Humour.* New York: Academic Press, 1972.

Goodlad, Sinclair. *A Sociology of Popular Drama.* London: Heinemann, 1971.

Haacke, Wilmont. *Handbuch des Feuilletons* (*Handbook of the Feuilleton*), 3 vols. Emsdetten, West Germany: Lechte, 1951–1953.

Habermas, Jürgen. *Strukturwandel der Offentlichkeit* (*Structural Change of the Public*). Neuwied, West Germany: Luchterhand, 1962.

Hackforth, Josef. *Massenmedien und ihre Wirkungen* (*Mass Media and Their Effects*). Kommission für wirtschaftlicher und sozialer Wandel, Band 112. Göttingen, West Germany: Schwarz, 1976.

Hall, Stuart, and Whannel, Paddy. *The Popular Arts*. London: Hutchinson Educational, 1964.

Head, Sidney W., and Gordon, Thomas F. "The Structure of World Broadcast Programming: Some Tentative Hypotheses." In *Gazette* 22, no. 2 (Deventer, Netherlands, 1976): 106–14.

Hesse-Quack, Otto. "Der Comic-Strip als soziales und soziologisches Phänomen" ("The Comic-Strip as a Social and Sociological Phenomenon"). In *Kölner Zeitschrift für Soziologie und Sozialpsychologie* 21, no. 3 (Köln & Opladen, West Germany, 1969): 680–703.

Holzer, Horst. *Illustrierte und Gesellschaft* (*The Illustrated Weekly Magazine and Society*). Freiburg, West Germany: Rombach, 1967.

Holzer, Horst. "Politik und Unterhaltung in den Massenmedien: Reaktionen des Publikums" ("Politics and Entertainment in the Mass Media: The Viewing Public's Reactions"). In *Massenkommunikationsforschung* 2. Ed. by Dieter Prokop. Frankfurt, West Germany: Fischer, 1973.

Hood, Stuart. *A Survey of Television*. London: Heinemann, 1967.

Huizinga, Johan. *Homo Ludens: A Study of the Play Element in Culture*. Boston: Beacon Press, 1950.

International Publishing Corporation (IPC). *Leisure*. IPC Sociological Monograph No. 12. London: IPC, 1975.

Jarvie, Ian C. *Towards a Sociology of the Cinema*. London: Routledge & Kegan Paul, 1970.

Kaplan, Max. *Leisure in America: A Social Enquiry*. New York: Wiley & Sons, 1960.

Katz, Elihu, and Gurevitch, Michael. *The Secularization of Leisure. Culture and Communication in Israel*. London: Faber & Faber, 1976.

Kaupp, Peter. "Die Regenbogenpresse. Inhalt—Leserschaft—Wirkung" ("The Rainbow Press. Contents—Readers—Effects"). In *Internationale Zeitschrift für Kommunikationsforschung* 1, no. 2 (Köln, West Germany, 1974): 168–87; 1, no. 3: 321–39.

Kaupp, Peter. *Die schlimmen Illustrierten. Massenmedien und die Kritik ihrer Kritiker* (*The Awful Illustrated Periodicals. Mass Media and the Criticisms of Their Critics*). Düsseldorf, West Germany; Wien, Austria: Econ, 1971.

Kempkes, Wolfgang, ed. *International Bibliography of Comics Literature*. Detroit: Gale Research Company, 1971.

Klapper, Joseph T. *The Effects of Mass Communication*. Glencoe: Free Press, 1960.

Knilli, Friedrich, ed. *Die Unterhaltung der deutschen Fernsehfamilie* (*Entertaining the German Television Family*). München, West Germany: Hanser, 1971.

Kracauer, Siegfried. *From Caligari to Hitler. A Psychological History of the German Film*. Princeton: Princeton University Press, 1947.

Kübler, Hans-Dieter. *Unterhaltung und Information im Fernsehen* (*Television Entertainment and Information*). Untersuchungen des Ludwig-Uhland-Instituts der Universität Tübingen, Vol. 37. Tübingen, West Germany: Tübinger Vereinigung für Volkskunde, 1975.

Kutter, Adrian. *Die wirtschaftliche Entwicklung der deutschen Filmtheater nach 1945* (*The Economic Development of German Cinema since 1945*). Biberach an der Riss, West Germany: no publisher given, 1972.

Langenbucher, Wolfgang R., and Mahler, Walter A. *Unterhaltung als Beruf?* (*Entertainment as a Profession?*). West Berlin: Spiess, 1974.

Langer-El Sayed, Ingrid. *Frau und Illustrierte im Kapitalismus* (*Women and Women's Magazines in Capitalist Society*). Köln, West Germany: Pahl-Rugenstein, 1971.

Leigh, John. *Young People and Leisure*. London: Routledge & Kegan Paul, 1971.

Lundberg, Dan, and Hultén, Olof. *Individen och Massmedia* (*The Individual and Mass Media*). Stockholm: Norstedt & Soner, 1968.

Mann, Peter H. *Books: Buyers and Borrowers*. London: Deutsch, 1971.

Mann, Peter H., and Burgoyne, Jacqueline L. *Books and Reading*. London: Deutsch, 1969.

Marcuse, Herbert. *One Dimensional Man*. London: Routledge & Kegan Paul, 1964.

McLuhan, Marshall. *Understanding Media: The Extension of Man*. New York: McGraw-Hill, 1965.

McQuail, Denis, ed. *Sociology of Mass Communications*. Harmondsworth: Penguin, 1972.

Meijden, J. H. van der. *Massacultuur en Televisie* (*Mass Culture and Television*). Amsterdam: Elsevier, 1974.

Mendelsohn, Harold. *Mass Entertainment*. New Haven, Conn.: College & University Press, 1966.

Menningen, Walter. *Fernsehen: Unterhaltungsindustrie oder Bildungsinstitut* (*Television: An Entertainment Industry or an Educational Establishment*). Stuttgart, West Germany: Kohlhammer, 1971.

Nordenstreng, Kaarle, and Varis, Tapio. *Television Traffic—a One-Way Street?* Reports and Papers on Mass Communication No. 70. Paris: UNESCO, 1974.

Parker, Stanley. *The Future of Work and Leisure*. London: MacGibbon & Kee, 1971.

Plath, David W. *The After Hours. Modern Japan and the Search for Enjoyment*. Berkeley: University of California Press, 1964.

Prager, Gerhard. ed. *Fernseh-Kritik. Unterhaltung und Unterhaltendes im Fernsehen* (*Television Criticism. Entertainment and Entertaining Programmes on Television*). Mainz, West Germany: v. Hase & Koehler, 1971.

Prokop, Dieter, ed. *Massenkommunikationsforschung*, Bd. III: *Produktanalysen* (*Mass Communications Research*, Vol. III: *Product Analyses*). Frankfurt, West Germany: Fischer, 1977.

Rapoport, Rhona, and Rapoport, Robert. "Four Themes in the Sociology of Leisure." In *British Journal of Sociology* 25, no. 2 (London, 1974): 215–29.

Rosenberg, Bernard, and White, David M., eds. *Mass Culture: The Popular Arts in America*. New York: Free Press, 1957.

Rosenberg, Bernard, and White, David M., eds. *Mass Culture Revisited*. New York: Van Nostrand Reinhold Co., 1971.

Rüden, Peter von, ed. *Das Fernsehspiel—Möglichkeiten und Grenzen* (*The Television Play—Possibilities and Barriers*). München, West Germany: Fink, 1975.

Rüden, Peter von. *Unterhaltungsmedium Fernsehen* (*The Entertainment Medium, Television*). München, West Germany: Fink, 1977.

Sato, Tomoo. "Sociological Structure of 'Mass Leisure.' In Its Relationship to Television." In *Studies of Broadcasting* (International Edition) 3 (Tokyo: NHK, 1965): 83–149.

Smistrup, Gert. *Fortsaettes i Naeste Nummer . . . Masselaesingens Mekanik (Continued in the Next Issue . . . The Mechanics of Mass Literature)*. Kφbenhavn, Denmark: Berlingske Forl., 1971.

Smith, M., *et al.*, eds. *Leisure and Society in Britain*. London: Lane, 1973.

Stephenson, William. *The Play Theory of Mass Communication*. Chicago: University of Chicago Press, 1967.

Sylvester, Regine. "Zu den Aufgaben und Problemen der sozialistischen Unterhaltung in Film und Fernsehen" ("Some Thoughts on the Responsibilities and Problems of Socialist Entertainment on Film and Television"). In *Filmwissenschaftliche Beiträge* 13 (West Berlin, 1972): 176–91.

Szasz, Thomas S. *Pain and Pleasure*. New York: Basic Books, 1957.

Tamura, M. "Leisure of the Japanese." In *Studies of Broadcasting* (International Edition) 8 (Tokyo: NHK, 1972): 27–47.

Thompson, Denys, ed. *Discrimination and Popular Culture*. London: Heinemann, 1964.

Tudor, Andrew. *Image and Influence. Studies in the Sociology of Film*. London: Allen & Unwin, 1974.

Zeppenfeld, Werner. Tonträger in der Bundesrepublik Deutschland (Recorded Sound in West Germany). Bochum, West Germany: Brockmeyer, 1978.

Zöchbauer, Franz. "Der Unterhaltungsfilm in sozialpsychologischer und sozialhygienischer Sicht" ("The Entertainment Movie in Social Psychological and Social Hygienic Perspective"). In *Publizistik* 15, no. 1 (Konstanz, West Germany, 1970): 38–49.

Zweites Deutsches Fernsehen (ZDF). *Mainz bleibt Mainz. Die Unterhaltungssendungen im Zweiten Deutschen Fernsehen (Mainz remains Mainz. Entertainment in German Television's Second Program)*. Mainz, West Germany: ZDF, 1965.

INDEX